The
House
of
Northcliffe

The
House
of
Northcliffe
A Biography of an Empire

Paul Ferris

WORLD PUBLISHING
TIMES MIRROR
NEW YORK

Published by The World Publishing Company
First American edition
First printing—1972
ISBN 0-529-04553-2
Library of Congress catalog card number: 76-149420
Printed in the United States of America

WORLD PUBLISHING
TIMES MIRROR

To my mother

Contents

Illustrations

The author and publisher are grateful to all those
who have allowed them to reproduce photographs in their
possession. With the exception of the undernoted, all the
photographs are reproduced by permission of Sir Geoffrey
Harmsworth. Numbers 2 and 16 are reproduced by
permission of Mr C. W. Crofts; numbers 5 and 15 are
reproduced by permission of Mrs Macneil-Dixon; and
number 31 is reproduced by permission of United Press
International.

Acknowledgements

Many of the documents consulted and used are in the North-cliffe Papers which have been collected by Sir Geoffrey Harmsworth, who used them in the official biography, *Northcliffe*, which he wrote in collaboration with Reginald Pound. These include letters, Northcliffe's diaries for 1886 and from 1891 to 1906, and office memoranda. A selection of these papers was deposited with the British Museum in 1967, to become available to the public in 1972. In addition, Sir Geoffrey has a great deal of material relating to Northcliffe and the Harmsworths generally in his private papers. These include the diaries of Alfred Harmsworth (Northcliffe's father) for 1867, 1868, 1870, and 1874; the diaries of Sir Leicester Harmsworth for 1932, 1933, and 1934; miscellaneous family papers, and the personal recollections of friends and relatives. I have been given full access to this material by Sir Geoffrey, who has also talked to me at length.

For permission to quote from other family papers, I must thank Mr St John Vyvyan Harmsworth, Mr Cecil King, and Mrs Collin Brooks (letters of the first Lord Rothermere). Other members of the family who helped with documents and interviews, and to whom I am grateful, are: Lord Harmsworth; Mr Hildebrand Harold Harmsworth; Mr Eric Harmsworth; Mrs Daphne Macneil-Dixon; Mrs Christabel Bielenberg, and Mrs Barbara Macdonald.

The letter from King Edward VII to Balfour is reproduced by gracious permission of Her Majesty the Queen. Extracts from Cabinet & Foreign Office papers in the Public Record Office are quoted by permission of the Controller of HM Stationery Office. Other copyright material is quoted by permission of the following: Trustees of the British Museum (letter from Balfour to King Edward VII); the 6th Earl of Rosebery (letters of the 5th Earl); Mr Oliver Woods (letters of J. L. Garvin).

I am grateful to Mr William Rees-Mogg, editor of the *Times*, who let me see and quote from the paper's archives, and Mr Gordon Phillips, the archivist; to Mr Gavin Astor, who let me see the Astor Papers; to the First Beaverbrook Foundation for access to the Lloyd George, Bonar Law, St Loe Strachey, and Blumenfeld Papers; to Mr Victor Bonham-Carter of the Society of Authors, for information about W. L. George; to John Walters, Broadstairs area librarian, for information about 19th-century Broadstairs; to Unilever, who let me consult their library material about the Lever libel case; to the *Observer* librarian, Ann Melsom, and the *Daily Mail* librarian, Tom Kelly; and to the Royal Society of Medicine.

The use of copyright material from the following books is acknowledged: *Insanity Fair* by Douglas Reed (Cape); *Doctor's Progress* by R. McNair Wilson (Eyre & Spottiswoode); *Uphill* by Evelyn Wrench (Nicholson & Watson); *Politicians and the Press* by Lord Beaverbrook (Hutchinson); *My Northcliffe Diary* by Tom Clarke (Gollancz); *Northcliffe's Return* by Hannen Swaffer (Hutchinson); *Winston S. Churchill* by Randolph S. Churchill, Companion Volume 1 (Heinemann).

Many people helped with information and advice. They include Mrs Ivy Bartholomew, Dr R. D. Catterall, Mr C. W. Crofts, Mr James Drawbell, Mr Denis Gifford, Mr Derek Hudson, Mr Burland Jacob, Mr Lajos Lederer, Mr Michael McNair-Wilson, Sir Oswald Mosley, Mr Malcolm Muggeridge, Dr J. R. Pedder, Mr Reginald Pound, Mr Frank Price, Air Commodore Seymour-Price, Sir Campbell Stuart, Dr J. Russell Rees, Miss Constance Russell, Mr A. P. Ryan, Mr Harold Snoad, Mr A. J. P. Taylor, Lady Vansittart, Dr J. Stuart Whiteley. And I apologise in advance to any whose names have been omitted.

I

A Million Little Villas

IN 1888, the year after Queen Victoria's Golden Jubilee, a man of more than average imagination might have seen the glowing prospects of the coming age. Those morning commuters in their black coats and top hats, pouring into the smoky vale of London by steam train and horse bus, were a new generation of educated citizens. Their children would read, learn, grow, multiply, and cover the face of the earth with literate Britons. More and more of them would live in cities, in rows of pink and yellow villas with net curtains on the windows. A sense of people, of gathering millions with names, voices, votes, desires and money, was in the air, as real as the smell of paint and mortar in the ravaged fields above London, where builders were running up homes for clerks and greengrocers to rent at ten shillings a week. The mass market for everything was trembling on the edge of being born. Beecham's Pills were making a fortune for Mr Beecham. Railway companies competed to take working men and their families to the seaside. Mr Lever was selling four hundred tons of soap a week, and whenever an epidemic of diphtheria or typhoid struck a town, his agents hurried there to take advantage of the germs and sell some more. Standards of living had been rising for years; cocoa and cigarettes and black-lead to polish the hobs sold briskly to the New Victorians.

A man with a vivid imagination might have seen beyond the villas, the fly-blown windows, the greenish gaslight, and the maids on their knees with their skirts tucked up, to the problems of time and space in the city age. Leisure would percolate the masses as thoroughly as Fry's Cocoa and Wills' Woodbines. They would have time, the commodity that only the rich had had before. They would grow aware of a future crammed with delicious things to be desired and had. Soon people with money would be concentrated in cities where salesmen with products could get at them. The world was full of new flavours, and the West was smacking its lips. The sourness came later.

Industrialists and entrepreneurs everywhere, exploiting the revolution, would become household names – Levers and Cadburys and Morrises in Britain, Fords and Bells and Singers in the United States. They stumbled on their future, as Alfred Harmsworth, the innocent genius of newspapers, stumbled on his. The year 1888 is significant because this is when he began his first magazine: on borrowed money, compiled in an attic of one of those raw villas within walking distance of the new Underground railway, born out of Alfred Harmsworth's feeling for the crowd and what he could do to them with words. The Harmsworth family descended on Victorian London like a band of pirates, but it was Alfred who made the cutlasses and gave the orders. He started a chain of magazines, then moved into newspapers. He invented the modern British newspaper, founding the *Daily Mail* and *Daily Mirror*, buying and re-animating the *Times*. He understood advertising before anyone else in journalism, realising that mass consumption meant mass selling. Fleet Street was dominated by his ideas, his style, his arrogance, and his growing eccentricity, in a way that will never happen again: he was king of the industry when it was expanding. He ruled the little world of newspapers for over twenty years, and, more lastingly, created styles and habits of reading and perhaps thinking that were called 'vulgar' and 'trivial', until the years went by and such words ceased to have any meaning for an age of mass markets. The Harmsworths caught and distilled into print the spirit of a guilt-free, imperialist Britain, loving every minute of its power. Unscrupulous in achieving his ends while pretending to higher motives, Alfred both caught and helped to heighten the spirit of fear and rivalry that led to war with Germany in 1914 – impossible, now, to distinguish between the Harmsworths seizing history and the Harmsworths being seized by it. Alfred and his brothers accumulated more titles per pound of flesh than any family of their generation. Alfred became Lord Northcliffe and Harold became Lord Rothermere, both viscounts. Cecil became a baron, Leicester and Hildebrand baronets. Their fortunes added up to tens of millions. They were not particularly happy, nor, apart from Alfred, particularly talented. Looking back at them now, they are like fragments of an explosion. What counted in the Harmsworths was energy.

In the early summer of 1888, Alfred was a pale, fine-featured man of twenty-two, newly married to a girl called Mary. He was a journalist, so no one took his prospects seriously. After an economical honeymoon by the sea at Folkestone (twenty-two and six return, second class), they had set up house in Pandora Road, a newly-built terrace on the edge of the northern suburbs. One end of the road ran into fields and builders' debris; commuters used a footpath to get them to West Hampstead railway station a quarter of a mile away. Pandora Road is still there, red brick drowned in seas of red brick. Alfred and Mary's neighbours included an architect, a builder, and an artist; the road was hardly up to the standard of older avenues nearby, with physicians and a retired general or two. Drainpipes swarmed up the front of their house, and the attic was crowned with a lightning conductor in curly iron.

It worried Mary more than it worried Alfred. She came from a family with social pretensions, still living in an older house in the area, and her father, a City businessman, reproached her because she learned to type so that she could help her journalist husband. It seemed a waste of her French and German governesses. Alfred presumably had too many obsessions on the boil to care about fine social distinctions. In later years he was never keen to discuss Pandora Road, or any aspect of his early days, except in a carefully edited version. But he must have been uneasily aware of his own parents, living in shattered gentility a mile away. His father was a barrister who took to drink and fell apart, slowly and with dignity. His mother bore fourteen children in twenty years, beginning with Alfred. Eleven survived; most of them still lived at home when Alfred married.

There was enough gall in his family background to egg him on to success, but nothing to account for the depth of his obsessions and the peculiar nature of his will. At the time of his marriage in April 1888, he and an Irish partner ran a dismal publishing business from an office near Fleet Street. He had been planning a magazine since the previous year, and launched it two months after he married with a thousand pounds borrowed from a retired soldier and a line of credit from a printer. Magazines came and went weekly in those days, groping among a public that was learning to read. Education finally became compulsory for British children in 1880, when enough schools had been built to give full effect to the Education Act of ten years before. Editors slowly grasped the possibilities.

Alfred Harmsworth went in for the 'scrapbook' type of magazine that already sold widely: a world of undemanding facts in short paragraphs. He called it *Answers to Correspondents* in an attempt to come close to his public, marketed it efficiently and used it to indulge one of his fancies, that the essence of life was information.

He once said with pride that his empire was founded on useless information. This is not to say there was anything shoddy about his methods: he was the careful technician, collecting material from books and interviews, writing it up in a brisk, nononsense style, assuming, with the arrogance of the natural journalist, that what interested him would interest his readers. TERRORS OF TOP-HAT WEARING, declared the unobtrusive headlines in the first issue, AN ADVENTURE WITH A MONEYLENDER, CAN SNAKES KILL PIGS? DO WOMEN LIVE LONGER THAN MEN? Alfred's interest in the mechanics of journalism came out in HINTS ON STORYWRITING and BEHIND THE SCENES IN A NEWSPAPER OFFICE. A more private interest in pain and fear came out in NARROW ESCAPES FROM BURIAL ALIVE and THE STRANGE THINGS FOUND IN TUNNELS. It was all his own work, reflecting what he cared about. One significant article (considering that he was later spoken of as a possible Prime Minister) was headed POLITICIANS' PECULIARITIES, and began: 'We constantly receive queries as to the height of Mr Gladstone or Lord Salisbury, or other prominent men.' It was too early for *Answers* to have received queries about anything, but Alfred had the spirit of the thing; there was a public that would be vaguely interested, as he was vaguely interested, to know that Tall Members of Parliament included Robert Peel and Fat Members included Lord Elton; that the House of Commons contained three Smiths and one Jones, that Mr Gladstone stood five feet nine inches, that three MPs had glass eyes and one a cork leg.

6

More than thirty years afterwards, when Alfred Harmsworth was rich, tired, and not far from death, a writer who had worked for him and been dropped, W. L. George, took his revenge in a novel called *Caliban*. The *Times Literary Supplement* (by that time owned by Harmsworth) dismissed it as a 'masquerade'.* One of his editors thought the book a shrewd study of his master's psychology, exploring a mind 'closed to ideas', yet 'infinitely interested in them'. In the novel, Alfred is thinly disguised as Richard Bulmer, founder of *Zip*.

Zip is to be filled with jokes, and funny stories, and facts, oh, thousands of facts. If there's a coronation going on, we'll tell you all about the other coronations, where they happened, and who was there, and what they wore. If there's a good murder, we'll tell you how other famous murders were done. And who was killed. And by whom, and why it happened. And lots of interesting things like ... oh! anything.

Richard stands at night above Maida Vale, in Harmsworth country, watching the gaslamps like fireflies, hearing the slow trot of bus horses drift up, and the rapid clip-clop of hansom cabs bringing the theatre-goers home. A sense of multitudinous people and houses, of facts and *things*, entrances him. He visualises the public,

a creature that slobbered over its bib and cooed with content over the results of races which it didn't bet on, and pictures of the underclothes of actresses in another continent, and details of the weddings of royalties it had never seen ... He felt that the public was like a great ape begging you to scratch it, and he was willing to scratch it; after all, perhaps the poor thing itched.

The real Harmsworth was a knot of wilder, deeper sympathies and aversions, caught between love and hate for the public; driven by a need to dominate others lest they dominate him, and to escape the dark corners of his nature, which had little to do with conscious theories about mass marketing. But Richard Bulmer has an echo of Harmsworth, the young Victorian, who, fascinated by mass living, was anxious to understand and use it:

* W. L. George, 1882–1926, had been a controversial novelist at one time; he held 'advanced' views about women. The *T.L.S.* review of *Caliban* spoke crossly of 'a tireless and feverish elaboration of detail', but shied away from the book's sparkling portrayal of Harmsworth. George's obituary in the *Times* six years later was a mean piece of writing, full of sneers.

A personal revelation told him that mankind did not really care for politics, but for politicians; not about religion, but about comic curates. With rapturous certainty he realised that most human beings hated their work, and that by natural reaction they loved the pleasures accessible to them: home carpentry, the rosebush, cheap, tasty dishes. Sometimes when he walked north of Regent's Park, towards Highgate, he looked at the rows of villas that were just running up, and told himself that all those houses were alike, all those gardens alike; thus they must be let to people whose tastes were all alike. If one could discover that taste one would be able to sell the same newspaper all along the row, just as one sold the same quality of tea.

Alfred looked for the taste and found it, though it was a year or two before the fortunes of *Answers*, its owner and the Harmsworths began to look secure. He wrote copiously, filling space where necessary with jokes and paragraphs stolen from other magazines, usually American – after all, the mass audience was virgin territory; everything was new to it. A page each week could be filled with 'Curious Facts':

Kissing originated in England.
Betting men send more telegrams than any other class.
Mr Gladstone wears number nine in boots.

Working between the attic at Pandora Road and a poky office in Paternoster Square – soon replaced by something smarter in Fleet Street – Alfred gave early signs of a savage sense of propriety that was to be a useful weapon. Slang and the mildest vulgarities were excluded. One early editorial assistant, looking through items that had been clipped for use in *Answers*, wondered if it was proper to print a joke that read: I knead thee every hour, As the baker said to the dough.

The joke, such as it was, lay in a pun on the hymn, 'I need Thee every hour'. He blue-pencilled it, to the approval of Alfred, who made him office censor.

His life was already lived on more than one level. He was the father of a five-year-old boy, being brought up by the child's mother in an Essex village. To his older acquaintances he was still the young journalist. To the newer ones he was a proprietor, more of a manipulator than a scribbler. At the Priory Lawn Tennis Club in West Hampstead, not far from Pandora Road, the solid suburban members eyed Alfred and his pretty wife with amusement and then a trace of envy. In the next few years, four of them overreached themselves in business and were ruined. It was assumed they had been trying to emulate Harmsworth. No doubt they were giving way to the dangerous new middle-class appetite for keeping up with and overtaking the Joneses. It was an appetite that Alfred understood, and exploited from the start.

giving + Lareshef's

und

2

Descended from Kings

THE HARMSWORTHS came from Hampshire, where they were labourers and smallholders, ordinary stock that was so ordinary that at times the family has been worried to think how it could have led to such distinguished descendants. This may be only an instance of the Harmsworths' grandiose streak; instead of being proud of their peasant origins, they yearned for important ancestors. Just conceivably there is a grain of truth in the family legend that somebody, somehow – in its extreme version, a person of royal blood – introduced the super-genes into a line of horny-handed countrymen.

The name of Hannah Carter floats through the family dream, belonging to a real enough woman of uncertain background. She was born around 1804, into another long-settled village family in the southern part of Berkshire, near the boundary with Hampshire. Her forebears were farmers and cobblers. The fanciful story that circulated among later Harmsworths, neither openly believed nor dismissed, was that Hannah was the natural daughter of Frederick, Duke of York – the grand old Duke of York who had ten thousand men, and 'marched them up to the top of a hill and marched them down again'. The Duke was a son of King George III. Any possible connection with the Carter family's district of pasture-land and little villages hangs on the fact that as Commander-in-Chief of the British Army (until he resigned because of a promotion scandal in 1809), the Duke of York was a professional colleague of Arthur Wellesley, later the Duke of Wellington, whose ducal mansion at Stratfield Saye was a mile across the county boundary into Hampshire. But Stratfield Saye, bought with money subscribed for Wellington by the nation, wasn't acquired until 1817. The tenuous connection means nothing.

The only certain soldier in Hannah Carter's life was a Berkshire veteran, Thomas Wickens or Wiggins, who fought in the Peninsula wars against Napoleon. He served under Wellington, the Army commander in the Iberian Peninsula, and became an old soldier in his thirties, suffering from rheumatics, nursing wounds received in the Battle of Albuera in 1811. A village girl in her teens might have found his scars and memories romantic. Hannah Carter married him in the village of Swallowfield when he was thirty-six, twice her age. They had no children and their married life lasted only a few years. When Thomas died in 1829, he was living in the Royal Hospital in Chelsea – a forty-three-year-old Chelsea Pensioner, who left what money and effects he had to the sergeant of his hospital ward.

After an unsuccessful marriage to a colourful figure, Hannah settled for something more mundane: a Harmsworth called Charles. Charles was born in 1805, attended Odiham Grammar School, and went to work as a carrier, his journeys taking him to London, forty miles away. By 1837, Charles and Hannah had met, courted, and presumably married, though no record of the marriage has been found. In 1837 they were in business in a small way in London, and their first child, Alfred, was born. This was to be the impoverished barrister, the father of Lord Northcliffe, Lord Rothermere, and the rest. He grew up a dreamy man, talented but ineffectual, drinking heavily and sliding into chronic alcoholism. His birth certificate describes Charles, his father, as 'coale dealer', but Alfred Senior (to distinguish him from Alfred, later Northcliffe) liked to hint at royalty. When he came home after a few drinks, he was apt to call jovially to one of his sons to pull off his boots, adding that he couldn't be expected to do it himself because he had the blood of kings. Alfred Senior was a hopeless romantic; the family legend may be all his own work, a leg-pull founded on scraps of hearsay that he later elaborated and half came to believe.

Hannah, his mother, had a sufficiently striking personality to serve as a basis for elegant fictions. It was she who managed the coal and greengrocery business that the Harmsworths ran in Portland Town, a respectable district of small houses, shops, and offices on the edge of the recently opened Regent's Park. Mrs Harmsworth had more children after Alfred Senior, though only one, a child called Sarah, born in 1844, survived infancy.

Vivacious and clever, Hannah was a round-faced woman with a masculine sternness about her features, in a photograph of 1863. The Carter family is supposed to have regarded her as 'not one of them', and to have known that some mystery surrounded her birth. She could have been an illegitimate child, fathered by an outsider on a Carter girl who worked as a servant at a country house. The first Lord Rothermere (a grandson of Hannah Carter) was heard to say mysteriously that the secret of the family lay in Burghfield, another village in that corner of Berkshire. Common-land straggles around Burghfield. The place has a tradition of 'heath people', gipsies and itinerants moving in and out of the district. Might that be the link with Hannah, some brief encounter there with a travelling man? Whatever it was, Alfred Senior later called one of his suburban residences 'Burghfield House'. The first Rothermere used the name for a house in Scotland. The district held some importance for Alfred Senior. He returned to it more than once as a young man, and left oblique references in his diary to people and places. The Harmsworths breed mysteries, and take a secret delight in covering their tracks. For a family that was to produce the most rampant publicists and investigators of their time, they have managed to keep their own affairs remarkably private.

The Hannah Carter story can be explained by the romancing of Alfred Senior, who admired his mother all the more because Charles, his father, faded out at an early age – as he himself would do. Charles was an alcoholic who died at fifty-two, after a long illness. His mind clouded in the last years of his life; the cause of death, in 1857, was 'diseased kidneys'. It may be that the 'mystery' about Hannah, guessed at by Alfred Senior and turned by him into something more agreeable, is simply that she and Charles were never married. There may even have been a suspicion that Hannah's children were fathered by someone other than Charles. The next generation's desire for a family background that would prove they were not only legitimate but well connected could have done the rest. Cecil and Leicester, two of Northcliffe's brothers, agreed in 1932 that it was 'unthinkable' that a 'humble Hampshire peasant circle' should have produced someone like their father, Alfred Senior. Any connections were worth having. The brave Thomas Wiggins who was Hannah's first husband was transformed into a captain by the time Alfred Senior died, a cousin of some legal dignitary called Sir John Wickens. There were vain attempts to connect Wickens the Vice Chancellor with Wiggins the infantryman. The chain of supposition would vanish altogether except for a curious likeness among some of the Harmsworth women this century to the British royal family, in particular to Queen Elizabeth II when she was younger. As she got older, Sarah, the sister of Alfred Senior, is said to have resembled George III. It must be imagination, of course; people making pictures from the firelight. But the legend stays there, entangled in the family narrative.

Alfred Senior and his sister Sarah grew up in Portland Town with their ailing father and hard-pressed mother. Around them, London grew up. The divisions of society were still accepted as inevitable. The groans of the poor would have been loud in the ears of a family that had not long come from the country, and established itself precariously with a bit of trade, a bit of property. Victorian London guaranteed nothing except a changing scene and the unchanging struggle for place. Commercial prosperity provided the means to build a new London, and as it grew out of slums, cesspits, old gardens, and scrubby hills, it was there to be fought for, evidence in stone and iron of the rewards that were available to those who were diligent, lucky, or clever. In the middle of London, the ancient 'rookeries', the tenement quarters thick with criminals that lay behind the shops and arcades, were being eaten into by developers. Mayfair, St James's, and Notting Hill were carved out. Offices and hotels sprang up, while on the rim of London, pushing into the fields, the suburbs were on the march. Portland Town would soon disappear, swallowed and outmoded by the new district of St John's Wood, running up to the western slope of Primrose Hill. Even the burial ground that adjoined the High Street where the Harmsworths lived would be closed and superseded by fancier cemeteries. Charles Harmsworth, who died in 1857, was just too late to be buried in his own parish. Six of his children were there already. 'A beautiful blossom, Mouldering to dust', said the stone above Charles Albert, died 1 September 1841, aged eighteen months – 'Ascended to heaven, To dwell with the just.' Two alive (Alfred Senior and Sarah) and six dead was unfortunate, even for those days; some genetic flaw, presumably from the short-lived Charles and his Hampshire ancestors, ran through the family.

Alfred Senior as a young man was vigorous enough. He was well-built and clear-eyed, with a lock of hair on his brow that people said was Napoleon-like, and a soft, full mouth. His manner was easy-going and dignified; his education well up to standard for a shopkeeper's son. In his teens he went through a wild phase, but that passed. Hannah and Charles had sent him to a small boarding school two miles from home, and at fourteen he moved on to a teachers' training college in Chelsea. At seventeen he was ready to be a schoolmaster.

Then came some crisis in his affairs. The faint outline is still visible – he was away from home for months, perhaps because of a girl, perhaps someone connected with the Swallowfield district. The Harmsworths were friendly with a family called Wood; Alfred Senior and Fred Wood went to the same school. A fragment of Fred Wood's diary for 1855 reports on 30 January that Harmsworth has 'not returned yet' to St John's Wood, and fears for his safety. At the beginning of April there is still no word from him; finally, on 14 April, Fred receives a letter. The dates connect with an entry in Alfred Senior's diary for 1874, when he was making one of his sentimental journeys to Berkshire. It was a Saturday in October:

By train to Reading – on foot to Beech Hill – thence Three Mile Cross and Spencer's Wood. Saw my mother's birthplace. Lord keep her soul. Thirteen years since I saw these places. May's Hill – nearly twenty since I stood and looked back so unhappy. Saw C. surrounded by her children and her mother.

May's Hill is a thickly wooded ridge. Down the road, through the trees, the hamlet of Beech Hill is visible. It was to Beech Hill that he looked back. That was 'nearly twenty' years before; 1855 would have been nineteen years. But why was he unhappy and who was C.? Alfred is known to have had a lover before he married; was she a girl from a village, and was it on her account that he stayed away from home in 1855? His own son Alfred would leave home at seventeen because of a girl.

Whatever happened then, his future was already determined. There would be girls and a spot of gaiety and a glass of wine with friends; specifics against the melancholy that was all too liable to creep into his brain. He would write poems, make speeches, abhor vulgarity. People would like him, his courtliness and clever tongue would carry him along; it would never come to anything. He depended on style, not action; those kings and queens kept rattling about in his head. As a youth his tastes were already too flamboyant for the Woods, who once refused to let Fred go into lodgings with him.

For years, all he did was teach half-heartedly. He was at a grammar school in Cornwall; then he was in London; then, in 1861, in Dublin, fourth master at the Royal Hibernian Military School. For much of his time in London he had been at a loose end, developing a taste for drink, getting to know the girls and pubs on Hampstead Heath. By the time he reached Dublin, Alfred Senior had taken himself in hand and struck out on a more sober career. Moving in polite middle-class circles, he met Geraldine Mary, the daughter of a prosperous land agent, William Maffett. The Maffetts were Protestants, originally a Scottish family from the cattle-rustling regions near the English border. They had been in Ireland for centuries. William Maffett was a hard bargainer, described as the cruellest business man in Dublin, but he liked Alfred and encouraged the match, against opposition from his own family. The English suitor's charm worked better with the old man than with Geraldine's numerous brothers and sisters.

Geraldine was twenty-four when she met Alfred, a plump, good-looking girl with auburn hair and serious features. She said it was his laugh that first appealed to her. She had more practical ambitions for him than he had for himself, a fact that would have been hidden from William Maffett under layers of soft talk. Alfred's lassitude may have been hidden from Alfred, since he was never short of schemes and hopes; all that was missing was the will to act, and Geraldine, who had some of her father's character, supplied that from the start. Alfred wrote her soulful letters about mysterious Unions and the Laboratory of life. In return she persuaded him to become a barrister, aiming at a law practice in England by becoming a student of the Middle Temple. Although this meant visits to London, he was

15

able to do his studying in Dublin. By the time they were preparing to marry, in September 1864, he had hopes of a decent career. But his hopes always slid into the easiest channel. He hoped for a slice of Maffett's business and fortune when he died, and he hoped for subsidies while he lived. A few months before the marriage, one of Geraldine's sisters died. In his letter of sympathy to Geraldine, written from London, Alfred wondered hopefully whether Maffett would be softened by his loss. He asked her to speak to her mother about a small house near Dublin that they had been to see. 'I am afraid of its being let if I do not stir myself. We should save something by vegetables. There is a nice greenhouse. Think of it, darling, and speak to your Mama. Ever your true Alfred.'

They were married on 22 September, at the fashionable St Stephen's Church, in the presence of the reluctant Maffetts. Two of Geraldine's sisters refused to go, until their father warned that anyone who was not at the wedding would be cut out of his will. On the marriage certificate Alfred described himself as 'gentleman'; his father the coal-dealer, now dead seven years, was posthumously promoted to the same rank. Alfred and Geraldine rented the house they had been to see – Sunnybank, a modest Georgian dwelling with its front towards the River Liffey at the end of a small garden, its back towards a street of grey and white cottages and a high wooded bank. The place was Chapelizod, a village on the road leaving Dublin to the west; the name is corrupted from 'Chapel of Isolde'. There were vegetables and apple-trees, a cosy fireside by which to study *Principles of Equity* and *Smith on Contracts*, an income of two hundred and twenty pounds a year, and a bright fog of prospects somewhere ahead. The rural setting, with rooks quarrelling in the trees and the Liffey rushing past the garden, hinted at better things to come. There were always a few pounds in the cash-box; there was always Maffett's friendship.

Geraldine was pregnant almost at once. Before the baby was born, Maffett had died and the family's pent-up dislike of Alfred had been released; worst of all, there was to be no place in Maffett's business. Maffett was a rich man, and Geraldine's share of the estate should have been thousands of pounds; instead, his fortune became entangled in family disputes, and the lawyers got most of it over the years. The baby, a boy, was born at ten to seven in the evening on Saturday, 15 July 1865. He was christened Alfred Charles William, after his father and two grandfathers. Within a year, Geraldine was pregnant again, and a daughter, named after her mother, was born in December 1866. It was time for a man who wanted to advance to make a move, before his family grew too burdensome. Alfred Senior had mixed feelings about London. Geraldine coaxed him into agreeing that it was sensible to continue his studies there and be called to the Bar. But he could never shake off his melancholy. The future was uncertain, Sunnybank was safe; long before they went to England he was thinking nostalgically of the house, as if they had already gone away from it. In company he could shine; left to his own thoughts, his spirits sank. The Liffey froze in January 1867, coal was short, and he began to worry about starvation. Should he break up the goat house for fuel? He walks on his own, returning for dinner at 5 p.m.; the coal arrives; calm again, he reads *Principles of Equity*. Disaster is always round the corner. Thinking of train crashes, he buys a railway key so that he can let himself out of a locked compartment. In London temporarily to eat regulation dinners at the Middle Temple, he imagines he has a narrow escape when the ice breaks in Regent's Park and fifty skaters are drowned. When he takes Geraldine for her first outing after the birth of their daughter, he manages to see a man having a fit on the way home.

They left Sunnybank in March 1867, their departure mildly complicated by Fenian rumblings in the district. The Fenian revolutionaries were after the blood of the English. Knockings and ringings at the house were turned into a melodrama by Alfred Senior. He sat reading law with a sword on his knee, waiting for the worst while Geraldine went about the packing. The Harmsworths left without incident, stayed at various temporary addresses, and set up house in London later that spring. The address was Alexandra Terrace, in St John's Wood, not far from Hannah. No silver stream ran past the windows. They had a railway at the bottom of the garden, and all night they could hear the trains.

3

The Two Alfreds

ALFRED SENIOR was twenty-nine, beginning to be chronically poor in the middle-class way. Two years later he passed his exams and became a barrister. He assisted his seniors, appeared intermittently for a railway company, and earned enough to keep a step ahead of his creditors. Small sums came from Ireland, gratefully received; half a five-pound note, cut in two for security, would arrive for Geraldine from her mother in one letter, followed by the other half a few days later. He switched loans among his friends and sold family pictures. His income as a barrister in the first year after he was called to the Bar totalled a hundred and forty pounds, a disastrous drop from the Sunnybank days. It was well above the poverty line for a working man, but working men lived in a different style, and, if they were lucky, had wives who had been brought up to economy. Geraldine, who couldn't knit or sew, had been brought up to servants and a well-stocked cellar, and Alfred Senior was not the one to suggest lowering standards. He wanted a share of current prosperity. The British middle classes were blooming. A late Victorian writer estimated that between 1851 and 1881, the number of salary earners who were assessed for taxation on incomes of between a hundred and fifty and a thousand pounds a year rose from three hundred thousand to nearly a million. At the end of the century, the early social surveyors discovered that nearly a third of Londoners were living in poverty. Few people cared, except those who were living in poverty; certainly not the middle classes. An income of a few hundred a year would buy a comfortable house, servants for the dirty work, and some of the new range of clothes, furnishings, and household appliances that were coming on the market.

It was not that Alfred Senior had a grasping nature. He

wanted the presence that went with plenty rather than the plenty itself. He wanted to be a legal and literary figure. He founded the Sylvan Debating Club, which met in a pub to argue whether 'Government supervision of social evil would be beneficial', or to discuss the merits of horse flesh as a food; they ate some before voting. He wrote tepid poetry and long-winded articles that no one would print. A gulf opened up between the outward man, charming the ladies and amusing the fellows, and the inner person, haunted by the passing years, the bills, and the children that Geraldine kept conceiving. He has an eye for flighty girls and seems to like them large. '*Saturday 23 May 1868.* Met Haycock at 6.30 at Adelphi Terrace – went to Adelphi together ... *Saw the finest woman I ever saw in stalls where we were.* She was extremely large, but well bred, with a charming countenance (about 22).' In court he has his minor triumphs, between the long gaps without work, and afterwards he can be relied upon to entertain his friends. At home, hung over, he vows to give up drink; or sits alone, musing on 'my fleeting years and purposeless life' – that was on his thirtieth birthday, when he still had prospects, but was already enjoying his sadness, having a wonderfully gloomy time with those backward glances.

The children must have wearied him almost as much as they wearied Geraldine. For over twenty years they arrived on average once every eighteen months, adding up to a fine specimen of the unstoppable Victorian family. Sometimes there was barely a year between them; once, less than a year. Alfred and Geraldine had been born at Sunnybank; baby Alfred, nicknamed 'Sunny', spoke his first recorded words on Wednesday, 21 August 1867, aged two; he said 'Open door, papa' at the house in Alexandra Terrace. The next two children were Harold (April 1868) and Cecil (September 1869), both born in Alexandra Terrace. By 1870 the rent was too much for them, and they moved to Rose Cottage, a small wooden house in the Vale of Health, on Hampstead Heath. There, two boys and a girl were born: Robert Leicester (November 1870), Hildebrand (March 1872), and Violet (April 1873). Leicester was named for a family friend, George Robinson, who had helped with money. He was a gas-company engineer from Leicester. Friends dissuaded Alfred from calling the child Hildebrand St Barbe, but he fancied the sound of Hildebrand, and kept it by him for the next boy.

From Hampstead the family moved a few miles south again, back to St John's Wood and its terraces. Charles (December 1874) and St John (May 1876) were born at a house in Grove End Road. By the time Maud arrived (December 1877) they were in Boundary Road, in the house called 'Burghfield'. Maud died an infant. Then came Christabel (April 1880), Vyvyan (April 1881), and finally two more who died as babies, Muriel (May 1882) and Harry Stanley Giffard, originally called Guy Lovel Alfred (October 1885). Geraldine was then forty-seven; she had eight sons, beginning with Alfred, the eldest, who was twenty; and three daughters.

The years of child-bearing and housekeeping enhanced Geraldine. Like figures in a weather-house, Alfred Senior slipped into shadow as she moved outwards. She was not demonstrative, not an openly loving mother; fat and red-cheeked, solid and commonsensical, her virtue was dependability. She was a religious woman; strict in her moral standards. Her husband's lapses strengthened her, and he must have come to depend on her increasingly. His mother had died in the autumn of 1874; her illness throughout the summer preyed on his mind and brought uneasy dreams. In one, he owned an estate of park and meadowland; a stranger's cattle came to graze there; a naked boy appeared. He dreamt of swallows, and awoke crying out at a white figure beside the bed. Geraldine lit a candle, but he promptly fell asleep again and began to dream that he was catching rabbits, the only one of a large party who was successful. Even that went wrong. 'There was still a confusion and a sadness,' he wrote in his diary, 'with a hearse and a train on the Great Northern Railway.' His sister Sarah told him once of a dream where she vomited gold and silver. Now, he dreamt he plunged his hand in a stream and brought it out filled with gold and silver fish. A month later Hannah Harmsworth, formerly Wiggins, formerly Carter, was dead, and he was making the return journey to May's Hill and the Berkshire villages; thinking of his mother's last words – 'How happy we shall be at our next meeting', 'Cling to thy Redeemer in the days of thy youth', and 'Alfred! Alf! Alf!'

In the other world of yellow fogs and whistling locomotives,

Geraldine counted the slices of bread and jam, while reach-me-down clothes arrived from Sarah's family in brown paper parcels, and torrents of tiny feet echoed through the house. Alfred was the boss child; his sister Geraldine, a big, handsome girl, did the smacking. The house in Boundary Road was the one where they all found their strength, or lack of it; they were there eleven years, trampling the garden to a wilderness, bashing the woodwork in their ground-floor playroom. It contained one large table, two heavy forms for sitting on, and cupboards screwed to the wall for school books and the remains of toys. A toy in the Harmsworth playroom had a life of something less than an hour; when relatives made a dolls' house as a birthday present for the young Geraldine, it was duly pulverised; she didn't cry.

They were big, assertive children. Alfred grew from pretty to handsome, with his father's fair, straight hair across his forehead, strong blue eyes, and the full Harmsworth face moulded into a fine nose and lips. He seems to have assumed his superiority from the start, and to have persuaded others to agree. One of his mother's cautionary sayings was, 'Those who ask shan't have, and those who don't ask won't get.' This was no problem for Alfred, who used to answer, 'Yes, Mother, but I take.' A child of long silences, he is said to have hated noise; perhaps he hated it no more than many children do, but was better at imposing his wishes. Mrs Jealous, the wife of a journalist neighbour in the Rose Cottage days, remembered Alfred, aged eight or so, visiting her parlour and curling up in an armchair with books and newspapers – 'He seemed to be in a world of his own, of which he was chief and king and sole possessor. His supreme delight was to be and think he was the sole possessor.' It may have been less of a delight than a necessity. Harmsworth childhoods lacked affection. Was there a sense of loss behind Alfred's assertion of his rights? The lifelong contrast between his devotion and his mother's unbending manner is a clue; he loved her exaggeratedly and demonstratively, without much visible response.

Mrs Jealous's husband George ran a local newspaper. Alfred liked to visit the composing room on press days, and on his eighth birthday, Jealous gave him a toy printing set. He had an appetite for print and journals. He was to have a passion for the mechanics of the medium, the journalist's weakness for cold, damp proofs, soft-leaded pencils, and the instant authority of putting words in type. Words, like facts, existed in themselves, rather than as the means to understanding abstractions. It was always true of Alfred, even when he owned the *Times*. Among the authors he liked were Dickens and Defoe, perhaps for their hard gloss of descriptive prose, reporting the English scene. His childhood reading also included 'penny dreadfuls'. Although these were losing ground to magazines of the 'clean-limbed, brave young English boy' variety, the dreadfuls continued to pump out ill-printed tales of crime, torture, vampires, and creaking vaults. When Alfred became an editor himself, items in his early magazines pointed to a good grounding in the horror comics of the day.

Alfred was bold. Harold, three years younger, was cautious; his family nickname was 'Bunny'; he was good at arithmetic. Cecil was gentler than the family average. Leicester and Hildebrand both had the heavy family look, big-limbed and well-fleshed, that helped to widen the gap between the older and younger boys. Charles was a slow little boy who was found to be mentally subnormal; St John a quick, happy child, good at games. Vyvyan, who wasn't born till Alfred was fifteen, grew up in awe of so many hulking brothers and sisters.

Their formal education ranged from very little in the case of the girls to Marylebone Grammar School for Harold, Cecil, and Leicester, and a boarding school in Lincolnshire, Stamford Grammar, for Alfred. Before that, like the others in their turn, he attended a private establishment next door to their house, run by two ladies. At Stamford, where he stayed for less than two years, Alfred was caned fiercely and often by the headmaster, a clergyman. Years later the headmaster wanted help from his former pupil, who took his revenge and refused him. Alfred at school was high-strung and volatile, known as 'Dodger', a nickname he didn't like to be reminded of afterwards. He left Stamford when a particularly violent blow by the headmaster split the ball of his thumb and caused blood-poisoning. Moving to a day school in St John's Wood, Henley House, when he was thirteen, he blossomed into a school hero, captain of the cricket and football teams, noted rider of early bicycles, founder and editor of the school magazine.

Academically he was a failure, which disturbed Alfred Senior, as much as anything disturbed him now. The law was a noble profession; writing for the papers, his son's suggestion, a vulgar trade. Alfred Senior liked to take his sons to hear debates at the Sylvans. He advised them to practise speaking, to study good writing, to be as weighty as possible – lightness, he said hopefully, would come later on. His hopes and illusions were neverending. He thought trams were vulgar and football not as nice as cricket, which called out 'the best faculties of mind and body', whatever that meant. He was a nice, boozy, fatuous romantic who gave his sons the best he could, and whose broken hopes are reflected in some notes that Alfred, then Lord Northcliffe, dictated in 1921 when he was sailing round the world, a year before he died. The notes were for an approved biography of himself that one of his employees was to write; they suggested the childhood that never was. The Harmsworths' father, said Northcliffe, was 'very fond of teaching them outdoor life and seeing that they learnt their cricket, and, in Alfred's case, fencing and boxing'. Sadly, there was no fencing, no boxing, and no cricket coaching, though the boys used to visit Lord's cricket ground near their house. 'It was the custom of the Harmsworths,' dictated Northcliffe, 'to spend a long holiday in Ireland every summer.' Not really: when they could afford it they went to a genteel watering-place near London, Margate or Broadstairs, for a fortnight among the bathing machines and bandstands. But the family reputation had to be guarded. In retrospect Alfred Senior was to become a distinguished member of the Bar, a grand-nephew or a cousin of Vice Chancellor Wickens, the ghost who had been conjured from the memory of Private Thomas Wiggins of the 57th Foot Regiment. His sons, and especially Alfred, were tigerishly loyal to his name. When Keble Howard, another Northcliffe writer, produced a flattering biographical novel, *Lord London*, in 1913, the book's innocuous portrait of the hero's father aroused Northcliffe's anger. The book made the parent an Irishman who played the flute and smoked a pipe – 'rather a dreamy man, rather aloof, rather difficult to know well'. 'You know nothing whatever about me,' snapped Northcliffe. 'I am not in the least cross about it, except that the absurd caricature of my father has given the greatest offence to my family.'

Northcliffe was repaying the debt he felt to a disappointed parent. Alfred Senior saw his son leave Henley House School at

the end of 1881, when he was sixteen. He watched him try to be
a journalist, writing articles that weren't accepted. He watched
him experiment with vulgar money-making ideas. There was a
liquid to revive silk hats. There was a patent medicine called
Tonks's Pills, manufactured from soap in the Harmsworth
kitchen, advertised with handbills in St John's Wood shops.
Alfred had the ideas and gave the orders; his brothers and sisters
obeyed. He knew there was money in everyday products backed
by advertising. The big patent-medicine firms were well into
their stride, making a fortune from thin air and cheap chemicals.
He knew that journalism promised money as well as other satis-
factions; print carried authority. Then, or soon after, the possibilities of raw information began to stir in his thoughts. Other
thoughts stirred. The Harmsworths had a parlour-maid, Louisa
Jane, a village girl from Essex who had entered domestic service
in the great city. Afterwards it was recalled that she used a lot of
face-powder. Alfred had tried experiments with words and pills;
now it was time to try sex. With no school and no office job, he
was around the house at odd hours. Well before the spring,
Louisa Jane Smith was pregnant. There must have been some
awful moments in Alfred Senior's study, more awful for the
father at forty-four than the son at sixteen. Geraldine herself
was pregnant again (the child, born in May, later died). It
would have been ridiculous if it hadn't been a nightmare.

The solution was typical of Alfred Senior: Alfred was sent off
in the summer of 1882 on a miniature Grand Tour of Europe as
travelling companion to a well-connected clergyman, the
Reverend E. V. R. Powys. Powys, a younger son of Lord
Lilford, had advertised in the *Times* for a secretary-companion.
The trip was explained away, then and later, by the need for
Alfred to convalesce after an attack of pneumonia, brought on
by a long-distance bicycle ride. No doubt he was ill, but no
doubt the illness had something to do with his emotions. His
frame of mind and state of health were bound up with one
another throughout his life. The scenes that followed the news
about Louisa Jane would have been enough to bring on one of
Alfred's 'nervous attacks', with or without the aid of a virus.

He was well again by the time he and Powys set off from
Boundary Road in a hansom cab, waved goodbye from the windows by the assembled family. Appearances were maintained.

Money had been found for his clothes, and he travelled in a
light grey suit that was unlike the Sunday Best style of dress that
his brothers were used to, coarse cloths of beetle-black and navy
blue. Alfred and friend jingled down the road to Victoria and
the boat train, and a leisurely tour of France that kept him out
of the way for months. Perhaps Alfred found a moral in it. God,
a figure he never gave much thought to, was being good. Having
done a wicked thing with a girl, Alfred qualified for a holiday
abroad. It was apparently possible to disregard the conventional rules and have a more agreeable set for oneself. The baby
was born on 5 November 1882, in the village of Southminster.
It was given the names of Alfred Benjamin; no father was
shown on the birth certificate; the Smith family rallied round
and looked after Louisa.

When he returned to London, his mother wouldn't have
Alfred back at Boundary Road. He lodged at more than one
address with friends, among them Herbert Ward, a young man
who had been a sailor and adventurer, and would soon be an
explorer with Stanley in the Congo. They shared a cottage in
Hampstead, then a room near Clapham Junction, south of the
river. When Ward went to Africa, Alfred was joined by a former
school friend down from university, Max Pemberton. All this
time he was writing articles and stories for magazines, at last
with some success. He wrote for *Weekly Budget*, *Young Folks'*
Tales, and *Youth*, and found himself earning three pounds a week
or more. At *Youth*, an impecunious magazine, he was made
editor. Before it ceased to exist he improved his education in
printing, engraving, and editorial budgeting. He was made a
fool of in print by boys from Eton College. The captain of the
school conceived an elaborate practical joke, inventing an Eton-
ian custom called 'Slunching the Paddocks'. ('On a certain day
all the Collegians and Oppidans are provided with a coarse sort
of pudding, which is put to the following use: after dinner is over
they all go to Weston's and School Paddocks and throw this
pudding all over them. This is called "Slunching the Paddocks",
the pudding being called "Slunch".') Alfred was invited to
Eton, entertained, and told all about Slunching. The account
appeared in *Youth*. It must have hurt when he found out, an
early lesson in coping with a public that could be manipulated if
you were clever, but was always liable to bite you if you weren't

careful. As an employer, he was suspicious of public school men, or pretended to be.

For the next few years, until 1887, when he was twenty-two, Alfred made the beginnings of a solid career in journalism. He was not going to be distinguished; as a writer he appeared to have enthusiasm but no style, curiosity but no conscience. His idea of a good article was a catalogue of facts, clearly set down, about something of popular interest that wasn't controversial. A few years later, when he was too successful for it to matter, he said that most of the articles had been 'poor stuff'. Just as television journalism in its early days was able to point a camera and record a scene, relying on the novelty to excuse the superficiality, so early 'feature' journalism for the newly literate public of the 1880s was able – or compelled – to offer small doses of bland mixtures. To some extent the novelty has never worn off, and soft, innocuous articles about nothing in particular have become one of the staples of journalism. In the 1880s they were as new as the typewriter. Alfred was so adept that it's unlikely he wrote them as pot-boilers: he really cared about famous ventriloquists or the origin of the bicycle or a visit to a newspaper wholesaler:

On the morning of Saturday, 27 November an opportunity was afforded the writer of visiting Messrs W. H. Smith and Son's establishment in the Strand. It is questionable whether now-a-day folk, whose custom it is to patronise the railway station stalls every morning, ever pictured the scene of bustle and commotion ...

and so on for two thousand words. He might attend a Friday-night debate on 'Is there such a thing as progress?' but the things he wrote about were 'Stage Villains' and 'Old Clothes Men' and 'Some Curious Butterflies'. He didn't slave day and night; Pemberton, his fellow-lodger, found him often lethargic and disinclined to work; it was the stabs of wilful energy that counted. He was growing fond of Mary Milner, whom he had met at a children's party years before. He spent his time between her house, his lodgings in Hampstead, Boundary Road, and publishing offices. He got up late on a Saturday morning and went to the British Museum, dressed in black cape and glossy silk hat, to potter about in the Reading Room, among the students and old men, looking up articles on photography. Over

he weekend he began to write an article on 'How to take a
photograph', between visits to the Milners, finishing it in time
o post on Tuesday. When snow and ice persisted in the winter
f 1886, he went with Mary to see the skating at Hampstead,
nd presently produced an article on 'Forgotten Frosts'. He
lidn't do vivid or Bohemian things or try to live as gentlefolk
upposed journalists to live, raffishly if they were successful and
eedily if they were not. He had pedestrian tastes, his thoughts
lways wandering back to journalism. He was earnest and ambitious, almost enough to put him in his father's category of
ulgar, if he hadn't been so handsome and sure of himself. Colds
nd sore throats and toothache bothered him unduly; he didn't
ail to let people know when he was ill.

There must have been dozens of other young aspirants in
London, churning out copy on the passing scene, supplying raw
material for the new mills of journalism. Many of the cheap
magazines were based on the scrapbook principle, a collection
f oddments with something for everybody. Some said so in the
itle – like *Scraps* and *Tit-Bits*. *Tit-Bits* was the most successful,
begun a few years earlier by the former owner of a vegetarian
restaurant in Manchester, George Newnes. Alfred made it his
chief source of income. The success of *Tit-Bits* made him want
o do the same himself, only better. He needed his own outlet;
he had to be a 'sole possessor'. He tried to borrow money to
begin a magazine, approaching the fathers of his friend Pember-
on and his sweetheart Mary. No one would oblige, and he became an editor again, this time of a more promising magazine,
he Iliffe family's *Bicycling News* in Coventry, where the factories
were in the middle of the bicycle revolution.

The job, offered on the strength of his articles, plunged him
nto a sales-fight between cycling magazines in the spring of
1886. Soon he had enlivened *Bicycling News* and improved the
circulation. Pedalling about Coventry on a solid-wheeled
machine, or trying to look like a junior ironmaster with a curly-
brimmed bowler and a big cigar, Alfred was a busy young
fellow. He enraged contributors by butchering their articles
(one of them called him a 'yellow-headed worm'), printed
hoaxes that worked on others as well as the Etonians' had
worked on him, stirred up controversies, employed a woman
correspondent to champion the cause of feminine bicycling, and

still found time to burrow in the local library for the ingredien
of more *Tit-Bits* articles. He conceived a slogan for *Bicycli
News* in the purple style of patent-medicine advertisements, '
Comes as a Boon and a Blessing to Men, The Popular Penn'ort
the Racy B.N.' Alfred made his magazine talked about. Th
was what he did best; that was the way to go.

4

Interesting Things

BY THE START OF 1888, the family apart from Alfred were set for a steady grey future. Harold was a clerk with the Board of Trade in the City, earning twenty-five shillings a week. He was nineteen, with prospects. Britain was entering its great imperial years, and even an employee of the Mercantile Marine Office could expect rewards. If he worked diligently and obediently for most of the rest of his life, he could one day earn six hundred pounds a year. Since inflation was not a late Victorian concept, this meant that when he reached his peak as a salary-earner – say, in 1915, when the British Empire would be richer and happier than ever – he would be able to buy more comfort than his father had ever afforded. Harold was a careful youth, always ready with mental calculations of pensions, mortgages, and rents.

Close behind him but with a more academic turn of mind came Cecil, eighteen years old. Cecil, 'Bouffles' in the family, having failed to get into the Civil Service as a clerk, had gone to Trinity College in Dublin, his fees paid by Mr Robinson of the gas company, and was distinguishing himself at English literature. He was interested in religion and good works; he had been brought up a conventional Anglican, and some of his more religious friends thought he had a calling as a clergyman. Leicester, seventeen years old, was also a possible candidate for the Church, having acquired a reputation for piety as a child with bouts of praying. At the moment he was learning to be a Civil Servant, working as a boy clerk with the Inland Revenue. The only other career that needed to be thought about yet was Hildebrand's. He too was in Dublin, relieving the strain on Alfred Senior in Boundary Road; he lived with the Maffetts and attended Dublin High School. A cheeky boy, fond of jokes, with a half-baked ambition to enter Parliament, he might, with luck, be found a stool in a stockbroker's office; more sums, more toiling, loomed ahead of Hildebrand.

Alfred floated above this world of steel pens and heavy ledgers. The family followed his progress with pride, perhaps with a trace of fear. He had gone to Coventry; now he was coming back to London; now he was going to be a publisher. An Irishman called William Carr, engaged to a woman who had been a girlhood friend of Geraldine, the Harmsworths' mother, had crossed from Dublin with fifteen hundred pounds that he wanted to invest. Introduced to this friend of a friend, Alfred, who had resigned from *Bicycling News*, persuaded him to sink the money in a publishing partnership. In Coventry he had failed to talk the Iliffes into backing a popular weekly magazine that he wanted to start under the title of *Answers to Correspondents*. In London, Carr was willing to back him, but not to start the magazine. Carr & Co, with offices in Paternoster Square, near Fleet Street, went into business with a series of booklets called *A Thousand Ways to Earn a Living*. The firm published a magazine for the owners of private schools, *The Private Schoolmaster*, edited by an unprepossessing barrister friend of Alfred Senior, Edward Markwick, who was also in the partnership.

Alfred and Carr eked out a living in an office eight feet by ten. Hangers-on drifted in, looking for commissions to write articles or hoping to borrow half a crown from Carr, who was known to have a soft heart. Alfred was not known for his soft heart. His sense of protocol was as well developed as his father's. He lectured an office boy for abbreviating 'chambers' to 'chmbs' in an address on an envelope. Another office boy left because Alfred insisted that juniors wear Eton suits and top hats. Alfred was charming as long as he wasn't contradicted; angry when he was. Worst of all was to be insulted in front of others. One day he had a furious row in the office with his cousin, Arthur Hendry, the son of Aunt Sarah. Sarah had married a Mr Hendry, who used to knock her about. He died and left her free to marry a solicitor, Francis Miller. The Millers were more prosperous than the Harmsworths. Like her brother, Sarah thought or hoped there might be blue blood in the family. But where he was flowery and splendidly vague, 'Auntie' was a loud, plump lady with a cockney accent. In the family checklist she was to be written down

as 'vulgar', a word that was used like a bullet to dispose of anyone whose manners didn't fit. Auntie was good value. She liked
to tell spicy stories. Her version of the family legend, even less
probable than Alfred's, hinted at a connection with the Duke of
Wellington. The Millers had an engraving of the Duke outside
the dining room, where, it was hoped, visitors would notice a
facial likeness as they were going in to dinner. Arthur Hendry
was accustomed to regard the Harmsworths as poor relations.
He started the row with Alfred by calling him a liar and a
swindler. Alfred never forgot this. Insults from the family that
had once provided cast-off coats and trousers were particularly
disagreeable. They had a stand-up fight; Carr, enjoying it immensely, had to separate them. It was the most expensive outburst of Arthur's life. He was still trying to beg or borrow from
Alfred, more or less unsuccessfully, thirty years later.

News about Alfred travelled fast through the family. They
heard he had taken over the London agency of an American
sporting journal called *Outing* ('The Gentleman's Magazine of
Recreation'), and publicised it with a band of 'superior sandwichmen' who marched up and down the West End with
advertising boards, dressed as fishermen, huntsmen, and yachts-
men. They heard he had raised more capital for Carr & Co from
a certain Captain Beaumont. Beaumont, a retired officer of the
Royal Welch Fusiliers, had been introduced by Markwick the
barrister, and took to Alfred at once; he had homosexual lean-
ings. Alfred, although his own tastes were the other way, was
remarkably handsome at that age. The money, about a thousand pounds to begin with, belonged not to Beaumont but to his
wife. Fourteen years older than her husband, she was referred to
in the office as the 'C-in-C'. Alfred's letters to the Beaumonts in
south-east London sent affectionate greetings to them both. The
first injection of Beaumont capital was spent mainly on *Outing*, a
venture that never looked like succeeding, with articles on
'Mask and Foil for Ladies' and 'Hints to Football Captains'.
Carr & Co remained a powerhouse of misdirected energy.

Scraps of gossip about Alfred's long-awaited magazine, the
Answers to Correspondents he had thought of in Coventry, continued to circulate. Probably the family were more interested in
his forthcoming marriage to Mary (sometimes called Molly)
Milner. The Milners, like the Harmsworths, were keeping up

appearances. Mr Milner had lost money in the sugar trade. Mrs Milner cultivated her family tree, hoping to pin down a rumour that she was related to the Earls of Rochester. Mrs Harmsworth, married to one social climber, was unlikely to be impressed by another. She was not keen on the marriage, though resigned to Alfred's determination. There was much borrowing and scraping within the family as the date in April approached. Alfred's engagement ring was paid for by Markwick. It wasn't even possible for Cecil and Hildebrand to come over from Dublin. Cecil was so short of clothes that his appeal for a new jacket and trousers had to be met by having an old black coat of Harold's mended and dyed; trousers, the younger Geraldine wrote to Cecil from Paternoster Square (where she was learning to type), were beyond her powers.

The wedding was on 11 April 1888, at Hampstead Parish Church; performing the ceremony was Alfred's travelling companion on his continental journey, the discreet Mr Powys. Alfred and Mary left for their honeymoon in Folkestone, according to the wedding report '*en route* for the Continent' – they weren't – and Mrs Harmsworth, driving home in a hansom, said in tears to her eldest daughter Geraldine, 'They will have so many children and no money.' She had no need to fear; least of all that she was losing a son. Geraldine, never given to kissing and cuddling her children, regarded them as more of a burden than a joy. As an adult, Alfred embraced his mother daily, in the flesh when he could be with her, in letters and telegrams when he could not. What he missed in childhood he exacted till he died. He wrote to 'darling Mother' from bed on the morning of his wedding day. From Folkestone that night came a postcard to say he and Mary had arrived safely.

Alfred's wedding seems to have been the signal for him to embark on *Answers to Correspondents*. Before he left Iliffes, the Coventry publishers, they had promised him credit at their printing works. In the spring of 1888 he decided that this, together with a further thousand pounds if the Beaumonts could be persuaded to invest it, was enough. The Beaumonts were at their villa in Italy. Markwick, best man at the wedding, was sent as an emissary. He travelled to the Continent via Folkestone, where Alfred and Mary were staying in a boarding house by the sea, and they waved him off when he caught the steamer to

Boulogne. On 19 April he cabled a one-word message from Italy: 'JOY'. Alfred roughed out the title block for his magazine on a current copy of *Tit-Bits*, and contacted Iliffe's about printing.

The Beaumonts were gambling on Alfred – nothing published by Carr & Co had been notably successful – and Alfred was gambling on his view of the public's taste in this unmapped area of the entertainment industry. Popular journalism for millions had to find its level, which might have been anything from an attempt to imitate the serious journals, to a collapse into the scurrilous and scandalous. At the time it didn't seem to be an extension of the entertainment business. Entertainment was still a cottage industry by comparison with what happened later; it was impossible to foresee how it would thrust its way into the centre of people's lives, let alone to relate magazines and newspapers to it. *Tit-Bits* was steering a wobbly course towards some undefined objective in which education, information, and improvement played a part. The new journals that arrived and vanished week by week were all part of the great educational egg that the Victorians had laid; tappings came from within, the shell trembled, and those with curiosity wondered what would emerge when it cracked. Nobody knew, certainly not Alfred, who, if he had stopped to think, might have clouded his mind with speculation. As it was, he assumed that whatever came out of the egg would like what he liked. He liked *Tit-Bits*, and burned with desire to improve on the formula.

When Alfred and Mary moved into Pandora Road, the plan was already unfolding. They were not like the neighbours, whose menfolk either strolled out at gentlemanly hours, or marched to the railway station in the early morning, their glossy top hats bobbing about like the funnels of ships. Alfred, always careful about dress and anxious not to be censured for it, wore a top hat with the rest; but the rhythm of his life was different. He was neither a leisurely stroller nor a clockwork suburbanite. Some mornings he went to the City. Other days he left later for the West End or to catch a train for Coventry. Often he didn't go out at all, except to take letters to the pillar box in the next road but one, where a postman made twelve collections each day, from 7.40 in the morning until ten minutes to midnight. Proofs and manuscripts flowed in and out of

33

Pandora Road. Mary Harmsworth might have looked a little wryly at Mrs Beeton's *Book of Household Management*, published twenty-seven years before, with its advice that 'As with the commander of an army, or the leader of any enterprise, so it is with the mistress of a house. Her spirit will be seen through the whole establishment.' The spirit that ran through their little rooms was less Mary's than Alfred's, since he worked there so much – in the attic, in the poky drawing room, often in bed in the mornings. He liked bed; his energy fluctuated and needed cosseting.

When *Answers to Correspondents*, price one penny, finally appeared on the streets two months after they were married, some of Beaumont's money was quickly spent on sales-promotion. Many copies were given away, a device that Alfred claimed he invented; vendors leapt around Fleet Street with bundles of the magazine, which was never in danger of dying because its proprietor, having poured his talent into the pages, was sitting back and waiting for something to happen. Nor was his financial backing as slender as it sounds. As late as the 1930s, it was possible for a journalist to launch a successful magazine in London for just over a thousand pounds. Alfred had his thousand, at Victorian values, as well as credit at the printer's. But from the start, he needed money to publicise the magazine, to run competitions and sales-promotion schemes. Journalism didn't mean casting words into the wind, it meant firing them like bullets; aim and velocity mattered.

The first issue to appear was Number 3. Answers to genuine questions from readers could hardly be expected when there had been no magazine to write to in the first place. By starting with Number 3 (Numbers 1 and 2 were printed later), Alfred was able to pretend that letters had been received, and invent questions to provide convenient openings for the articles he had written. Even when genuine queries came in, it's unlikely that many of them were suitable. The formula was an attempt to provide a novel excuse for printing miscellaneous articles. With so many new magazines, novelty was important. *Answers* had to appeal quickly and positively to large numbers of that indistinct mass of people that filled the sulphurous carriages of the Underground railway, sang rude songs in the music halls, and appeared in the streets with flags and cheers on national occasions, like the Queen's Golden Jubilee the year before. Since it was such an early exercise in mass entertainment, the impresario had little information on which to found his judgments. Alfred could do nothing beyond making the basic assumption that his readers' inclinations would match his own. In a world full of things, there were tedious things and interesting things. 'Mask and Foil for Ladies' was a tedious thing. So were column after column of Parliamentary reports in the newspapers. Interesting things were snappy, chirpy, instant.

'What the Queen eats' was a headline that demanded to be looked at; the reader might be a superior person, but if he was human his eye would travel down the column: 'The Queen's favourite foods are boiled mutton, of which she partakes at least twice a week, venison, salmon, boiled fowl, and silverside of beef.' If the reader was not a superior person, the items that crammed the skinny off-white pages of the early issues would open windows on the world of other people's experience. Television would learn later to grasp the mind with anything that moved; first, magazines had to learn to grasp it with images in print – 'How Madmen Write', 'How Divers Dress', 'How Dickens Read', 'An Electrical Flying Machine', 'A Year only Eighty-Seven Days Long', 'Horseflesh as Food'. Horseflesh had been one of the subjects debated by the Sylvans. Alfred understood the economy of journalism: wait a while and everything recurs. Old clothes had been one of his topics for *Tit-Bits*. Here it came again, 'A Mysterious Trade' ('In every town there are old clothes shops . . .').

Even at the time it was possible to laugh at this outpouring of useless information. Issue Number 4, the true second issue, on 23 June 1888, listed some of the sarcastic questions that were coming into the office: 'Why are no bus conductors bald?', 'What is the present weight of cat-fish per pound?' 'Were this a comic paper,' said the editorial, 'we should immediately invite the gentlemen who have evolved these brilliant efforts to take up substantial appointments on our staff; but as we are a serious journal (though not without our humorous side), we can only regret our funny correspondents' ruthless shedding of innocent ink.'

The breezy editorial style was kept up through the early months, when circulation remained between twenty and thirty thousand and the printing bill mounted at Iliffe's. Alfred tried everything he could think of. Competitions were a mainstay of *Tit-Bits*, so week by week he invited his readers to send in the best Scottish joke, or guess how many people walked across London Bridge in a day, or name the twelve most famous living Englishmen (Gladstone won easily; eight of them were politicians. The only names that were remotely connected with the entertainment business were Tennyson the poet, Spurgeon the preacher, and Ruskin the writer).

After offering a junior clerkship in the *Answers* office as a prize, Alfred ran a further competition to guess the age, height, and colouring of the winner (it was a short dark woman). One ingenious competition was to vote for 'the ten greatest advertisers in Great Britain'. This enabled Alfred to print the names of firms he wanted to have as advertisers (for good measure he listed the first twenty-three that his readers voted for), as well as interviews with some of them. Advertising was a subject that *Answers* kept returning to in articles. Authorship was another. Dickens, Alfred's favourite author, occurs dozens of times. Grinding up and down the line to Coventry, writing himself silly every week, Alfred had no option but to deal with the things that interested him.

Torture, cruelty, and painful death interested him. Always good copy for journalists, suffering was dwelt on in issue after issue, with that lingering on grisly detail that betrays a morbid interest. This was 'penny-dreadful' country. The 'penny dreadfuls', the cheap fiction that boys read when nobody was looking, were a long-standing bee in Alfred's bonnet. He liked to regard his publications as a clean break with such nastiness. An 1888 *Answers* condemned the way in which 'shop boys and factory hands, pit boys, and telegraph boys, devour them eagerly and fill their foolish brains with rubbish about highwaymen, pirates, and other objectionable people'. But highwaymen and pirates (soon, in any case, to be featured in many Harmsworth magazines) were only one aspect of the dreadfuls. Hideous shrieks and ghastly torments were another. Alfred developed a taste for them, perhaps without realising.

Articles in nearly every issue reported on what it felt like to be hanged, or speculated as to how long a severed head might be conscious after beheading ('I found that the eyes followed me,' a

Saigon executioner was reported as saying; in another issue it was a French executioner, remembering how 'on one occasion a woman's head made a faint effort to speak to him'). Pressing or burning to death as a punishment, and children suffocated in trunks, occurred regularly, as did burial alive and mistaken assumptions of death ('It was decided that the cardinal should be embalmed. During the process of cutting the patient awoke, and, with screams of agony, attempted to struggle with the operator; but it was too late, the wounds proved fatal'). Dreadful things happened in railway tunnels. The story of the Underground railwayman, who, walking along the line before the trains started running, found a HUMAN FINGER ('The finger had been torn off roughly, and in a manner which must have caused the owner pain of the most terrible kind'),was used in Number 3 of *Answers*; two years later it appeared in the first issue of another Harmsworth magazine. Madness and tales from asylums were popular. As Alfred's grip relaxed on *Answers* and other hands took it over, the grislies faded out. There were fewer screams; more healthy cries of 'Ouch!'

One essential difference between Alfred and his rivals was that he had a deeper, richer curiosity. He liked the scrap-book idea of interesting items; at the same time he used articles to penetrate situations and institutions. He was not interested in ideas or controversy; why men should go on strike, or whether Darwin was right about men and monkeys, and the bishops wrong, were matters that lacked the comforting normality of everyday life and sentiments, the skin-deep world of streets and shops, crimes and marriages, jokes and gossip. The subjects of the early reporting-in-depth were modest. In 'Mysteries of a Hashish House', a reporter went to an opium den in Soho, tried a pipe for himself, and reported a dream of 'dragons, angry seas, beautiful music, fairies, noisome caves, and hissing lizards'. In 'Confessions of a Ticket-of-Leave Man', a serial article that ran to book length, a convicted forger who had been released on parole recounted his prison experiences. Alfred extracted the story from him and banged it out on the typewriter in many sessions. It made a good, flinty series, full of well-observed clichés – 'The distant tones of a barrel organ, the whistling of some careless errand boy, the rattle of passing carts, all seem to eat into one's very soul at these times, and throw into hard contrast one's own helplessness and horrible position.' This was Alfred at full stretch. Later instalments included illustrations, among them, inevitably, the treadmill, the cat o' nine tails, and one captioned 'Ready for the lash' ('The lash falls with a dull thud on the shoulders of the man, which in most instances bleed at once').

If the 'Confessions', begun in February 1889, had raised the circulation dramatically, Alfred's career might have been different: it would have fed him the message that the public shared his appetite for miscellaneous information, plainly served. But that would have been a different public: a different world. Readers already wanted a little extra. Sales rose steadily but not excitingly; the printers, now a London firm, while Iliffe's were fended off with promises, still breathed down their necks. The first annual meeting, in June 1889, reported a circulation of forty-eight thousand and a gross profit for the year of £1,097 3s 1d. Alfred's head was just above water. He kept offering the public straight journalism and a variety of tricks, and in the end it was a trick that won. Besides the competitions, 'special offers' of books and pens had been made early on. An 'Answers Puzzle' of coloured balls in a box, suggested to Alfred by a visiting American, had been mainly responsible for lifting sales permanently above thirty thousand. A few months later, Alfred glimpsed a more effective idea. The family legend has Alfred and Harold walking beside the Thames and meeting a tramp. He tells them what he would like most in life; they offer it as a prize, and a stir runs through the nation. The tramp is probable enough. Tramps can still be found on warm nights sleeping on the Embankment, close to Fleet Street, wrapped in newspapers for blankets. In the 1880s, before it became a through-road for traffic, complete with underpass, the Embankment was a fashionable boulevard; with De Keyser's Royal Hotel at one end, by Blackfriars Bridge, and the broad sweep of road, trees, and gardens following the river to Westminster. The tramp would have smelled their cigars and asked them for money. Alfred was an habitual collector of other people's experiences; he didn't look deep but he looked often. He had sharp senses. He swept up everything around him and identified them in rapid glances – the outsides of other people's newspapers, tin advertisements for starch and mustard, species of birds and trees, which way the wind was blowing, whether the tide was in or out. Harold, suspicious behind his moustache, would have been too nervous to start interrogating a tramp. He wouldn't have cared, anyway. Alfred worked on the basis of the old journalistic axiom that everyone has a story to tell, if the reporter knows how to get at it. Perhaps he just wanted value for his shilling.

The tramp talked; one of the things he said was that happiness was a pound a week for life. It was a sum you could live on then. The idea became Alfred's, and he offered the tramp's random wish as a prize in 'The Most Gigantic and the Simplest Competition the World has ever seen'. Simple things made people tick. Readers had to guess how much gold and silver coin would be in the Bank of England's banking department on a certain afternoon. *Answers*, which had just moved to new offices in Fleet Street, sent out sandwichmen with orange-coloured boards. It printed ecstatic accounts of what a pound a week for life could mean – 'How many sordid anxieties, how many trying incidents, how much trouble might be saved by the possession of even half this income ... On this sum the young man who has been waiting to marry could probably be united to the object of his affections, and what an heiress would be the girl who secured the prize!'

No one thought that whoever won the prize might live into a time when a pound a week would be a pittance. 'Pound a week' fever raged; postcards poured in. A year before, a competition to choose the most popular works of Charles Dickens brought 5,516 entries. Now more than seven hundred thousand cards were delivered, for twenty temporary clerks to sort. Each entry had to be countersigned by five witnesses, none from the entrant's address, so that Alfred was not far wrong when he boasted later that for eleven hundred pounds – the amount required to capitalise a pound a week – he publicised *Answers* to nearly five million people. The winner was a soldier, Sapper Austin, who came within two pounds of the correct amount. He married his sweetheart immediately, just as *Answers* had hoped, but died eight years later of tuberculosis. A pound a week was a poor man's dream.

Alfred's dreams were deep and ruthless; they manipulated luck instead of fishing for it. The Christmas issue of the magazine that announced the result of the competition sold two hundred and five thousand copies.

Even the modest success of *Answers*, in the months before Alfred met his tramp, was enough to make it glisten with promise for the bulky young Harmsworths in their offices and schoolrooms. Harold, the first to join, was reluctant at first. He had to be coaxed by Alfred into giving up his pensionable job in the Civil Service. The boy who was good at sums joined the boy who was good at words as company secretary at two pounds a week. He was twenty-one, already better with balance sheets than with people. Under his painful shyness, which later would harden into a shell, was an energetic young man who liked horseplay. But he brought with him a cold draught of middle-aged pessimism. Neither the soft-hearted Carr nor the restless Alfred had much idea of careful budgeting and book-keeping. Harold, an altogether sterner and grimmer figure, jolly in spasms, bustled about the office, fearing ruin every time money had to be spent. A few years later, when the magazine empire had taken shape but before it lost its sense of humour, a billiards magazine run inside the company caught him in a limerick:

> There was a young cueist named Harold,
> A fluker of shots, double-barrelled.
> 'How much? More expense?
> Frightful rush – loss immense!'
> You know him; you've heard it; that's Harold.

Brother Leicester went to Fleet Street in the evenings, to help judge competition entries. Soon he had left the Inland Revenue and was travelling from town to town in the North of England, organising teams of boys with barrows to carry bundles of *Answers*, marking off the streets on a map as they sold the magazine door-to-door. Brother Hildebrand, aged seventeen, had joined straight from school, and was writing scatter-brained letters to Cecil, in Dublin, from towns in the West of England. Delighted to be finished with the seedy trousers and washable rubber collars of his schooldays, he worried lest his friends in Ireland heard he was knocking on doors, doing the dirty work of selling. Brother Cecil won prizes at Trinity College but was soon sucked into the machine. Presently sad letters would arrive from friends who had gone to be missionaries in India, asking what had happened to the old Harmy. With his tall figure, reddish face, and air of gentle dignity, he was earmarked as Archbishop of Canterbury in Hildebrand's juvenile scheme of things. But Cecil found himself making up jokes, writing headlines, and pottering about the office, trying to look like a journalist.

The family affairs were beginning to centre on Alfred. His father was too far down the slippery slope when *Answers* was launched for the event to have much impact. The family address had changed again, for the worse, to a jerry-built house facing a cemetery in Salusbury Road, still within a mile of Pandora Road. It was narrow and raw-red, like tens of thousands of London dwellings put up by speculative builders in the second half of the century. Londoners never took to apartments, but insisted on four walls and a roof; what they ended up with was all too often a relentless machine in bricks and mortar for crushing the spirit. There would be a scrap of garden for a lilac or a privet to wither in; many chimney pots to pump out smoke and make black November fogs; and inside, a world of dark corners and knobbly fittings, with steep staircases where maids or children ran up and down half the day in cold weather, carrying buckets of coal to feed the grates.

Writs came from creditors, and once there was a bailiff, sitting in the hall. The house was still full of children, from Geraldine and Harold, who were grown up, to Christabel and Vyvyan, who were not yet ten years old. Aunt Sarah Miller continued to condescend. One day, when she was taking tea with them in the front parlour, Alfred Senior leaned expansively on the mantelpiece, which came away from the wall and crashed into the fireplace. 'What do you expect if you live in the country?' she giggled, thinking of the half-developed fields and muddy roads outside her brother's house.

The petty domestic scene had finally swallowed him. Hannah Carter and the myths of blue blood were far away as he sucked his pipe and drank his brandy, shut away in the study. Swallowfield and the Berkshire villages were a dream. So were the naughty girls of Hampstead Heath. So was Sunnybank, with the Liffey under the windows as he had lain in bed with Geraldine, whispering about the old days – even then they were sweeter than the new days. But weak as he was, it must have been from him that Alfred inherited a sense of desire. The Maffetts gave him harshness through his mother. His father gave him something for the harshness to work on. Alfred Senior, wrapped up in mysteries and romances, was unlike his sister Sarah. She was the earthy peasant daughter. He was the descendant of kings – in his imagination. The imagination was the seed.

On a cloudy Saturday in July 1889 – soon after *Answers* had completed its first year of publication – Alfred Senior and Geraldine went to a friend's garden party in Hendon, a few miles away. The day was cool; he wore thin clothes; that night he was ill, and vomited blood. Leicester went by Underground for a doctor, who knew what was wrong and held out no hopes. Alfred Senior had cirrhosis of the liver, and was dying of drink, like his father. He died in the small hours of the Tuesday morning, aged fifty-two. His wife and sons crowded into the little bedroom at the top of the stairs, but Alfred, whose twenty-fourth birthday fell on the Monday, was staying with Mary in Broadstairs, and hadn't been told of his father's illness. A telegram was sent to tell him, followed by a letter to say there wasn't enough money to pay for the funeral. Because of the garden party and the overcast afternoon, it was possible to say or infer that Alfred Harmsworth, the well-liked barrister, had caught a dangerous chill; a harmless enough fiction. But it was appropriate that even in his dying, the facts had to be edited and made respectable.

5

Fairy Tale

IT WAS NEVER CLEAR what kind of person Harold Harmsworth, later the first Lord Rothermere, really was. There are violent inconsistencies in the views of those who knew him, as often happens with rich men. Some remember him as kindly and generous; others as gross and boorish. A clumsiness in personal relations afflicted him all his life. Once, when he was a rich old viscount living in hotels, dreading the coming war with Hitler, he upset a niece by making offensive remarks over lunch. She left the table in anger. Next day she received an enormous diamond brooch from Cartier, with her uncle's compliments, but no message. She christened it 'The Bomb'. Bombs of diamonds and rubies and banknotes were his standard solution. Like some peppery millionaire in a black comedy, he was capable, as on another occasion, of presenting a gold cigarette case inlaid with gems to a sister who didn't smoke. Harold had the makings of a fairy-tale uncle, but crucial ingredients were missing.

A fairy tale, beginning about the year 1890, with Alfred and Harold on the brink of riches, is one way of looking at the Harmsworth story. A later Harmsworth publication likened it to 'some brilliant, glowing fairy story of the East'. Later still, Leicester took a more sober view when he opposed the writing of a frank history of the firm's early days, on the grounds that the truth would be undesirable. The sustained ruthlessness of the operation seems to be what he had in mind, with Harold playing a part that was as bleakly unattractive as it was necessary to Alfred's success. They came, saw, and conquered swiftly. They had to be quick, since every success by a magazine publisher was an incitement to others to do the same. Arthur Pearson, a clergyman's son, had joined the fight between Newnes and the Harmsworths with his own variation on the

popular theme, *Pearson's Weekly*. Below these journals of information, all striving modestly to educate as well as entertain,
was a cruder, ruder level of publication, the early comics. This is
where the brothers turned next. In May 1890, a few months
after 'A pound a week for life', they started *Comic Cuts*, an
eight-page weekly costing a halfpenny. This began as a trashier
version of *Answers*, with some of its jokes and articles pirated
from early issues; the 'Ticket of Leave' serial reappeared without a blush in Number 1 of *Comic Cuts*. Columns of jokes were
the other standby when space had to be filled. It was the age of
the joke, especially the pun. 'The police magistrate may not
enjoy himself even when he is having a *fine* time.' 'It is never too
late to mend. This is why the bootmaker never has your boots
done at the time promised.' 'Why is a ship the politest thing in
the world? – Because she always advances with a bow.'

Two months after *Comic Cuts* the Harmsworths launched their
first illustrated magazine, *Illustrated Chips*. This also cost a halfpenny. Old jokes and articles came round again. Number 1
repeated the report on strange things found in tunnels, complete
with torn-off finger. The usual sprinkling of grislies over the
opening months showed that Alfred was in charge – skulls
squeaked in dissecting rooms, ghastly things happened down salt
mines and up chimneys. *Comic Cuts* and *Chips* were not primarily
meant for children; they were intended for adults who had read
little or nothing before. This is apparent from editorial comments. A note in another Harmsworth magazine of 1893 men-
tions that with its large circulation, *Comic Cuts* is 'naturally read
by a large number of juveniles'. These, it seems, are incidental.
Using each publication to advertise the others, swamping the
market with cut-price goods – a penny was still the usual cost of
a magazine – the brothers began to reap total weekly circulations
of half a million or more. The idea of a range of magazines that
would overwhelm the opposition seems to have occurred to
Alfred even before he launched *Answers*. He called it the
'Schemo Magnifico', with a nod in the direction of an education
he never had, and kept the details in a folder with the title
written across the front. 'Schemo Magnifico' was locked up in a
safe, and stayed in his office till near the end of his life, when he
tore it up and flushed it down the lavatory.

Alfred wanted big circulations from the start. Why he wanted them so badly is the story of his life. But his genius was intermittent, brooding, romantic; it didn't run to the grinding routines of management. From the beginning, and especially *in* the beginning, Harold the pessimist took the necessary action to see that the magazines were cheap and solvent. He was always nagging Alfred about the fees paid to contributors. Alfred insisted on paying well, when they paid anything – many articles and drawings in early issues were robbed from foreign magazines.

Where Harold cut costs to the bone was with paper and printing. As the level of profits rose astonishingly through 1890 and 1891 – twenty, thirty, forty thousand pounds a year – Harold prided himself on paying skeleton prices for raw materials. The quality of the paper was appalling. A memo from Harold to Alfred (10 February 1892) gives the game away:

> If I were you I should not extend that small type in *Answers*. To a person with weak eyes like myself it is almost unreadable. Our bad paper and cheap printing will not stand much in the way of small type. To railway travellers also the small type will of course be unreadable.

Never mind: it would serve for the reader. Eighty years later, library file-copies of early Harmsworth magazines flake between the fingers like dead leaves. Rival contemporaries which were nothing like as successful are still smooth and glossy; they didn't have a Harold Harmsworth to curb their extravagance and make their owners millionaires.

There was ruthlessness of another kind in the way the Beaumonts were squeezed out of the business. Captain Beaumont, with beard and dark glasses, was a man of parts, an amateur musician and a notable chess player. Carr, the Irishman (who had gone back to Ireland to handle the selling there), used to greet him on the rickety stairs in Paternoster Square with biblical quotations about the virtues of giving. Beaumont and his wife had given a good deal – they did it for profit, but it was risk capital, and without it Alfred would have been slower to start. On one occasion Beaumont had a hundred pound note wheedled out of him as a competition prize. His relations with the Harmsworths remained cordial through 1890 and most of 1891. He loaned Alfred four thousand pounds against a short-term mortgage on a house in the country, Alfred's first major step towards raising his standard of living from the Pandora Road level. He bought a bicycle for the fourteen-year-old St John. But his friendliness may have proved distasteful to the Harmsworths in the end, so that what seemed like a trivial disagreement in October 1891 grew into a quarrel. A fourth magazine was about to be started, *Forget-me-Not*, aimed at ladies (later an enormous success, when it aimed at shopgirls). Beaumont was offered a one-tenth share for a thousand pounds. A few days later, on the grounds that he had raised some minor quibble, Harold lifted the price to two thousand five hundred pounds. Beaumont protested that he had already accepted the offer at a thousand pounds, and wrote to Alfred in a tone that suggested it was a tiff among friends – Harold, he said, had been seedy and out of sorts the week before, which must explain his bad manners. But the brothers had closed their ranks; as Harold said in a letter to Alfred, capital was nothing beside talent. They wanted no more of Beaumont or his money. The row was long and complicated. Alfred appeared to convince himself that Beaumont was a snake in the grass; but the note that comes through the office letters and memos is one of resentment that the Captain was there at all to share in the family's private pleasures. Eventually he was bought off with an annuity for life of two thousand four hundred pounds a year. There is a hint of threats to Beaumont, of some scandal involving homosexuality that hung over him and strengthened the Harmsworths' hand. Edward Markwick the barrister, best man and emissary, had already lost his nerve and sold his shares. He died long after, a poor man, unable to afford a gramophone. Alfred, Lord Northcliffe, sent him one, together with a plaque showing Northcliffe's profile, a detail that enraged Markwick's family, who considered he had been hard done by. But the Harmsworth nature, as shown by Harold and especially Alfred, was proud and self-sufficient. They wanted to be surrounded by people they had chosen, not the original partners who would be likely to claim rights and privileges.

The archetype of the Harmsworth executive had joined the firm at the end of 1889, a stringy young man called George Augustus Sutton. The son of a London coachman, Sutton had learned shorthand and typing, and was engaged as Alfred's first secretary. There was no fire in Sutton, only a limitless capacity for serving his employer with loyalty, discretion, and hard work. His manner to the brothers verged on the obsequious, but for juniors he had a sharp tongue. He had slanting eyebrows; they called him 'Satan'. When Alfred lived in Pandora Road, Sutton would arrive there most days after breakfast, and work in the house all morning. In the afternoon he might accompany Alfred on a walk over Hampstead Heath, silent when his master was silent, speaking when spoken to. Then back to Mary Harmsworth's tea and toast, sitting awkwardly on his chair and fingering a starched collar that always seemed too tight for him, with a long evening of work to follow. Alfred trusted few men throughout his life; Sutton was one of them, and it was to give him power and position beyond anything he dreamt of in the days when he was scribbling Pitman's shorthand in his notebook and trotting round to the pillar box.

They were all bent to Alfred's will – even Harold, who, with growing confidence, emerged as a man with a commercial mind of his own. His idea of good business was to grab it now in case tomorrow was too late. His pessimism told him that if everything was ephemeral, what could one expect from a business built on words? He liked the word 'grab', grab the profits, grab the cream, slighting the magazines in a way that irritated Alfred. For him they remained a reward in their own right, extensions of himself in print that glided like ghosts into people's minds – not an unsatisfactory handful of people but multitudes, sitting in kitchens and parlours and railway compartments, waiting for something to happen. He made something happen; he showed them interesting things.

Alfred was not the romantic journalist in exaggerated form, whose notions were trimmed by Harold to fit commercial realities. Harold was a balance-sheet man. He cut costs and was alert to the danger that the firm might over-reach itself, as new enterprises often do. It was Alfred who supplied the basic philosophy, who realised that the age of cheapness was coming. The world was waiting for watches and cigarettes, silk stockings and aspirins. Alfred saw this from the start, which is why he never failed to take advertising seriously. An item in an early *Comic Cuts*, under 'What the Editor Says', shows his brisk approach. He is writing (if the author is Alfred, as it almost certainly is) to herald the start of Volume 2. (Everything was

heralded in Harmsworth magazines. The columns were loud
with trumpetings about how well they were doing, what treats
and innovations they provided.) There had been opposition to
the idea of halfpenny papers, from newsagents who thought it
meant less money for them. The editor berates them for their
wicked prejudice – writing in an aggressive style that is an improvement on the freelance Alfred of a couple of years before;
he is beginning to find subjects where he can let himself go. 'I
am not a socialist,' he declares, 'but I cannot help saying that
whenever a man tries, like myself, to do anything for the working classes, immense difficulties are placed in his way.' Newsagents opposed the halfpenny magazine, he says, but the British
working man rallied round, followed by the upper classes. 'This
is the age of cheapness. Things get cheaper every year. You can
get a good watch now for ten shillings. Thirty years ago, it
would have cost you four or five pounds.'

Mixed up in the double-talk about helping the workers, the
commercial philosophy shines hard and clear. Basic costs of raw
materials and manufacture fell steadily in late Victorian times.
A magazine proprietor could exploit this twice, first by bringing
down the cost of production, second by selling space to the advertisers of other cheap goods that were coming within the reach
of millions. Here were fine pickings for the journalist and the
salesman. Alfred was both. An early sign of this interlocking of
interests was the succession of *Answers* products that were marketed. Harold's letters to his brother are full of references to the
Answers pen, the *Answers* watch. He was always investigating
new possibilities, cigarettes and tobacco, tea and coffee. There
was even an *Answers* toothache cure, which they tried on the
clerks; the dentist who manufactured it assured Harold it was
harmless. And in the magazines the advertisements began to
creep in for Hudson's Soap and Beecham's Pills, for cocoa and
corsets, Mazawattee tea and bicycles; offering treatments to
stop blushing, cure baldness and red noses, grow moustaches
and increase the height by up to four inches with a device known
as Universal Elevators.

One of Alfred's talents was to rise above the sordid details, to
avoid any taint of money-grubbing. There is something elusive
about him; he devises the machine and sets it in motion, yet he
is never there to get oil on his clothes. He laid his plans well in

advance like a good industrialist and carried them out swiftly and effectively, yet he always gave the impression that he was doing something else. When *Comic Cuts* appeared, its slogan was 'Amusing without Being Vulgar'. Vulgarity and nastiness were rampant in their contemporaries, according to the Harmsworths. They would help stamp them out. By later standards, it is the Harmsworth style that looks vulgar. The drawings in *Comic Cuts* and *Chips* are unbearably crude, the embryonic strip-cartoons childish, the humour thin. But Alfred, aiming hopefully at millions, looking for adults, adolescents and children, anyone as long as they could read a little and were in need of amusement, was shrewd enough to see that his readers wanted the obvious. They didn't want cleverness; they wanted a few drawings, which were a novelty, and a few items that would make them laugh or say 'Oo!' The quality of the paper and the artwork didn't matter; what mattered was buying something cheerful with a halfpenny.

The vulgar opposition that Alfred crusaded against was not always cheap and nasty. *Ally Sloper's Half-Holiday*, which claimed a circulation of a third of a million, was illustrated to a much higher standard than any Harmsworth magazine, printed on good-quality paper, and agreeably witty. But it lacked the Harmsworth punch, with the tiny black headlines scattered everywhere, and it cost a penny. It faded away before the Harmsworth onslaught. Alfred's charge of vulgarity was mainly but not wholly cant. *Ally Sloper*, like other journals of the day, went as far as it could, while remaining respectable, in showing women's thighs and bosoms. Drawings of actresses and singers in brief theatrical costume appeared regularly. A weekly series called 'Tootsie's Friends' showed girls apparently dressed for pantomime or music hall, legs and shoulders bare, often gripped at the crutch by anonymous knicker-like garments. Another series, 'Fashion Fancies', later included such daring illustrations as 'The Ladies Cycling Club Costume', where a pretty girl wore a knee-length frock embroidered with cycling motifs, among them a wheel that fitted neatly on each breast, with hub-caps where the nipples were. The lady looks demure, innocent, just fractionally naughty. But she would have looked naughtier at the time, and if there was one thing Alfred couldn't stand, it was smut. No one ever told dirty stories in his presence. He liked to make love to women, when he had time and there were no better things to do, but that was part of his other life. He once forbade a mistress to go to the *Folies Bergère*, as unsuitable for ladies, and it's unlikely that he saw any irony in this. Individual women were to be taken and enjoyed, but women as a species were pure and inviolate. He was well in the tradition of his times. An early *Answers* remarked that 'An oath from a woman's lips is unnatural and incredible. I would as soon expect a bullet from a rosebud.' When Alfred said he eschewed vulgarity, vulgarity affecting women and sex is what he had in mind. It was a genuine dislike, which presently he exaggerated and used as a bludgeon against competitors.

If Harold was later the rich uncle in the family fairy tale, Alfred was the prince. His suits came in light colours, like the one he wore for his first trip to the Continent. In a photograph taken against the garden wall of Salusbury Road, about the time of Alfred Senior's death, a select family group confronts the camera in their best black clothes, some with caps, some with bowlers, all of them dark and heavy looking – except Alfred, who wears a pale, crumpled suit, and faces the group, bareheaded, letting the camera see his profile. He looks like a supernatural figure come down from a cloud to breathe life into the dead landscape, with its solemn sons and daughters standing amid the back-garden rubbish. Alfred always looks clean, hair shining above small ears, full cheeks free of beard or moustache. This is how he wanted to be seen, the spotless figure who stands above the dirt. His strait-laced mother brought him up to be pure. It was not pure to lust after the family servant. His life was a series of façades. The itch of the flesh, the taste for sadism, the hunger to make others obey, were concealed behind potent freshness and youth. A woman writer who had not met him before went for the weekend to his country house in Kent, to discuss serial stories for his magazines. She waited in the flower-filled drawing room, her feet sinking into the carpet 'as into moss', in the approved serial-fiction style. A dogcart swept past the window, the reins held lightly by a fair-haired boy with dazzling blue eyes. He wore a light grey suit and white shoes, and he looked, she thought, as if he had been playing tennis all his life. Nearly all the journalists who described Alfred called him 'boyish'. Visitors to Kent remembered Alfred and Mary as boy and girl, playing on bicycles and throwing tennis balls for the dogs.

The country house of these idyllic scenes was a more modest place than the readers of magazine serials were used to. It was called Elmwood, a two-storied building in brick and flint, in the village of St Peter's, just inland from the North Foreland. Lighthouse, low cliffs, and the sea were visible through trees, and steamers coming up inside the Goodwin Sands with pilots on board for London, sixty miles to the west. It was the German Ocean then, not the North Sea. At night, the lighthouse rays lit up the ceilings of bedrooms at Elmwood. Broadstairs, a small but growing seaside town, was nearby. It was unfashionable and cheaper than Margate, a few miles in the other direction, in the days when Alfred Senior took his family there for summer holidays. It suited Alfred when he took holidays of his own, and he found Elmwood one afternoon when he was returning to his lodgings in Broadstairs; a rambling house, big for a suburb but small for the country, behind high walls in eight or nine acres of garden. The original dwelling, a Tudor farmhouse, had disappeared under later rooms and outhouses. It was square and nondescript, like a rectory in a copse, with bay windows and ugly chimneys. The price was four thousand pounds, paid for in September 1890 with the help of Captain Beaumont's loan. Harold, reluctant to commit himself, told Alfred that he could probably count on receiving ten thousand pounds in the next twelve months. Harold wasn't keen that he should buy Elmwood outright. Why not rent it instead? In five years' time, he suggested, looking down his nose, a thousand-acre estate would be more in Alfred's style.

But Alfred's style didn't fit other people's stereotypes. The district suited him. Broadstairs had strong associations with Charles Dickens, his favourite author; a part of *Nicholas Nickleby* was written there. It freed him from the suburbs without plunging him into the wilds, or ensnaring him in the farmlands and mansions of the rich man's acres around London. For a country residence whose owner was in business, Elmwood was a long way out of London, almost a two-hour journey by train. This didn't matter to Alfred, who worked at home for most of the week. He was twenty-five when he moved into Elmwood, in April 1891, and began, like a boy with a magic lamp, to follow the simple regime of pursuing his desires.

6

Pike and Goldfish

NEW HARMSWORTH MAGAZINES were appearing at an average rate of one every six months. *Forget-me-Not* for the ladies began in November 1891. *Funny Wonder* for those who liked comical pictures followed in July 1892. (Soon it had bold drawings of 'people who have laughed at *The Wonder*'. Among them was Mr Gladstone, who thought it a 'marvellous production', and John Burns, the militant trade-union leader, who found it 'just the paper to enliven the homes of the working man'.) Total circulation sailed above a million. An *Answers Supplement*, later renamed *Home, Sweet Home*, appeared with stories in December 1892, and total sales went to a million and a half. Harold had registered a title for a new comic, *Funny Bits, or Roars of Laughter*, but already the market was growing more sophisticated, and it never appeared. At the end of 1893 came two more story-magazines, *Halfpenny Marvel* and *Union Jack*. The year after came an uplift magazine, *Sunday Companion*, with a greeting on the cover from Samuel Smiles, and another fiction series, *Pluck Library*. The list begins to lengthen into a history of British periodical publishing.

Alfred, dressed for tennis, gave the orders from afar. He could stay away for days and weeks at a time because he had brothers he could trust, at the centre of the small group of young editorial assistants. Anyone aged thirty was an old man; the Harmsworths, 'those annoying and irritating Harmsworths' as they described themselves in one annual report, established a youth-cult and waved their youthfulness in the face of their elders. Leicester had the makings of a journalist. He thought of the title *Forget-me-Not*, which had the right touch of gentleness and sweetness for the feminine market, and became its first editor. Cecil battled with the editor's column in *Comic Cuts* and for a while was in nominal charge of *Answers*. His style was too delicate for journalism, and he seems to have been written off as a disaster at an early stage. One *Answers* contained the same joke twice, which carried economy too far; Harold advised Alfred to send Cecil an ultimatum, adding that they had better pretend there had been a deliberate mistake in that issue, with a prize of a guinea offered to anyone who found it.

Proofs, manuscripts, printers' make-ups, memos, advertisements, and ideas poured out of Elmwood. There were ideas for articles, typefaces, new writers, comic-strips, and themes for serials. Alfred's interest shifted towards fiction. He paid good prices for stories of love and bravery. Conan Doyle, beginning his career as a writer from a house in the suburbs, was paid a hundred and fifty pounds for a long tale, 'The Doings of Raffles Haw'. Sometimes Alfred saw his authors in London; often they went to stay at Elmwood, where they played tennis or billiards, walked on the sands or loafed under the elms on the velvet lawns, while Alfred suggested colourful characters and striking plots, laying down exactly how much love there should be, how much incident, how much dialogue. He would spend a morning discussing a story about poisoning or prisons.

His everyday life was simple, not in any ascetic way, but by virtue of his directness in taking what he wanted, no more and no less. He went to a shirtmaker for his shirts and a tailor for his suits. He took lessons in fencing and the mandolin, and gestured to his father's memory by making a token effort to sit his preliminary Bar examinations; a tutor taught him Latin and history for a few months, before he lost interest. Mary was hankering after a gayer social life, sharpening her claws on the long evenings at Elmwood when they had quiet dinner parties with neighbours; or the days of fishing expeditions, the trips to local bookshops. She wanted to glitter and be seen glittering, not spend the morning giving orders for dinner and waiting for Alfred to finish talking to one of his boring journalists; then out for lunch to a neighbour who showed them how his new electric light worked, followed by an afternoon looking at his rare Oriental coins, because it was raining too much to go home. Alfred's youthful gaiety was too youthful at times; he didn't have a proper regard for the social end-products, he didn't strive to be the fashionable man about London. A world of conventions and delicious social disciplines, of carriages and Mayfair evenings, was there, waiting to be breached. Alfred neither respected it nor was particularly interested. A new camera would keep him happy for hours. He would go over to Canterbury to watch cricket, take a party to the sands to play hockey, organise shooting matches with a toy pistol, or play all evening with a model steam-train. There were compensations for Mary, a chance to be the pretty hostess at an August garden party, with a marquee, a fortune teller, and the Blue Hungarian Band playing waltzes. They visited the theatre in London, to see new plays by the fashionable Mr Wilde, *Lady Windermere's Fan* and *A Woman of No Importance*. They saw Beerbohm Tree in *Hamlet*. Alfred didn't think much of *Hamlet*; he preferred a musical comedy like *The Mikado*, or a popular singer rendering 'Come into the Garden, Maud'. Mary found still better compensations – a diamond necklace costing two hundred pounds from Alfred, a shopping trip to Paris, a settlement of twenty-one thousand pounds in railway stocks.

Travel was one of the fashionable things they did from the beginning, taking it in slabs in the early months of the year, when the English upper classes flocked to the Continent in search of sun, gambling, medicinal springs, and affairs in strange bedrooms. London to the Riviera took thirty hours. The Casino with its gaming rooms at Monte Carlo, reached direct from the railway station by a flight of stairs, was still comparatively new. It would be years before common people began to sneer at it as a symbol of decadence, serving a class that died slowly as the old Europe died. In the 1890s it was the modern way of having fun. Alfred said he was afraid to gamble seriously lest it get a hold on him. He liked travel for what it showed him, fresh vistas of interesting things. Their first trip was a seven-week cruise to the Mediterranean in 1892. His mother and Hildebrand were among the party that saw them off from London in the morning; at dusk on the February afternoon their ship was off the North Foreland, and they saw the lights of Elmwood. They gambled a little at Monte Carlo, drove around Turkey eating hard-boiled eggs and oranges, and visited the Pyramids. People reading *Answers* were observed in Sicily, Port Said, and Gibraltar, where the soldier in charge of the visitors' book had a copy. Next year they went to Paris and Monte Carlo, and the year after that to

Hannah Carter, Northcliffe's
grandmother, the village girl
who was fondly thought
to have royal blood.

Geraldine, Northcliffe's
illegitimate daughter.
Some said she looked
like Queen Elizabeth II.

The two Alfreds, father
and son.

The Harmsworths about
1889, soon after the death
of Alfred Senior. Alfred
wears the light-coloured
suit. Then come his wife,
Mary; Christabel; St John;
Edith Bell (Irish cousin);
Hildebrand; Vyvyan *(at
front)*; Harold; unknown;
Violet; Mrs Harmsworth;
and Cecil. These were the
years they all wanted to
forget.

Canada and the United States, the beginning of a long love-hate relationship; the first thing Alfred noticed, with annoyance, was American bureaucracy at work, keeping them on board the *Teutonic* all night because the liner was a few minutes late reaching the quarantine anchorage in New York Harbour. He found the streets of Manhattan muddy and sordid; the Waldorf Hotel palatial.

Alfred's restlessness was noted from the start. A trade paper remarked in 1892 on the 'entirely original methods' on which the office was run – 'to begin with, Mr Alfred Harmsworth is hardly ever there'. He was always lying on divans and staying in bed late; he needed long holidays to conserve his energy, it was said. His energy seemed to ebb and flow, there when it had to be, gone when he didn't need it. He was the sort of man who would rise from the dinner table, and, as he did once at Pandora Road, tell his guests he had to lie on the sofa because he suffered from 'flushings of blood to the head' after meals. His health was enigmatic, liable to give him trouble, or perhaps provide a refuge, when the world became too pressing. He was unwell when *Forget-me-Not* started; the row with the Beaumonts prostrated him, and for weeks he was 'seedy' and 'not well, in bed', and 'suffering from overwork'. No doubt he was suffering from Beaumont. His father, faced with similar problems, would have written about them lugubriously in his diary, squeezing out the bittersweet drops from each crisis. Alfred's diary, which he kept for some years from 1891, reveals nothing but the surface of what he did and who he saw, with an occasional flash of opinion. To those who knew him he had a sharply defined, sometimes overpowering personality, arrogant and self-opinionated, charming and humorous, easy to be attracted by, difficult to be intimate with. Writing in his diary he skates over his feelings. He is neither happy nor unhappy, glad or sorry, good or bad. Pleasures with women, which Alfred Senior hinted at more than once, appear not to exist. The nearest the diary comes to affection for Mary is where he calls her, once or twice, 'wifie' and 'wifelet'. The atmosphere is that of the romances he commissioned for his magazines, tales like *The Smiths of Surbiton* which Keble Howard wrote for him a few years later. It was the age of the delicate euphemism, interpreted by people in general, and certainly by Alfred, as good taste. This is how Mr Howard, working to the proprietor's specifications, saw a bedroom scene between man and wife:

A long pause, and then the girl, bracing herself for an effort, murmured:
'Ralph?'
'Yes, kiddie?'
'There's something I want to tell you. I can do it better in the dark.'
'What is it?'
'Can't you – can't you guess?'
'Can't I guess? Let me see. Oh!' He tried to read her eyes through the darkness. 'Do you mean,' he said solemnly, 'that I may call you little mother?'
She spoke no word. Yet the angels of God heard her answer.

It was not how Alfred lived, it was not how anybody lived, but it was a convention with the force of a law. One entry about Mary in Alfred's diary touches reality for a moment, when he refers to a surgeon's visit to perform a minor operation on her at Elmwood in April 1893. They hope for 'great things' as a result, presumably that she will be able to conceive; after five years of marriage, they were still childless. The diary contained only a vestige of Alfred. It was all façade. He was a secretive, slippery man. When he moved to Elmwood, his natural son, christened Alfred Benjamin, was eight years old, living in a village barely thirty miles away, across the Thames Estuary. Discreetly, surreptitiously, payments were being made to Master A. B. Smith's grandmother, who had been bringing him up since his mother, Louisa Jane, got married, a few years after her liaison with Alfred. That was the private Alfred. The public Alfred went to the other extreme, raising the bogeyman of 'vulgarity' in magazines in order to make a virtue of how clean and wholesome his own publications were. *Comic Cuts* might be rubbish by educated standards, but since the patronising attitude to the masses that prevailed made it possible for politicians like Mr Gladstone and John Burns (and Lord Randolph Churchill, and many others) to endorse the rubbish, it left Alfred free to concentrate on areas where he was unassailable, and proclaim the good news that *Comic Cuts* was 'A pure Paper for every Home and for Every One of the Family'. He gives the impression that he believed in what he was doing. This was one of Alfred's strengths; he could take a view of things that was commercially advantageous, but make it sound as if it came from the bottom of his heart. Perhaps this is the secret of success for all good publicists: they turn what would be hypocrisy in clumsier operators into a crusade. It would have been commercially disastrous to depart from the moral standards of the time. As a magazine proprietor, Alfred not only conformed to them, he wallowed in them.

His preoccupation with pain and madness, as shown in the early magazines, may have been important. Perhaps he feared them both as the violent outcome of dreams and fantasies. Years later, he told a nephew, Cecil King, of two experiences when he was a boy, each time when he was alone with one other person, in a compartment of a no-corridor train. In the first, it was a woman. As the train left a station, she shouted at him: 'I'm going to have a baby – now!' He leaned out of the window and stopped the train. On the other occasion, it was a man, who stared at Alfred and produced a knife. Alfred was terrified, until the man used the knife to cut off the leather window strap, and carve it into a pair of braces. Why remember those particular stories? There is a menace in both episodes, a glint of terror. If Alfred was aware of a taste for dark fantasies, he would know they must be kept under control lest they break loose and consume him. The more he hides them, the more they creep out to colour his judgment when he is doing something else, innocently choosing subjects for little articles. His life is to be bound up with the idea of control, of regulation. He must dominate a world that will get the better of him unless he is watchful. He must dominate his own nature. This may have been connected with the need to fight for his mother's affection, in the face of a big, aggressive family. However Alfred's psychology is interpreted, some explanation must be hazarded to explain what it was that changed an enterprising editor and salesman into a force, a will, that was not entirely normal.

Most of the time he seemed calm enough, with passing outbursts of irritation. His voice was soft; softer still when he was angry. Sometimes he bit his nails till his fingers bled. As he grew older, his cruel streak was turned against people who worked for him. In the early Elmwood days there is little to report; except that for a time he is said to have kept an aquarium with two compartments in his bathroom. On one side of a glass partition swam goldfish, on the other a pike. When it amused him, he would lift the partition and study the results.

Alfred demanded bigger and bigger circulations. Harold's letters to him at Elmwood in 1891 and 1892 reflect the brothers' obsession with sales. A typical letter at the end of 1892 would begin with the week's figures, and sometimes contain nothing else: *Answers* 360,000, *Comic Cuts* 430,000, *Chips* 240,000, *Forget-me-Not* 120,000. Harold and Alfred discovered a new spur to circulation about this time, the use of long, two-column advertisements for the magazines' serial stories, placed in local papers. Religious newspapers were also used; the *War Cry*, journal of the Salvation Army, refused to accept the advertisements.

Although circulation was meat and drink to both the brothers, their approach to it was different. Alfred loved his magazines for themselves, and if the sales of one of them looked unhealthy, he sought to improve the journal and thus the circulation. Harold was always inclined to reach for the knife. If 'grab' was one of his words, 'knife' was the other. When the *Sunday Companion* faltered, he wanted to knife it. Alfred had to intervene and say no. Harold cared about money for its own sake. Alfred enjoyed his money, spending lavishly on fine linen, vintage wines, Henry Clays, the best physicians, the best suites at the Metropoles and Waldorf Astorias. But he was always ploughing it back, into his life and into the business. It comforted his body and strengthened his hold over people; it wasn't the key to Alfred, experimenting with a new scale of persuasion. He told people what to buy and read, and they bought and read it. Very quickly, he had become the world's biggest magazine publisher. He had served up the jokes that made him laugh and the articles that interested him. Now he was finding a new vein, the stories that stirred him. With *Halfpenny Marvel* and *Union Jack* in 1893 and *Pluck Library* the following year, Alfred plunged into the market for boys' stories of adventure, war, and travel. Each issue was built around a complete tale of twenty thousand words or more, jammed into fifteen or sixteen book-sized pages. The Harmsworths sold these magazines partly on their merits as blood and thunder, partly as an antidote to the allegedly poisonous influences of that snake in the literary paradise, the penny dreadful.

Popular fiction in Britain for much of the nineteenth century had a powerful undercurrent of crime and horror. Magazines with tales of fiends, vampires, brigands, deformed lunatics, horse-stealers, and highwaymen made many publishers' fortunes. These were naturally read with pleasure by growing boys, and were naturally condemned by their elders, who found them a convenient way of accounting for evil tendencies in the young. The idea of supplanting the dreadfuls with tales that could be advertised as exciting but healthy had occurred to a publisher in 1866 (the year after Alfred was born), and resulted in a story magazine called *Boys of England*, which was soon widely imitated. The new wave avoided the regrettable tendency of the dreadfuls to present criminals as heroes, but its stories were well spiced with violence and were not above torture. Alfred's authors worked on the same principle, including plenty of fighting, killing, tying-up, flogging, and general beastliness, written in terms of unmistakable goodies and baddies. Baddies were apt to be non-English. Women, as usual, were rosebuds:

Coming up to her he seized her roughly by the arm.
'I will make you listen to me,' he cried. 'You *shall* be mine –'
Two hairy hands circled round the Spaniard's throat; his face turned purple.
May heard the terrible howl which she had heard at night, and looking up she saw the form of a huge gorilla. Its great fangs were revealed as it snarled viciously.
The frightened girl uttered a cry of terror; the powerful animal released its hold of Victor's throat, and seizing him round the body with its hairy arms, carried him into the bushes.
One shriek of agony awoke the stillness of the forest; then a death-like silence reigned. That was the last ever heard or seen of Victor.

The Harmsworth stories had to be red-blooded without going too far. With women only one approach was possible. Heroines were demure in speech and safely wrapped in voluminous clothes, in contrast to some of the penny-dreadful ladies, who had been known to reveal a calf or a shoulder. Violence was essential; no one seemed to mind as long as it was done in what could be presented as a good cause. 'The Torture Chamber' contained a long account of the suffering of brave Alan Chester,

Englishman, being pulled apart on the rack in a castle dungeon
– Spanish, again.

No answer came from the English chieftain's compressed lips. His
broad chest heaved convulsively, but no shriek for mercy escaped
him. The only sound that now dispelled the silence of that death-like
vault was the shriek of those rusty wheels, torturing a brave man to
his death.

When the *Marvel* was still in the planning stage, Harold wrote
to Alfred to suggest they call it the *Boys' Weekly Reader*. 'It sounds
respectable,' he said, 'and would act as a cloak for one or two
fiery stories.' They had to be all the more careful because they
kept lashing the penny dreadfuls and blaming them for juvenile
delinquency. It was here that Alfred improved on *Boys of England*
and the other magazines of healthy fiction; he made what he
was doing into a crusade. Week after week, his other magazines
cross-advertised *Marvel*, and *Marvel* advertised itself, as healthy,
tasteful and with a tendency to elevate, as against the 'vile
trash', the 'deleterious rubbish' of the gutter-press. It could be a
turning point in a youth's life, announced the anonymous
editor, if he gave up 'penny horrors' and began to read 'our
pure, healthy tales'. Readers were told that 'if we can rid the
world of even one of these vile publications, our efforts will not
have been in vain'. Any magistrate or policeman who made a
scapegoat of lurid fiction, as some of them did, was sure to find
his words reported with satisfaction by the Harmsworths. A
respectable lad, charged with stealing thirty pounds from his
employers, had fallen into the clutches of the dreadfuls. 'The
father of the prisoner said his son's mind had been completely
turned by reading trashy literature. The magistrate said that the
books mentioned could only do harm to all who read them, and
he was glad to see that at last an attempt was being made to
issue pure, healthy literature, at a price within the reach of
all...' When a boy of fourteen who had stolen nine pounds was
found on a pier at Liverpool, armed with a revolver and a knife
and looking for a ship to America, he pleaded penny dreadfuls
in mitigation. He had wanted to go to the Far West. The magistrate ordered twelve strokes of the birch rod, to which the *Marvel*
retorted that it was the man who published the books who ought
to be punished. 'Police Sergeant' wrote to say that the boys in

blue supported the 'great undertaking' of the *Marvel*. 'Thanks, Sergeant,' replied the editor.

Other editorials hammered away at the wonderful value for money and the true-to-lifeness of the stories. Cynics who doubted the existence of owl men, as described in 'The Slave King', were put in their place:

It may interest them to know that, according to a leading scientific journal, American naturalists are just now deeply interested in the discovery of some owls of an unknown species at New Jersey. The birds have faces like monkeys, covered with white down nearly an inch long, and their wings, sparsely covered with feathers, have a spread of three feet.

The voice of Alfred, who always cared about birds and animals, can be heard. He coloured every issue, usually with relentless boasts and promises, harping on the theme of purity and wholesomeness. He was creating publicity, whipping up interest, attaching importance to his story-magazines instead of letting them be recognised as exciting pulp-fiction. His approach was factual, up to a point: penny dreadfuls existed and contained much crude writing. It becomes difficult for critics to put a finger on his cunning. Perhaps he convinced himself that it wasn't a stunt; that the crusade was necessary for England. In any case, he had learned what ingredients went to make a successful publicity campaign: simplicity, cheek, topicality, and repetition.

Alfred was seeking new horizons. By 1894 he had a nest of magazines and a printing works. A public company called Answers Ltd had raised new capital without affecting family control. Mary fancied a house in London where she could entertain: she wanted progress in this direction. She already had lovers. The Harmsworths were getting glimpses of the fashionable world. At Willis's Rooms, a West End restaurant, they saw the Prince of Wales at one table, the beauteous Lily Langtry at another; Alfred wrote it down in his diary. An agreeable future of entertaining and being entertained, of sinking into the thick, delicious syrup of Edwardian society by sheer weight of income, lay ahead if he wanted it. The rest of the family were still bogged down in suburbia, mentally and sometimes physically. If the men had waited a few years and looked around judiciously, they might have found better brides than they did. Most of the Harmsworths married poorly. Alfred was an exception:

Mary was clever, pretty, enterprising, good with showy things – reception rooms, jewellery, rose gardens. Harold's wife, Lilian, was sharp-witted and flighty, a blonde with blue eyes who watched her figure. Her father ran a hardware business and presently went bankrupt. (Mary's father, too, was in financial trouble soon after she married Alfred. It was as though the Harmsworth turbulence sank little craft that came too near the wake.) Lilian's mother came from a family of fierce Baptists. As a child, Lilian told her sister that she prayed she would marry a very rich man and have three sons. Long after, the sister said: 'Never pray to God, in case he hears you and gives you what you think you want.' Cecil married his cousin, a Maffett girl called Emily (she spelt it 'Emilie' because it looked more elegant). Aunt Em was not too popular with the Harmsworths, perhaps because Cecil was weak and charming, and she was thought to be taking advantage of him. Later on she gave innumerable impecunious Maffetts direct access to the Harmsworth cash. Some of her relatives regarded her as vaguely sinister, a bird of ill omen. Mrs Harmsworth Senior tried to stop the marriage, as she had tried to stop Alfred's. Leicester, anticipating trouble from that direction, married in secret; the news was not broken to Mrs Harmsworth until just before the first child was born. Leicester's wife, Annie, was another who failed to arouse much warmth. Her father was a stonemason's labourer. 'Vulgar' was fired at Annie triumphantly. She was an odd companion for Leicester; but Leicester was an odd man, not casually eccentric like some of the lightweight Harmsworths, but bearing down upon people in dark clothes and black boots, his face pale and potato-like, dry-tongued and coldly witty. He must have known that his talents resembled Alfred's without matching them, and suffered inwardly, by never being able to avoid comparison with the family genius. Alone in the family, he had a collector's taste for silver, pictures, books.

Among the girls, Geraldine was the only one who was off her mother's hands by the mid-nineties. She married into a well-to-do Dublin family of Protestant doctors and booksellers, the White Kings, and went off to India as the wife of Lucas, an official in the Indian Civil Service. Her children were born in hill stations on the rim of the Empire, miles from anywhere; with the family from place to place travelled a piano and English glassware from the Army & Navy Stores, all sent out by steamer. Geraldine was clever; she and Lucas King formed one of the brighter spots in the family. Violet and Christabel lived in comfort with their mother, who had been whisked out of Salusbury Road as soon as *Answers* prospered; the house with poky windows and shaky mantelpieces was erased from memory, as though it had never existed. Next-generation Harmsworths who asked about the early days were told of Rose Cottage or Boundary Road; not the jerry-built house by the cemetery. Mrs Harmsworth, soon to have a substantial fortune in cash settled on her, was installed in a better district some way down the Edgware Road towards the West End; later, continuing in the same straight line, in a town mansion at Marble Arch, with a painted porch and a footman to answer the door. The younger boys also lived with their mother, when they were not away. Hildebrand had been taken off the road and sent to university; St John was there too.

All this was founded on half a dozen magazines. The empire grew month by month. This was where Alfred's energy burned; not at the business of entering society, which doubtless would come to him in the end. *Union Jack* and *Pluck Library* were nicely timed to catch the upsurge of imperialism with tales of Empire and armies. *Union Jack* was heralded by the *Marvel* in an editorial that said there was no connection between the two; it even praised the promoters for being so brave as to start competing. Soon the tales of Britons in strange lands were pouring out ('More than forty natives sprang on Cyril, and, though his resistance was desperate, he was quickly reminded how surely numbers tell, even though they be black ones'). Alfred and his magazines were edging on to the national scene. The Empire in the last decade of the century covered one-sixth of the earth. According to influential writers like Rudyard Kipling, the British administered it by a kind of divine right. Portions of Africa were still being added. Matabeleland had been taken from the Zulus by the Chartered Company (the British South Africa Company), using police and machine guns, at the end of 1893. The British public treated this as a brilliant victory. Imperialism began to look more warlike and aggressive in the 1890s. For years Britain had turned its hopes away from Europe and the growing continental armies, and fixed them on the more amenable Empire.

Now the annoying Europeans were criticising Britain, coveting her possessions and impudently competing for her trade. It was a time to be firm and build battleships.

A new serial for *Answers*, 'The Poisoned Bullet', by William Le Queux, began in December 1893, a story of war and invasion, with Britain treacherously attacked 'one evening in 1897' by the forces of two foreign powers, France and Russia. It was presented as fiction that could easily become fact, buttressed with quotes from retired admirals. This was another clue to Alfred's future. Like everyone who read newspapers he knew that Britain was drifting into new waters; the difference with Alfred was that he immediately wanted to do something about it, something big, impressive and exciting. His nature was to leap straight from desire to satisfaction, without preliminaries. The house he lived in, his rather muddled life of work and leisure mixed up together, were the result of doing as he pleased. He was like desire personified and put into action. Once his interest wandered, anything could happen. In common with many, his interest wandered to Britain's place in the world. The subject of Empire was in the air. Patriotic sentiments were abroad, in songs and plays and speeches, made harsher by threatened change and signs of rivalry across the Channel. Here was another crusade, simple and popular: Be strong, have guns. It didn't replace his other interests – nothing ever did, with Alfred; everything accumulated, weighing him down. But it moved him on from the world of *Comic Cuts*.

Just now [said an editorial in the *Marvel* early in 1894,] when the supposed superiority of other European navies over our own is attracting so much attention, it may interest our readers to know that (according to Government papers just issued) the trade of the British Empire is nearly equal to the combined trade of France, Germany, Austria, Russia and the United States.

But to protect that trade we naturally want a very powerful navy, capable of withstanding the attack of a combination of any two other powers.

We would strongly urge all those who are interested in our navy, and have the welfare of our grand country at heart, to read 'The Poisoned Bullet', now appearing in *Answers*. It is a splendid story, and deals with the great crisis it should be every man's desire to avert.

The serial, the first of many about Britain with its back to the

wall, ran for months, with the country invaded, massacre at
Eastbourne, carnage in the manufacturing towns, treachery in
high places. 'This extraordinary work,' claimed *Answers*, 'is
based upon the prognostications of the best living authorities on
modern warfare. It deals not with the vague, shadowy, and
distant future, but with the almost immediate present.' The
style was lurid. When the battles looked like ceasing, Harold
pressed for more. Electric mines shattered French gunboats ('the
dark green water was tinged with the life-blood of the hapless
victims'), Indian troops manned the Surrey hills, corpses
strewed the outer suburbs. Germany was on the same side as
Britain; the Ruskies and especially the Frenchies seemed more
natural enemies than the Englishman's stolid, hard-working
German cousins, whose Emperor was Queen Victoria's grandson. Finally the invaders were cornered between Dorking and
Horsham, and slaughtered – 'Britannia had husbanded her full
strength until this critical moment, for now, when the fate of her
Empire hung upon a thread, she sent forth her valiant sons, who
fell upon those who had desecrated and destroyed their homes,
and wreaked a terrible vengeance.' The serial was headed
throughout in newspaper style: A GLORIOUS VICTORY! – UTTER
ROUT OF THE ENEMY – DEFEATED BY LAND AND SEA –
£250,000,000 INDEMNITY – THE REIGN OF PEACE – END OF
THE GREAT WAR OF 1897.

New kinds of journalism were calling him, new approaches to
power were in sight. In W. L. George's novel *Caliban*, the hero
who is meant to be Alfred says: 'I'm a second-rate man. He cuts
more ice than the first-rate man. He's like Napoleon, nearer to
the earth, nearer to the common people.' Napoleon was an
amusing idea; a connection; a recurring fantasy in his life. 'I
have been to Paris,' wrote Mrs Harmsworth Senior to Cecil in
December 1894, when he was on a world tour with Leicester.
'Had a very gay time,' she added. She had been there with
Alfred. They had had a 'Napoleonic craze', and 'nothing suited
us but what belonged to that great man – especially as the
waiters said Alfred is exactly like him – and of course you
remember dear Papa's Napoleonic lock. We have got china and
pictures of him and were going to try for more, but the Parisian
shopkeepers know how to put it on, especially when they see the
English come along.'

Alfred's supposed resemblance to Napoleon was amusing, nothing more. Like the imagined family likeness to the Hanoverian kings or the Duke of Wellington, it stuck in people's minds, never quite serious but never quite forgotten. It pleased Alfred to think he looked like Napoleon, the man of will. It would keep cropping up.

7

In the News

ELMWOOD was a comfortable, tree-screened house that verged on the ornate where Mary Harmsworth showed her hand with black oak and potted palms. Alfred's requirements were that annoying callers should be told he was out, that servants should wear thin shoes that didn't squeak, that soft blue and black pencils were kept sharpened beside his bed, that the telephone was working. The trunk line to London often broke down. It was not the most convenient place for a man in the communications business to live. But Alfred grew more, not less, attached to it. He would hurry back from business, in the 'Kent Coast' or 'Granville' train. He had a billiards room built, equipped with an organ and a little piano, which he played while his guests got on with their billiards. He bought many gadgets, including the amazing new phonograph, using it to record cylinders of instructions for despatch to London.

The shady fish-pond was unexpectedly large; Alfred feared fire, and wanted ample water close at hand. Beyond the lawns and rose-gardens was a heated glasshouse where alligators from Florida lay under the bubbling mud. Nearby he had a work-bungalow, furnished with a table and tray of pens from the original *Answers* office, a few pieces from Pandora Road, and a blackboard with chalks for scribbling down ideas. After a few years nothing changed at Elmwood. One day in the future, when she no longer went there, Mary would have the house redecorated, either thoughtlessly or spitefully, while Alfred was away. When he saw what had happened, he had everything replaced in exact copies of the originals, down to the wallpaper, curtains, and cheap pieces of china.

In the hall, for many years, stood a stuffed polar bear. On the lawn was a long white lifeboat, the *Mary Harmsworth*, sunk to the level of the rail; on hot afternoons visitors reclined in it against cushions to take tea and cucumber sandwiches. Bear and boat were trophies from an Arctic expedition that Alfred sponsored in the summer of 1894. An American polar expedition spurred him on to organise one for Britain. He commissioned a young traveller, F. G. Jackson, who sailed in the *Windward* and brought back modest scientific results. The maps of Franz Josef Land, now Russian, still show a Mount Harmsworth. Alfred said it cost him thirty thousand pounds.

About the same time (it was the day his bungalow was finished) he declined an offer to be Conservative candidate for Folkestone. He had been toying with a career in politics for at least two years. His energy and shrewdness impressed old hands. They thought they saw a conventional Tory inside the eager young businessman with the beautifully cut frock coat and golden forelock. Alfred may even have thought so himself. American reporters didn't yet bother to interview him when he arrived in New York, but against a British background he caught the eye. He matched something in the public mood. In Tudor Street, between Fleet Street and the river, Alfred's comings and goings at the *Answers* office caught the eye of less successful journalists across the road, at an evening paper called the *Sun*. London had nine evening newspapers at the time, most of them trying to cater for the popular market. Some had caught a whiff of the new American journalism, with its sensational crusades and bold style of presentation. But so far brightness had failed in Fleet Street. The great grey sponge of British public life sucked it up and made it disappear. Pushful young men at the *Sun*, which was known to be in trouble, kept their eyes open for opportunities. Two of them, the assistant editor, Louis Tracy, and the chief sub-editor, Kennedy Jones, managed to see the books of another foundering paper, the Conservative *Evening News and Post*, and set themselves up to act as brokers. Jones was the aggressive one, a Scot with Irish blood and a gangster's face. He knew about the Harmsworths. He had seen Alfred stepping out of his carriage and pair in Tudor Street, under the white facade, the glaring gold sign *Answers* and the triple row of windows with boxes of flowers on the sills. That was long before the area ran downhill. Newspaper offices and printing works then had some of the glamour of television studios later on. The hot smells of ink and machinery that come through gratings and dirt-encrusted windows meant progress in 1894. Jones and Tracy contacted the Harmsworths with the information that the *Evening News*, though losing money, still sold up to a hundred thousand copies every afternoon. Harold was cautious. He had heard unsatisfactory reports of Jones and Tracy, and thought it unwise of Alfred to identify himself with the Conservative Party. He advised a small offer, with only a small percentage of any profits for Jones and his partner.

The negotiations crept forward. Alfred liked the idea of being a newspaper proprietor; he had already made abortive inquiries about buying a suburban daily. He and Harold probably feigned indifference to keep the price down. For a week after Jones and Tracy brought the offer, Alfred stayed at Elmwood, fishing, playing tennis, and working in the bungalow, while Harold negotiated. Another week, and the sale was clinched, at a price of twenty-five thousand pounds, to include printing plant and a ramshackle building. Harold referred to it ironically as 'our gold brick', and set to work to cut the cost of paper and other ingredients, while Alfred and Kennedy Jones, who was soon appointed editor, improved the contents. Headlines grew a shade bigger and blacker, cross-headings sprouted, paragraphs became shorter; led by Kennedy Jones, the sub-editors were at work like moles, burrowing out of sight, early members of a new race of journalists who made blue-pencil marks on other people's articles and turned newspapers into a visual experience. The little items that Alfred loved were shovelled into the columns: 'Hunting for a Ghost', 'Baby Farming in Belgium', 'Blew herself up with a Cartridge', 'Rider Haggard in a Smash' (he was riding a bicycle). Fragments of world news off the agency tape machines were presented as 'News Flashes Brought by the Electric Wire from All Quarters of the Compass'. A tired formula today, though still to be seen in tired newspapers, it was a novelty then. It was part of Alfred's philosophy of selling through emphasis. The news was a product that must be sold if it was to reach large numbers of people. How coherently this was seen inside the cup- and gluepot-littered offices of the *Evening News* isn't clear; probably not at all. Enthusiastic young men were experimenting with a new kind of popular entertainment. Sport and crime were served up alongside a daily short story, a women's column, and (against the wishes of Jones) a column of short feature-articles called 'Some Interesting Items' that looked like extracts from old Harmsworth magazines, and sometimes were ('God, man,' said Jones, 'you're not going to turn the paper into an evening *Answers*, are you?').

Politics came sparingly and in small doses. Crime, especially if violent, was the most consistently featured kind of news. This was in the tradition of sensational Sunday newspapers like *Lloyds Weekly News*. It went against the high ideals of Alfred, who had been condemning the newspaper exploitation of crime only a few months earlier, in *Answers*. But Kennedy Jones knew the power of a bloody deed. Part of his value to Alfred was no doubt that the hard-as-nails journalist could be used to exploit the crime reporting that the proprietor wouldn't have cared to be seen advocating, however much he may have liked it in private. Every day had its exciting deaths, some traditional ('MYSTERIOUS MURDER of an aged chemist at Nottingham – no clue'), some up-to-the-minute ('PROFESSOR AND POISONER. Kills fifteen victims by cholera bacilli – sensational suicide'). Alfred can be seen hovering on the edge of the late Victorian crime wave. In July 1894, Harold had had occasion to complain (on the grounds of boredom) about still more articles in *Answers* on the insides of prisons. In September, his first month as a newspaper proprietor, Alfred spent a morning at Chelmsford Prison, where he went with an *Answers* contributor to see a local murderer, James Canham Read. Read had shot a pregnant girl. A long unsigned article in the *Evening News*, with drawings, lingered on Read's red socks, his good appetite and the small chamber in the prison yard that fascinated Alfred: 'The man who is executed at Chelmsford is pinioned in his cell, is walked quickly from there to this strange little room, with its gaudy, dark red paint and unpleasantly clean whitewash, and is sunk into eternity in less than sixty sec. after he leaves his cell.' Read was tried, found guilty, and duly hanged in the red and white room. During the trial, Alfred was in Paris, where daily telegrams showed him how the reports were helping to push up circulation. It rose from a hundred and eighty-seven thousand on the first day to three hundred and ninety thousand on the last. When Read was hanged in December, there was still enough interest in him to raise the sales to three hundred and thirteen thousand. A reporter had a look at the dead man in his coffin, pronouncing the face slightly blue and the neck a trifle chafed. On the opposite page, 'A Madman's Act', the report of a killing in Kensington, kept the pot boiling.

Editorial content was one side of the operation; advertising was the other. Small ads were hailed as though they were a Harmsworth invention – 'twelve words for sixpence, same price as a telegram.' Enormous display advertisements for Lipton's Tea and Carter's Little Liver Pills were lured on to the back page, not by cheaper rates – Harold raised the price – but by the atmosphere of excitement and the growing circulation, which was emphasised daily. A typical device, and one with important consequences, was to have the sales certified by an accountant. The figure thus represented 'net sales' rather than the number distributed, which might include a large number of copies that were returned to the publisher unsold. 'Net sales' became a war-cry, with other newspapers dared to do the same. When the *Evening News* first used it, three weeks after the Harmsworths took over, the figure was a hundred and ten thousand, little more than under the previous ownership. Alfred was boasting about a circulation that was essentially the same as it had been six months before. It was the style of the boasting that counted, though soon enough the sales were responding to the overall impact of Harmsworth style, providing a continual feed-back of results that justified further claims. By early October the paper was making a profit of eighty pounds a week; by the middle of the month, a hundred and seventy.

As the figures improved, the case for beginning a daily news-paper, already attractive to Alfred, became stronger. A week after the *Evening News* began to look like making substantial profits, he wrote to Cecil and Leicester, who were still going round the world, to tell them that one was being planned for the following February. Most of the letter was taken up with cir-culation figures – wherever Harmsworths went, vital statistics followed them.

All the papers are doing well: *Forget-me-Not* has been fluctuating between 145,000 and 148,000 for a long time. The autumn double number, price twopence, went well, doing 148,000. *Home Sweet Home* is 75,000. *Answers* is as high as it was this time last year. We are giving away for a Christmas prize a flourishing shop in any kind of business the winner chooses. The halfpenny books, the *Marvel* and the *Union Jack*, are rising splendidly. We are just about to start another which will appear 26 November called *The Pluck Library*. The *Wonder* is doing more than it ever did before. *Chips* went down but is now rising. *Comic Cuts* is steady, 425,000.

There was a P.S.: '*Sunday Companion* rising steadily.'

A new daily was discussed that winter, without the plans maturing in time for February, or for any date in 1895. Alfred decided to make a serious attempt at politics, and spent much of the year working to get into Parliament. In March he had agreed to stand as Conservative candidate for Portsmouth, and between then and July, when there was a general election, he and Mary were in the town for most of the time, undergoing the peculiar rituals involved in being nice to the electorate, from admirals and their ladies to naval stokers with large families. Deputations from the dockyard waited on him. He stood beaming while Mary declared bazaars to be well and truly opened, and allowed himself to be hypnotised on the pier. He went on board warships, sat through a ghastly concert at the Central Conservative Club, saw the fire brigade turn out, attended sports days, and became in rapid succession a Forester, a Buffalo, an Oddfellow, a member of the Lodge of Druids, and an apprentice Freemason (he completed his initiation by the end of the year). To help his campaign he bought a local newspaper, the *Evening Mail*, in the names of Harold and Kennedy Jones, and ran an invasion story, 'The Siege of Portsmouth', in which a foreign power struck at Britannia through her great naval base.

Patriotism was the theme of his electioneering. He commissioned a song that was sung twice nightly at a local music hall by a woman wearing a Union Jack:

> The soldier brave fights for his flag,
> His martial valour shields it.
> The sailor staunchly mans our Fleet
> But here's to the lad who *builds* it!

As a political campaigner, Alfred was tireless and ingenious, but without experience. At one public meeting he said he was in favour of ordinary sailors becoming officers; the chairman hissed at him not to talk like that, for God's sake: the British seaman wanted to be led by gentlemen. Alfred must have hated being out of his depth. His true-Blue colleagues may have unsettled him as well. Garden parties and weekends at country houses had the usual hard core of Tory aristocrats, and his fellow-candidate – there were two Conservatives, two Liberals – was the Honourable Evelyn Ashley, an elderly son of the Earl of Shaftesbury, and once private secretary to Lord Palmerston. Even at the height of his power, Alfred is reliably said to have been uneasy in the company of those he regarded as his betters by birth. In Portsmouth he would have been painfully on his best behaviour.

The Parliament he hoped to enter in 1895 had had a few weeks of Conservative rule, as a result of the unexpected fall of the Liberal Government in June. Before that, the Liberals had held office for three years – the first two of them under the leadership of Gladstone, who moved to the sidelines in 1894, to become an old man looking on at the new currents in politics. The Conservatives were well placed to make the most of the rising mood of imperialism; they were that sort of party. Their leader was Lord Salisbury, who had just lost one of his fieriest lieutenants, Lord Randolph Churchill (he died insane in January 1895). Among the Liberals, one of the coming figures was a Yorkshireman in his early forties, Herbert Henry Asquith, who had been a successful Home Secretary under Gladstone, and who confidently expected that one day he would be leader of the Liberal Party. Another emerging name was that of David Lloyd George, the dashing Welsh solicitor who seemed to have sprung fully armed out of some Celtic legend to champion the rights of Wales and natural justice. He had become a Liberal MP in 1890, at the age of twenty-seven. At the election he kept his seat, and so did Asquith, but in general the Liberals were swept away, and a Conservative Government ruled again. In Portsmouth, Alfred and the earl's son managed to lose. Alfred declared that they had had 'a good square licking', offered his congratulations to the Liberal victors, which were angrily rejected because the campaign had been so ill-natured, and said he would try again soon. But he never did. Overwork or disappointment or both made him unwell after his defeat. The party would have liked him in Parliament, and in December he was invited to stand for Brixton, a safe Conservative constituency in south London that became vacant when its MP went to the

House of Lords. Most of the electorate were 'educated and comfortably wealthy members of the middle class', according to the *Evening News.* Alfred considered it over a weekend and declined on the last day of the year. By this time he had other designs on the middle classes. Years later he told his private secretary that the Portsmouth campaign had been 'like wading through a sea of filth', which may have been his way of saying that he found it easier to manipulate people from outside politics than from inside. Lacking a sustained interest in political ideas, he found it more agreeable to regard politicians as schemers and place-seekers, tainted with self-interest from which the Press was miraculously free. 'Do you think that the bitterness and intrigues of politics have delights for me?' he told an interviewer from Pulitzer's New York *World* in 1899.

Events moved with Alfred, as usual. The day after he said no to Brixton, he was caught up in a development that was to set him on a new course as a journalist. In South Africa, British imperialism had lurched forward with a piece of muddled filibustering, the 'Jameson Raid'. The news filled the London papers on 1 January, and Alfred, who spent a day or two at the office while the crisis was at its height, found himself involved in the kind of politics he cared about, running a newspaper that could reflect the heat and smoke of events, and by so doing influence them. Leander Starr Jameson, a doctor of medicine, was the administrator of the Chartered Company, the unofficial British vehicle for exploiting as much of South Africa as it could lay hands on. Mashonaland, seized a few years earlier, was being busily developed by British settlers as a new piece of Empire, called Rhodesia after Cecil Rhodes, managing director of the Chartered Company. Rhodes was industrialist, politician, and fanatical imperialist, an empire-builder whose obsessions were eccentric even by the standards of his day. The Jameson raid was an unhappy by-product. It was directed against the Transvaal, one of the regions which later came together to form the present South Africa, and which in 1895 was a more or less independent republic run by descendants of Dutch settlers, the Boers (from 'boor', the Dutch for farmer). Rhodes, who was Prime Minister of Britain's Cape Colony to the south, wanted the Transvaal and its goldmines for the Empire. Paul Kruger, President of the Transvaal, a God-fearing old man who disliked the English and their buccaneering ways, had no intention of cooperating.

The particular thorn in the flesh that caused Jameson to act was the situation in Johannesburg, the boom town of the Transvaal, where business men, gold miners, prostitutes, and crooks of all varieties were pouring in from Europe and America. Kruger looked with disfavour on this mass immigration (though not on the prosperity that accompanied it), fearing it would upset Boer authority. But to British patriots, their fellow-countrymen in Johannesburg were a downtrodden minority that had to be saved from what Rhodes called 'a pack of ignorant, retrograde Boers'. Rhodes planned a rising in Johannesburg, supported by an armed raid from outside. At the end of December Jameson was waiting on the border with a force of a few hundred Chartered Company police, half a dozen machine guns and one piece of field artillery. Even Rhodes hesitated before ordering an invasion of what was supposed to be friendly territory, but on 29 December his friend Jameson (who was later the inspiration for Kipling's poem 'If') decided it was time to march on Johannesburg and hurry the rebellion along. Rhodes finally sent a telegram telling Jameson not to move; by the time it arrived, he was over the border and heading for disaster. The column was halted and broken up, no one rebelled in Johannesburg, the ammunition ran low, and on 2 January the invaders surrendered after a promise that their lives would be spared. Joseph Chamberlain, the British Colonial Secretary, denounced the raiders, as he had to, but popular feeling in London was on the side of brave Dr Jameson and his raid. 'Technically incorrect it may have been,' said the *Times* on 1 January, before details were known, 'but the sense and the feeling of the nation will recognise that technicalities could not have been suffered to stand in the way where the lives and the property of thousands of their fellow citizens were at stake.'

Alfred's *Evening News* took this rich mixture of pride and anxiety, and flung it into the paper under enormous headlines. He had met Rhodes and breakfasted with him several times in 1894, finding him, said Cecil, a man after his own heart. On 31 August 1895 he had been privileged to buy five hundred shares in the Chartered Company at a price of eight pounds ten shillings each; his investments, made with Harold's guidance, were usually in dull securities, and pure gain is unlikely to have been his motive for this speculative stake in Rhodes's organisation. Nasty rumours circulated afterwards that the Harmsworths had been corrupted by South African gold, that Alfred was in Rhodes's pocket. This was not Alfred's style at all. His shareholding in Chartered embarrassed him later on, and he regretted having taken it (it was not even profitable, as it turned out); but he supported Rhodes because imperialism seemed to him natural, praiseworthy and as enthralling as a good yarn in the *Union Jack*. It's possible that Rhodes, who was very wealthy, did make some investment in Harmsworth enterprises, with a view to providing himself with a platform; allegations that he did so have never been proved or disproved. If he did, it was even more foolish of Alfred to accept Rhodes's money than it was to put his own money into the Chartered Company. But corruption hardly enters into it; Alfred had too much pride and truculence to let himself be bought so easily.

At the *Evening News*, stories were allowed to flood the pages with black type and short paragraphs, giving the paper an excited, disordered look that not even the bloodiest crime had done before. There was no attempt to keep news and comment separate; patriotic sentiments overflowed into the writing and the editing. On 1 January the main headlines read:

IS CHAMBERLAIN BLUNDERING?
KRUGER HAS CUT THE WIRES, AND WE DO NOT KNOW WHAT IS GOING ON AT JOHANNESBURG.
UNARMED ENGLISH AT THE MERCY OF THE BOERS.
THE LAST CHANCE FOR BRITISH PRESTIGE IN SOUTH AFRICA.

On 2 January:

DR JAMESON'S MARCH.
SOME FACTS WHICH TELL AGAINST MR CHAMBERLAIN.
ARMED BOERS IN JOHANNESBURG.
AND ENGLISHMEN IN DANGER SING 'GOD SAVE THE QUEEN'.

On 3 January:

DR JIM'S DEFEAT.
THE BOERS SAY THEY CONQUERED HIM AFTER HARD FIGHTING.

HIS MISSION OF HELP CRUSHED – JOHANNESBURG AT THE MERCY
OF KRUGER.
WHAT WILL THE END BE?

It was the mood of stirring stories of adventure in Harmsworth
novelettes. BRAVE DR JIM cried a huge headline across a drawing
of Jameson that filled half the front page on 8 January. Under-
neath, the caption read: 'May his march to the relief of our
brothers and sisters in the Transvaal be crowned with success!'
There was eager speculation about 'Maxim v. Maxim' (the
Maxim machine-gun was the latest in weaponry), followed,
when it became apparent that Dr Jim and his men were inside
Boer prisons, by irritable speculation as to why there had not
been 'terrible slaughter' before he surrendered.

A second sensation sprang from the first when on 3 January
the German Emperor sent a telegram to Kruger congratulating
him on having repulsed the 'armed hordes'. This infuriated even
the critics of Jameson and Rhodes, and focused British attention
on Germany as an unfriendly rival. International attitudes were
crystallising into the shapes of the future. Ultimately, Alfred's
claim to be something more than a popular entertainer and
commercial innovator would rest on his attitude to Germany.
His special correspondents and leader writers would be hammering the Huns (a label that one of his writers first applied to
the Germans) well into the next century. The *Evening News*
leading article on 4 January 1896 headed HANDS OFF! was a
fore-runner of hundreds. It attacked the Kaiser, calling him
'hot-blooded and eccentric', and accurately judged his telegram
to the Boers to be part of a deliberate policy, not a momentary
blunder. 'It is,' said the article, 'of a piece with the hostile
utterances of the German Press and the unfriendly attitude
which Germany has uniformly maintained towards us since the
throne passed to its present occupant, whose brain is filled with
dreams of extending his colonial empire.' The Jameson Raid,
the resignation of Rhodes as Prime Minister of Cape Colony,
and above all the German menace, dominated the news for
weeks. The *Evening News*, referring matter-of-factly to 'English
grit' and 'the British bulldog', invoked Shakespeare: 'Come the
three corners of the world in arms, And we shall shock them.'
Crime reporting continued to fill many columns, but the South
African crisis had opened up the paper, and given its proprietor

a permanent theme: the place of Britain in a changing world. It was never so parochial again. To what extent this was a direct result of Alfred's instructions, rather than the general response of journalists to shifts of public feeling, is impossible to say. The tide took him as it took everyone; his talent was for seeing the way they were going.

8

Mighty Presses

EARLY IN 1896, Alfred was preoccupied with his plans for a daily newspaper, now, at last, being finalised. He found time for plenty of relaxation, from billiards matches with the staff of *Answers* (he and Harold were the worst players among the brothers) to bicycle rides around Kent and East Anglia. For three weeks of March he was in Scotland, fishing. In the middle of April he spent a few days in Paris. All this time, men and machines were being collected for the newspaper that had now been under discussion for more than a year. Various titles had been rejected, among them *Express* and *Herald*. *Arrow* was originally Alfred's favourite. The solution came from Leicester, who had heard newsboys shouting *Mail* to sell a local paper in Birmingham, and thought the word had penetrating power. Alfred added 'Daily', to make *Daily Mail*.

Many of the staff came from the *Evening News*, with Kennedy Jones in day-to-day charge (Louis Tracy, his partner when they first approached Alfred, had sold his share of the paper and gone to write novels). There was a sharp break with the magazines, which had been staffed with Harmsworths and competent hacks. For the newspaper, Alfred and the rough-tongued Jones recruited the best they could find. Alfred wanted something more than hard-boiled professionals. He loved 'experts', and could never get enough of them. J. E. MacManus, appointed acting editor, was a qualified solicitor. H. W. Wilson, the chief leader writer, had an honours degree from Oxford. Ignatius Rubie, the foreign editor, was a doctor of medicine and a musician who had lived in Paris.

What they discussed, meeting in pubs and one another's houses, has gone up in smoke like a thousand other discussions on how to run a newspaper. Certain key decisions were taken, or emerged, or were forced on them all as time went by. Alfred coloured most of them. It was to be a 'writers' paper', with journalists encouraged to develop their own styles. Foreign news was to be used prominently, from the paper's own correspondents where possible. Politically it would be impartial in orthodox party politics, but imperialist and aggressive over Britain's place in the world. Advertising would not be allowed to dominate the paper. Sub-editing would be thorough and exact once the copy arrived in the office, and to make sure that it arrived abundantly, news would not be treated as an Act of God that happened or didn't happen, according to fortune; there would be feature articles (many of them directed at women), and in general anything that interested the public would be seized on, highlighted, explained, made vivid and wrung dry of the last drop of value before being abandoned. Most of these elements are now commonplace in newspapers, but at the time they seemed more like fragments flung off by Alfred's brain. Some were not original; it was the velocity that counted. Alfred's presence dominated the endless discussions, if not Alfred himself – the days when he could sit in on all the office arguments were coming to an end. He stated the policy and poured out ideas for his clever young men to work on, and there was never any doubt that he was going to stamp the paper with his personality. It would put many sides of him into print, the professional concern with good writing, the disinterest in formal politics, the boyish passion for Empire, and the cunning simplicity involved in hooking the interest of the average reader by sensing the average reader's appetite, and feeding it without mercy. Alfred had no illusions about the need for popular ideas to be simple and vivid. He sensed human needs because his own were so pressing. He lifted out of the air, or from the back of his mind, a picture of a public that was uncatered for by the communicators of the day. He used his talent as a journalist to define the market in which journalism was going to flourish. 'The new century was close at hand,' wrote one of Alfred's men years later, 'and hundreds of thousands of people to whom the old papers had nothing to tell were ready and eager for the *Daily Mail* to rise up and interpret its meaning.' Behind the dutiful exaggeration is the truth that Alfred exploited.

On the technical side, there was no risk that happy thoughts would wither for lack of machines. Mechanical typesetting on the linotype, introduced from America, was still a novelty. The *Evening News* was hand-set until 1902. Alfred ordered eight linotypes, though for years after he insisted nostalgically that parts of the *Mail*, including the leading article, should be set by hand. Three small rotary presses were bedded down in the basement of Number 2 Carmelite Street – an existing building near the river, a few hundred yards from the magazine headquarters in Tudor Street. The premises there were cramped. Alfred was to have a small room, with Sutton, his secretary, next door. The editorial staff totalled fourteen. The acting editor would have to work behind a curtain in a corner of the news room. The reporters would have one unreliable telephone clamped to the wall. But for once, the idea was not to cut the costs. Alfred planned the opposite, basing his calculations on the fact that the falling price of newsprint – thanks to new processes – and the extensive use of machinery, meant that anyone who chose could produce a comparatively lavish newspaper that was nevertheless cheaper than anything then available. His slogan, 'A Penny Newspaper for a Halfpenny', didn't appeal to Harold, who regarded the talk about cables from foreign parts and high-quality newsprint as evidence that the project had gone to his brother's head. The family fortune had been made on cheap productions, excitingly marketed; the idea of throwing it away on a grandiose newspaper scheme appalled him. Kennedy Jones, his eye on crime and racing as the staple diet, tended to take Harold's side, to Alfred's annoyance. What Harold didn't understand was that his brother was staking his future on the *Mail*. It was his vehicle into the world of affairs. For the first time, they had serious arguments. To protect the newspaper, Alfred decided not to put Harold in charge of the management. If he had, as Leicester said once, they might have ended up with a farthing paper for a halfpenny. Offended at his exclusion, Harold sulked and stayed away from the office in the final stages.

Many dummy editions were produced. Red, blue, and yellow posters appeared on hoardings. Advertising got under way. Regular announcements in the *Evening News* from the beginning of April emphasised the price, quality, and amount of money that was being spent, a hundred thousand pounds. Alfred claimed in 1903 that it had cost half a million pounds, which (despite a personal income for 1896 of forty-two thousand pounds and investments outside his own companies of eighty thousand pounds) would have been beyond his means. In 1921 he let a company booklet claim that it cost less than fifteen thousand, which sounds like boasting at the other extreme. The date of publication began to appear: 'Four leading articles, a page of Parliament, and columns of speeches will NOT be found in the *Daily Mail* on 4 May, a halfpenny.' 4 May was a Monday. As the day approached, Alfred stepped up the level of publicity, striking the note of harsh good-humour that was to characterise the paper. '*Read this aloud to your friends*, said the *Evening News* on the Friday before publication. 'Read the following words slowly to your friends, and note the effect: "Monday morning is coming, and with it the first number of the great new halfpenny daily paper, the *Daily Mail*. Every one is ordering a copy of his or her newsagent or bookstall ..." If after reading this once to a number of friends you fail to notice the effect, try it again on another circle.' It was the sort of absurd announcement that people read aloud in order to show other people how absurd it is; and remember.

Alfred knew he was producing a newspaper against slight opposition. In America, his efforts would have gone unnoticed. There, mass readership in a vigorous new society was being catered for by the newspapers of Pulitzer and William Randolph Hearst, with violent politics, roaring crusades, and juicy scandals. Alfred's revolution, operating within the framework of solid, oak-beamed England, was a much quieter affair, though no less far-reaching in the end. Looking back, what it lacked most noticeably was a social conscience. In America, genuine social anger was harnessed to the drive for circulation, producing the tradition of 'muck-raking' journalism. In Britain this wouldn't have worked. Things were too stable, anger was too upsetting; 'muck-racking' remains an alien phrase, a comment on the man who does the raking rather than on the muck. Alfred had no desire to start looking for social evils, and no need. What he had to keep in mind were the tastes of a new public that was becoming better educated and more prosperous, that wanted its rosebushes and tobacco and silk corsets and tasty dishes, that liked to wave a flag for the Queen and see foreigners slip on a banana skin. Nobody else seemed to be keeping them in mind. London's morning papers competed gently with one another – the *Times*, the *Daily Telegraph*, the *Daily News*, the *Morning Post*, the *Daily Chronicle*, the *Standard*. To Alfred, they lacked initiative and were emasculated by having to follow a party political line. There is a story of Alfred as a beginner going into Spiers and Ponds, a restaurant by Ludgate Circus where editors and managers went for their lunchtime chop and bottle of wine. His umbrella is neatly rolled; his Napoleon's lock falls over one eye as he surveys the room, recognising the men who run Fleet Street. They look grey and pathetic; no problem.

Alfred liked to describe the start of the *Mail* as 'rather like the beginning of a battle', and muse that 'newspaper warfare is very like trench warfare. Each party sees very little of the other.' He spent the week in London, staying with Harold on Friday and Saturday. His diary on Sunday, 3 May reads: 'Came down from Harold's to the *Mail* office, where I worked all the afternoon. After a severe struggle got the paper to press with many mis-givings at 1.20 a.m.' Alfred autographed the first copy off the machines and sent it by messenger to his mother. Four editions were printed between then and 7 a.m., by which time the first copies were already being opened in railway carriages and propped against breakfast teapots.

It would take a few hours to know the result. If Alfred went for a stroll after the presses stopped, he saw a fine, clear morning, with the sun in a blue-white sky above the City, and a rising tide filling the river between the Embankment at the end of Carmelite Street, and the wharves on the south bank. His diary says he stayed at the Salisbury, an hotel off Fleet Street. The office legend, which eventually got into print, was that Alfred spent two days and nights on the premises, then went home and slept for twenty-two hours; Leicester, the cynical brother who was enough of a journalist himself to know how legends started, thought that Alfred probably invented it.

Wherever he was, the reports that came in through the day went beyond anything he expected. He had said he wanted to sell 100,000, hoped privately it would be 150,000 and ended the day with 397,215. His remark to Kennedy Jones as orders con-tinued to pour in, 'We've struck a gold-mine,' must have rung sweetly in Jones's ears: the crime sub-editor with the pushful manner had been given a seven-and-a-half per cent share of the paper. Alfred kept absolute control, with fifty-one per cent. Harold had twenty-four per cent, Leicester seven-and-a-half, and Cecil and Hildebrand five per cent each.

As for the paper itself, those eight sheets of superior newsprint with advertisements on front and back, for students of the media they are as absorbing as shards and post-holes are for archaeologists; for anyone else they are no more than a mild curiosity. It seems a typographical mouse after so much labour. Dainty headlines stand up straight, single column by single column. Alfred was looking for dignity, taking two steps backwards from the *Evening News* style of headlines on a crisis afternoon. But the promised news from the wide world had been accommodated. He had special cables from Bulawayo, where African natives were rebelling; from Pretoria, where the Boers were still being tiresome; from New York, where the papers were pro-Boer and anti-British; from the Sudan, where British cavalry had routed Dervishes on camels; from Teheran, where the Shah had been assassinated; from Budapest, celebrating Hungary's thousandth birthday. The only prominent piece of domestic news on the main news page concerned the Reading Murders, where a woman accused of killing babies was on trial. Elsewhere you could read that London horse-buses were being re-routed or that a curate had been cited as co-respondent in a divorce case. Sport and financial news were given much space.

All this represented better value for money than newspaper readers were accustomed to. They were also offered a page headed 'The Daily Magazine', where Alfred's department of useless information went a stage further, and, with better resources than in the past, began to provide something more than glorified extracts from encyclopaedias. The aim was 'to amuse, interest, and instruct during the leisure moments of the day'. Articles included one about courting procedures among the Boers, and another about the finances of the Australian cricket team that was visiting Britain. The first episode of a serial story was included. So were two columns 'exclusively for ladies', who were told how to make a school frock and a new bonnet. As a later *Daily Mail* writer suggested, at that time women were 'not quite reckoned as part of the population. Public affairs were not for women ... Popular amusements were not for women, restaurants and places of public entertainment were not for

women. The appearance of a woman on a bicycle provoked
derision. If one smoked a cigarette she proclaimed herself a lost
soul. If a woman were a *grande dame* she might dress herself in
suitable but sober splendour, and if she belonged to the well-to-
do classes she should sufficiently advertise the opulence of her
husband. But if she were of the people the fashions did not exist
for her. It was her duty to be dowdy, if not shabby, and to
follow on respectfully with succeeding styles of attire when, and
not until, her betters had done with them.' It would be fanciful
to suppose that Alfred was catering for women, or for anyone,
who belonged to 'the people' of the lower orders. But at least he
was catering for the wives of shopkeepers and clerks, the growing class that came between the conventionally affluent and the
sordid poor.

His first leader page, with its political gossip and society notes,
gave some clues to the kind of readers he was looking for, and to
the philosophy of the paper, in a short leading article headed
'The Explanation'. 'The main difference between the *Daily
Mail* and its competitors,' it announced, 'is the absence of the
advertisement supplements of two and four pages added to most
of them some years ago. The *Daily Mail* gives *exactly* the same
news, but fewer advertisement sheets.' Having put the advertisers in their place, the article went on to say that what distinguished the paper was 'not so much economy of price as
conciseness and compactness. It is essentially the busy man's
paper. The mere halfpenny saved each day is of no consequence
to most of us. The economy of the reader's time effected by the
absence of the usual puzzling maze of advertisements is, however, of the first importance.' The writer must have been Alfred,
cheekily flattering his readers by assuring them that a halfpenny
was beneath their contempt, while the slogan on page one, 'A
penny newspaper for a halfpenny,' suggested the opposite.
Alfred had his finger on the pulse of the nation's snobbery. He
saw that the readers wanted a cheap newspaper but were anxious not to be put in the cheap-newspaper-reading class. They
were, typically, young men on the make, busy and trying to look
busier, aspiring to prosperity. The new easy-payments style of
living was opening up for them; small ads in the first number of
the *Mail* offered 'charming semi-detached villas' in the suburbs
for fifty pounds down and a four-hundred-pound mortgage, and

'clothes in the latest West-end styles', made on credit for 'clerks or other gentlemen who are in regular employment'.

Alfred's appeal to aspirations is straightforward enough. More puzzling is the cavalier way he refers to advertising. Instead of putting in a kind word, he goes out of his way to disparage it. Yet from the beginning, the Harmsworths had been anxious to attract advertisers to their magazines. The *Mail*'s first issue contained prominent display announcements for cocoa, pianos, and meat extract, besides many columns of small ads. The explanation seems to be that Alfred, now that he was a newspaper proprietor and a man of wider horizons, wanted more than ever to feel independent. He resented the power of advertising because he saw it as an insidious threat to his position as 'sole possessor', although in the world he was helping to bring about, the power of the advertisers was as real a fact as paper, ink, and printing presses. All his life he would have rows with his advertising departments and demand that the ads be kept in their place, while at the same time building up his newspapers on a base of advertising revenue. He did more than anyone else to make the Press dependent on advertising. The difference between this situation and the one he originally wanted may have been a small element in the dissonance that finally shook him to pieces.

The thin end of the advertising wedge was apparent a few weeks later, when the *Mail* was using part of its first leader, 'The Explanation', as a 'filler' at the foot of a column. The passage about the busy man's paper and the 'mere halfpenny' was copied word for word. But the sentence that originally referred to 'the economy of the reader's time effected by the absence of the usual puzzling maze of advertisements' now talked about 'the economy of the reader's time effected by the terse summarising of the news of its special correspondents'. Alfred had come into line; he must have hated it.

Proprietors and editors from the early magazine days. Cecil is third from right, Harold second from right. Extreme right is Arkas Sapt, later the man who put photographs in the *Mirror*.

Cecil spent long hours in the magazine offices before it became obvious that he wasn't cut out for jokes and thrilling stories. He once wrote of a family publication as 'the huge *Girl's Friend*'.

In this 1898 issue of the Harmsworths' *Illustrated Chips,* the artist
depicted some of the brothers in a front-page strip. In frame 3 are Cecil
(left) and Alfred. In 9, Harold has hands on hips, while Leicester, Alfred
and Cecil look on from right.

9

Family Party

A BIG HOUSE with servants and gardeners, visited daily by respectful tradesmen who called at the rear entrance and always closed the gate when they were going, was as solid and enduring as a castle in the days when the *Daily Mail* was finding its level, and England was still bemused with its own greatness. Poynters Hall at Totteridge, on the northern outskirts of London, was not the biggest or most palatial of the Harmsworth houses. It was a dark, inconvenient place, hated by some of the family but acknowledged by them all as the point to which they returned in the end. Poynters was where Mrs Harmsworth Senior lived from 1897, radiating an influence that reached them wherever they were. She was at the centre of a fine web of deference. They were a close family, not a united one; cross-currents, jealousies, secrets, divided them. Perhaps Mrs Harmsworth's sons and daughters needed a fixed point in their not particularly well-rooted lives. Alfred needed her physically – to be able to hug her, kiss her, attend her with little presents and endearments – but he was a special case. They all looked on her as the family rock, as they had done when they were children.

By the time she went to Poynters she was a stout lady of fifty-eight, pink-faced and heavy-limbed, inclined to frown, not given to gaiety. Photographed at the front door, wearing yards of black cloth like a tent, she stares crossly into the sunlight as though seeing a tramp off the premises. She had a violent temper. Usually she was not assertive so much as stubbornly sure of herself, her piety and her commonsense. The natural order of things included man's obedience to God, and children's obedience to their mother. Half jokingly, but half seriously as well, she expected and received from her grown-up sons a standard of good behaviour, as in childhood. When Leicester said 'belly' one day, she slapped him on the wrist and told him not to use such language. When Alfred came in from golf, he would be told not to go into the drawing room with his brogues on. Since nasty things tended to be unmanageable, they were excluded from conversation. She had as little as possible to do with Charles, the mental defective, a big, slow man who was set up with his own house and companion in Sussex. She once declared that she couldn't stand the sight of him. Alfred's illegitimate child was like the memory of a bad dream. Drink was another skeleton at Poynters, waiting in the cupboard. Her husband had died of it. One of her sons-in-law – Lucas King, the official in the Indian Civil Service who had married Geraldine – was too fond of it. Drink was not brought to the table at Poynters, though she must have known that Alfred, Harold, and the rest enjoyed a quiet glass of whisky or champagne before going in to dinner. They deceived her because she wanted to be deceived. Interviewed by an American newspaper in 1899, Alfred (aged thirty-four) wriggled and said he was a teetotaller without being a fanatic. When he was aged fifty-two and she was staying with him in an hotel, she kept notes in her diary of what he drank with his meals, half a bottle of claret here, a bottle of champagne there.

Poynters and its thirty-five acres cost nine thousand pounds and was a present from the elder sons. Mrs Harmsworth's income included four thousand pounds a year from Alfred, soon increased to six thousand. She could live well. Life in any big house must have seemed as permanent and natural then as it seemed precarious and artificial later on. Poynters was a rambling old mansion in the Queen Anne style, many windowed, roofed at different angles. It faced the main road, which divided it from a block of common-land that had houses, a pub, and a duckpond at the far end. This was the village of Totteridge. London was seven or eight miles to the south, near enough for the Harmsworth sons and their not always enthusiastic wives to arrive by motor-car, as they were able to do from about 1899 – Alfred drove his own car in England for the first time on 30 March that year. The house had some quality that made it less attractive than it should have been. Mrs Harmsworth had seen it by chance, as Alfred saw Elmwood, and liked it at once. Others found it depressing even in fine weather, with the sombre grounds sweeping down to an artificial lake, and a summer-house that no one ever went to. In winter it was a damp, misty place. Cecil used to blame the heavy clay soil. St John, elegant and pleasure-loving, would flee from it to warmer places as soon as decency permitted.

Electricity never reached Poynters, but gas, coal, candles, oil-lamps, and plenty of maids kept it lit and fuelled. Mrs Harmsworth liked her boudoir at sixty-five degrees fahrenheit. The maid who lit the fire there used to throw metal polish on the sticks to make them burn up quickly, and, if that didn't work, breathe on the thermometer when she heard her mistress coming. It was an economical household. Mrs Harmsworth's personal maid kept the key to the store cupboard. Every morning another maid had to read to her, from a slate, a list of left-overs in the larder. Sometimes no one had bothered to write on the slate, and the maid would improvise quickly, 'Two cold sausages and a piece of apple tart, Ma'am.' 'And what do you propose to do with them?' Mrs Harmsworth would say.

The staff consisted of a butler, chauffeur, cook, parlour-maid, under-parlour-maid, two kitchen-maids, and personal maid, together with a couple of gardeners. The wages bill for them all would have been well under three hundred pounds a year before the first world war, supplemented by tips from visitors, most of whom were members of the family (one notable exception was Sir Thomas Lipton, friend of King Edward vii, grocer, leading advertiser in the *Daily Mail*, and devoted friend of Mrs Harmsworth). Servants were expected to be invisible but always available. Mrs Harmsworth liked punctual obedience to a summons, but objected strongly if she encountered a servant on the stairs. Before the maids went to a dance in the village, they had to line up for inspection.

It took less than ten years for the Harmsworths to find their way to the golden land, safe from poverty and drudgery; once they were there, it might never have been otherwise. Grandchildren appeared, pretty creatures in embroidered frocks and floppy hats, shepherded by nannies. By the turn of the century, Harold's wife had the three boys she had wanted. Leicester and Annie were producing a large family. Leicester's coating of gloom was as thick as ever; one of the children's compulsory outings was to the family grave. Cecil and Emilie had three children. Hildebrand married a doctor's daughter in 1900. A few years more, and Vyvyan, Christabel, and Violet were married, leaving only Charles and St John. Sons and daughters with their wives and husbands came for weekends, called for tea, stayed at Christmas, ate enormous Sunday lunches, and walked them off afterwards on the lawn, the Harmsworth menfolk padding along with a characteristic family walk, almost a shuffle, as if they were trying to kick their own feet. Four of them were generally regarded, by the servants and other people's children, as the 'heavies': Alfred, Harold, Leicester, and Cecil. They were solid, dignified men with polished motor cars, their waists growing thicker and their vehicles getting bigger with the years. Christabel, the last to marry, lived over the road in a house on the edge of the common. She would look across on a Sunday morning, see the Rolls-Royces in the drive, and say, 'Oh God, they're here.'

Hildebrand was heavy in build but not in nature. When he worked on the editorial side of the magazines, which he did for a while after going to Oxford, his speciality was jokes and puzzles. Later, when he turned gentleman of leisure, he became notorious for his practical jokes and elaborate wagers. He liked being rude to people for the pleasure of seeing them lose their tempers, but when he visited Poynters, which wasn't often, he was popular with any nephews and nieces who happened to be there. He used to arrive by train and climb the hill from the station, trousers hitched up, face purple with exertion, pockets bulging with slabs of nut chocolate; the children called him 'the nut-milk-chocolate uncle'. Hildebrand made one or two brief attempts to relate his adult life to the grandiose visions of adolescence, which had included himself as Leader of the Conservative Party, Cecil as Archbishop of Canterbury, Leicester as Bishop of London, Harold as Chief Secretary of Ireland, and Alfred, rather lamely, as literary figure. In 1900 he tried and failed to get into Parliament as a Liberal. Three of the brothers were Liberal candidates at the same election, showing their independence of Alfred, who was nominally a Conservative. Cecil was beaten, though he was successful later on; Leicester was elected narrowly for Caithness, in the far north of Scotland, where the original intention had been for Harold to contest the seat. Harold was nervous about speeches and public appearances, so Leicester went instead.

All the heavies came to regard Hildebrand as a clown. His fondness for billiards in office hours had irritated Alfred in the early magazine days. It was permissible to drop out of sight and not attempt to be weighty in the manner of Alfred, Harold, and Leicester. (Cecil was a semi-heavy, conscientious and upright, a gentle, fussy figure who didn't quite belong.) St John was on the way to being a beautiful person, with a handsome body that he used to the full for sport and women. Vyvyan liked living in the country, wearing old clothes, doing his own hedging and curing his own bacon. Easy money, the Harmsworth income spilling over into their pockets, encouraged them both to be eccentrics of a sort. But both knew their place in the family pecking order. Hildebrand didn't, somehow. Because he was older and had worked for the family near the beginning of the firm, canvassing in the provinces, his shareholding was nearer in size to those of Cecil and Leicester. He was substantially better off than his younger brothers, which helped him not to give a damn about anything. He laughed at the heavies for their dignity; Leicester, he used to say, was like a public building coming into a room. The heavies resented it. Leicester was in correspondence with Jerome K. Jerome, the author, in 1926. 'Are you the Harmsworth with whom I seem to remember playing poker in some chambers off Fleet Street?' wrote Jerome. Leicester replied testily, 'I am not a poker player. I think it must have been my brother Hildebrand.'

Money, arriving quickly and painlessly, with tax negligible and labour cheap, blew them overnight into prosperity. Upper-class Edwardians may have been less sure of themselves than they have come to appear. They knew that the world where 'pleasure fell like a ripened peach for the outstretching of a hand' was slipping away; they overdid the act in order to postpone the reality. The Harmsworths, in fact, were inexperienced at pleasure. They didn't set their sights high. None of them became dazzling social figures. Alfred apart, they were dull dogs by the standard of sophisticated London. But they surrounded themselves with comforts and reassurances appropriate to their station. Poynters was one of a thousand houses where gardeners were always cutting armfuls of roses, and cars with low registration numbers and wheels like locomotives stood in the drive. There were pleasures and there were obligations. In July, a long table was laid with ham, beef, and strawberries, in the shadow of a tree on the lawn, near the white-painted croquet hoops. Clutching babies, wearing their best clothes, a dozen ladies from the village were entertained and later photographed, sitting stiff-backed and frozen-faced. The picture was pasted in the family album, along with picnics on moors and Sir Thomas Lipton on a horse: 'Poor women's treat, Poynters, July 1903.'

Alfred was the most regular visitor at Poynters. He went for lunch, for dinner, to stay the night, for weekends, before he went abroad, as soon as he came back. When he slept there, his room was next to his mother's. His relationship with her was central to his life. It's too easy to say that Alfred was in a perpetual muddle, with which he needed her help. He organised too many successful enterprises for it to be true that he lacked a grasp of essentials – on the contrary, he knew exactly what the essentials were, in any situation affecting his newspapers. But his mind was disorganised. Things and facts haunted him; he liked them for their own sake, indiscriminately. In the end the daily torrent of information about strikes, wars, crimes, politics, books, plays, and society floated him away. It filled his correspondence files with letters on assorted subjects that he didn't seem able to stop writing. This wasn't true in the early years of the *Daily Mail*. But even then, the feeling of pressure building up is noticeable. His mother gave him something to hold on to. She became more desirable as he grew older. He sought constantly to make each the centre of the other's life. His favourite way of signing letters to her was 'Your Firstborn'; he had to keep reminding her.

Alfred began to travel a good deal, often with the implication that he was worn out, escaping a breakdown. One evening at the end of 1896, seven months after the start of the *Daily Mail*, he thought of going to India. He had been unwell and run down for weeks. Ten days later he sailed with his wife and a friend, and was away until the end of the following February. In April he was in Paris for a week, shortly after receiving 'certain advice' about his health, and at the end of 1897 he took a party to Egypt, via France and Italy, for eleven weeks. From Egypt he wrote to Fred Wood, his father's old friend, with whom he kept up a warm friendship, to say that 'One of the many crimes of middle age [he was thirty-two] is that I am so absorbed in business that I neither see nor write to old or, indeed, any friends. Indeed I am become a sort of hermit.' While in Egypt, he told Fred Wood, 'We live in a kind of glorified houseboat and sail thirty or forty miles a day, shooting, exploring, photographing as we choose. That piece of brown stuff I enclose I took from a tomb four thousand years old. It is a piece of mummy cloth. As my dear father would have said, from journalism to robbing the dead is but a natural and brief step.' The trip to Egypt was purely a holiday. Soon his trips were increasingly likely to be interrupted. Staying at Cannes early in 1899, an editor arrived to talk about a magazine; Kennedy Jones came to discuss enlarging the *Evening News*. 'Seedy. Liver attack. Walked up mountain with Jones,' says the cryptic diary.

As a newspaper proprietor, Alfred's circle of acquaintances widened rapidly. When Lord Rosebery, who had headed the Liberals before they went out of office, resigned the leadership of the party in October 1896, Alfred went to interview him and stayed for lunch. Rosebery found him 'an interesting young man'. Alfred, looking for interesting things, found Rosebery 'merry and sunburned', though when the name of Gladstone was mentioned, 'there was, I thought, a note of sadness in the cheery voice'. At the same lunch he met Asquith, who was presently to be offered and to decline the Liberal leadership. A year later Alfred had moved into the orbit of country-house weekends, if he wanted them. He stayed with George Nathaniel Curzon, a rising young Tory politician, at his house in Reigate, where other guests included Asquith and his wife Margot. Alfred said he heard 'a great many interesting things about the inner life of politics', many of them apparently from the talkative Mrs Asquith. He became friendly with the private secretary to Lord Salisbury, the Prime Minister. Winston Churchill, nine years younger than Alfred, was another new acquaintance. They met a number of times in the latter part of 1898. In 1899 the *Daily Mail* supported Churchill in an unsuccessful attempt to enter Parliament as a Conservative, and Churchill wrote to Alfred, thanking him for his support and for 'your adventurous expedition in the motor-car' – Alfred had tried to drive to Oldham at short notice, but turned back after six punctures. He might have been less enthusiastic if he had seen a letter that Churchill wrote to his mother, Lady Churchill, that year about a quality magazine she intended to start: 'Your title *The Anglo Saxon* with its motto "Blood is thicker than water" only needs the Union Jack and Star Spangled Banner crossed on the cover to be suited to one of Harmsworth's cheap Imperialist productions. I don't say that these have not done good and paid but they are produced for thousands of vulgar people at a popular price. People don't pay a guinea for such stuff. And besides there is a falling market as regards Imperialism now.'

Politicians on both sides were friendly to Alfred, partly for obvious reasons ('Harmsworth is very civil and will report the speech at Dover well,' Churchill wrote to his mother in October 1898), partly because they were intrigued. Sir Charles Dilke found him 'the most remarkable man I have ever seen', not excluding Bismarck and Rhodes. Lord Rosebery still found him interesting when they became next-door neighbours in Berkeley Square, where the Harmsworths moved in 1897; they used to take morning walks in Hyde Park. It occurred to Alfred that it was time he had a title. George Newnes of *Tit Bits* had been given one; why not Alfred Harmsworth of *Answers* and the *Daily Mail*? Applying the principle that those who don't ask won't get, he wrote blithely to an influential acquaintance, the Earl of Onslow – Under-Secretary of State for India – on 18 October 1897, pointing out that Newnes's baronetcy from the Liberals had been of 'enormous commercial advantage'. On the Conservative side, 'owners of newspapers of comparatively slight influence are rewarded and my predecessors in the *Evening News* received recognition, though the journal was a failure. However, I would rather say nothing more on the subject: the Party leaders are no doubt quite ignorant of the revolution which the *Daily Mail*, in its infancy at present, is making in London journalism.' Alfred concluded by saying that no doubt the Government, with its enormous majority, felt it could dispense with young men, especially one like himself who would 'never sacrifice my belief in the need for a strong Imperial and foreign policy to any personal disappointments and annoyance at the favouring of opponents. Pardon that worst of bores, the man with a grievance ...' Alfred was a little premature with his request, but at least the Conservatives would not be able to say that they didn't realise he wanted a title. Some time before July 1902, when Lord Salisbury ceased to be the Conservative Prime Minister, he offered Alfred a knighthood. Alfred declined, fearing that to accept a lesser honour would compromise his chances of a greater.

Instead of Alfred moving into other people's circles, they began to move into his. Ellen Terry, the actress, took his arm when they went down to dinner at a party. He and Hildebrand had lunch with W. G. Grace, the cricketer, at Lord's. He was quickly recognised as a potential patron by the infallible noses of poets and writers, who, as usual, were not as affluent as they considered they ought to be – W. E. Henley, Rudyard Kipling, Conan Doyle. Max Beerbohm found Alfred 'quite amazing and interesting'. Because he became famous so quickly, in an exciting industry that lived on publicity, he was an obvious target for people who wanted something. They rained letters on him seeking newspaper space for good causes, jobs for relatives who wanted to write, and of course money. Ellen Terry wanted him to appear in a charity matinee as 'Napoleon crossing the Alps on a little gee-gee'. Max Pemberton, his boyhood friend, who had become a journalist on Alfred's magazines, asked if his wife could be put nominally on the staff, in order to qualify for a free trip to Madeira. Meeting Sir Douglas Straight, editor of the *Pall Mall Gazette*, Alfred remarked in his diary that he was 'one of the first friends of my father I have met who did not want anything.'

His old friends included Pemberton ('I don't have to think when I'm with him,' said Alfred) and Herbert Ward, the adventurous youth with whom he had shared lodgings, and who had become an explorer, author, and sculptor. The friend he saw most of was a man who worked for him, Reginald Nicholson, whom he had met through mutual acquaintances at Broadstairs. Nicholson, four years younger and a suave attendant on the Harmsworths, became a private secretary, overlooking the household finances, travelling abroad with Alfred and Mary, sometimes going alone with Mary to look at country houses she thought of renting. He was the socially accomplished complement to George Sutton, who attended dourly to business letters and office management at the magazines. Nicholson and Sutton were the two men that Alfred trusted most, apart from his brothers, and it's likely that Sutton knew more than any of them about his love life. Mary Harmsworth began to have affairs within a few years of her marriage. When Alfred began isn't certain. Eventually he achieved a reputation for being an impulsive lover, on the lines of Lloyd George's dictum that 'Love is all right if you lose no time'. He is said to have used the couch in his office. Secretaries were among his partners.

Alfred's son, Alfred Benjamin Smith, was brought up in Essex and apprenticed to a local carpenter when he left school. As Alfred became widely known, the possibility of blackmail occurred to the man who had married the boy's mother, a gasworks employee. Alfred immediately had the child taken away from the grandmother who had been looking after him, and made other arrangements in London. This was in 1897. A young Cambridge graduate called Francis Bluett Duff, just down from university, wanted to be a private tutor, and had his name on the books of an agency. That summer he was asked to call at the office of a firm of Bloomsbury solicitors, where a heavily built man with fair hair and glowing eyes was introduced to him as 'the Client'. The Client explained in a soft, quick voice that he was interested in a boy aged fourteen whose upbringing had been somewhat rough, and who was now to be turned into a gentleman. This romantic explanation was followed by a few questions from the Client, who turned abruptly to the solicitor and said, 'This is the man I want. I never make a mistake.' A salary of two hundred pounds a year and expenses was arranged, and Duff was told to keep quiet about the matter, and not to inquire into the identity of the Client. Duff soon recognised him from photographs, though it was another year before Alfred revealed who he was, one day at Waterloo Station. Alfred seemed to enjoy secrecy for its own sake. While Duff bought the boy clothes, gave him lessons, took him to theatres, and travelled with him to France and Spain, Alfred hovered in the background, sending messages through intermediaries. One Sunday in December 1897 Duff received a telegram from the solicitor, asking him to dinner at Berkeley Square. When he arrived, he found that the host was the Client, delighted with his subterfuge. (Mary was away in the country, where they had both been staying. Alfred had returned alone on the Friday, claiming to have hurt his ankle while hurrying, by himself, to overtake a shooting party.) Duff and the boy lived in Hampstead. Alfred called there once, after dark, to discuss his son's future. He wore dark glasses and wouldn't enter the house, so Client and tutor walked up and down the road like conspirators, talking in whispers. Alfred Benjamin was an excitable boy, not unintelligent, with large eyes and thick lips, recognisably his father's son. Alfred hoped he would do great things in journalism. There was now little hope of a child by his wife, though doctors were unable to find any reason for her failure to conceive.

In other respects the family advanced as Alfred had hoped it would, with satisfying speed and dignity. It made itself secure with houses, possessions, and servants. It attracted attention in high places. Something unseen was burrowing at the roots of the society that the Harmsworths had entered so confidently. But it was too early for anyone to suspect that the Harmsworths themselves were agents of change, undermining their own castle.

I O

Empire at Noon

ALFRED DIDN'T BELIEVE it was thinkers who led the world: it was men of action. He was interested in ideas only when they could be expressed in something solid and touchable, a machine or a telephone, or a brave man raising the British flag above a new territory. He loved mechanical inventions and spoke shrewdly about them. 'Before steam was discovered,' he told a doctor friend once, 'Englishmen were road-minded. The bicycle and the internal-combustion engine have made them road-minded once more. Road-minded people don't think like rail-minded people. The rails steer you, but on the road you steer yourself. Believe me, that's tantamount to a change of character.' He liked to rush around England and France in Panhards, Daimlers, Renaults, and Gardner-Serpollets, free from restraint.

At the *Daily Mail* his ideas appeared in solid form six days a week. He was frequently away, but his spirit blew up and down the corridors, and his voice came over the telephone, when it worked, suggesting topics or complaining about dullness. Old-fashioned newspapers, Alfred wrote in 1897, had 'not kept pace with the people in quickness of movement, in the desire to obtain the largest result with the smallest loss of time'. Readability, instead of being desirable, became an end in itself. His hand can be seen in the earliest feature-pages, with the regular appearance of stories about pain, as in the early magazines. 'Awful Punishment' was an account of tarring and feathering ('As soon as the tar sets, the victim's suffering begins'). 'How the Shah's Assassin Will be Tortured' was linked to the news from Persia, and described in detail what happened to previous Persians who tried to kill the Shah ('Lighted candles were stuck in slits cut in their bodies'). On the news pages, topics of the day were carved from thin air to help combat dullness. Weather and public holidays were recognised as matters of importance to people who were going to spend the day picnicking on Hampstead Heath or going down the Thames by steamer, and who would be interested to read about themselves doing these things. Whit Monday, three weeks after the *Mail* began, provided the best part of a page of news. A roving correspondent went to Hampstead and wrote down what he saw.

A girl in a long jacket and a dress of 'pile 'eliotripe' remarked to me 'Cheer-O' as she gaily squirted some water in my eyes from an engine known as a 'ladies' tormentor' – always the outward and visible sign of a holiday.

The *Mail* was a strange phenomenon, light-hearted but awake to serious matters, gossipy but literate, cheap but not nasty. Long speeches by politicians were reduced to a few paragraphs or thrown away altogether, and the resulting space given to leading articles about 'The Wonderful Weather' (on a Wednesday) and 'The Fine Weather' (the following Tuesday, in case readers might not have noticed). Or, if the editorial fancy so decided, there would be short leaders headed 'Spain and America' or 'Trains Habitually Late' or 'Will Men Fly?' Since most people had minds that were untrained to do more than peck at things, let them peck at a variety of small dishes every day. Inspired by a letter about the wisdom of husbands and wives taking separate holidays, a leading article appeared on 'Husbands and Holidays'. A lively correspondence followed. As this was fading out, 'Swimming and Sex' appeared with naughty speculations about mixed bathing. ' "Husband's Holidays" appears to be about dead,' wrote Alfred to J. E. MacManus, the acting editor, from Elmwood (7 August 1896), before going over to Canterbury to watch the Australians play Kent at cricket. 'I think we should work up "Swimming and Sex" until we can get another good discussion.' The subject was duly worked up. The chairman of the Beach Committee at Brighton was interviewed, and proved as willing then as local spokesmen have been willing ever since, to provide the public with a laugh at their expense.

He answered perfectly frankly that it would never do either at Brighton or any other English seaside town that he knew. Look, he said, at the thousands of excursionists who come down to Brighton every day in the summer, from all classes, and from all parts of London. SOMETHING VERY UNPLEASANT would be bound to happen before long.

Letters, signed with initials or pseudonyms like 'Poppy' and 'Beware', kept the debate going. It spread to America, where the *Mail*'s man cabled what the New York *Herald* said in a leading article: 'There is no social or moral danger resulting from the practice in the United States.' Non-events were being recognised as news that was worth flashing around the world. There is no evidence that Northcliffe invented news (as Hearst was inventing news of the Spanish–Cuban war at this time), but he invented 'talking points' regularly. For weeks the personal column of the *Mail* was filled with fake advertisements. 'Uncle Jim – Come home at once. All is forgiven,' said one in the first issue. 'Bring the pawn tickets with you. Niece.' Next day Uncle Jim replied: 'Am sending the tickets, but cannot come home just yet for reasons of my own.' 'Oak' told 'Ivy' that he was leaving her for ever and sailing to Africa. ('Ivy' to 'Oak': 'If you go to Africa, I shall follow.') 'Brown Eyes' and 'Light Suit', 'Diana' and 'Apollo', corresponded furiously. Ladies with red parasols or grass-green hats who had been noticed by adoring young men were beseeched to send their names and addresses.

Letters to the editor were another outlet for imaginative journalists. If readers were slow to write letters, Alfred would have them invented in the office. Years afterwards he began a furious debate in the *Times* about the morals of modern dancing with two faked letters. A *Daily Mail* letter in August 1898, headed 'Should the Clergy Dance?' and signed 'Pained Parishioner', arouses suspicion. The parishioner had been shocked to see the curate of his church at a hall in Ostend, dancing with 'a person with dyed hair and rouged and enamelled cheeks'. This was accompanied by a leading article ('Dancing Curates') and followed by nearly thirty letters spread over a week or two, defending or attacking dancing clergymen. No sooner was this topic waning than another item of guaranteed reader-interest (a genuine one, this time) appeared, when a clergyman-headmaster was fined two pounds for flogging a boy. 'The Ethics of Flogging' was worth forty letters from such correspondents as 'An Old University Boy' and 'Floreat Etona'. 'Present-Generation

Schoolboy' took the line that was frequently heard in leading articles: 'What England wants is not namby-pamby boys, but boys full of energy and pluck, such as were the Spartans.'

The absence of an active 'social conscience' seems to contrast with so much alertness in other directions, but was in keeping with the times. When it came to the poor, Alfred's paper took the orthodox view, that poverty and its accompaniments were regrettable but unavoidable. In the *Mail*'s first week, a small news item reported the inquest on a baby aged seven months, the third child of an out-of-work London stagemaker to die of starvation. A doctor told the coroner that the parents were 'hard‑working people who had been very unfortunate'. Two days later another item described how a potman had been charged with causing the death of his wife by neglect. Unlike the baby's death, this received an editorial comment, which thought 'the horror of the story' was intensified by the fact that the husband had been earning enough to keep his wife. Feckless bread-winners could be censured in leading articles; starving babies were natural accidents.

A better deal for the motor-car or a more efficient public telephone service was the kind of campaign that appealed to Alfred. The *Mail* claimed it was the first newspaper to take up 'the great telephone question'. It nagged away at the monopo-listic National Telephone Company until the Government let the Post Office compete. These themes were central to the paper. They meant that news was not merely being gathered: it was being organised. When Alfred and his editors decided to deal with the poor telephone service or the export of old horses for the continental horseflesh market (another early favourite), they were looking for readable copy. The test was not whether the subject 'mattered', as long as it mattered to the man on the Clapham omnibus who paid his halfpenny and wanted half an hour's relaxation. The *Mail* soon achieved a reputation for assiduous news-gathering. It was true that its resources, intell-igence, and high spirits made it, at the time, a revolutionary medium for reporting. But the reporting was selective. If a subject caught the fancy of the editors, it might become a campaign that lasted a week or a month. While it did, the subject was news; afterwards, it wasn't. Nor was it possible to distinguish between 'news' and 'comment', when campaigns were fought in the news columns. The size and wording of headlines themselves became a form of comment when they pushed the story in a particular direction. When a headline announced: SOLVED AT LAST. A REMEDY FOR THE VAGARIES OF THE TELEPHONE, it was as pointed a comment as a leading article. The line between 'news' and 'comment' is always difficult to draw; the *Mail* didn't try very hard.

Besides domestic campaigns of many colours, the paper took a clear view of world affairs. Militant imperialism had quickened in the country. Innumerable articles in the *Mail* proclaimed Britain's greatness and warned of the dangers that threatened her, from Kruger and the Boers to the Kaiser and his generals. In the paper's first birthday issue a leader headed 'England's Power and England's Duty' referred to the world's crisis spots, among them South Africa. It observed that 'a certain greatness of spirit is demanded from a great nation', and concluded that 'if Kaisers cross our path or meddle with our concerns they may discover that we can strike, and strike hard'. What gave the *Mail* its special character was that instead of relying on armchair criticism, it spent large sums on sending correspondents to report on matters it considered important. This was a natural extension of Alfred's desire to know interesting things, but the scope had widened and the information was no longer useless. To employ a newspaper as an instrument of inquiry was nothing new in itself; the difference was that Alfred's *Mail* could use new methods of communication – cables and telephones – backed by sophisticated printing machinery, and was so financially successful that it could pour money into these and other areas. British newspapers were moving on to a new level of editorial spending.

A series of articles on 'Germany as She Is' in August 1896 reported from Berlin on the danger of a country that was both a military and commercial rival. The writer, like so many of his successors over the next half-century, looked with suspicion at German smartness and discipline, from heel-clicking porters to tram-drivers wearing close-buttoned uniform. Most of the *Mail*'s early reporting was competent; some of it was outstanding. A shy young journalist of twenty-seven, George Warrington Steevens, had been advised by Charles Dilke to seek a job with the paper. He began by writing bad leading articles but was discovered to have a talent for description when he was sent to report a horse show. Alfred admired his writing and saw him often. Steevens, with a good degree from Oxford, was the quiet, bespectacled reporter who dawdles unobtrusively, fingering his pencil in his pocket, looking for the exact, scholarly phrase. He was a meticulous observer of surfaces at a time when there were no film cameras to take over the function of 'colour' reporting. They sent him to wander about London, and he described the deserted City on a Sunday afternoon: 'When you walk your boots thud and ring like a steamer's engines; when you halt you could hear the flower drop out of your buttonhole.' In 1897 Alfred sent him to Germany to produce a series of sixteen articles headed 'Under the Iron Heel'. Like all the best headlines, this told readers exactly what to expect. Steevens described forts on the island of Heligoland that no one could photograph, and lumpish private soldiers who would obey orders like machines. He saw hatred piled on envy. His articles, prejudiced and highly readable, stemmed directly from Alfred's concept of style in journalism: the simple message hammered home in good prose, the world reduced to crisp paragraphs. This is not to sneer at Alfred and his editors, only to note that they bowed to the inevitable by accepting that a mass-circulation journal had no option but to be simple, crisp, and readable; even the pre-judice was necessary, since who could have tolerated a news-paper that looked as coldly at the warts and eccentricities of its own countrymen?

Steevens described the Kaiser, riding among his people. Over the years the *Mail* was to make friendly gestures towards Germany, between bursts of vituperation; but this early piece of purple prose, and others like it, for which Alfred was responsible, helped to prejudice the British against the Germans:

Between the walls of acclamation came riding the Kaiser. A man of middle age, sitting constrainedly and bolt upright; a dead yellow skin, hard-pencilled brows, a straight, masterful chin, lips jammed close together under a dark moustache pointing straight upward to the whites of his eyes. A face at once repulsive and pathetic, so harsh and stony was it, so grimly solemn. A face in which no individual feature was very dark, but which altogether was as black as thunder ... He looked like a man without joy, without love, without pity, without hope. He looked like a man who had never laughed, like a man who could never sleep. A man might wear such a face who felt himself turning slowly to ice.

Lord Salisbury and Mr Asquith may have smiled at such an outpouring, but the words would have echoed in the ears of smart clerks and busy commercial travellers, bringing the straightforward message that there was something very unwholesome about Germany.

The following year Steevens was sent to Africa, where he reported the exploits in the Sudan of a British hero, General Horatio Herbert Kitchener. Steevens's articles, 'With Kitchener to Khartoum', chronicled the extension by force of British rule from Egypt to the Sudan, culminating in the battle or massacre of Omdurman, where howling Dervishes were mown down in thousands at long range by Maxim machine-guns, Lee-Metford rifles, and shrapnel. According to Edgar Wallace – another *Mail* foreign correspondent in the 1890s – Steevens's articles ruined Kitchener by creating the legend of a ruthless man of ice and blood, who spent the rest of his life trying to live up to his newspaper caricature. Steevens was one of only two British journalists allowed to interview the lordly Kitchener (who once pushed through a group of reporters outside his tent, saying 'Get out of my way, you drunken swabs!').

Africa provided more and more exciting copy as the century neared its end. War with Kruger and his intransigent farmers in the Transvaal, prophesied for so long, began in October 1899, and the Boer War became the first large-scale test of the *Mail*'s capacity for sustained reporting of a major international crisis. Alfred and Kennedy Jones sent special correspondents from London, supported by local correspondents in the war areas, with instructions to cable whatever news they could gather. The cost was enormous; the bill for unused cables on some nights ran into hundreds of pounds. But the material that did get into the paper – carefully edited and presented, with maps and diagrams – made the reputation of the *Mail*, in Fleet Street and with the public. On some days circulation went above a million, making it by far the biggest in the world. Special trains took the papers to most parts of Britain, exploiting, for the first time, the fact that the country had enough readers to provide a mass market, yet was small enough to be covered by trains running through the night, carrying newspapers that began to go to press late in the evening.

Steevens was one of the special correspondents. He sent back neat despatches with obscure datelines. 'The wind screams down from the naked hills on to the little junction station,' he wrote from some spot in the middle of nowhere. 'I wonder if it is all real? By the clock I have been travelling something over forty hours in South Africa, but it might just as well be a minute or a lifetime ... South Africa is a dream.' Two months later Steevens died of typhoid in the beleaguered town of Ladysmith, remarking, 'This is a sideways ending to it all.' Alfred was grief-stricken when he heard the news, early on a Saturday morning. He sent for his fastest car and drove to see Mrs Steevens at her house in the suburbs. When he arrived he was sobbing, declaring that he would never forgive himself for sending George to Ladysmith. A tragedy for Mrs Steevens became, by a familiar process, a tragedy for Alfred; he told her that the blow had destroyed his power to think or work. He was genuinely upset but incapable of effacing himself. Later he made sure that Mrs Steevens was well provided for, with a pension of five hundred pounds a year.

South Africa was a very bad dream. 'Black Week' in December 1899, when British forces suffered three defeats, can be seen, without too much exaggeration, as the end of an era. It gave a psychological jolt that tipped the British forward into the twentieth century. 'It is our habit calmly to accept what God sends without losing patience, faith, and hope,' said the *Mail* in a sobered voice. Leading articles complained bitterly about inferior artillery and blundering generals, making the paper unpopular with many politicians, and giving Alfred a new dimension: a voice of the people, or at least some of the people, against their bumbling masters. Men like Rhodes and Kitchener of Khartoum – who was hurriedly sent out to South Africa as chief of staff to a new commander in chief, Lord Roberts – were more to Alfred's taste than politicians at Westminster. In the late 1890s, Alfred and Rhodes met frequently when the latter was in London, often breakfasting together. After the Jameson Raid, Rhodes moved steadily into the shadows, although he kept insisting that his career was only beginning. Alfred backed him with the *Mail* until he died in 1902. The decline of Rhodes, like the miserable progress of the Boer War, can be read now as portents of inescapable change. Nothing seemed inescapable then, and Alfred was merely a violent partisan of the imperialists who thought that the Empire had suffered a temporary setback. Many Liberals in Britain strongly opposed the war, especially as it became more punitive; Lloyd George made his Parliamentary reputation with fierce attacks on the Government for browbeating the Boers in order to keep native labour cheap, and ensure large profits for Rhodes's shareholders. Alfred was not interested in reporting the views of pro-Boer dissenters, except to mock them. The *Mail* saw the war as a beautiful episode that united the British. When the town of Mafeking was relieved in May 1900, with wild celebrations in Britain that cost a hundred thousand pounds for flags and fifty thousand pounds for fireworks (if the *Mail*'s arithmetic was right), the paper said approvingly that the war had 'brought about a recrudescence of the military spirit which, when kept within due and proper bounds, tends to national order and national greatness'. As for the effect of national rejoicing on the young, it would (said the paper) awaken military ardour and remove the need for conscription. The article was headed 'Why the Foreigner Does not Rejoice with Us', and reflected once again the feeling that Britain was alone – its war against the Boers being seen by many in Europe as aggressive colonialism. Alfred supervised that issue of the paper and perhaps wrote the article, driving up from Berkshire, where he and Mary rented a country house, to spend a Sunday evening in the office. When he was not abroad or fishing in Scotland, Alfred ran the paper himself about three days in four. The printers were used to seeing him in the composing room, standing in his shirt-sleeves with his waistcoat pocket full of pencils, always liable to take a dislike to a page, when the damp yellow proof was handed to him, and say 'Make me another!' as he crossed it out.

He continued to support the war as it degenerated from textbook manoeuvres and pitched battles, into guerrilla fighting. The last organised Boer army was defeated in August 1900, but the war dragged on for nearly two years after that. Kitchener, left in charge of operations, developed a scorched-earth policy, burning Boer farms, fencing off the countryside and controlling it by blockhouses, and herding women and children into 'concentration camps', as they were blandly called. It all seemed necessary, given an enemy who wouldn't follow the rules and give the Maxims and Lee-Metfords a chance (as the exasperated Kitchener wrote home 'The Boers are not like the Sudanese, who stood up to a fair fight. They are always running away on their little ponies.'). Alfred, like millions of people in Britain, seems to have gone along quite happily with Kitchener's methods. There was widespread agitation in Britain against the concentration camps, where disease was rife, but the *Mail* had no patience with it. An Englishwoman, Miss Emily Hobhouse, visited the camps and exposed the scandal. Kitchener called her 'that bloody woman'. The *Mail* dismissed her as a trouble-naker who 'is not impartial, has no balance in her judgments, and does not know anything of war or its history'.

The Boer War gave Alfred a personal stake in great affairs, which was both pleasing and profitable. The *Mail* circulation rose to unforeseen levels. There were other benefits. The Harmsworths produced a best-selling fortnightly magazine that could be bound and made into volumes, called *With the Flag to Pretoria*, on the lines of an earlier one prepared for Victoria's Diamond Jubilee, *Sixty Years a Queen* (which, written for two hundred and fifty pounds, made a profit of fifteen thousand). 'Sensationalism' was an early stick to beat the *Mail* with. It made the most of the war, but it was sensational only in that it approved and encouraged people's natural appetite for excitement. Once newspaper journalism conceded that the appetite existed, it was reasonable to attempt to satisfy it. It left papers like the *Mail* in an exposed position when they made mistakes, as inevitably they did. The *Mail*'s reports of the 'Boxer Rising' of 1900, when white residents in Peking were falsely reported to have been massacred by Chinese revolutionaries, tainted the paper's reputation for years. It was not the only paper to report the massacre, but it plunged in more vigorously than the rest. It also had more to lose when the truth came out: the *Mail* stood for the new journalism, good or bad. On 2 July the *Mail* was reporting FEARS OF MASSACRE. On 5 July 'Our Special Correspondent at Shanghai' wrote (in the issue of 6 July) that it might be 'almost taken for granted' that the worst had happened: rape, torture, public executions, and the murder of all foreigners in Peking. The text betrays slight self-doubts, but the

presentation and headlines report facts, not fears: THE GREAT
TRAGEDY. TERRIBLE STORY OF PEKING HORRORS. On 13 July
the Special Correspondent confirmed the reports, and on 16 July
enormous headlines (for those days) sealed the story with THE
PEKING MASSACRE. ALL WHITE MEN, WOMEN, AND CHILDREN
PUT TO THE SWORD. AWFUL STORY OF THE SIXTH AND SEVENTH
JULY. The *Mail* declared: 'It will be seen that the terrible story
confirms in detail the Shanghai cablegram published exclusively
in the *Daily Mail* on Friday last' – i.e. on 13 July. But what
about the Shanghai cablegrams published earlier? These were
conveniently overlooked. The massacre had been feared on 2
July. It had been reported as a fact, as far as the ordinary reader
was concerned, on 6 July. Now it was being said that the massacre
took place on 6 and 7 July, by which time the *Mail*'s man in
Shanghai had already reported under the headline THE GREAT
TRAGEDY. The episode smells of over-eagerness. In fact, there
had been no massacre, as the *Mail* and everyone else discovered
on 31 July. The Chinese may have had reasons of their own for
spreading the rumours, but the British Press was not unwilling
to believe them. Newspapers had always had a vested interest in
bad news. Once a mass-circulation Press came into existence,
seeing the world in hard, bright colours, it was inevitable that
this sort of thing would happen more often.

There was another side to Alfred's patriotism. He liked to
wave a flag but he didn't close his eyes to national shortcomings.
He saw to it that his writers knew about the economic war that
was developing, as other countries began to eat into Britain's
overseas trade. Enemies encircled Britain. The situation –
threats met with defiance – may have mirrored his private view
of life. Germany was the obvious rival; the United States the
most serious. At the end of 1900 Alfred made his second trip to
the United States, seven years after the first. This time he was a
celebrity. In his buttonhole when he stepped ashore he wore a
lily of the valley that his mother had given him. 'People say that
no young man's coming has ever stirred up the United States so
much before,' he wrote to her. Pulitzer had invited him to edit
his daily newspaper, *The World*, for a day. Alfred produced a
tabloid version on 1 January 1901, calling it, once more, 'The
busy man's paper'. Hearst, who jibed at it, thought that Alfred
looked like 'a mixture of Napoleon, Edison, and the left-hand

cherub leaning over the frame of Raphael's "Sistine Madonna".'
Edison was one of the famous Americans Alfred met, along with
Mark Twain, the Vanderbilts, and the Astors. He took a journalist's look at the American scene, and didn't like what he saw.
'This is the most progressive and growing of countries,' he wrote
to his mother. 'The wealth and energy appal one.' Back in
England, recovering from an infection he picked up while fishing in Florida, he wrote in May to a journalist friend, St Loe
Strachey, editor of the weekly *Spectator*, to say that 'I don't think
the colossal nature of their huge business combinations is at all
understood here, and that their movements are directed almost
entirely against our commerce, the only prize they think worth
capturing.' A second letter said he had been dismayed to find
that 'with identically the same machinery that is used in my
business, the American workmen contrive to make an output of
fifty per cent more per man. Inquiries in other businesses showed
the same thing to exist.'

England was being overtaken, despite an upsurge of exports.
By 1900 her output of coal and iron had been surpassed by the
US, her output of steel by both the US and Germany. The
problem niggled at Alfred and he gave it space in the *Mail*,
reflecting the new attitude, and, with a circulation of three-
quarters of a million, helping to make it as well: the mysterious
two-way process of the mass media was beginning. Articles
announced that 'Uncle Sam takes his coat off' and described
how 'commercial America is making a big bid for the Rand [the
South African goldfield district], and commercial America is
being aided and abetted in its plans by a pathetic, worn out,
vitiated commercial England'. Alfred was taking it upon himself to be a national lighthouse, warning of reefs ahead. In
Russia for a holiday in 1903 – looking at tombs, a tramcar on
ice, guns left behind by Napoleon – he wrote to Strachey to say
that 'I have not seen any English newspaper since I left home so
I do not know whether our national march backwards is proceeding more or less rapidly than usual.' He added his impression that 'Russia regards us [as] of about as much importance
as Belgium.'

Alfred looked at the British and the British looked at him – a
poorly publicised figure by later standards, increasingly anonymous in his own publications, but nevertheless a large silhouette

on the skyline, with unusual features. People seemed impressed by his size but uncertain of his direction. There was Dilke's 'most remarkable man I have ever met'. Lord Esher found him (in 1901) 'clever, vain, not very intelligent about anything except organisation and money-making, but full of aspirations for power. The man interests me, as all self-made men do.' He was interesting; he was puzzling; there was no obvious category in which to put him. An American reporter looked at him for the *World*, shortly before the New York visit when he edited the paper. Alfred received him in Room One at Carmelite House, the five-storied headquarters built to contain all the newspapers and magazines that had recently opened. The reporter noted concealed electric lighting, easy chairs, and statuettes that were 'dreams of beauty'; he missed a black bust of Napoleon. Alfred confided that concentration was the secret of success, and held up three predictable heroes; Rhodes, Kitchener, and Joseph Chamberlain, the Empire-minded Colonial Secretary. He had no ambitions beyond newspapers, he said. This was improbable. A novel published at about the same time, Marie Connor Leighton's *A Napoleon of the Press*, sought to portray him as a national figure. Mrs Leighton and her husband Robert were writers of serial stories for the Harmsworth magazines (among them the famous 'Convict 99'). Mrs Leighton was fond of Alfred; she thought his nose resembled Napoleon's. She must have known that the role she visualised for him, like the plots of her stories, would be acceptable. In the book, the wife of 'Alfred Chantrey', proprietor of the *Daily Post*, tells him what he must do:

You must keep on sweeping clear the path of reform, and working disinterestedly for the greatness of the Empire and for Imperial Federation. What does it matter, after all, if the worry of life here at the centre of things kills us a little sooner than it would do in the country? There are a good many lying out in South African graves who died too soon for want of the reforms which you are pledged to carry out . . .

That was how Alfred saw himself. It was only six years since he became a newspaper proprietor, and linked his name with anything more important than *Answers* and *Comic Cuts*. Now, aged thirty-five, he was hankering after some statesmanlike role, sliding crabwise into politics while renouncing any interest in being a politician.

But he had nothing to say as an orthodox politician that made his opinions worth a second thought. He kept his originality for Fleet Street. His business philosophy had hardened into an obsession with size and excellence, each to be dependent on the other. He was fond of the phrase 'simultaneous newspaper', by which he meant the same newspaper produced in more than one centre at the same time; the *Mail* had led the way with offices and printing plant in Manchester. Writing in the *North American Review* in January 1901, Alfred said that 'given the man, the capital, the organisation, and the occasion, there seems to be no reason why one or two newspapers may not presently dominate almost the whole of Great Britain.' Alfred regarded himself as that man.

We shall see – or our children will see, [he wrote] journalism brought to a standard of excellence hitherto unattained . . . The simultaneous newspaper combination will possess the ablest directors, the most skilful editors, the most brilliant writers and a monopoly of the news service.

It was an innocent expectation, if Alfred really believed it, as he probably did. Size and monopoly, in this rosy dream, would lead to excellence; millions would read a dazzling *Mail*; opposition newspapers would be crushed by quality. The truth was more complicated: serious journalism and big circulations were not as compatible as Alfred liked to think, and the one had frequently to be achieved, in later years, at the expense of the other. Where he was right was in realising that newspapers were an industry, and so, like all industries, could not afford to ignore the realities of profit, promotion, and large-scale competition.

In his daily routine at the *Mail* he was still very much the executive editor: fuller, heavier, more imperious, but still the journalist who wrote headlines and pored over proofs. The magazines saw little of him after 1900. Leicester was the principal Harmsworth there; the other brothers who had joined the firm were drifting out of it, apart from Harold. He was financial controller, except that, in the case of the *Mail*, he lacked ultimate control of the budgets. With the exception of Alfred, no

Harmsworth had anything to do with the editorial side of the newspapers. The *Mail* built up a powerful staff, attracting journalists with its high rates of pay and air of general excitement. A permanent editor was appointed at the end of 1899, Thomas Marlowe, a fierce-looking Irishman, unkindly described as a sheep in wolf's clothing. Alfred made the appointment a trial of strength. Marlowe's predecessor, S. J. Pryor, had been sent to South Africa to organise the Boer War reporting. When he returned, expecting to find himself still in the editorial chair, Marlowe had been made 'managing editor', and thought this gave him seniority. A silent daily battle for physical possession of the editor's room ensued, watched with fascination by the office. Alfred must have found it almost as good as the goldfish and the pike. Each man tried to arrive before the other in the morning, then remain sitting at the desk all day. Marlowe proved the stronger; one version of his victory has it that he brought better sandwiches; another, that he had a stronger bladder.

To all but the most senior at Carmelite House, and perhaps to them as well, Alfred was a mysterious figure. He would descend on the office, turn everything upside down, and disappear for a day or a week. He spied on people: it was a way of protecting himself. He had been known to arrive unannounced at the magazine printing works at four o'clock in the morning. At the *Mail* he did the same. One morning in the small hours, when only a sleepy 'late man' was on duty in the news room, watching the tape machines and thinking about his bed, the swing door crashed open. A man in heavy leather coat and cloth cap, with goggles pushed above it, came in. Motorists still looked like pilots in 1901. It was Alfred, dusty from a drive.

He halted with his hands behind his back and said, 'Who is in charge of this paper?'

The sub-editor was only eighteen. He stood to attention and said, 'I am, sir.'

'And what,' said Alfred, 'would you do if the King died?'

This was the ancient fear of late men. Queen Victoria had died not long before, as it happened, though conveniently early in the evening. The sub-editor rattled off the routine processes for ordering a page-change. Alfred listened, nodded, and disappeared as suddenly as he had come.

At other times, the office wouldn't see him for long periods. In 1901 he was out of the country for nearly five months on six separate trips. Three months of this covered his American visit. which ended with illness in Florida, followed by another two months of intermittent ill-health in England, with depression, rashes, boils, and prostate pain. It was put down to 'malarial fever'. Well again by the end of May, he sent ten thousand pounds to the London Hospital. The rest of his travelling that year was in France. In 1902 he was on holiday for much of the time, in Paris and Monte Carlo from the end of January until the middle of April, visiting Germany for the first time in July. He motored in the West Country with his mother and in Scotland with Mary and the inevitable Reggie Nicholson. Altogether he had between four and five months' holiday. He seemed to fling himself into leisure as violently as he flung himself into work. Even at a time when the upper classes believed in four-day weekends and prolonged stays at Grand Hotels, he did himself well. A newcomer on his staff, Evelyn Wrench, was invited to stay with him on the Riviera. He ate his breakfast on a white marble verandah, overlooking orange trees and the sea: hot-house strawberries, scrambled eggs, bacon shaved as though with a razor. 'It was an entirely new world,' he wrote. 'Money did not count. A lunch given by my host at Ciro's cost as much as my weekly income.' Alfred set great store by bodily comforts.

The impression that he was beginning to leave with everyone was of an abnormally single-minded man. He was no less capable of demanding and taking in the widening spheres of his life now, than he had been when he first wrote articles and fancied Louisa Jane, the servant girl. He demanded and was taking a place for himself as a national figure. His qualifications for this were strong patriotic sentiments, a perceptive newsman's grasp of trends, and unrestricted access to a readership that by sheer weight of numbers commanded respect. Alfred seemed to think them sufficient; others would have to think so as well. At his newspapers and magazines, and especially at the *Mail*, which was the one he cared about most, his single-mindedness had happy results, journalistically speaking. He demanded liveliness, readability, a close and genuine interest in the passing scene; and he saw that everything must be subordinated to the end product. Threats to the Empire made admirable copy because they touched sensitive chords in his readers. It was not that Alfred was dishonest, whipping up a patriotic fervour he didn't believe in, in order to sell papers. His own feelings were usually those of the majority. He cared about Rhodes and the Boers, about cars and telephones, about Swimming and Sex and The Ethics of Flogging. They were all News, they all crowded in, aspects of the world that he could marshal in columns and reduce to order. Before they overwhelmed him, facts must have been a sedative to Alfred; they removed the need to think. His weakness as a journalist was not that he sensationalised events but that in the end he was curiously indifferent to them. One or two causes stayed with him all his life, in particular the threat of Germany. Otherwise he manipulated words and causes with a kind of magnificent numbness. His aim was relevance, not truth. 'What does the *Mail* mean?' asked a 1905 article in the *Bystander*. 'Not always what it says, we fear. It may not always be entirely truthful ... but it is always interesting and always on the spot. You cannot get away from it.' That was Alfred's strength. As long as they were entertaining, one story was much like another. 'Talking points' made newspapers come alive: wars, women's hats, letters about everyday topics, real or invented. Some moral cogwheel was missing from the machinery of Alfred's judgment.

In 1906 he was caught up in an odd episode concerning the Belgian Congo. King Leopold's officials and troops had been systematically despoiling the region since the early 1890s, gleaning rubber and ivory by means of slave labour and a reign of terror. British public opinion grumbled at what it heard from the Congo, and the *Mail* reported the grumbles in a low key. The subject was a sensitive one in a country that practised its own colonialism. They were deep waters, and Alfred can hardly be blamed for avoiding them. But he was pressed to do something about the Congo by his friend Herbert Ward, who had lived and explored there with H. M. Stanley. Ward wrote from France in 1903, asking him to expose the 'awful misdeeds committed by those infernal Belgian serfs of that arch-criminal Leopold', and enclosing a pamphlet about Congo atrocities by E. D. Morel, a young social reformer. Alfred did nothing, but three years later, when Morel asked to see him, he agreed. Morel was about to publish a book called *Red Rubber*. Alfred listened to his story, then cross-questioned him at length, asking him why he was doing it and who was backing him. Morel replied that he had no ulterior motive. As though satisfied at last that here was an honest man, Alfred said he would review the book himself, on the leader page, and Morel could write the leading article to go alongside it. The Congo would be the talking point of the day. So it was, on 20 November 1906. The leader referred to the 'popular movement' against the Congo Scandal. Alfred's anonymous review declared that what *Red Rubber* had to say about Leopold of the Belgians was 'the most appalling indictment of personal rapacity, cruelty, expropriation of life and labour, maladministration and tyrannical atrocity ever recorded on irrefutable proof against any one man in any country or in any age.' The *Mail* was hitting out: Morel must have been delighted. But there the campaign ended, apart from a few news items. Morel thought that Alfred had been influenced, missing the sad truth, that he had lost interest. He was bolder than most in taking up a controversial topic that caught his fancy, and quicker than most in putting it down again when his attention moved elsewhere. Food and gardening and holidays and atrocities were all grist to the mill. Some causes had a lasting appeal, some didn't. The book was 'the most appalling indictment ever recorded', but those were only words. One of many sayings attributed to Alfred is supposed to have been borrowed from Kennedy Jones: 'Everything counts, nothing matters.' The words have a hollow thud that fits very well.

I I

Lord Northcliffe

ALFRED was a man who consistently tried to do too much. His talents as publicist and entertainer equipped him for success; the calm assumptions he made about his destiny, combined with his need to feel he was in personal charge of his empire, ensured that in the end he would over-reach himself. His progress had been so spectacular that it may have seemed to him that he had some special understanding of his period that was denied to ordinary men. Journalism for women is an example of his insight and the way his preoccupations multiplied. While his newspapers were writing about Rhodes and Kruger, he saw to it that they wrote about clothes and cookery as well. Women readers were there in millions. Alfred saw them; so could everyone if they looked, yet other newspapers were slow to copy him. Harmsworth magazines, meanwhile, were carving out a mass women's market, pioneering a school of journalism. *Forget-me-Not*, the magazine that provoked the quarrel with Captain Beaumont in 1891, became one of the most prosperous Harmsworth publications by discovering what appealed to women. Leicester, whose idea the title was, edited it for years, steering it away from its early gentility to something more starry-eyed. What appealed to women, it seemed, were not interviews about different schools of music, or even 'A Chat with the King of Dressmakers'. Harold complained from the start that the readers were too frivolous for this kind of thing. By 1900 the Harmsworths had seen the way ahead and *Forget-me-Not* was full of material that its editors knew was going to work: Are Flirts Always Heartless? – How to Kiss and When to Kiss – Does a Woman Value Love more than a Man?

Other Harmsworth magazines helped to open up the women's market, among them *Home, Sweet Home* (1892) and *Home Chat*

(1895). Advice about love, marriage, and beauty was combined with sentimental fiction that paved the way for the paper-covered 'romances' about mill-girls and rich young men with flashing eyes, that sold in millions before the first world war.

The magazines were pushed down Alfred's list of personal priorities without disappearing altogether. The name 'Harmsworth' was lost from the magazine imprint in 1901, when he and Harold launched a new company called Amalgamated Press to run the multiplying periodicals, with Alfred as chairman and most of his brothers on the board. His connection with the magazines was increasingly confined to suggesting or approving new ones – often encyclopaedias, histories, and fiction libraries published in parts. But he was always liable to descend on *Answers* or *Comic Cuts* with comments on a particular serial, or a complaint that an artist was drawing thin policemen when all the world knew that the British bobby was a fat and cheerful fellow.

Nothing was too trivial if it caught his attention. It was years before he showed signs of regarding some activities as too undignified for a man in his position. In 1898 – the year after he wrote to Lord Onslow to sound him out on the possibility of a title – he let *Illustrated Chips* devote its front page to a strip cartoon headed 'Weary Willy and Tired Tim have a lively time at Tudor Street', which showed the two familiar characters invading the magazine's offices, and being chased out by recognisable Harmsworths. Harold, Leicester, and Cecil are all there, and so is Alfred, dressed in a light-coloured suit, charging from his room armed with a paper-knife (' "Now for it!" Timothy was heard to remark – "now to scatter the double-dyed villain's giblets." But as soon as the Editors saw them, they armed themselves, and prepared to assault the visitors. "Great Billiards!" cried the gents, "we have tumbled into Sweeney Todd's by mistake!" '). There is an eccentric light-heartedness about the would-be statesman with a paper-knife, the young publisher of *Illustrated Chips* who sees himself as a figure of national importance – not tomorrow but already today. He could appeal to people over the heads of established authority, so why bother to follow the rules for dignified behaviour? Perhaps there was also a failure to grasp reality. He was Alfred Harmsworth: he made his own rules. So he did; but there were limits.

When it suited him, he was happy enough to engage in orthodox politics. These revolved around questions of Empire and
defence. He was sucked into the interminable debate about
'Free Trade' versus 'Protection'. That obsession of the day concerned the merits of regarding the Empire as a family of growing
nations that needed to be encouraged by special trading terms
with the mother country. This was 'Imperial Preference' or
'Protection'. Its protagonist was Joseph Chamberlain, the
Colonial Secretary. Chamberlain resigned from A. J. Balfour's
Conservative Government in 1903, in order to preach Protection
without inhibition. Some Conservatives and most Liberals advocated Free Trade. What made the debate so violent was that
Protection might mean higher prices for food. Thus the free-
traders accused the Protectionists of wanting to impose 'food
taxes'. Alfred was caught between wanting to support Protection, as a good Empire man, and wanting to hammer food taxes,
as a good journalist who knew how unpopular dearer bread
would be. He was prepared to go either way. During the summer, before Chamberlain began his campaign, Alfred's men
were reporting the extent of popular feeling. Among the investigators was his son, Alfred Smith, now a budding journalist aged
twenty, who called to see the Smiths in Essex and stayed the
night with them: they were proud of his notebook and pencils.
He may have been the 'Walking Inquirer' who wrote at length
on the leader page on 10 September about a tour of East Anglia
and Essex (a third of the people he spoke to had never heard of
Chamberlain's fiscal policy). Alfred Harmsworth had already
decided to campaign against Protection and 'stomach taxes'.
The man who appealed to him as a political ally was his next-
door neighbour, the Earl of Rosebery, the Liberal Party's
elder statesman and the foremost Liberal Imperialist. Rosebery had come to regard Alfred as an amusing young
fellow, always up to something. He sent a note round
in 1902 to say he had been expecting a visit – 'but I suppose
you are ascending Mont Blanc in a motor car, or something
of the kind'. On 1 September 1903, Alfred, after some preliminary conversation, wrote to him from the *Mail* office, to suggest a programme of speeches designed (among other things) to
oppose Chamberlain's Protectionist policy. Alfred suggested
'with the utmost respect' that 'you consent to the arrangement

of a series of speeches which will allow us the chance, by no means a sure one under any circumstances, of carrying our Press campaign to a successful issue by giving us the support we ask'.

Rosebery was astonished to receive what sounded like an ultimatum; this was no longer amusing, it was ridiculous. J. A. Spender, the Liberal editor of the *Westminster Gazette*, was with Rosebery when the letter arrived. He laughed when he read it. So did Rosebery, a little grimly. He declined politely to be put in Alfred's pocket, writing to him to say that 'I doubt if such a letter as this was ever addressed to a public man in this country'. But Alfred, by his own jaunty standards, was merely being practical. Presently he became more practical. A campaign alongside Lord Rosebery would have been a useful criculation-builder, in a political controversy that was good for newspaper sales in general. By October, Chamberlain was promising that the dearer food resulting from Protection would be offset by reduced prices for other goods. Alfred changed direction. The *Mail* announced: MR CHAMBERLAIN AT GLASGOW – HIS GREAT SPEECH – DETAILS OF HIS FISCAL POLICY – NEW MEASURES FOR NEW TIMES.

But Alfred remained anxious about stomach taxes, as he showed in a letter to Chamberlain that he drafted, but apparently never sent, in October 1903. Alfred was about to launch a newspaper for women called the *Daily Mirror*. He was ill with influenza and liver trouble. The letter has a new ring of harassment and self-importance:

Unfortunately I, who am on the eve of embarking upon a new morning journal in which undoubtedly my journalistic reputation is at stake to say nothing of very large sums of money, am laid low by an annoying temporary indisposition, and inasmuch as it is essential for me to recover my health it may be that it will be impossible for me to come to Birmingham before 2 November, on which date I am publishing the journal in question.

As to the fiscal question, your ultimate object and mine are the same, namely the cementing of the British Empire by the improvement of trade at home and in the Colonies by means of Protection. I discussed this question in the old days constantly with Cecil Rhodes. As to the bringing about of this object, I should much like to have the opportunity of discussing it with you at some future date for I feel that my knowledge of the feelings and thoughts of the poorer classes which I gain by circulating among them almost ten million copies a week of my publications and also of the people in the Colonies among all of whom I have businesses established apart from the personal knowledge I have gained by travelling, might be of great use in bringing about this gradual understanding of the advantages of Protection. My great fear is that unless it is possible to kill the food-tax cry the task will be a very long one and I know of no one who can carry on the task after you . . .

The impending newspaper was a further example of Alfred's capacity for advancing on all fronts at once. The *Daily Mirror* seems to have been put together at the last minute, compared with the preliminary work that went into the *Mail*. It was to be a women's newspaper – edited by them and read by them. It wasn't meant for the naughty New Woman who smoked cigarettes and had unthinkable notions about the vote. Alfred hoped it would attract bright, home-loving ladies, who in turn would attract advertisers of clothes, jewellery, and furniture. Advance publicity described it as 'the first daily newspaper for gentlewomen'. The first issue contained an optimistic article by Alfred which promised that the paper would be so arranged that 'the transition from the shaping of a flounce to the forthcoming changes in Imperial defence, from the arrangement of flowers on the dinner table to the disposition of forces in the Far East, shall be made without mental paroxysm or dislocation of interest.' The result of these contortions was that the paper disappeared between two stools. It was neither regarded as a serious journal of events, nor was there any appetite for the stale genteelness of its society reports and hints on the use of the chafing dish ('or cookery above stairs, as it is sometimes called'). The *Mirror* began on a Monday, price one penny, and sold 265,217 copies. This was quickly seen to be a result of the Harmsworth reputation. Sales fell by nearly half on Tuesday, and by the end of the following week were below a hundred thousand, and sinking fast. 'The desire not to read the *Mirror* had become contagious,' Alfred wrote later. The ladies on the staff seem to have been almost farcical in their inefficiency, though later accounts may have made them a convenient scapegoat. Alfred is supposed to have sent in champagne to revive those who fainted under stress. Some innocent girl, sub-editing an article from Paris, is credited with the headline, OUR FRENCH LETTER,

hurriedly changed by a man on the staff to YESTERDAY IN PARIS.
It is strange that Alfred should have tried such an experiment.
Years later he told an audience of women journalists how a
'prim but fascinating' lady in a neat black costume, in charge of
production at the *Mirror*, was inundated by proofs and printers
as the evening wore on, until she dissolved into tears and a man
had to be brought in, to send the paper to press. Women production editors would still be a novelty, seventy years later. Perhaps an exaggerated Victorian respect for Womanhood misled
Alfred, both about women readers and women journalists.

As circulation fell and losses rose towards two and three thousand pounds a week, there was talk at Carmelite House of stopping the paper. Alfred chose to blame the staff rather than the
concept. After three weeks the lady editor was replaced by a
Scotsman, Hamilton Fyfe, hurriedly bought up from the *Morning
Advertiser*, the brewers' newspaper. The women were sacked.
They tried to soften Fyfe's heart by leaving presents on his desk;
he said it was like drowning kittens. When their tears dried and
they had taken their three months' salary in lieu of notice, they
may have recovered their spirits by observing that the *Mirror*
became less popular after they had gone. Circulation was forty-
five thousand when Fyfe took over; by the end of the year it had
lost a third of this and was barely thirty thousand.

The paper was saved by a drastic change of style. More space
was given to pictures, the page-size reduced, the price was cut to
a halfpenny, and it was sold as the *Daily Illustrated Mirror*. In a
way the episode was in character. Alfred was exploiting a technical innovation. Techniques for using half-tone blocks to print
photographs on newsprint were primitive, and no one had yet
succeeded in doing it on high-speed presses. An improvident
technician on Alfred's pay-roll, Arkas Sapt, who had been
experimenting with picture reproduction for years, was encouraged to keep trying, and succeeded in producing smudgy
newspaper photographs. These, combined with drawings that
reproduced easily, were sufficient to justify calling the paper
'illustrated'. But the innovation had been forced on Alfred before
it was ready. The *Mirror*'s photographs were derided for a long
time. Nor was there anything new about the idea of a pictorial
newspaper; the *Daily Graphic* had been a modest success for
years. Alfred had to make the best of a bad job, and with his

usual skill succeeded in doing so. After the change-over on 28 January 1904, circulation rose from a rock-bottom of twenty-four thousand to one hundred and forty-three thousand in a month, and Alfred, the irrepressible publicist, made a stunt of the failure: he filled two pages with graphs, sales-figures, and his jaunty account of 'How I Dropped One Hundred Thousand Pounds on the *Mirror*.' But the *Mirror* and its pictures never held much appeal for him. He had been compelled to go 'down the market' to sell it, an echo of the early magazine days that probably he would have preferred not to hear. Compared either with the *Mail* or with the original 'newspaper for gentlewomen', it was a second-best. It dealt in fragments of news; Kennedy Jones was the editorial overlord, and the headlines echoed his efforts with crime reports on the *Evening News* – 'UNCLE'S FLAT. Young lady's adventure with three young men', and 'PEER'S DAUGHTER. Only one dress, and a cup of tea a day. Three years of fraud.' Its justification was that it made money – increasingly, as the pictures got better and the sales kept rising. But some memory of the *Mirror*'s awkward birth was incorporated in its character. It was more than thirty years before it found a decisive role, as a people's newspaper of a kind that Alfred didn't dream of in 1904, and went on to achieve the biggest daily sale in the world.

A few months after the *Mirror* became illustrated, Alfred achieved one of his ambitions, by being made a baronet. If he saw himself as an unconventional figure, he wanted the conventional honours as well. He received the title in the Birthday Honours List on 23 June, drawn up by the Conservative Prime Minister, A. J. Balfour, who once went on record as saying that he never read newspapers. It appears that it was not the Conservative Party that suggested the award, but the King. Edward VII had been on the throne since January 1901, a vigorous monarch whose engaging manner combined a taste for pleasure with a sense of duty. In a private letter to Balfour, written from Sandringham on Christmas Day, 1903, King Edward said that

the name of Mr Alfred Harmsworth has been mentioned to me for an Honour. It seems that Lord Salisbury offered him once a Knighthood, which he declined; but I understand he is most anxious for a Baronetcy. He is a great power in the Press and strongly supports the Government as well as Mr Chamberlain's policy. Should you wish to recommend his name to me, I will certainly give my consent. He is married, but has no children.

Why should the King have intervened on behalf of Alfred? Whatever the reason, the royal command resulted in the baronetcy six months later; in between, on 26 February, the King saw Alfred in person. The first letter of congratulation came from Mary Harmsworth, who wrote to 'My darling "Sir Alfred" ' to say that 'the happiest thought of all to me is that *we began* life together and have been together through all the years of work which have earned you distinction and fortune so young.' One could read into her emphasis a hint that she knew she was being supplanted by other women; similarly with the way she signs herself, 'Your loving *wife*'. J. A. Spender wrote amiably to say that 'I have always in my own mind intended you to be a marquis – I don't quite know why, but that title alone seems exactly to suit your disposition'. He added, tongue in cheek, that 'Baronets, according to the writer of the thrilling stories in the *Daily Mail,* are either dull men or very bad men. It will be for you to create a new type which shall be both exciting and virtuous.' Spender, a few years older than Alfred, insisted on declining titles all his life. His idea of journalism was austere and totally different from Alfred's, but the two were friendly for many years; when Alfred thought that Spender's paper, the *Westminster,* was in difficulties, around 1902, he offered a loan of up to a hundred thousand pounds. It was important for Alfred to be liked on all levels. To St Loe Strachey, the other journalist friend who came into the same category as Spender – influential, without trying to command a large circulation – he found time to write, on the day the baronetcy was in the papers, in the tone of a man who realises that he might be criticised for accepting: 'I had not much time to decide, and I thought it best to do it for many reasons not unconnected with our business.'

Alfred remained Sir Alfred Harmsworth, Bart., for less than eighteen months. Balfour resigned office on 4 December 1905, and a Liberal Government was formed. The ex-Prime Minister submitted his list of Resignation Honours to the King the same day. The King approved the names, but added four of his own. Two of them were baronets, now to be made barons. Balfour wrote to the King on 5 December:

Sir A. Harmsworth and Sir E. Stern have very recently been made Baronets on Mr Balfour's recommendation: and for this reason he did not add them to the list of those who were to be made Peers on the change of Government. But Mr Balfour quite recognises that they are (in different ways)gentlemen to whom the Party owe much, and who occupy great positions in the country; they would, without doubt, have, at no distant date, received the further honours which it is now proposed to confer upon them, and Mr Balfour will be happy to add their names to the final list ...

Four days later, Alfred got his barony. The Conservative Party was angry because it interfered with promises made to other journalists. The usual explanation of Alfred's peerage has been that it was a reward for his services to the party in pumping money into a moribund North Country newspaper, the *Manchester Courier*. He bought this in 1905, and spent nearly fifty thousand pounds in trying, with small success, to make it a tower of Conservative strength in the North. Rewards for services rendered to political parties, especially when measurable in hard cash, were common enough. At different times and in different ways, honours could be bought directly by contributions to party funds; the practice became accepted in the early part of the twentieth century, and notorious under Lloyd George after 1918, but even Gladstone sold two peerages in 1891. Alfred's is not generally thought to have been purchased outright; the official history of the *Times* newspaper says that it was paid for, but it gives no evidence, and apparently had none. If it was a reward for the money Alfred had spent on the *Manchester Courier* and the *Southern Daily Mail* in Portsmouth, then it would be true that he had indirectly bought his barony. The letters between Balfour and the King suggest otherwise.

The King's circle of friends included industrialists and self-made men, pushing their way into Edwardian society. Sir Thomas Lipton, family friend of the Harmsworths, was one of them. The King might have been sympathetic to a man like Alfred, if his interest was awakened. One Harmsworth story is that Mrs George Keppel – the admiral's daughter who was the King's most durable mistress – was involved on Alfred's behalf, and that a hundred thousand pounds changed hands; it's not clear whether she or the King is supposed to have received it. There is no evidence for it, and the tale is improbable. One of

Alfred's mistresses, a mysterious woman with aristocratic connections, could have played some part. But Alfred's tracks are
well covered.

The title gave him trouble. He wanted it to have a connection
with the countryside around Elmwood, and suggested Kingsgate, a village nearby. This sounded too regal for the College of
Arms, which suggested that he adopt 'Lord St Peter's' or 'Lord
Broadstairs'. Evelyn Wrench was sent round to the college, but
failed to change their mind about Kingsgate. When someone
suggested 'Lord Elmwood', Alfred said, 'No, it's the wood they
use for coffins.' Finally he thought of a stretch of coastline in the
middle of Broadstairs known as the North Cliff. It was marked
only on large-scale maps, and is now called Stone Bay. Alfred
made it into one word and added an 'e' to produce 'Northcliffe'.
This also enabled him to sign himself with the Napoleonic initial
'N'. The college approved; he became Lord Northcliffe.

Off to Monte Carlo for Christmas, 1905, he could look back
on a year in which his affairs had noticeably gathered speed.
Aged forty, he continued to advance on all fronts. His other
activities during the year included launching the *Continental
Daily Mail* in Paris and buying a Sunday newspaper, the
Observer, for five thousand pounds. Alfred, his son, went there to
work on Saturdays. A public company, Associated Newspapers,
was formed in April to run the *Mail*, *Evening News*, and *Weekly
Dispatch*, the latter bought from Newnes in 1903. This company
marked the formal beginning of the British newspaper industry.
For the first time, investors bought shares in a newspaper as they
might have bought them in a soap factory or a railway. Control
remained with Alfred. In the *Mail*'s nine years he had spent three
hundred thousand pounds on buildings and equipment, all out
of profits. His newspaper group now included journals in Manchester, Leeds, Glasgow, and Portsmouth. Total readership was
estimated by the *Financial News* to be not less than two million,
and was probably much more. The Amalgamated Press produced six monthly and twenty-eight weekly magazines, from
Answers and *Forget-me-Not* to *Golden Stories* and *Girl's Friend* (once
described by Cecil, in print, as 'the huge *Girl's Friend*').

The composition of the readers, those shadowy millions with
their pennies and twopences, was beginning to fascinate the
industry. The *Financial News* speculated on who bought the

magazines: pale-faced waitresses, tired-looking shop assistants, 'sentimental typewriters' (the old word for typists). 'Does she make her own ill-fitting blouse? *Home Fashions* will give her the latest Paris model. Has she a taste for fiction? The *Heartsease Library* will dull her senses.' Behind the sardonic tone of the *Financial News* is uneasiness: they were only silly girls and ignorant women, but their numbers were vast, their weekly pennies a small fortune. Even more than newspapers, the magazines were supplying the mass market that Alfred had foreseen.

Alfred the journalist-tycoon was famous enough to be the subject of laborious jokes as well as laborious novels. A booklet called *Change for a Halfpenny* satirised him as the producer of an elixir called Napolio, guaranteed to expand the imagination, fortify invention, destroy reticence, render domestic privacy impossible, convert an accident into an assassination, and produce Marvels out of Nothing. His correspondence was growing all the time, some of it necessary to the business, some of it the result of his capacity for having views on everything. Amid the letters about tariff reform, the price of newsprint and the situation in Germany, one can even pick out the threads of a private life. In the summer of 1905 he wrote to Katharine Furse, the widow of Charles Furse, a painter. The Furses and Harmsworths had been friendly for years. Alfred said the police had informed him of a highly improper postcard addressed to him from Davos. It was in her handwriting, and read 'What a S–x!' He asked what he was to do about it. Presumably there was no embarrassing sequel. Life proceeded in an orderly fashion. Alfred, Lord Northcliffe, remained well in control.

12

Drama of Mystery Woman

T HE THREE WOMEN who mattered to Northcliffe were his mother, his wife, and his Irish mistress, Kathleen Wrohan. His mother became an obsession. His wife gave him a well-managed social background, suitable for the country's leading (before 1914, its only) mass communicator. But she slipped away to the edge of his private life in the years after 1900. On 15 July 1903, he wrote in his diary: 'My birthday. First year wife has been away on my birthday.' She had never been given a share of the business, but her allowance was enormous. She entertained on a large scale, often with her husband beside her as host, bored with the small-talk. From August 1901, she had a mansion in the country as well as the house in Berkeley Square. This was Sutton Place, a stately home of the sixteenth century, built in the reign of Henry VII. It was only thirty miles from London, much nearer than Elmwood, and in Surrey, a more domesticated county than Kent. The house had dozens of bedrooms, sweeping lawns, and a famous hedge of wild roses; Northcliffe added a golf course. He didn't own the house but leased it, at £1,700 a year, and never cared for it much. It was really Mary's house.

In public, Northcliffe was a considerate husband. He went to extravagant lengths to defend his wife's reputation. Edward Marshall Hall, a King's Counsel rising to prominence as a barrister, was unwise enough to make a remark about Mrs Harmsworth when he appeared in a libel action against the *Daily Mail* in 1900. He declared that his client, an actress, was entitled to 'the same consideration as that of any lady in the land including Mrs Alfred Harmsworth'. Northcliffe retaliated by denying the barrister publicity. When Marshall Hall's name did appear, which was not often, it was given as 'Mr M. Hall'. In

February 1905 he was infuriated to see the first line of a paragraph in the *Mail* that read: 'Mr   M   Hall, K.C., who appeared ...' It looked as if the reporter had written 'Mr Marshall Hall', and that this had been set in type, but changed at the last minute, and the line of type hurriedly reset. This would account for the large space surrounding the 'M'. Marshall Hall complained to the editor that it lent colour to what he had heard, that the paper bore a grudge against him. A few days later someone had whispered in his ear, and he was writing to Northcliffe to apologise for his remark of five years before. It made no difference; the sub-editors continued to write 'Mr M. Hall'.

Mrs Wrohan bore Northcliffe three children. She was a striking woman, rather fleshy as she grew older, with a long nose, fine deep eyes, and a plump bosom. In a photograph of 1903, perched at the wheel of a car, the oval face is hard and handsome; the picture is dedicated to Pine, Northcliffe's chauffeur. By this time she was well-established as his mistress. Her manner shifted between gay and imperious, with a hot temper and a pressing need to get her own way about everything. She spent Northcliffe's money like water. Her background was mysterious, and the Harmsworth family later spent considerable sums in vain attempts to discover who she was.

Mrs Wrohan was well connected. Her address book was packed with upper-crust names. Well over a hundred of them had titles; they were mainly British, but included a sprinkling of French, Italian, and Russian aristocrats. She knew Colonel Sir Augustus Fitzgeorge and the Earl of Munster, Lady Macdonald of the Isles and Viscountess Portman, Lady Troubridge (who wrote serials for Northcliffe), and Le Duc d'Oratino, c/o the Grand Hotel, Naples. Garvin was in the address book; so were Reginald Nicholson and Sutton. Sutton was one of only two people whose birthdays were noted (the other was Northcliffe, listed as 'N'). Mrs Wrohan and Sutton understood one another, at the least; perhaps there was more between them. Some of the names may have been those of lovers; one explanation of her mysteriousness could be that she was a girl of humble origin who worked her way up as a society courtesan. She is said to have been engaged to a kinsman of the Duke of Norfolk, and to a Swiss chocolate manufacturer called Peter. (This would have been Daniel Peter, the man who invented milk chocolate; he lived in London between 1894 and 1906.) In one account, Northcliffe is supposed to have met Mrs Wrohan in Lady Glasgow's drawing room; in another, in an hotel where she was working; in yet another story, they met through a typewriting agency that she is said to have managed. Some of the stories pitch her high in the social scale and some low. The most extravagant makes her out to be an illegitimate daughter of King Edward VII and Lady Londonderry, an echo of the Harmsworth dream of royal connections. Northcliffe's former chauffeur, Pine, interviewed in 1946, described her as being a great friend of the Duke of Westminster and of Queen Alexandra; a signed photograph of the Queen was among Mrs Wrohan's effects when she died. It is possible that she was a friend of the King; he had plenty. This could explain his desire to advance Northcliffe.

The name 'Wrohan' is assumed to have been an invention. She was using it by 1901; a book that passed to her daughter, *The Love Letters of Prince Bismarck*, has 'K.W. 5/9/01' written on the flyleaf in her hand. It was this daughter, Geraldine, who claimed to have been told by her mother that Edward VII was her grandfather. Mrs Wrohan's own story of her origins, as told to a family friend, was different. The friend, who doesn't seem to have believed it for a minute, was Fred Wood, the contemporary of Alfred Senior. He was old by now, and she used to tell him her troubles. What she told him about her birth was an involved story of being a bishop's daughter in Southern Ireland, educated at a convent, running away with the music master and marrying him when she was sixteen. He deserted her and went to America, where he died. Fred thought she was an awful liar. The only verifiable element of the story is that she was Irish: she spoke with an Irish accent.

People were trying to find out about Mrs Wrohan long before most of the family had ever heard of her. One early inquirer was a redoubtable lady called Louise Owen, also Irish, who joined Northcliffe as a secretary in 1902, and spent the rest of her life more or less devoted to him. She said he was the most marvellous person who had ever crossed her path. Unfortunately she was an awful liar, too. She was a possessive and secondary mistress who took pains to play down Northcliffe's relationship with her more successful rival. According to Louise, Mrs Wrohan was employed by Northcliffe to do contract typing; when Louise questioned a payment of twenty-five pounds soon after she went to work in Carmelite House, Northcliffe replied: 'She needs it. I knew her years ago.' Mrs Wrohan had a flat in Brick Court, one of the blocks of barristers' chambers in the Temple. Northcliffe paid the rent. Her name didn't appear in the Post Office directory, though she occupied the flat for years. Louise Owen is said to have gone there once, in an effort to find out more about her. She pretended to faint at the front door so that she would be carried inside. She seems to have seen nothing more incriminating than a sheet of *Daily Mail* stationery in a typewriter. The only persons supposed to have known Mrs Wrohan's identity, apart from Northcliffe, were a London solicitor, Montague Ellis, and her private secretary, Sophie Fenton. Both are dead. Miss Fenton used to annoy people by saying: 'If you only knew who she is!' One promising clue, followed up by the Harmsworths in recent years, was an allowance of a pound a week that Mrs Wrohan paid to a woman in Northern Ireland, Mrs Isabella Osborne. She sent it via a solicitor with strict instructions that Mrs Osborne should not know where it was coming from, and described Mrs Osborne as 'my distant relative'. There is a theory that Mrs Wrohan was, in fact, either her sister or her niece. But nothing was ever substantiated.

She travelled widely in Europe, and was often to be found near Northcliffe, staying at an adjoining hotel. She would shadow his movements from place to place. Letters and postcards trailed after her, sometimes readdressed three or four times before they caught up with her. A card from Switzerland, sent to Savoy Court in London, would be passed on to the Hotel Ritz in Paris, who would send it back to an address at Dover Street in London, where someone would forward it to the Cliftonville Hotel at Margate, or perhaps to Elmwood itself. Mrs Wrohan often stayed at Elmwood. Mary Northcliffe no longer went there. Mrs Wrohan led a busy social life, much of it disconnected with Northcliffe, and was probably no more constant to him than he was to her. She once wrote pointedly to his solicitor to say that no man could serve two masters, though sometimes he tried to serve two mistresses.

Another of Northcliffe's Edwardian girl-friends was a popular novelist, Baroness von Hutten. The baroness, born in

Pennsylvania of Irish–American parents, came to Europe as Miss Bettina Riddle and married a Bavarian aristocrat, Baron von Hutten zum Stolzenberg, in 1897. Life in his castle didn't appeal to her, and they were divorced ten years later, when she was already Northcliffe's mistress. She said she was in love with him, though that didn't stop her taking a shrewd view of her lover. She was nine years younger than Northcliffe, a beautiful young woman with a sexual reputation. J. A. Spender and his wife, who were frequent visitors to Sutton Place, disapproved of the affair. It lasted for several years, made easier by the fact that she was a professional writer whose stories Northcliffe bought for his magazines, and so could be entertained openly. She joined house parties at Sutton Place; on 20 October 1906, she was there with guests who included Sir Douglas Straight (the editor and friend of Alfred Senior) and Mrs Katharine Furse (who sent the improper postcard from Switzerland). Earlier in the year she was being taken, at night, by Evelyn Wrench – now promoted to a position of trust on Northcliffe's staff – to Queenborough. This is a small town on the Thames coast, midway between London and Broadstairs. It would have been convenient for a discreet meeting place with Northcliffe, who told Wrench that there was no one else to whom he would entrust the mission, apart from Sutton and Nicholson.

On her first visit to Sutton Place, her spirited manner annoyed Northcliffe, who pretended to want some sign of feminine submission (though it is equally likely that he fancied women who took a dominant role sexually; both Mrs Wrohan and the baroness sound tough customers). Northcliffe plucked a leaf from the ivy on the wall and handed it to her, saying: 'Take it to remember this visit by. You'll never come here again.' They walked on the lawns and she pointed admiringly to the high chimneys. 'This is the only chance you'll have to see them,' he said. She was able to cope with him. In an hotel in Paris once, he lost his temper because of some imagined slight from her, and flung himself on the carpet in a rage, in front of her and a friend. She waited till he had finished rolling about, and gave him a comb to tidy his hair. She learned not to take him at his face value, to accept that deceit and elusiveness were part of his nature.

There are times when Northcliffe as a person seems to dissolve into words and gestures that mean nothing except that he is signalling some private distress. He demands to be noticed, to be the centre of attraction: the message often seems to be no more than that. The baroness was with him in a Paris restaurant once when he walked across to a table where a newspaper editor was sitting, and slapped his face. The man jumped up, waving his napkin. They exchanged cards, and Northcliffe told her he was going to fight a duel. She didn't take it seriously, and the following day Northcliffe was grumbling that she didn't seem to care whether or not he was killed. It's hardly conceivable that he fought any duel; more likely that nothing happened; possible, even, that the incident was arranged to impress her. His streak of make-believe could detach him from reality. He was sane, but one feels he could have been saner. At one time he kept a dummy telephone on his desk in the office, with a hidden bell-push that he operated with his foot. The bell would ring, and Northcliffe would have an animated conversation with a Cabinet Minister or a general; sometimes he succeeded only in mystifying his visitor, who wondered why the conversation was so one-sided. Tom Clarke, a news editor of the *Daily Mail*, and a friendly witness, described how the telephone trick was worked on him (probably after 1918). The phone rang as he entered the room, and Northcliffe, waving him to a seat, said: 'Oh, yes, the Prime Minister wants to know ... oh ... yes, I see ... Say that I am in conference with an important visitor, and I'll let him know.' Clarke described it 'as the comic dummy phone', but the joke is obscure. To Northcliffe, the only true reality was Northcliffe.

The affair with the baroness lasted for several years. When it ended, she was very upset. Her brother became medical adviser to the *Mail*. Once, when she visited him at Carmelite House, she passed her old lover on the stairs. His dark, enraged look left her trembling. A man who was with her asked what was wrong. 'That was Northcliffe,' she said, 'and he doesn't like me any more.'

Events propelled Northcliffe into situations that left him with less time for his brothers. A few years before – around the turn of the century – he was still active in their lives. He decided about 1900 that they should all have their portraits painted for him to hang in the dining room at Elmwood, and they dutifully sat for Mr Edwin Ward, R.A. He issued an edict that they should join the Automobile Club, and they joined. He said that at least one of them should learn French, and St John, down from university, lived in France with a tutor. But they were striking out on their own. Harold, with a large stake in the business and a keen awareness of his worth as a careful, ruthless manager, was already a rich man, with a country seat at Horsey Hall, in Norfolk.

Leicester, a Member of Parliament since 1900, had bought a magazine of his own called *Golf* in 1898, though within a few years he was moving over to business. When he proposed to sell his family shares, Northcliffe protested, but without success; Sir John Ellerman, the shipowner, bought them. Leicester resigned from the board of Amalgamated Press in 1906, and his relations with Northcliffe became cool. He had a strong gambling streak, putting money into oil companies and the French-made Darracq motor-car, which he helped to import into Britain. He was also building up a collection of paintings and books, later the finest private library in Britain. His houses were hot and dark, full of treasures but tinged with gloom. Unlike Northcliffe, who had no taste, and Harold, whose taste was erratic and liable to be exploited by artful dealers, Leicester was a genuine collector. He was acquiring paintings by Fantin-Latour for a few pounds when most people regarded them as pretty pictures of flowers.

Hildebrand clung to his Harmsworth shares, but he, too, wanted to go his own way. He helped Cecil start a magazine, the *New Liberal Review*, in 1900. Northcliffe failed to persuade him to take over *Vanity Fair*, a magazine he had acquired, and Hildebrand resigned from the Amalgamated Press in 1905, a year before Leicester. In 1908 he bought a London evening newspaper, the *Globe*, and lost over eighty thousand pounds in three years.

St John was the most surprising of the defectors. He bore a strong physical resemblance to Northcliffe, who hoped he would use his education in the interests of the firm. But St John took an early opportunity to escape. In the summer of 1902, while staying in Provence, where his tutor had a villa, he visited a local spring of medicinal waters, bubbling into a pool among the vineyards, near the village of Vergeze. This was a poor man's spa, known to the Romans but not much developed in two thousand years. A Dr Perrier ran it and bottled the water. Early next year the older and wiser Harmsworths were alarmed to hear that St John was selling his family shares in order to buy the Perrier spring. Presently he was designing new bottles in the shape of the Indian clubs he used for exercise, writing the advertisements and talking to the family friend, Sir Thomas Lipton. Sir Thomas talked to his friend the King; the King began to drink Perrier Water, which was granted the Royal Warrant in 1905.

The Harmsworth girls did nothing exciting. Geraldine King had seven children, six of them born in India, one, Cecil,* at Poynters Hall when the family was on leave. Then she came to a full stop, and did nothing for the rest of her life; a heavy, once-lovely, idle woman, who bewildered and upset her children with her powerful but destructive personality. When her husband retired, in 1905, he was a district commissioner with medals, although his achievements, like everyone else's in the family, were now overshadowed by Northcliffe's. They settled in Ireland, in a large house on the edge of Dublin, and lived there with ten servants on a comfortable income of three thousand five hundred pounds a year, two thousand pounds of it from Northcliffe. When there was friction, he would threaten to stop the money. Geraldine was a queenly woman whose emotions grew inward like toenails. Violence seemed to be pent up inside her, as it was in Northcliffe; a lasting shadow of the bleak Harmsworth schoolroom where toys were relentlessly smashed. Cecil, the only second-generation Harmsworth to make a name for himself in Fleet Street, found her loveless, capricious, sometimes cruel; she thrashed him with a walking stick and scoured his ears with a handkerchief and a hatpin. Geraldine was in awe of Northcliffe, but not entirely so. One spring day at Poynters, Northcliffe arrived feeling unwell and went straight to bed. Presently a message was sent down that the children were making too much noise. Outside, the cuckoos were singing hard. 'I suppose he'll be sending down to stop those birds next,' said Geraldine.

Violet was like Geraldine, but greedier and craftier, according to Cecil King; she married an Army officer, Wilfred Wild, in 1908. Violet gambled, gossiped and made the rest of the family uneasy about what she might do next. But Wilfred was

* Named after his Uncle Cecil, who at first tried to deter Geraldine from using his name, on the grounds that it would be wiser to flatter the head of the family and christen him Alfred.

fond of her, and so was Harold, who used to ask her what she was up to, and subsidise her stock-market flutters. Christabel, the youngest girl, was interesting for what she wasn't as much as for what she was. She had the heavy good looks of the family, coupled with a kinder, more placid nature. Together with Cecil and Vyvyan, she lacked the harsh, aggressive traits that made for family success. The sharper Harmsworths were inclined to patronise her. But Christabel was no fool; she was just nicer. As a girl, living at Poynters in a suite of her own, she was lonely. The man she decided to marry in 1905 was a cheerful, not very clever Irishman called Percy Burton, whose father was a bank manager with debts. He met Christabel when he was a secretary to Cecil Harmsworth, and endeared himself to Northcliffe by not appearing to be after his money. Northcliffe wrote to St Loe Strachey that Percy was an agreeable contrast to 'the fortune-hunters who follow shark-like in the wake of my turbine: he is exactly what I would have chosen for her. Christabel has been fortunate enough to escape them, and I rejoice greatly.' But he added: 'I hope that his marriage will make him work harder.'

The trouble with marrying a Harmsworth was that an assured income sapped the will to work. Percy was amiability itself. He wore shockingly loud suits, made by a bookmaker as a sideline, which Christabel insisted he change for something milder before he took her out. His mother-in-law was afraid he might turn out to be one of the feckless type of Irish, for whom, as one of the diligent, she had nothing but contempt; when Christabel announced her engagement, Mrs Harmsworth's only comment was: 'Well, he's good-looking, and if you've got that, you've got something.' Percy and Christabel settled into one of her properties, the Old House on the edge of Totteridge Common, across the main road from Poynters. Mrs Harmsworth, sixty-seven when they married, wanted to have a daughter near at hand, and Christabel was in and out of Poynters all day. Percy founded an advertising agency, which did well from the Northcliffe connection, but he liked to combine business conversations with a round of golf. 'By the ninth hole,' he used to say, 'the thing's in the bag.' Money slipped painlessly through his fingers. But the Burtons were normal; nothing very good or very bad was ever going to happen to them.

As a family, the Harmsworths had been lucky. The sun had

shone for them. In 1906 they had their first disaster, one summer evening when St John was being driven by his chauffeur from Norfolk to Totteridge. He had been staying at Horsey Hall, Harold's country house, where, as some of the family knew, he was carrying on a quiet love affair with Harold's wife, Lilian. St John is said to have been in love with her. On 18 July, being driven back the hundred miles to his mother's house in an open car, they ran into mist along the Great North Road. The chauffeur followed the line of telegraph posts. Not far from Hatfield he must have failed to notice that the posts took a different route. The car veered off the road, mounted a grass bank, and overturned. St John found himself lying on the ground paralysed, unable, at first, to close his eyes. His spine was broken. He was taken to a cottage, where he remained for weeks, too ill to be moved, attended by doctors from London; straw was put down outside to deaden the noise of vehicles; the cottagers were paid to move out. The police superintendent in charge of inquiries was paid thirty pounds for his trouble, and the Chief Constable of Hertfordshire received another thirty-five guineas to distribute in 'police expenses'. It was the beginning of an enormous expenditure over the years on servants, doctors, travel and other comforts, that made St John's life more tolerable without doing anything to cure him. When he was well enough he was brought back to London, packed in sand to stop the jolting. He recovered the use of the upper part of his body, but was paralysed from the waist down. Northcliffe had come hurrying back from Newfoundland, where he was fishing and visiting the Anglo–Newfoundland Development Company, a complex of paper mills that the Harmsworths were setting up to ensure supplies of newsprint from outside Europe. (Harold was the overlord; the concept was Northcliffe's.) All summer they hoped in vain that St John would improve. Lilian helped to nurse him, to the distress of Harold. Then, gradually, they came to accept that he would be a cripple for life.

He became the man in the wheelchair, expensively dressed, attended by nurses and manservant, impatient of fools. His Rolls-Royce in kingfisher blue had a special door so that he could be carried in and out. His hands grew stiff and wasted. One of Herbert Ward's daughters, Sarita, a girl of eighteen, became engaged to this beautifully tragic figure, and was promptly

taken to America by her father. When she became engaged
to someone more suitable, a diplomat, St John wrote vindictively
to Ward to complain about his daughter's behaviour. But St
John's accident became an excuse for almost anything. Most of
his letters are optimistic; occasionally he falters. 'My mind
never ceases day and night in searching for a means of escape
from my prison,' he wrote to Cecil, after eleven years as a cripple. 'To the world I may seem a madman, but, dear Cecil, you
cannot imagine the mental agony of this existence.' What saved
him, though it gave endless trouble to the family in general and
Northcliffe in particular, was the Perrier business. He had made
it into a local industry, with a plant that was turning out five
million bottles a year by 1906; Mussolini was one of the masons
who helped build the works. For the first few years the firm lost
money, despite such efforts as an agreement with the Wagon-
Lits company by which he paid them three hundred pounds a
year to carry Perrier Water in their restaurant cars in France and
Germany. By 1909 the business was showing a small profit. The
trouble was that St John dreamt of expansion, and ploughed the
money back. He wanted a bottle of his mineral water on all the
best tables in Europe. It gave him a purpose in life, and he was
ruthless in pursuing it. His private finances were disordered, and
the letters he wrote, mainly to Northcliffe, applied a perpetual
thumb-screw. He knew there was plenty of money in the family,
and he wanted all the comforts it could buy; no one could blame
him for writing letters that proved he couldn't manage on three
thousand pounds a year. 'As a free man,' he would say, 'this
would be more than enough, but as an invalid it is soon
swallowed up.'

Money, and the way it poured out of his banks into other
people's pockets, irritated Northcliffe at times. His purse seemed
bottomless, with an annual income rising towards two hundred
thousand pounds, but the supplicants were never-ending. He
was a man whose wealth and power were implicitly advertised
to millions every day. His family, immediate and distant, had to
be looked after, to the extent of more than twenty-five thousand
pounds a year. Included in this was five hundred pounds for
Aunt Sarah Miller, now a widow, who wrote polite letters to
dear Alfred and feared lest he might remember old offences and
turn against her one day. (In 1891, when he was beginning to

be rich, he had refused to lend her two hundred pounds, writing a letter that left her half frightened and half resentful.) Mary Northcliffe's family, the Milners, were provided for. The widow of W. E. Henley, the poet (who dedicated a bad poem about motoring to Northcliffe), had her rent paid till she died. Northcliffe lent money to his doctors and his employees. Edgar Wallace was helped, and so were Max Pemberton and Reggie Nicholson. Sick journalists were sent hampers from Fortnum and Mason. Charities got their donations.

Mrs Wrohan added her share of expenses. Apart from allowances of thousands of pounds a year, she spent heavily on jewellery and clothes. She ran up huge bills with London stores; Debenham and Freebody's were owed thousands, and the bills would end up with Northcliffe. Presumably she was worth it. In later years he spoke ruefully of women. It may not only have been Mary who moved to the edge of his life. It may be that Mrs Wrohan was never near the centre of his life in the first place. If he ever wrote love letters, to her or to anyone else, they have disappeared. One suspects he didn't bother, or that, if he had tried to bother, he wouldn't have known how.

13

Power Game

NORTHCLIFFE made one of the most expensive mistakes in the history of newspapers in 1906. Only someone of brutal courage and wrong-headed determination would have done it, and only a prosperous organisation could have paid the bills at the end. The episode concerned soap, improbably enough, and it introduces a new level of intensity in Northcliffe's progress through life and Fleet Street. It arose from a perfectly proper interest by the *Daily Mail* in the making and selling of household soap, but rapidly got out of hand and resulted in libels so gross that Northcliffe's newspapers seemed like machines without operators, stamping out material that no one knew how to stop.

The manufacturer whose path crossed Northcliffe's so violently, Mr William Lever, MP (later the first Lord Leverhulme), had been developing the soap industry at the same time that Northcliffe was developing the newspaper industry. He was probably the first to introduce a pure soap, about the time that *Answers* was launched, and by 1906 his factory at Port Sunlight, named after his best-selling brand, had an output of three thousand tons a week. Soap had ceased to be a sign of household affluence, and large sums were spent on advertising it to a mass market. Among the brand-names that Lever invented were 'Lux' and 'Vim', still going strong after seventy years. In 1906, increased competition among manufacturers, together with a sudden rise in the cost of raw materials (the oils were in demand for margarine), led Lever to seek protective combinations within the industry. Firms would be interlocked by secret exchanges of shares. When the combinations became known, they would be explained as a means of saving costs in manufacture and advertising, so as not to pass on all the increases to the consumers. It was one of those commercial exercises, no doubt unavoidable,

that manufacturers like to push through as discreetly as possible
in case people begin to complain and ask questions. As an immediate measure, Lever also wanted to raise the price of the
one-pound tablet of Sunlight Soap. This was difficult because a
pound of soap cost threepence, and an increase to the next
feasible fraction, threepence-halfpenny, was not justified. Instead, the price was left unchanged and an ounce was taken off
the pound bar. Shops were told about it in a notice on delivery
cartons – printed inside the flap, in order, it was said later, not
to disturb the design.

Conditions were ripe for confusion and bad feeling. Northcliffe
was precisely placed to make the worst of things. To begin with,
he needed campaigns. The art of manufacturing news was becoming highly developed at Carmelite House. No other proprietor or editor had appeared to compare with Northcliffe,
either as a generator of excitement about trivialities, or as a
shrewd judge of major trends. He had known exactly what to do
about telephones, cars, Boers, the Kaiser, and the disgraceful
export of British horses to make sausages for Belgians; he knew
exactly what to do about soap. Given an objective, Northcliffe
was difficult to divert. His life was run on lines that encouraged
him to be what he was now universally called, 'The Chief'. Day
by day (when he chose to attend) he went up to the first floor at
Carmelite House, past murals of Greek muses and winged ladies
with blunt nipples, to the cool peacefulness of Room One.
There, he sat with his back to long windows, facing glass-
fronted cabinets filled with sets of mint volumes in dark reds and
greens: Hardy, Dickens, lives of politicians, histories of wars.
Long after his death they were still there, frozen in time, behind
locked doors. His editors and managers came to receive instructions and exchange views; only rarely to argue. With the quiet
voice went unquiet eyes, deep blue and riveting. He lolled in an
armchair or lay on the great dark-green couch with his back to
the light, his low voice snapping shut on sentences like a well-
oiled door, or, at times, trailing off into silence. His approach to
visitors could be paternal, gentle, humorous, and warm. It could
also be mean and aggressive. Then the voice became still softer;
he drew back his lower lip on his teeth and delivered needle-like
words, as if he meant to inoculate the listener with a bite. His
power was all around him, visible in every morning's paper. He

had not only invented the popular Press, but looked like domi-
nating it for years to come. The *Daily Express*, started by Arthur
Pearson in 1900, was a weak competitor. Existing papers had
copied the *Mail* without achieving its forceful ingenuity. With
his efficient pursuit of modern-mindedness, Northcliffe even
made inroads into so-called 'serious' journalism, which too often
missed the point of the progress into the twentieth century that
it was supposed to be reporting.

Northcliffe was cleverer than they were. When he heard, in
the late summer of 1906, that moves to set up a soap combine
were on foot, he thought he recognised a parallel with America,
where monopolistic trusts, then under attack by Theodore
Roosevelt, were a major political issue. His own dream of an all-
powerful 'simultaneous newspaper combination' was conveniently overlooked. A soap trust sounded unpleasant. One day
there might be a newsprint trust. In any case, the Lever combine
that was being stealthily put together in August would do immediate damage to the Press by reducing rivalry and thus
advertising. This was a prime object of Lever's scheme, and a
powerful reason for Northcliffe to oppose it. In September,
Lever and other manufacturers began to suspend and cancel
advertising contracts, and many thousands of pounds' worth
were withdrawn from the *Mail*. Lever was resigned to having
news of the combine leak out in September, but it was not until
the beginning of October that Press comments began in earnest.
Northcliffe's papers were puzzled or neutral at first; then, from
18 October, suddenly hostile. The *Mail* found shopkeepers ready
to criticise the manufacturers, and quickly inflamed their grievances. No attempt was made to distinguish between 'news' and
'comment'. Northcliffe was not interested in discovering the
truth, which would have led to different conclusions, but in
printing as many stories as possible to sustain his case. News and
leader columns were packed with invective and biased reporting.
'Prices have been artfully raised to the public,' said the *Mail*,
'not always in a straightforward manner, but by the subtler
process of diminishing the quantity in the packets and packages,
and giving the ignorant customer fifteen ounces, or even less, to
the pound'. Lever Brothers were accused of dismissing employees,
trying to bribe the Press, using unsavoury fish-oils and grinding
the faces of the poor. 'If ever hunger and poverty followed upon

the ruthless operation of a great "combine",' cried the *Mail*, 'it waits upon the Soap Trust. It goes straight at the throat of people living on the verge of starvation.' This was a novel display of social conscience. The *Mirror* specialised in cartoons in which 'Mr Soap Trust' of 'Port Moonshine' picked pockets and gave short weight. No one seemed to worry whether letters to the editor were genuine. One sneer at the soap firms, published in the *Evening News*, was later challenged by Lever. The paper said the letter had been received without name or address, adding innocently that *they* hadn't written it. The letter said:

I'm a tradesman in a small way, and I'm thinking of trying a short-weight Lever dodge, just to make ends meet. There's my yard measure; well, I've cut six inches off that. Then my scales; I've stuck a chunk of putty below the end I weigh the soap in; no, I made a mistake, not soap, cheese I mean. Then I'm getting a false bottom put in my gallon measure. And the painter is coming in the morning to add to my sign above the door, 'Yard measure, scales and gallon according to Lever.' I'm not greedy for money, but I must make ends meet. A Would-be MP, West Kensington.

Other newspapers reported the Soap Trust affair and criticised Lever, but without Northcliffe's venom. After two weeks of the attacks, sales of soap were falling. A letter from the *Daily Mail* to Lever, on the day the campaign began, had already passed on a 'sincere assurance' from Northcliffe that it was his 'aim and intention to maintain the strictest impartiality'. This impertinence was followed, at the end of October, by a verbal message from Northcliffe received via a firm of advertising agents, that if Lever resumed advertising in the Northcliffe papers, the attacks on him would cease. Lever refused, with the result that the campaign went ahead, Lever shares slumped, the sixteen-ounce bar was restored, and the soap combination abandoned. 'The British Lion Destroys the Greedy Soap Trust', was the heading on a *Mirror* cartoon on 26 November; it showed the British Lion standing triumphant over the sprawling figure of Signor Soapo Trusti. 'The *Daily Mirror* cartoons,' it added, 'were among the great factors that smashed the Soap Trust and restored the sixteen-ounce pound.'

There was certainly a case for investigating Lever and the soapmen. The manufacturers were reorganising the industry. Bars of soap had got smaller without most people realising, whatever

Lever said about small print on the retailers' cartons. Newspapers rightly suspected that the soapmen, whatever they were up to, were acting in their own interests. But only large-scale villainy would have justified Northcliffe's attack. No evidence of this was forthcoming. As the *Times* pointed out, a classic trust with evil intentions would hardly begin by raising prices and so alarming the public. Lever took legal advice. The case went to F. E. Smith, later Lord Birkenhead, who sat up all night with the papers, drinking champagne and eating oysters, and delivered a one-sentence opinion before breakfast: 'There is no answer to this action for libel, and the damages must be enormous.' The case came to court the following July, 1907. A few days before the hearing was due, Lever was offered a public apology. Having seen his soap combine killed and his company grievously damaged, he was hardly likely to agree. In the witness box he obstinately refused to concede one of the main points that Rufus Isaacs (later Lord Reading) tried to make for the defence, that a threepenny bar of Sunlight Soap was supposed to weigh one pound. Because of evaporation, Lever insisted, it was sold as threepennyworth of soap, not sixteen ounces, whatever anyone might have thought to the contrary. The case collapsed on the third morning, when Isaacs tried to settle for ten thousand pounds outside the court. This was refused, and in an extraordinary courtroom scene soon after, Isaacs made a series of offers in a stage-whisper, culminating in one for fifty thousand pounds. 'That's a substantial offer,' said Lever. 'I'll take it.' By the time other firms had claimed, and damages had been awarded against other Northcliffe newspapers, the bill came to more than two hundred thousand pounds: the largest sum ever awarded till then by a jury in the English courts, and worth one million six hundred thousand pounds by present-day values. Northcliffe had been responsible for the campaign – he wrote much of the copy himself, with instructions that it was not to be altered – and a good deal of the money came from his own pocket, though he tried, against opposition from other directors, to charge it all against profits. Harold, his worst fears justified, imposed harsh economies on the papers. His personal situation, it is said, was happier: he bought Lever shares in anticipation of the verdict.

Northcliffe spent much of 1907 out of the country, prudently

lying low. He was reported to be unwell. A postcard to Katharine
Furse from Germany, written ten days after the fifty thousand
pound award, read: 'The first words I have written for a month,
and against orders.' Northcliffe was making himself ill with
worry again, retreating from the world. But why should he have
put himself in such a position? No doubt he saw himself threatened by Lever's plans to cut advertising. Once involved, he was
reluctant to be seen withdrawing under pressure. It may have
been tempting, also, to emerge as a popular champion. This was
exactly what he had failed to do over the issue of Protection
versus Free Trade, which had ended in equivocation, as far as
the *Mail* was concerned, not long before. Northcliffe had neither
attacked food taxes, nor defended Protection, whole-heartedly.
Politics, he had been learning for years, were involved and tiresome. But the Soap Trust issue appeared simple, finite, and an
excuse to deliver some enjoyable hammer-blows. The *Mail*
always needed causes. Its circulation, though healthy enough,
remained well below the peak reached in the Boer War, until
the next war started in 1914. Northcliffe used the *Mail* in a carefully calculated way. Years before, when Edgar Wallace said he
wondered why an article he had written should have upset a
politician, Northcliffe replied gravely, 'You are little, Wallace,
but the *Daily Mail* is big.' In 1904, when writing to tell Strachey
that he shouldn't take too seriously some remarks about him in
the *Mail*, Northcliffe declared:

The most unfortunate part of the circulation of my paper, is the
fact that the immense number of people who see everything that
appears in it and the comment they make, magnifies every utterance.
We have been obliged to reduce the tone and colour of the paper to
far below that of any morning newspaper except the *Times*, and even
then such remarks as I made about you, will get magnified by hearsay. The position is a new and difficult one for a newspaper owner.
Had I published the *Pall Mall Gazette*'s ridiculous nonsense about
Russia the other day, there would have been a panic. During the
recent small Savings Bank smash, we were inundated with telegrams
and letters from bankers all over the country, asking us to leave
things alone, and we did so, but from one point of view, quite
wrongly.

Northcliffe trod carefully so as to avoid panic when a savings
bank closed; he abandoned discretion when the situation

appealed to him, as it did with the Soap Trust. His use of power was arbitrary. He might hurt others and he might hurt himself. Given the innocent, almost virginal state of the mass-communication business, it was the inevitable way for a strong man to proceed.

In Northcliffe's life, success and failure were so intermingled that it is difficult to strike a balance at any given point. He was one of those men who follow a course that seems often to owe nothing to the particular events in which they are involved. A blunder like the Lever campaign should have had some effect, apart from the need to dip into his pocket. Yet a few months later, it might never have happened. The next important event in his life was a triumph: by cunning, patience, boldness, and strength, he bought the *Times*, and became master of Fleet Street. Yet that, too, was to prove irrelevant. It was as though some deeply hidden purpose that owed nothing to the events that made headlines was slowly unfolding in Northcliffe's brain – as though Northcliffe's schemes and secrets, his newspapers and women, were all part of his imagination, all subordinate to the man who sat within the man, spinning out a lifelong dream of himself.

It was one of Northcliffe's persistent ambitions to buy the *Times*. He first tried to get it in June 1898. He approached the Walter family, the principal proprietors, and was rebuffed. Two years later he tried again, telling a go-between that he had Government stocks worth a million pounds, which he was willing to pay (his net worth that year was rather less than a million, £886,000 to be exact). In 1902 a diary entry in May said, 'Busy about negotiations re the *Times*,' but without sequel. In 1907 the paper became ripe for plucking, when a chronic financial crisis came to a head. Founded by the Walter family in 1785 (originally as the *Daily Universal Register*), it became an authoritative newspaper in the nineteenth century under successive editors, Thomas Barnes and John Delane. Since late Victorian days it had been in decline, losing touch with the wider public, hampered by ageing machinery, perpetually short of cash. But it had turned into an institution, occupying a special position in

British affairs, like the monarch or the Houses of Parliament. People regarded it as accurate, dignified, and impartial; its golden years had given it a reputation on which it rested comfortably. The editorial staff regarded themselves as more than mere journalists. What they produced was a record of public affairs, with due attention to Parliament, law, Church, foreign news, and the arts. The place breathed propriety and conservatism. (A musty smell that lingered in the editorial rooms for years was traced to the remains of dead rats, found behind mahogany bookcases when they were sold to raise money.) The offices faced the main street; behind them was Printing House Square and a small house with a garden, where the editorial staff dined nightly. Two men ruled the paper. The editor, George Earle Buckle, was a barrister and Fellow of All Souls. The manager, Moberly Bell, had been in business in Egypt; he became the *Times* correspondent there, and was later brought to London. With his hook nose and sallow complexion, he was said by irreverent colleagues to have been a pirate on the Nile who had kidnapped the real *Times* man and taken his place; he was known as 'the Pirate'. Bell wrote his correspondence with his own hand, and once had a learned exchange of letters with a man in Essex, broken off when it was discovered that the correspondent lived in a lunatic asylum. Bell and Buckle were men of substance who understood the nature of the institution, but even at its price of threepence, they were incapable of making it show a profit.

The Walter family were the chief but not the only proprietors of the *Times*. Eighty or ninety co-proprietors owned smaller shares, and complained at the lack of return on their investment. They forced a legal dissolution of the partnerships in July 1907, and left the Walters looking desperately for someone agreeable who would refinance the paper as a limited company. A City group agreed in private in November to put up the money, with Arthur Pearson as managing director. Neither Buckle, Bell, nor the lesser proprietors were told. Pearson, a capable manager, was a smaller version of Northcliffe, having begun with *Pearson's Weekly* soon after *Answers*, and progressed to the ownership of provincial and London newspapers, among them the *Daily Express*, which he founded in 1900. No one seems to have shown much enthusiasm for Pearson, but the scheme might have gone ahead for want of anyone better if Northcliffe had not heard a rumour that something was happening, one evening when he was reluctantly attending a dinner party, towards the end of 1907.

For months after that, he manoeuvred secretly. Much of the time he was on the other side of the English Channel, staying under an assumed name at the Hotel Crystal-Bristol in Boulogne, sending and receiving telegrams in code. Inquirers at Carmelite House were told he was having a rest cure in the South of France. The point of disappearing from London was to remove his name from speculation and put him beyond the range of the curious, while he moved behind the scenes, damaging Pearson and acquiring support for himself without revealing who he was. The money involved, a matter of three or four hundred thousand pounds, was no problem. The difficulty was to use his resources without having the door slammed in his face because he was revealed as Harmsworth of the Yellow Press. Occasionally he crossed to London, carrying his own bag and staying in the suburbs like an adulterer keeping a rendezvous. Mainly he idled in France with secretaries and aides, eating too much because of the tension and putting on weight, which he recorded, as always, in a weight book. (Whenever he lost a few pounds he would write 'Ha! Ha!' or 'Good boy'. When he touched fourteen stone he wrote 'Horrible'.)

Pearson proved too simple for the game that had to be played. His provisional agreement with the Walters was signed on 1 January 1908; the scheme itself had to be sanctioned by the courts. Instead of keeping quiet, Pearson couldn't resist boasting. Word reached Northcliffe in Paris. On 5 January a paragraph was planted in the *Observer*, Northcliffe's Sunday paper, to say that 'a very capable proprietor' was to take over direction of the *Times*. This led to excited speculation in Fleet Street, and forced the Walters to tell Buckle and the small proprietors, and then the world at large, what was happening. George Sutton and Kennedy Jones, liaising with Northcliffe in France, gleefully concocted a longer article for the *Mail* which damaged Pearson by praising him as a 'hustler'. From then on, Pearson's credibility as future managing director of the *Times* declined.

Jones and Sutton found a capable ally inside the paper in the shape of the Pirate, Moberly Bell. The manager had two motives for not liking Pearson: he thought him an inadequate chief for his beloved newspaper, and he knew that under Pearson he would lose his job. His first reaction to the idea of Northcliffe as proprietor was to say: 'Never.' On his side, Northcliffe seemed to be dragging his feet. 'The *Mail* is in my judgment a very much greater power than the *Times* will ever be, and we can make it an infinitely greater thing than it is,' he wrote to Sutton and Jones on 9 January. He ended: 'Do not allow yourselves, either of you, to be carried away by zeal. Personally, as I told you here when you spoke to me two months ago, I am content with what we have. You have also to remember that anything either of you does will be ascribed to me. Walk warily.'

This was bluff. Behind the caution and the double-talk, two realities emerged: Northcliffe itched for the *Times*; Bell would help him get it. Northcliffe, he concluded, was the lesser evil. He convinced Bell that he would run the paper on traditional lines, and Bell negotiated for the support of Buckle and Arthur Walter, the senior member of the family, concealing Northcliffe's identity and referring to him as 'X'. The crucial moment for Bell came early one Sunday morning in February, when Sutton arrived at his house to finalise the terms on which Northcliffe would take the *Times*. A lengthy letter of agreement that Bell had prepared, full of checks and balances, was swept aside. He ended by writing out a promise, still wearing his dressing-gown, to obey Northcliffe's 'absolute instructions' as proprietor. Sutton warned that if he didn't, the negotiations were at an end. Bell told no one about this surrender. Another five weeks of deviousness followed, with plot and counter-plot, before the sale of the *Times* to Northcliffe was approved by a judge, at a price of three hundred and twenty thousand pounds. His name was still concealed from all but a few. Just before he heard that he had won, he wrote to 'Darling Mumlo' from Versailles to say that 'we are most anxious that if the thing is accomplished it shall not be known for several years' – though in fact, it became widely known before the end of 1908. 'Hooray!' said Lady Northcliffe to Sutton, adding that the Chief was 'the only person in the world who could run it'. But when Northcliffe saw his mother, she made an odd remark. 'I'm sorry, Alfred,' she said. 'You have lost your horizon.'

To recuperate after the struggle, Northcliffe and his wife took a party for a holiday in Spain. J. L. Garvin, the *Observer* editor, was with them; so was the editor of *Punch*, and two of the inner circle, Evelyn Wrench and Reggie Nicholson. In Seville, where they rented a villa, Alfred and Mary dined alone at an hotel and drank champagne to celebrate their twentieth wedding anniversary, on 11 April. Wrench, who looked after the establishment, was now a favoured member of the staff, with shares in the *Mail* that Northcliffe had given him. He admired Northcliffe. He saw that the guests had all they needed as they lounged about the villa, with its broad marble patio open to the sky and garden filled with roses, or went for car excursions. Sexual pleasures enlivened the holiday. Lady Northcliffe was sleeping with Reggie Nicholson, and Wrench was unwise enough to catch them in bed together. Northcliffe, who knew of the affair, which probably had lasted for years, was indifferent as long as it was kept private. But when he discovered that Wrench, one of his young dependants, knew about it, he flew into a rage. To Wrench's astonishment, he marched into his room and began to threaten him. 'If you ever tell a soul,' he said, 'I will sack you on the spot.' The next time they met, Northcliffe went out of his way to be agreeable; he promised to help with an Empire-unity society that Wrench was planning, the Overseas League. But Wrench viewed him differently from now on. He wrote later (concealing the details) that it was the first time he had seen the ugly side of Northcliffe's nature.

That summer, overwork begins to haunt Northcliffe. The word keeps recurring, as though he realises that all the holidays in the world can't save him from the cables and letters that reach out to him in villas, in hotels, in Elmwood by the sea – still there with its Polar bear and sunken boat, the old furniture from Pandora Road in the bungalow, the paintings of rosy-cheeked brothers in the dining room. He wrote to a shareholder in the *Daily Mail* to say that 'I have been working consecutively at the paper – with only three days' intermission – since August 1907.' He liked to exaggerate his burdens. But the groans may have concealed a fear. 'What is the Wood Street Publishing Company?' he wrote petulantly to Harold on 25 July. 'I have already written to some bankers saying that I know nothing of it. Surely the company of which I am chairman is not starting journals for which I am responsible without my knowledge? In many ways the business seems to be getting out of hand. I am so overworked that there have been only three days in the last three hundred and sixty-five when I have not worked, and mostly all day long, from 7.30 in the morning. I am working, for example, all today.' His health was giving trouble. His eyes worried him. In September he was in Germany with Mary, sending postcards as they moved from place to place, stopping at Frankfurt to see an eye specialist, Professor Solm. The professor advised dark spectacles, and told him to use a magnifying glass to read the *Times*. Back in London, journalists who knew him by sight recognised the square, wrathful shape humped in the back of the Rolls-Royce, going fast along Fleet Street or the Embankment, eyes hidden by blue-tinted lenses. About to leave for an American trip in October, he drew up a new will, and signed it on the day he sailed. Mary would receive two hundred pounds a week for life; his mother, a hundred and twenty pounds. Among the cash sums were a thousand pounds apiece to a Miss Florence Skipper ('one of my typists') and Miss Louise Owen ('another of my typists'). Northcliffe's wife and mother went with him to America; so did Mrs Wrohan, who appeared in New York when Northcliffe was there, and moved to Niagara when he went to Canada. They were all back in London before Christmas, and Northcliffe was ill again. It was his stomach; it was his eyes; it was his nerves. An undefined state of ill-health, vaguely connected with the strain of living, became almost normal.

He embraced the *Times* and it embraced him back: their relationship was to be a disturbing exercise in energy versus mass, but for the moment Northcliffe disclaimed any radical intentions. An office legend says that on his first visit of exploration, opening doors at Printing House Square that had stayed shut for years, he found a room with a collection of ancient muskets and spears, souvenirs of forgotten campaigns. He asked what they were for; no one knew. 'I know,' said Northcliffe. 'They're to arm the staff with, if anyone brings you a piece of news.' It was the Chief's little joke. His little jokes circulated in the sombre rooms where men insisted on writing articles with pens instead of typewriters. He was not the saviour the *Times* would have chosen. He had got the paper because he was a determined man with a third of a million pounds in ready money; he knew it, they knew it, he knew that they knew it.

Mary Harmsworth *(right)* and two of Alfred's sisters, Christabel *(centre)* and Violet. They were dressed for a pageant at Broadstairs.

Sombre Leicester, who might have gone in for the Church. Instead he edited *Forget-me-Not* for the ladies.

Lilian Share, the businessman's daughter who married Harold and became Lady Rothermere.

Alfred as a young man never seemed old enough to be a power in Fleet Street. A shareholder who saw the brothers at a company meeting remarked, 'They're only boys!'

Alfred in his early years as proprietor of the *Daily Mail*.

Northcliffe wrote to tell people how little he meant to inter-
fere with the *Times*. He wrote to Wickham Steed, the paper's
distinguished correspondent in Vienna, to say that 'I am not,
nor ever shall be, the "Chief" of the *Times*'. Steed had been
emphasising the importance of keeping Northcliffe in the background, lest the paper's wells of diplomatic and political information dry up. Northcliffe told St Loe Strachey that not only
did he have no control over the *Times* except for machinery and
paper, which he was improving, but he had made it part of the
bargain that he should have no responsibility, since he was too
overworked as it was. To reassure others, perhaps to reassure
himself as well, he talked of leaving the *Times* to the nation in his
will, suitably endowed and run by trustees, like the British
Museum. This peculiar reverence for a newspaper seemed perfectly natural to those, like Strachey and Lord Esher, who were
consulted by Northcliffe. The Speaker of the House of Commons
would be one of the trustees; the Archbishop of Canterbury
another.

But reverence for a collection of presses, distinguished correspondents, sub-editors who wrote Latin verse, and memories
curling at the edges, was not Northcliffe's style. What he said
about the *Times*, then and afterwards, was riddled with contra-
dictions. It frustrated him because for the first time in his life he
had to argue with journalists who possessed an intellectual vision
of how a newspaper should be run, and who could not be set
aside without causing the *Times*, that maddening repository of
tradition, to liquify and vanish. But there was never any doubt
that he wanted to do something more with the paper than leave
it to the nation. His talk of not wanting to control it was more
bluff. The face darkens; executives' telephones ring furiously;
the master-brain is inspecting the monument from all angles,
determined to understand it and reduce it to order. From now
on, Northcliffe's prime need is to be in control. It was true at the
Times, and in a wider sense as well.

14

Signs and Symptoms

ONE of Mrs Wrohan's admirers sent her a postcard from Germany in the summer of 1908. It showed 'Count Zeppelin's airship in full flight', sailing fat and ominous across the sky. 'Germany is ablaze with airship enthusiasm and interest,' said the *Daily Mail*, noting that Zeppelin's voyage from Germany into Switzerland marked the first time that a military airship had crossed a frontier and passed over a foreign State. Germany, Northcliffe's old bugbear, never left him alone. The country intrigued him, as it intrigued many of the British. Its characteristics were both enviable and shocking. It believed in discipline and militarism; so did the British imperialist, as long as things were done in a decent British way, with due respect for the rights of others, which the Germans were supposed to regard too lightly. (The *Daily Mail* had been calling for a British version of compulsory military service since 1904.) Germany breathed smartness and efficiency. Visitors brought back tales of troops manoeuvring on the plains in autumn, but they also noticed the everyday energy, order, and cleanliness.

Northcliffe expected to find something remarkable from the moment he first went there, in 1902, going by train from Strasbourg to Stuttgart. He wrote in his diary: 'I shall never forget the first sight of Germany as we approached it from the other side of the Vosges mountains.' Six years later he was writing to Arthur Mee, who edited encyclopaedias for him at the Amalgamated Press, to say that 'Germany is new, masterful, alive, brutal, and horribly *nouveau riche*'. A critic could have used the same words about Northcliffe; perhaps he saw traces of his own character in the country. He liked to think he was an expert on Germany. Two of his mother's sisters, Grace and Caroline Maffett, had married Germans and emigrated there. 'My dear Evelyn,' he was telling Wrench in 1908, 'I have German relatives, I know them, they will bide their time, but *Der Tag* will come. Remember what I say.' He added that the Kaiser had tried more than once to get in 'personal touch', but 'I prefer to keep away from him'.

The natural corollary to saying that Germany threatened Britain was to say that Britain must be strong. Both countries were arming, and Northcliffe's propaganda, which continually demanded greater effort, was violently attacked by Liberal newspapers as warmongering. They called him 'an enemy of the human race'. Naval supremacy was the crux of the matter. Northcliffe shared and exploited a sense of outrage at German attempts to build a navy that would rival Britain's, which God and history had ordained as the arbiter of power in Europe. Other newspapers were uneasy about Germany, among them the *Times*, which, long before Northcliffe bought it, was aware that (as its Berlin correspondent remarked in 1902, in an inter-office letter), Germany was a *'new*, crude, ambitious, radically *unsound* Power'.) But where the *Times* worried about the Navy, the *Mail* raged about it. By 1908 the argument revolved around Dreadnoughts, super-battleships with twelve-inch guns, heavy armour, and powerful engines that made existing battleships obsolete. The first was launched in 1906; Admiral Sir John Fisher, the First Sea Lord, called her 'the Hard Boiled Egg, because she can't be beat'. Britain and Germany began a race to build Dreadnoughts. The word chilled and excited newspaper readers as much as 'missile' and 'nuclear strike' would do later. Early in 1909, the country was in a fever as the Liberal Government tried to decide how many Dreadnoughts to lay down that year: four, six, or eight. Garvin, who wanted it to be eight, would talk about it all through lunch with Northcliffe, or spend the weekend at Sutton Place, where the ladies fled from the Dreadnought discussions that went on from morning till night. Behind the scenes, armament manufacturers did their best to make the German Dreadnought programme sound bigger than it was. 'We want eight and we won't wait' became the popular slogan. Northcliffe ordered a contents bill for the *Mail* with the stark message: 8. The eight were built, with ten more in the next two years. Northcliffe's friends said he had helped in a patriotic campaign to give Britain a margin of superiority in super-battleships. His enemies said it was warmongering. It may even have been impractical: the British Dreadnought programme led Germany to build more of her own.

During part of the Dreadnought campaign Northcliffe was on holiday in south-west France, at the resort of Pau, on the edge of the Pyrenees. The air in Pau is soft and warm; Northcliffe went there when his health needed soothing. At the end of January 1909 he was telling people that he had ptomaine poisoning, one of his favourite labels for unwellness; this time he blamed something he ate on board the *Lusitania*. His doctors were telling him to spend more time in the open air. At Pau he saw something to take his mind beyond Dreadnoughts. He wrote a mocking letter to Moberly Bell at the *Times*, 'I can ... show you a man flying in the air, which would wake you up a bit.' Wilbur Wright was flying his new aeroplane there; Northcliffe helped him drag it out of its shed. More than two years before, when the first European flight was recorded, Northcliffe was on the phone to the *Mail*, telling them angrily that their four-line paragraph wasn't sufficient: didn't they realise that England was no longer an island? In 1908 he had a reporter with the Wright brothers at their camp in America, reporting on developments in the art of aeroplaning since they first got off the ground in 1903. In 1909 he saw flying as an extension of motoring, a sport with possibilities as a newspaper stunt, and a useful ancillary in war. Planes could be used for scouting, he thought. He wrote to the War Minister, Lord Haldane, to suggest the Army send someone down to Pau, where foreign Powers had observers reporting on this strange American bird that sailed to and fro above the foothills of the Pyrenees at forty miles an hour. Among the faces upturned in the winter sun was that of Mrs Wrohan, shadowing the Northcliffe party as usual, staying at a different hotel, sometimes being driven over to Biarritz for the day by Pine. Mrs Wrohan was a trial at times. Approaching forty, she was appraising the future, calculating how best to make the most of the next few years. Those who knew about Northcliffe and Mrs Wrohan said she was not the easiest of mistresses.

From shaky flying machines he returned to Dreadnoughts in London. 'We are living in the most tremendous times in the history of our Island and our Empire,' he wrote to Strachey. He relished his part on the stage, even if no one could be sure what that part was. Critics of Northcliffe as warmonger were confused

in the middle of 1909 when the *Mail*'s attitude to Germany
softened mysteriously. Northcliffe was in Germany for most of
May, seeing about his eyes, letting it be known once again that
he was taking life easy on medical advice. For a week or two
he was in and around Frankfurt, arriving in Berlin about the
middle of the month. He sent a sharp despatch to the *Mail* to
complain that rumours in London of Zeppelins over East Anglia
were making Britain look ridiculous in the German Press. Following his return to London, the *Mail* began a long series of
articles by a German writer called 'A German in England',
aimed at promoting unity between the two countries. A leader
in the *Mail* said that 'Nothing is more likely to produce a happy
effect on the future relations of the two great Empires than a
better knowledge of each other.' There may have been a private
reason for Northcliffe's momentary tolerance. In any case, it was
short-lived. By the end of the year he was commissioning the
Socialist, Robert Blatchford, to write an inflammatory series on
'Germany and England' that echoed the fears of G. E. Steevens,
eleven years before. Coming from such a quarter, the series had
considerable impact. 'I write these articles,' began Blatchford,
'because I believe that Germany is deliberately preparing to
destroy the British Empire; and because I know that we are not
able or ready to defend ourselves against a sudden and formidable attack.' Northcliffe and the *Mail* were back on course.

It was a commonplace, now, that the *Mail* reflected the broad
middle thoughts of the broad middle class. In the years before
1914 it continued to explore that undeveloped area of the Press
where large circulation and popular appeal could be allied with
a degree of influence in high places. The mighty often looked
down their noses at the *Mail*, but it was impossible to dismiss a
paper that was read by so many, and which spoke loudly and
clearly for so many interests without taking a predictable line in
politics. It reflected the world of cars, aeroplanes, and telephones, which was fascinating but beyond the reach of most of
its readers, and the other world of cheap goods and brand names,
from Sunlight Soap and Iron Jelloids to Lipton's Tea and
Player's Cigarettes, which was well within their grasp.

The *Mail* could have accepted more advertising and made more money. It was an expensive newspaper to produce, and although it prospered, it was not a source of enormous profits. These came from the magazines and novelettes. But Northcliffe was unwilling to exploit his invention to the limit. Big display advertisements, with flaring type and undignified drawings, upset him. He saw them as unruly beasts that refused to conform. 'Opening the paper,' he was reported as saying, 'I felt like a bird wounded by an arrow.' As soon as he had the *Times*, he was nagging them about vulgar ads. 'Page 8 had an advertisement of Debenham and Freebody's sale in huge type,' he noted sourly (4 January 1909). 'I enclose an advertisement of Cockles Pills. It is not right that these people should be able to advertise on two pages at once' (7 January). 'The appearance of the front page is marred by the large number of display advertisements in the lower half' (12 January). From Germany in May, where supplies of his papers followed him daily, he thought it worth cabling the *Times* advertising manager: 'FRIDAY'S ODOL ADVERTISEMENT HORRID'. His true objections are unlikely to have been aesthetic: rather, he wanted to keep the advertising in its place. It was useful but it had to be a servant; then it could be encouraged. Advertising was the core of his prosperity, a fact of life that he had exploited faster than anyone else. 'The King's crown is advertisement,' he said. 'The feudal castles were advertisement.' He adapted the principle for the twentieth century. What he chose not to see was that mass advertising was too powerful for his strait-jacket. It needed to push its way into the columns of newspapers. It needed to be strident and vulgar. Perhaps no one could have foreseen the march of the adman. But even with the limited insight of the time, there is a streak of dishonesty in the way Northcliffe simultaneously wrings his hands about the advertisements and exploits the advertising.

To the staffs of his papers, and to Fleet Street in general, the inconsistencies were part of the Northcliffe legend that grew year by year. He could be the kindly benefactor, remembering colleagues' birthdays, sending fruit and flowers to sick reporters. He could be the unbending proprietor who struck without warning. Walking to Printing House Square with a colleague, he suddenly swung to the left at Ludgate Circus. 'We'd do best to keep to the byways,' he said. 'We might meet some of the men

I've sacked. They lie in wait for me here.' His executives had to accept that life meant a torrent of memos, telegrams arriving in the night, phone calls before breakfast; interspersed with suggestions or orders that they take a holiday, often at the Chief's expense and in his company, which meant a burst of spacious but not very relaxed living in Paris or Seville or Monte Carlo. The line between his pleasure and his anger was thin; people were commenting on it by 1909. A senior editor observed how Northcliffe was harassed from room to room by the telephone, as people he had called in the early morning rang back to report. The editor remarked to him casually that he looked like becoming its slave. 'I am not the slave of the telephone,' snapped Northcliffe. 'I am its master.' Odd stories circulated; they were not only odd but true. A new male secretary joined him in Paris. Northcliffe asked if he had brought his typewriter. The man said no. 'Then go back to London and get it,' said Northcliffe, and the secretary went. He sent another secretary from London to Paris on a Sunday afternoon to buy two litres of a special milk, in which a doctor expressed interest as they were talking in Northcliffe's library after lunch. His rages were coming to be feared. His head printer, Tom George, saw him harangue the managing director of the Imperial Paper Mills about paper-breaks at the *Times*. Northcliffe kept him waiting for twenty minutes, then forbade George, who was the previous visitor, to leave. 'Now you're going to see how I treat a man when I'm angry,' he said. As soon as he was shown in, Northcliffe began to rage at him, waving his fists and puffing out his cheeks. The managing director tried to speak, then gave up. Suddenly Northcliffe seized the man's bowler hat from the chair, rushed to the door, and kicked it down the corridor. The visitor went after it, and Northcliffe closed the door and went on talking to George. Real or simulated, it was odd behaviour.

He was exacting as a journalist. Meticulous attention to detail, often on the basis of reports by secretaries and specialists, meant that he might pounce on the smallest error in an article. One of his techniques for softening up the *Times* in the first year of his rule – while the remarks about its being a 'hobby' and his having no desire to be 'Chief' were barely out of his mouth – was the daily communiqué, when he was in the country, of as much as two or three thousand words. This usually began with a statement of which machine had printed the copy delivered to him in bed (identified from the page-marks) and what the quality of the newsprint was like. Then it dissected the paper page by page, commenting on anything from lapses, scoops, and ideas to be followed up, to the position of headlines and the size of type. Such attention was calculated to make people uneasy. At the *Mail* he had long since ceased to appear in his shirt-sleeves in the composing room. But he would intervene in anything that interested him. A young features editor from the *Mail* visited him at the *Times*. The room was darkened. Northcliffe lay on a sofa, poring over a bundle of proofs, choosing a feature article for the following day. He picked one about barbers and how bored they became with their customers. What was the headline? he asked. It had not been written. Northcliffe heaved himself off the sofa and sat frowning at the proof. The features editor waited uneasily, looking at the green silk curtains, the green pen holders, the antique Persian carpet, the Chippendale furniture. Northcliffe's breathing grew heavier. After five minutes he looked up. 'Call it "The Barber's Secret",' he said.

He was not always intimidating. He never lost his delight in the mechanics of journalism, the clever idea, the strong sentence, the crisp headline. He was the eager editor, ready to pounce on 'a good piece'. Nor, as a journalist, was he always the irate boss who insisted on having his own way. There were matters of policy and grand strategy on which he would hear no arguments. But if he respected another point of view, on style or content, he could defer to it, as long as a change of mind didn't show him up in front of a third party. If at times he is the raging tycoon, he can also be the genial colleague, a squarish man in soft collar and red-speckled tie, beaming at his men as he hands out congratulations like cigars. That would have been his style on the July Saturday in 1909 when he entertained the *Mail* editorial staff at Sutton Place. He gave them lunch and talked to them about 'the very splendid paper' they were producing. He asked them to be impartial in politics, to encourage individual styles in writing, not to overdo words like 'disaster' and 'tragedy' in headlines, to stop being pessimistic about Britain's future and to encourage national achievement. He referred more than once to the 'enormous' and 'gigantic' power of their paper. As he talked, in a voice that was not always audible at the back, oversized robins hopped on the lawns; grey squirrels chased up and down trees. Both breeds were alien to the British country-side, introduced from America by Northcliffe the previous year. The American squirrels (already imported by someone else twenty years before) were breeding; the American robins, to Northcliffe's intense displeasure, were not. He spoke of a trip he was about to make to the group's 'vast enterprise' in Newfound-land – 'perhaps the vastest of its kind in the world' – and of how he might be 'a long time away'. Hints and intimations seem to lie behind the words. He might have been serving notice that in future he would have less time for them.

It was another six weeks before he made his trip. When he did, much of the journey across America and Canada was spent shut away in a private rail coach, reading dozens of local papers and endlessly criticising the *Times* to its weary manager, 'old Bell', who had been more or less ordered to accompany the party. Northcliffe would announce that he was retiring to his compart-ment for three days of absolute peace. Ten minutes later he would be hammering on Bell's door, waving a newspaper with figures about immigration, telling him to cable London. In Newfoundland at the end of the journey, he inaugurated pulp and paper mills at Grand Falls. The Harmsworths had constructed a town; overcome natural hazards; guaranteed themselves a new fortune. If Northcliffe was imperious, it was because he was aware of so much at his fingertips. American reporters asked him if an early war was likely between Germany and Britain, and he gravely answered 'Yes'. He was an arbiter; if at times he was eccentric and the subject of strange stories, that was taken to be a by-product of his stature.

But some people said he was ill. They noticed bursts of bad temper and excitability. Percy Burton, the golf-playing adman who had married Christabel, was violently castigated when Northcliffe heard that puffs for a patent medicine in which Burton was interested had appeared in the *Mail*. Northcliffe's mother remarked that he must be unwell because for the first time in his life he had contradicted her. Lady Northcliffe told Sutton early in 1909 that she dreaded a breakdown. In February, when Northcliffe was at Pau, he was writing to Sutton to say that he had 'gone through a terrible time. I have been feeble, slow, cross, and lacking interest in the sex, always a bad sign with your devoted Chief.' Northcliffe's interest in his health was morbid, and he was quick to give acquaintances a brief résumé of his condition, though what he said to different people was not always the same. Perhaps the visit to Germany in May is a key; at that point he was not acutely ill, but he was anxious about his health. Perhaps what worried Northcliffe was that he had, or might have, syphilis. A number of his contemporaries thought so, and it was to be whispered about as the explanation of many strange things over the next ten years. Later Harmsworths took pains to show otherwise. But it has continued to be widely assumed that Northcliffe's mental imbalance was due to general paralysis of the insane – advanced neurosyphilis.

Northcliffe left London early in the month, and on 5 May wrote to Bell from an hotel at Königstein, in the mountains outside Frankfurt; he said he had been 'ordered' there from Frankfurt. Lady Northcliffe was not with him. During the second week of May his eyes were examined again by Professor Solm in Frankfurt, and he wrote to a secretary in London: 'Solm says there is no disease, but he is worried that I am constantly requiring stronger spectacles. I expect his report to be sent on to me in Berlin.' Another letter shows him at Königstein on 14 May, and on 15 May he appears in Berlin, sending a stream of letters and telegrams with that date which means he is now with his entourage. Other correspondence from Berlin contains various references to his health. A long letter to Sir Douglas Straight complained about overwork. 'I am rather like a spider enmeshed in a web of its own making,' he said. 'One thing has led to another in my career, and lately there has come the *Times*, which I did not want but which I did not wish to see ruined.' To Kennedy Jones, at the end of a long letter about mechanical arrangements at the *Times*, he said: 'Doctor's report not very favourable.' The report warned him to exercise 'the greatest care and restraint' with his eyes. But it was apparently more favourable than Northcliffe expected. He wrote to Sutton ('My dear Sutkins') to say that 'Professor Solm considers my eyes greatly improved ... I must use stronger glasses, but otherwise they go well.' Northcliffe added that a careless chambermaid had thrown away his teeth – 'An infernal nuisance. No teeth and a painful eye treatment, not much of a holiday.' By the end of the month, having been to Paris to collect new teeth on the way, he was back in London.

The story that Northcliffe had syphilis was almost certainly believed by, among others, Evelyn Wrench, who thought he contracted it at some time between 1906 and 1908. This would explain the 'ptomaine poisoning' episode at the end of 1908 as second-stage syphilis, with rashes, fevers, headaches, and malaise, as well as acute anxiety. Another story, that Northcliffe was treated for syphilis in Germany from 1909, can also be made to fit the known facts; Frankfurt, visited by Northcliffe, was at that time the centre of experiments with a new drug against syphilis. Most of the later 'evidence' about Northcliffe and syphilis* comes from the direction of Printing House Square. A former editor of the *Times*, Wickham Steed (1871–1956), believed that Northcliffe had the disease. He passed on what he knew to Stanley Morison (1889–1967), the typographer and compiler of the official *History of the Times*. Morison may have had other sources, but it is likely that Steed was the principal one. The disease is only hinted at in the *History*, but Morison is known to have spoken freely about the matter. Among the people he told was Cecil King, a nephew of Northcliffe and until 1968 chairman of the International Publishing Corporation. In recent years King has repeated the story in print and on television, lending authority to what many journalists and doctors already assumed to be true. Morison said at different times that a French doctor told him that Northcliffe had syphilis (he was never named); that Northcliffe was being treated in Germany from 1909 or 1911 (the dates vary); that the proof was contained in two letters in the archives of the *Times* (they were never produced). Later in his life Morison seems to have modified this view, and been more cautious about Northcliffe's health.

Assuming that Morison was correct about the treatment in Germany, Northcliffe would have been one of the earliest patients to receive the anti-syphilis drug, 'Preparation 606', that had just been discovered by the German biochemist, Paul Ehrlich. Ehrlich, the father of modern chemotherapy, was the first man to develop a drug that acted specifically against an

---

* See Chapters 20 and 21.

infection – the so-called 'magic bullet'. His work was done as director of the Speyer-Haus Institute in Frankfurt, and large-scale experiments were carried out at a chemical works near the city. Ehrlich and his colleagues worked through hundreds of compounds, looking for one that was specific against syphilis. They reached number 606 in 1907, but discarded it as ineffective in their animal experiments. It was patented as a formality. A year later, a Japanese doctor joined Ehrlich, and, while re-testing compounds, found that 606 had been wrongly classified. From early in 1909 the drug was being widely tested, at first on mice, then on people. It was very successful, though treatment was painful and unpleasant, and the results not always lasting. The drug, later called Salvarsan, was described at a medical meeting on 19 April 1910, and soon the laboratories had to be guarded against intruders; a cartoon in *Simplicissimus*, the Munich magazine, showed Ehrlich interviewed by a deputa-tion of civic dignitaries, who beg him to stop interfering with such an aid to moral purity. It is possible that Northcliffe heard of the experiments and visited Frankfurt, hoping to have treat-ment; and that he was treated, either then or later. The 'painful eye treatment', otherwise unexplained, might be an echo of the painful injections. Northcliffe's anxiety about his eyesight might itself be a clue. Untreated syphilis can eventually cause blind-ness. Earlier interference with vision, beginning with dark spots before the eyes and leading to serious damage, can appear from two to five years after infection. People with syphilis are usually aware of the danger to their sight, and may be obsessed with fear of blindness.

This is purely guesswork, apart from the stories told by Morison and Steed. These must be treated with caution. Morison was not always scrupulous with his facts. Steed was an experienced journalist, a cosmopolitan figure with a high repu-tation. He was Vienna correspondent of the *Times* when Northcliffe bought it, and later editor and close associate of the proprietor. But he was also a man of erratic judgment, wise in appraising the international scene, not always wise in his own affairs. An indiscreet interview with an American reporter in 1921 caused him, the *Times*, and Northcliffe much trouble. His views could be strongly prejudiced. He believed in the malign powers of international Jewry. He had at least a mild obsession with syphilis, which he claimed to have observed in other famous people. In addition, Steed took the full brunt of Northcliffe's runaway tongue at the end of his life; he had a vested interest in showing that Northcliffe was sick. There is no suggestion that he invented the evidence. But he may have interpreted it to suit himself. His views on Northcliffe's health, in the form of memoranda and letters in the *Times* archives, cite contemporary medical hearsay, and his personal observations, in the period 1921–2. Steed believed that Northcliffe's syphilis led to insanity. The story that Northcliffe was certified as insane did appear in Morison's *History*, to the dismay of the Harmsworths. Morison was pressed by the family to divulge his evidence when the 'certified insane' episode appeared there in 1952. He turned to Steed for support, and Steed supplied him with further details, none of them conclusive, in two letters (these are conceivably the 'two letters' that Morison said contained the proof of syphilis). Throughout, the evidence for syphilis is entwined with the evidence for insanity. It has a veneer of authority but would not convince a venereologist. On the other hand, the only *conclusive* evidence that Northcliffe had syphilis would be the findings of clinical tests, and it is hardly likely that these would be available. The case is, by its nature, virtually unprovable. Steed moved in circles where Northcliffe's health was a matter of the greatest possible interest; he certainly believed in Northcliffe's syphilis until the end of his life. Another witness is Garvin of the *Observer*, who hinted at it in a letter he wrote in 1946, the year before he died, where he spoke of the 'fearful price' that Northcliffe paid for his pleasures with women. There is no shortage of hearsay on the matter.

The contrary case is easily argued. A blood test for syphilis shortly before Northcliffe's death is said to have been negative. Northcliffe's fears for his eyesight were natural for someone who read as much small print as he did – especially since he knew that his contemporary, Arthur Pearson, was going blind. His hypochondria, love of secrecy, and fondness for dramatising his health account for any peculiarities in his behaviour in Germany (the professor's report on his eyes was later circulated to all his senior executives, to make sure they were suitably impressed with the Chief's problems). Anxiety about his health and habits may even have had the effect on Northcliffe, familiar to venereologists, of making him neurotically convinced that he had syphilis, despite every assurance to the contrary. The disease is heavy with moral overtones. It was common in fashionable Europe at the end of the nineteenth century (a fashionable European is said to have given it to him). Northcliffe was rigidly orthodox in his public attitude to sex; dirty thoughts, dirty words, dirty jokes were frowned on; he would not allow advertisements in his papers to say 'rupture' or 'constipation'. Sexual disease, for someone of his upbringing, indulging strong sexual appetites that formed no part of his outward life, was something to fear: perhaps something to wish upon himself as a secret punishment. Venereologists recognise this condition, sometimes lasting a lifetime, in which nothing will convince the patient that he is free from syphilis. He both dreads and needs it. Northcliffe may have been obsessed with a disease he never had. The verdict on Northcliffe and syphilis must be 'not proven'. His nature was deep and strange enough in itself, though some illness certainly twisted it further at the end. Towards the end of his own life, Garvin wrote that 'Northcliffe's mention always lures me like a first-rate novel'. Garvin saw lights and shadows – 'farce, comedy, terrors within himself ... Northcliffe should be described as a most extraordinary and partly abnormal human being.' By 1909, what is certain, germs apart, is that disturbing forces were at work in Northcliffe.

15

Breakdown

THE ADVANTAGE of a brother like Harold was that however many new interests he developed, he remained loyal to Alfred. By 1909 he was planning to sell his shares in the *Daily Mail*. As a Liberal in search of party favours, it was prudent to keep clear even of nominal entanglements with Conservatism. He had no interest in the editorial side, and as a business the newspaper was too extravagant; he would have loved to take a knife to the editorial spending, to reduce the news content and make way for more advertisements. His heart was in the simple comics and novelettes which continued to make a fortune. When anyone at the Amalgamated Press wanted to spend more on a magazine, he would resist, saying it was time they returned to the 'fried fish and stewed eels' of the business. Harold was a plain, rather greedy business man who loved to make money – even to win it at gambling from young men in his circle, who would receive twice as much back as a present the next day, stuffed in an envelope. Harold was a great stuffer of banknotes in envelopes. What makes him look gross and gloomy is the contrast with Alfred. Viewed simply as Harold Harmsworth, tycoon, with interests in Britain and Newfoundland, large investor in Wall Street, prominent member of the Liberal Party, he is unremarkable. Only the scale of his operations – working from the base laid down by Alfred – made him different. Where a rich man might leave five pounds as a tip, he would leave ten. Hungry for affection, like Alfred, he used his money to buy it, or something that could be used instead of it. He vibrated with money, though at this time he may have been no richer than Alfred. He used it to measure other people, and they used it to measure him. The Liberal Party, which benefited from his contributions, had him down on the list for a baronetcy. Alfred said he was an obstinate man with a weakness for radicalism, but added that they were great personal friends. It seems they could trust one another. Harold was always at hand with good, grey, cold-blooded advice.

In December 1909 he was writing to George Sutton, on Alfred's behalf, in the matter of a lawsuit that was pending in the High Court: Kenealy v. Northcliffe. The action was being brought by a woman who had been sacked from the *Daily Mail*, Miss Annesley Kenealy. Her brother Alexander was the editor of the *Daily Mirror*, and for two years he had been trying without success to persuade her to drop the case. Now Harold wrote to Sutton with thinly disguised threats to Kenealy, suggesting that he spare no pains, including money, to stop his sister. But Miss Kenealy went ahead. The case, in which Northcliffe knew he would have to appear in court, may have been connected with a new bout of nervous debility. He had to be in London in January, a month he preferred to spend abroad. Miss Kenealy, an overdressed lady of uncertain age, conducted her own defence, amid laughter. She is said to have been in love with Northcliffe; so much the worse for her. She had been sacked in 1906, after four weeks of writing a column called 'Humanities'. when she went to interview the chairman of the London Hospital, the Hon. Sydney Holland, and ended by lecturing him on the horrors of vivisection. Northcliffe was polished and amusing in the witness box, saying gently that reporters should not introduce personal opinions into interviews. She pressed him to say what Holland had written about her. Northcliffe begged her not to force him, appealing to the judge, with smiles. The judge smiled back. Miss Kenealy kept insisting. 'My impression,' said Northcliffe, 'is that he said, "Why do you send this old Guy Fawkes down to worry me?" ' The court rocked. Holland popped up. 'Quite right, my Lord, that's what I did say.' The only point at which Northcliffe seemed to lose his temper was where the plaintiff dared to suggest that pressure might have been put on Alex Kenealy. That was quite untrue, he said. Rufus Isaacs, counsel for the defence – now Sir Rufus Isaacs, Solicitor-General – soon demolished her. She was only Miss Kenealy, the anti-vivisectionist crank. The jury found for Lord Northcliffe.

If the dates and addresses on his correspondence are to be

believed, which is far from certain, Northcliffe left immediately for La Dragonnière, Harold's new villa at Monte Carlo, allegedly to get rid of 'bronchial trouble' (before Christmas it had been 'indigestion'). Early in February he was at a London nursing home, writing letters that he headed 'The Asylum', complaining that the place was like a prison. His latest physician, Bertrand Dawson, was doctor to the Prince of Wales. 'Neurasthenia' and 'inflammation of the pancreas' were new complaints that friends were told about. One of his doctors said in a letter that he was undergoing a rest cure for 'digestive trouble brought on by overwork'. He was in the clinic for weeks, in theory cut off from work, in fact still scribbling obsessive letters to Sutton, complaining that page three of the *Mail* was dull or that the *Evening News* was badly printed. Then his movements are shadowy again. In March he was at Avignon. Early in April he came to rest at St Raphael, to the west of Cannes. There, staying at a villa overlooking the sea, it becomes clear that he was recovering from a breakdown. Being Northcliffe, he talked about it all the time. He wrote to Nicholson (who had been made assistant manager of the *Times*) on 1 April to complain that the paper was not watching the German Fleet closely enough. He went on: 'For myself I recover or recuperate very slowly. Energy is measured by ergs and I have expended some billions of them in the past. If I get back to the Sturm und Drang by June I shall be lucky. I am still in bed twenty or twenty-two hours of the twenty-four.'

Lady Northcliffe was with him at first, then moved away, leaving the field clear for Mrs Wrohan, who was staying at an hotel nearby. In a letter to Sutton, Lady Northcliffe said plaintively that her husband wanted the villa to be a private hospital, and that he had written to say it was more peaceful now that she wasn't there. Presumably she knew nothing of the mistress who was being whisked along the coast-roads, in and out of hotels and villas. Mrs Wrohan was having a busy time. She was writing letters to one of Northcliffe's solicitors, Henry Arnholz – a school friend of his who had written to congratulate Northcliffe when he became a baronet, and now looked after some of his private affairs. Arnholz dealt personally with Mrs Wrohan, writing the letters with his own hand; his partner in the practice knew nothing about her. She wrote to ask his advice, for a friend of hers, about the rules for the registration of births in England. Her friend wanted to know whether the mother and father had to be named, and whether it was necessary to register a birth at all. The question was pressing. The friend was Northcliffe; Kathleen Wrohan was pregnant. Aged forty or thereabouts, she was securing her future with children. Her letters to Arnholz in April say how worried they are about the Chief's nerves, and how important it is to keep little worries from him. One of the little worries was a dress bill at Debenham and Freebody's for four hundred pounds. She wrote to Arnholz, Arnholz wrote to Northcliffe, Northcliffe had a row with her about it, she wrote crossly to Arnholz about the state of Northcliffe's nerves, and how hard they were all working to keep the little worries from him. Mrs Wrohan would have been even crosser had she known that the invalid, far from being too ill to care, was writing to Arnholz to say that Kathleen's old debts must be settled by small payments over a long period. He instructed Arnholz not to spare her letters on the subject.

At the end of April, the *Daily Mail* prize for the first flight from London to Manchester was won, by a Frenchman; he received the ten-thousand-pound cheque from Marlowe, who referred to Northcliffe's absence through illness, adding quickly that it was not a *serious* illness. There had been too many rumours in London to risk further speculation. In May Northcliffe moved to Paris for electrical treatment, then a fashionable cure-all. He wrote to his mother to say she must 'come to the Ritz in Paris where I shall be ready to embrace you. I shall be in bed when you come 'cos I go to bed at 7 p.m. like a good boy.' Dawson, his doctor, was warning that he would not be able to go back to work in quite the same way as before. Northcliffe's next move was to England, in secret, using his valet's name for messages. He went fishing in Hampshire, then to Scotland, and finally back to Elmwood, where he made preparations for a trip to America in August. He was apparently well enough to travel, not well enough to work normally. Garvin, who had visited him at St Raphael, was pressing for decisions about the paper and himself; he needed more money, as usual. Northcliffe and 'Garve' had an up-and-down relationship, with much warmth on both sides. Telegrams and letters flowed between them.

DO NOT THINK ME CAVALIER [said Northcliffe in a telegram on 12 August] BUT I LITERALLY CANNOT CONTINUE ON THE DIREC-TORATE OF THE OBSERVER IF IT IS TO BE A PERPETUAL SOURCE OF WORK. I AM NOT THE LEAST INTERESTED IN IT FINANCIALLY AND ONLY CARE THAT IT AFFORDS THE EMPIRE A PEEP AT YOUR GREAT VISION ONLY PLEASE DO KEEP THE COUNTRY INFORMED ABOUT GERMANY THAT UNKNOWN QUANTITY CANADA AND INDIA ... AS TO GRIEVANCES LET THEM WAIT UNTIL I GET BACK I HAVE MINE TOO. AT PRESENT I AM BESET FROM 7 AM UNTIL BEDTIME.

Mrs Wrohan was due to give birth before the end of month. This may have been why Northcliffe wanted to get out of the country; the pregnancy may even have precipitated the breakdown. She was apprehensive about her age. Later it was put about (among those who had to be told anything) that the child was born in Paris. This was probably a cover; the con-finement was at 3 Brick Court, Mrs Wrohan's flat in the Temple, but the birth was not registered. Before it took place, Northcliffe instructed Arnholz to draw up a settlement on the unborn child of a thousand pounds a year for the first three years and six thousand pounds a year thereafter.

Arnholz also made a new will for Northcliffe, a seventeen-page document dated 18 August 1910, which split the estate into one-hundredth parts and allocated various proportions of the income to relatives and friends. It was an unwieldy document, promising troubles to come. Wills brought out Northcliffe's ten-dency to perplex and confuse. Besides a large income, Lady Northcliffe would receive ten thousand pounds immediately, and their London house, No. 22 St James's Place. Miss Skipper and Miss Owen, the typists, were still down for a thousand pounds apiece. There was no mention of Mrs Wrohan. The will shows Northcliffe thinking about who should succeed him. He wanted Kennedy Jones to become chairman of Associated Newspapers. Next day, 19 August, in a codicil to the will, he said he wanted his brother Cecil to be chairman of the Amalgamated Press.

Having put his affairs in order, Northcliffe, his wife, and a party sailed on 20 August in the *Mauretania*. The liner arrived in New York on 25 August, and on the same day Mrs Wrohan gave birth to a boy, who (once again) was named Alfred. The baby gave rise to anxiety at first. By the autumn it was stronger, and Mrs Wrohan was renting a house in Scotland, another temporary resting place in her pilgrimage up and down Europe. In October, having visited the paper mills at Newfoundland during his journey, Northcliffe was in Scotland, where presumably he saw his child, and then in Paris, still recuperating. The whole of 1910 seems to consist of spasmodic recovery from an illness that is never defined. It makes a tedious catalogue, important only because from now on, Northcliffe's health needs to be taken into account in any assessment of what he did and said. Some chronic condition of mind, body, or both was capable of virtually cutting him off from control of his empire. In a few months' time he would be as active as ever. But people would remember his illness. Physical disease may have been involved. His syphilis, if this is what he had, was still in its early stages. But the knowledge of it, together with the rigorous treatment involved and the uncertainty of a cure, could have helped disturb the balance of a mind that at the best of times was never at rest. If Northcliffe did have syphilis – or thought he had it – and even if his visit to Frankfurt in 1909 was coincidental or fruitless, he would have been alerted by the talk about Ehrlich's 606 in the spring of 1910. All Europe knew about it then. A course of injections, together with a mental breakdown, may be the reason for his prolonged stay in France. What is certain is that 1909 and 1910 mark a change for the worse in his health.

In Paris in November, as he began to take up the reins, he was suddenly incensed at what he regarded as the vulgarity of some of the magazines. He was losing a sense of proportion. He wrote to Sutton on 3 November:

Will you get hold of Cantle [one of the editors] and read this to him.

Tell him I will not have such vulgarity. The papers have got out of my hands during my absence, and I am having a difficult job to get them back.

Why is it necessary to employ a Parlour-maid in the stories, and life in the kitchen, about which, I daresay, Cantle is well-informed? Why not give manly School stories?

Compare this paper with the early numbers of *Comic Cuts* and *Chips*. They were interesting papers then, with very much bigger circulations than they have today, and they were not vulgar ...

There had been no shortage of convicts in the early numbers of *Comic Cuts*, but Northcliffe had forgotten. He sent another message banning all magazine headlines such as 'Behind Prison Walls'. But Sutton could no longer be relied on for total obedience. The Amalgamated Press, and Sutton with it, had taken on a life of their own. Sutton prevaricated, pointing out the expense of suddenly changing all the things that Northcliffe objected to, and asking what was wrong with 'Behind Prison Walls', anyway. The rumblings from Paris died down; the magazines continued to drift away from their master.

Lady Northcliffe was confiding to Sutton that she was disturbed by rumours about her husband; she said that 'the Chief looks to me better than he has done for ten years', but that he was 'rather nervous about himself and more inclined to run away from London'. On 12 November Northcliffe wrote to St Loe Strachey, replying to a letter of 23 June that 'excessive zeal on the part of my devoted Secretaries' had stopped him receiving until then. He went on: 'I have also your very kind letter hoping that I will not return to active work until next year. I can assure you that I have had such a fright that I shall do exactly as I am told'. Two days later his doctor, Vernon Jones, was writing (presumably so that Northcliffe could show the letter to someone) to say that he could now think about working two days a week – 'I believe that you will still continue on the "up grade", and that your full measure of health will be *completely* restored. I am sorry to have to still limit your work after all these months of enforced rest, but I am absolutely certain that it is *for the present* a necessity.' Another sign of Northcliffe's return was a series of trusts, drawn up by Arnholz on 18 November, that set his infant son on the way to being a rich man one day. Before the end of the year a second codicil to the August will added a share of the estate's income for the child for life. He was described as 'Alfred Wrohan, my godson'.

One of Northcliffe's most famous campaigns in the *Daily Mail* indicated that his hand was on the levers again, in January 1911. He read or was told about a pamphlet written in praise of wholemeal bread by a country squire, Sir Oswald Mosley, who baked it with his own stone-ground flour. Sir Oswald was a four-square Englishman who lived on the family estate in

Staffordshire. His pamphlet on 'bread reform' became the core of a daily campaign in the *Mail* to stop the nation ruining its teeth and bones with white bread. 'Standard Bread' was dangled before the nation as a material benefit with magical overtones. No doubt wholemeal bread was more nutritious than white, but the *Mail* might have been advocating a new religion. Northcliffe was reported to have said, 'See if I don't force everybody in the country to eat Standard Bread'. There was a story that he had been arguing with someone about the power of the Press, and had declared that he would prove it by changing the eating habits of the British. Doctors and headmasters were canvassed. Lists of bakers who made it were printed. Two or three solid columns of bread propaganda on the main news page were nothing out of the ordinary. Scientists spoke of dietary deficiencies. Old men recalled the wholemeal bread of their youth. The King ordered it for Buckingham Palace. BETTER THAN MEDICINE, cried the headlines. NATIONAL AWAKENING. BROKEN REED OF WHITE BREAD AS A STAFF OF LIFE. Demand for wholemeal bread rose sharply and a generation was instructed in the matter of nutrition. As a measure to combat rickets and improve the appalling diet of the poor, Standard Bread was admirable. Nevertheless the campaign seemed ludicrous to many people at the time and it seems ludicrous still. Given the state of the nation, it was too much fuss about bread. And the way it was rammed down the readers' throats suggests a delight in manipulating them, in bending them to the master's will. When an editor at Carmelite House remarked after a couple of months that people were tiring of Standard Bread, Northcliffe flushed, turned to his secretary, and dictated an instruction that an article on the subject was to appear in every issue of his papers every day for a year.

At the *Times*, to the dismay of Bell, Buckle, and the rest, Northcliffe tightened his grip. A scribbled memo to Reginald Nicholson the previous year suggested how the new proprietor would act when he recovered his powers: nastily. 'One can't change the leopard's spots,' he wrote, 'but a woman, a Bell, and a walnut tree, the more you beat 'em the better they be. *Get this into your head*. As soon as everyone realises that there is *one* Master at P.H.S. and that you are his agent there will be very little trouble and much progress.' Controversy over a naval matter early in 1911 provided a cause to fight about. The Declaration of London, signed in 1909, set up an international prize court and laid down a code for seizing contraband in wartime. Wars were still being fought by rules. The Declaration was now to be embodied in an Act of Parliament. Northcliffe (and others) opposed it because it weakened the navy's powers to blockade an enemy. The *Mail* and *Evening News* began to attack it. But Buckle and his colleagues approved the Declaration. In the light of events, they were wrong; put into effect it could have hamstrung the navy's blockade of Germany. Northcliffe warned them not to support the Declaration and told Nicholson: 'If resignations are offered, accept them.' He told Bell on 3 March that 'I do not propose to allow one farthing of my fortune to be used in connection with that which would injure this country. I trust these words to the wise will be sufficient.' Incredibly, Bell was still the only man at the *Times* who knew of the written promise given three years before to obey Northcliffe's 'absolute instructions'. There was much huffing and puffing in the office, but the proprietor was inflexible. This was Northcliffe in action at his best: determinedly pursuing a matter of importance. Learned arguments were being deployed in support of the Declaration. Northcliffe proceeded by commonsense and saw that the measure was naive and short-sighted. On 6 March he told Nicholson that he wanted cuttings of every news item and letter to the editor in connection with the Declaration, sent round to St James's Place by three o'clock in the afternoon. More ominously, he wanted all the original copy brought from the printer, so that he could see how the material had been sub-edited. 'The news has not been fairly given,' he said. The result of all this was that the *Times* remained neutral, neither accepting nor condemning the Declaration. (Later in the year the House of Commons passed the Bill that embodied it, without enthusiasm; the Lords rejected it.)

From this point on, Northcliffe was the master of Printing House Square. Bell, the old Pirate, acknowledged it by dying of heart failure as he wrote a letter, by hand, on 5 April. Nicholson replaced him as managing director.

Preach the daily text, [wrote Northcliffe to him in an undated letter]. *Paper falling heavily into debt. Something must be done.* All over Tibet are the sacred words on every mountain side – gigantic letters

OM PANI MANI OM, or such-like. Everyone says it, sings it. So should it be at Printing House Square ... Everybody who is anybody should have that drilled into him twice a day.

Another Northcliffe nominee, a young man called Geoffrey Robinson who had been Johannesburg correspondent, was in the office, being groomed for power, while hints were dropped about the state of Buckle's health. Robinson (later renamed Dawson for family reasons) had a woman friend who knew Lady Northcliffe. Lady Northcliffe pressed her husband to help Robinson, and Northcliffe, recognising a professional journalist with political and social contacts, took him under his wing. No doubt he hoped to find Robinson amenable to a supreme editor-in-chief: himself.

Northcliffe was caught up in patterns of change. He broke with Garvin at the *Observer* over the old issue of Protection. Garvin was a leading advocate, but early in 1911 Northcliffe finally turned against the policy he had dithered over for years. His colleagues tried in vain to discover what had changed his mind, but it was as useless to expect a logical explanation of his change of direction as it was to expect an account of the motives behind Standard Bread or the war on Sunlight Soap. He *felt* things. Perhaps he felt that in a period of social unrest, food taxes must once and for all be ruled out of the Conservative programme as unthinkable. He discussed the matter with Andrew Bonar Law, who was about to become leader of the Conservative Party, at a meeting arranged at the flat of Max Aitken, a young Canadian millionaire who had recently arrived in Britain and erupted into politics. Aitken, later Lord Beaverbrook, and the successor to Northcliffe as the leading Press Lord of his day, was not yet interested in newspapers. He was a natural fixer of men and policies. He observed with amusement how Bonar Law demolished Northcliffe's objections and left him muttering that no one could achieve what Joseph Chamberlain had failed to do. Bonar Law thought he had convinced him.'I feel sure now that you are going to be our greatest friend,' he said. But he had misread his listener. 'I have been your greatest friend in trying to rid your party of the food taxes,' replied Northcliffe. He might be bad at argument; people had noticed that at dinner parties he made statements and then fell quiet. But he had no intention of bowing to someone else's logic.

The differences with Garvin grew quickly. Northcliffe had seen him as a political conscience-figure, and, while frequently disagreeing, never interfered at the *Observer* as he did at the *Times*. Garvin had raised the circulation from a few thousand to forty thousand, and his success as an editor, together with the friendship between the two, made it a satisfactory partnership. But Northcliffe had the right of veto over all political articles. Sooner or later there was sure to be a clash, as the 'sole possessor' demonstrated his power. Northcliffe didn't sack Garvin. He gave him three weeks to find a new proprietor, who soon came forward in the shape of Waldorf Astor, the American millionaire who had recently become a Member of Parliament. Northcliffe and Garvin had parted company amid a shower of letters and telegrams. 'Either you get out or I do,' said one of Northcliffe's cables. 'God help the Empire,' said Garvin in a letter. He added, 'I love you all the same.' Northcliffe impatiently called him 'a very sensitive soul' in a letter to Aitken at the time. But Garvin, clever and talkative, was one of the few men who matched Northcliffe, who grasped that he was a strange, increasingly tormented figure, without letting the strangeness alarm or offend him. Most of Northcliffe's intimates were dependants, to use the kindest word, like Nicholson and Sutton. Garvin was his own man.

A troubled year in Britain, full of portents, saw Northcliffe as much out of his depth as most of his contemporaries. David Lloyd George, the Liberal Chancellor of the Exchequer, announced his National Insurance Bill in May, an ambitious scheme to insure workers against sickness and some of them against unemployment. Was this necessary progress or dangerous socialism? The *Mail* called it 'Mr Lloyd George's leap in the dark' on a Wednesday and 'A great step forward' on Friday, but presently settled down to criticise it on technical grounds, as protests grew from doctors and private insurance societies. Northcliffe and Lloyd George were marked out for one another in public affairs, the mass communicator and the man of the people. Lloyd George denounced property and privilege in unheard-of language. He and Northcliffe met first in 1909; a long talk at the House of Commons, at the time of Lloyd George's controversial Budget, left them on friendly terms. By 1911, the issue of privilege versus democracy had crystallised into a bitter

Parliamentary dispute over the powers of the House of Lords, which had finally damned itself by delaying the 1909 Budget. A measure to curb the Lords, the Parliament Bill, was introduced in the spring, regarded by Conservatives as a work of the devil that would wreck society. Northcliffe was not very interested. He wrote to Lord Robert Cecil in July 1911 to say that 'not only in the country but among the middle classes of London, no one knows or cares about the constitutional question. I heard the matter cynically treated by people associated with the Lords themselves.' It was another complex political issue for Northcliffe to be ill at ease with. There is no sign that he was deeply involved in the debate about class, privilege, and social reform. When the Parliament Bill was finally passed by the Lords, under threat of being swamped by new Liberal peers, the *Mail* took the orthodox Conservative line and declared in a leading article: 'The flood-gates of revolution are opened, and two-Chamber government is swept away.' The paper took a severe view of the strikes which had begun the previous year – another aspect of the same social upheaval – and which reached a bloody climax in the summer of 1911. It was Britain's most turbulent year since 1842, when the Chartists were hammering on the gates of polite society. Now it was 'the workers'. They saw Parliament and the upper classes standing in the way of their demands for a fairer share of the national cake. Military force had not been used against strikers on such a scale since Chartist days. An exceptionally hot summer with weeks of drought added to the tension. Gunboats were anchored off Liverpool, where a policeman was kicked to death and rioters shot dead. In Llanelli, troops charged with fixed bayonets, and ten people died over a weekend. Dock and railway strikes caused food shortages. A curious leading article in the *Mail* blamed the 'Celtic fringe' of Irishmen and Welshmen for causing 'the atrocities of barbarism', adding that wherever life went on as normal, 'there to a certainty the Anglo-Saxon predominated'. The inspiration may have been Northcliffe's: despite his Irish connections, he regarded the Celts with suspicion. It was the English, not the British, who appealed to him.

Northcliffe once told a secretary: 'All strikes are justified. Men don't risk starving themselves and their families unless their grievances are gross.' Perhaps he meant it. But he was not free to do anything about it, unless he risked harming his business. His newspapers had to be safe and stable. He pointed out to the same secretary, Russell Wakefield, that advertisers would give lavish patronage only to Conservative newspapers whose judgment they could trust. Wakefield, a bishop's son with radical views who joined Northcliffe in 1911, showed him some mildly revolutionary articles he had written. Northcliffe sub-edited them himself and printed them in the *Mail*, because, he said, it was a good way of pretending to be impartial. People knew that in the end the radicals would get the worst of it, as of course they did, in subsequent articles and letters to the paper. 'He wanted to create a phantom of impartiality,' wrote Wakefield, 'make the mob believe it had flesh and bones, and then dismiss it with a dull, uncompromising thud.'

Northcliffe's personal income fell to a hundred and eighteen thousand pounds in 1911 because of the effect of the year's strikes on *Daily Mail* profits. He knew that changes were coming. He wrote to Sutton in March 1912 that 'We may have to introduce profit-sharing, as Levers have done', adding: 'The old Capitalist regime has gone. We are doing it quietly in England, as usual. America will follow with dynamite and blood.' But the only possible line for his papers to take was that strikers should go back to work, that violence was wicked. It was not a subject for blood-stirring campaigns, like Dreadnoughts and the German threat. When he felt driven to it, he would attack the militants, as he did in the spring of 1912 over a national miners' strike. He ordered that it be called 'The Black Strike' every day for a week, with carefully damaging sub-headings such as 'Miners off to the Seaside', 'Dearer Bread', and 'Effect on the Fleet'. The following week it became 'The Selfish Strike'.

The changing social scene found Northcliffe on the defensive, looking less attractive, as men always do when they are seen clutching at the past instead of heralding a future, as he had been accustomed to do. Perhaps the most unbearable aspect of the rise of 'the worker', as it affected his own business, was the feeling that he was losing personal control. In later years he threatened to close down, rather than be dictated to by trade unions. Tom George, his head printer, described how a union delegation visited Northcliffe at the *Times*. The men were amicably received. As they were leaving, Northcliffe said goodbye to each of them, using Christian names, handing out cigars and telling them to come and see him again. As soon as the door was shut he began to rage, saying he hated the lot of them, and how dare they tell him how to run his business. 'They're trying to rule us, that's what they're doing,' he shouted. So they were, in a way. Northcliffe had made his fortune by giving people interesting things to read. He was encouraging appetites, for the goods they saw advertised no less than for the newspapers and magazines that the foods were advertised in. He was helping to tap reservoirs, opening valves that could never be closed again. The new generations would shake off poverty, but in its place would come discontent with their share of prosperity. By setting them higher standards, advertising would make them feel disgruntled with legs when there were bicycles, bicycles when there were motor-bikes, motor-bikes when there were cars. Such appetites were dangerous, part of a new temper among men who would not let themselves be ruled as in the past. Northcliffe encouraged the appetites without perceiving the implications. He made an industry out of selling information as a package, an assortment of news and advertisements that showed a rosy future beckoning. He did it very successfully. But a rosier future for the millions meant an end of the world as he knew it. Northcliffe's income in a 'bad' year like 1911 was a hundred and eighteen thousand pounds – equivalent to more than eight hundred thousand pounds in purchasing power sixty years later. With labourers bringing up families on fifty pounds a year, it would have paid the wages of 2,360 of them. No British-based industrialist today pockets 2,360 times a labourer's wage. Such calculations would have seemed irrelevant in 1911. Northcliffe was helping to ensure that his successors would have to make them.

To relax, as his doctors continued to tell him he must, he fished; stayed with his mother; travelled abroad. Advised to take up golf, he had a nine-hole course made at Sutton Place, bought a hundred and fifty golf balls, and spent an afternoon driving them down the fairway; in the end he collapsed from exhaustion and had to be helped back to the house. If he still relaxed with Mrs Wrohan, it was in the intervals between arguing about money and the child. Their relationship was deteriorating in 1911. In April, staying with him in Paris, she stormed out of the hotel and returned to London, complaining that the baby was not properly provided for. She offered to let Northcliffe have the child, and said dramatically that she would leave England for ever. Letters flew to and fro between Northcliffe, Mrs Wrohan, and the solicitors. Her allowance at the time seems to have been eight thousand pounds a year; old dress bills were a bone of contention. For a while Mrs Wrohan refused to see him, and he wrote asking Sutton to try to influence her. Sutton must have been successful, because in August, while the arguments about money were at their height she again became pregnant by Northcliffe.

In October he was in Scotland, golfing and fishing with Max Pemberton. On an impulse he crossed to Dublin and stayed at Sunnybank, the house outside the city where he was born, and which he had bought a few years previously. Writing to his mother before breakfast, lying in bed with the rain-swollen Liffey rushing by outside the windows, he declared that 'I think of you every second, darling', and sent her an apple leaf and rose leaf from the garden. His mother was an escape from an unmanageable life. And if his private affairs were confused, his business affairs sucked him dry. He was a newspaper proprietor in the old, individually-powerful sense, but he was operating under changed conditions that required a team of directors and managers. There were too few of these; they were not easy to find, and it is questionable whether Northcliffe was over-anxious to find them. He insisted on personal authority; thus he was plagued by the troubles of the *Times* and Amalgamated Press, which spewed out its magazines without the central direction he longed to give it. The magazine empire had been beyond his control for years, but he was slow to face the truth.

Writing to Sutton from Nice in March 1912 he said that

my best attempt at a holiday was spoiled by *Times* friction (of which you did not hear) just as by Amalgamated Press friction. Before that it was Beeton [one of his managers] and Newfoundland and so on and so on and so on *indefinitely*. The business is a Frankenstein. *It gives me no peace whatever.*

Northcliffe had created it; now he had to live with it. He encouraged the very conditions he bewailed. Peace, one has to assume, was not what he wanted.

16

Family Pride

OF THE EIGHT Harmsworth brothers, four went into 'public
life' in one form or another. Alfred became Northcliffe, an
extra-political figure who wanted a share in running the country
on his own terms. Harold, though he never tried to be a Member
of Parliament, entered politics via his wealth and connections,
notably the fact that Northcliffe was his brother; before the first
world war he hob-nobbed with Liberals, among them Lloyd
George. Leicester was Liberal MP for his constituency in the
north of Scotland; politically undistinguished, sardonic about
the great, preoccupied with making money and collecting things.
Cecil, who should never have tried, became a Liberal MP in
1906. He was pushed by the corporate pride of the Harmsworths
rather than by any ambition to be a public figure. Every
Harmsworth believed in the family future.

Cecil was a disappointment. Although he could sound self-
important at times, in the Harmsworth manner, he was essentially a withdrawn and self-effacing man. One has the feeling
that he went into politics in order to please Northcliffe. He was
tall and dignified, spoke well, wrote prettily, and owed it to the
family to enhance their name. He first represented Droitwich,
and before the general election of January 1910 was asking
Alfred for newspaper support. Losing his seat, he was returned
for Luton in 1911, again with help from Alfred, who suppressed
criticism of his brother – 'I have kept the wolves from you,' he
wrote, 'but I assure you that they have strained at the leash. We
receive a daily torrent of abuse from the district.' Cecil became
parliamentary private secretary to the Minister in charge of
agriculture, and attended to engines for fishing boats and the
decrepit-horse trade with Belgium. His diary, rigidly discreet, is
filled with placid family affairs. He lists his children's fantasies,

dwells on nightingales and marsh marigolds, describes country weekends. He loved fishing. The Conservative paper at Luton make jokes about his 'piscatorial exploits', and printed a poem about his absences from the House of Commons; he clipped it out and pasted it in the diary. If they had not been Harmsworths, an inquiry from Alfred, in July 1912, as to whether he wanted a title would have seemed misplaced. But Harold was a baronet, soon to become a baron. It was only natural that Cecil should move up behind him. Cecil demurred, however. His means were not adequate; he would rather not be put in the position of having to decide. This was not the accepted family style. The matter fell through. Cecil, it was apparent, lacked push.

All the Harmsworths were wealthy enough to lead the good life in one form or another. Regularly in the early months of the year they would encounter one another at Monte Carlo, where Harold's villa, La Dragonnière, built high among pine and olive woods, was the family hub in the south of France. Harold and Lilian were still together, but only just. Their sons, Vyvyan, Vere, and Esmond, were growing up. Great hopes were pinned on Vyvyan, who had an air of uplift that some attributed to his mother's Baptist background. Harold was not at ease with Vyvyan. Sir Harold in his forties had solidified into the total businessman. Words and ideas meant little to him; perhaps people didn't either. On the Riviera he was an assiduous pleasure seeker, a gambler who would sit back and watch a secretary play roulette on his behalf for large stakes, a trencherman who ate slices of rich paté like cake, a *bon vivant* who was easily bored, who needed a circle of associates to listen when he had something to say, and amuse him with gossip when he hadn't. An associate remarked that he had two separate minds, one to carry on a conversation, the other to sift information. Although some people found him amiable enough, his coldness and remoteness were increasingly apparent. He owned various houses, but was more often to be found at hotels.

Poynters Hall at Totteridge was still the house they all returned to. The grandest mansion in the family was Sutton Place, where Northcliffe and his wife entertained at weekends. Visitors in summer saw the famous hedge of wild roses, a hundred yards long and burning with colour. The men might visit the garage and see a row of motor cars laid out for inspection, polished tins beneath to catch the oil, clean sand spread in front. If they were not the most brilliant social occasions in England, they were formidable gatherings – politicians like Bonar Law and Arthur Balfour, journalists like Garvin and Wickham Steed, Henry Irving the actor, Grahame-White the pioneer airman. It was the world before the war. They ate enormous meals and walked two-by-two on the gleaming lawns. Victor Trumper, a famous Australian cricketer, in the country for a Test series, was invited to play for the editorial staff against the mechanical workers at the firm's annual sports meeting. Northcliffe gave instructions in advance: the printers would go in first and declare their innings in time for the editorial team to bat immediately after lunch. The Northcliffe party included Sir Edward Grey, the Foreign Secretary, and the Curzons. At 2.30 he led his guests to the edge of the lawn, where footmen had arranged divans for them to recline on as they watched the mighty Trumper. Trumper fussed about, patting the grass and taking his stand, but was out first ball, to a Linotype operator on the *Mail*. As he walked off, Northcliffe and party rose and went back to the house.

Northcliffe had little affection for Sutton Place. It was low-lying, near a river, strangled by trees, reminiscent of long, very long weekends. He claimed he couldn't sleep in the house, and after 1910, whenever he had to stay there, he used a bungalow on a hill a few miles away. The locals began to call him the 'mad lord' and gossiped about sexual goings-on that were supposed to take place there. But if he didn't like the house, it pleased him to be seen in it. He worked in the library, where his desk was lost in so much space. 'Little rooms are no good for big ideas,' he would inform the young men who came down from the office to receive orders, waiting awkwardly while he brooded by the fireplace or whispered into the telephone. One disadvantage of Sutton Place, or of any social setting that exposed him to his wife's friends, and friends of friends, was that he found himself dogged by favour-seekers. Women, especially Conservative Party women, were always requesting free use of his columns for their charities, or openings for their sons and lovers. Caught by a woman who had been persecuting him all weekend, one breakfast-time when he called in at the house on his way from the bungalow to London, he pushed his secretary towards her,

o pine. the most careful & best chauffeur I have ever known! K. Wrohan. 1903.

Mrs Wrohan in the driving seat. The picture is dedicated to Northcliffe's chauffeur, Pine.

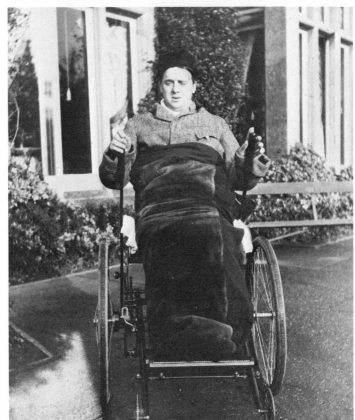

St John, the man in the wheel-chair, crippled for life at the age of thirty.

Wife—Mary Northcliffe,
who enjoyed life in
high society.

Mistress—Kathleen
Wrohan, who likewise
moved in only
the best circles.

murmuring 'Keep this bitch away from me' loud enough for her
to hear, and fled to the car. But he was far from indifferent to
rank and class. He suffered from the English disease of chronic
social uneasiness. He was particularly attentive to criticism of
his papers from peers or clergymen. He had been known to insist
that sub-editors insert the definite article before a title, making
it 'The Lady Blank', to change 'my maid' in an article to 'one of
my maids', to complain that journalists all lived in vulgar
suburbs like Camberley. Some of this was probably due to Lady
Northcliffe. In the matter of what others thought about him, the
Times and what it thought about him professionally was more
important. Many at Printing House Square still regarded him
with dismay, especially when, following a series of moves that
gave him control of still larger blocks of shares, he determined in
1913 to make the paper profitable: after five years of ownership,
there was still no prospect of a regular dividend. Northcliffe's
interest in the *Times* became intense. The paper was given a
circulation manager. Kennedy Jones, the rough diamond, was
put aside. Geoffrey Dawson, who had succeeded Buckle as
editor, was informed that the monks of Blackfriars, as Northcliffe
liked to call them, lacked foresight, initiative, prevision, or flair,
and that the *Times* was an institution, not a newspaper. But
Dawson, although appointed by Northcliffe, kept some independence. The paper continued to have its mysterious inner life.
Dawson and the staff embraced a sense of history and purpose
coiled within their corporate self, which they knew, and
Northcliffe knew, could not be prised away without destroying
the character of the paper. They needed Northcliffe to make the
paper pay, and if he (or someone) had not brought in fresh
capital in 1908, it would already have ceased to exist. He needed
its bland, maddening, unbreakable assurance of superiority, its
contacts in high places, even its combined command of (so it
was said) twenty-three languages, living and dead.

Dawson let the changes blow around him. The first major
move was to reduce the price from threepence to twopence, in
May 1913. Northcliffe preceded this with a burst of dismissals
and complaints that the paper was not sufficiently prepared for
its 'final plunge', despite its talented staff. He followed it, when
the price-reduction was seen to be failing, with the opposite
statement, that Dawson lacked 'a single person ... however

willing, that is really competent'. As with the *Mirror*, he blamed the journalists first, then sought a managerial solution. He warned that if the experiment failed, 'there is but one thing left, to make the paper a popular, penny journal'. Did Northcliffe care for the character of the *Times*? Delane and Barnes must already have turned in their graves when, as part of the preparation for the twopenny *Times*, Northcliffe put fake advertisements in the personal column to brighten up the front page, and organised a stunt with woman-appeal by inspiring a faked letter, signed 'A Peeress', on the morality of 'modern dancing'. Russell Wakefield wrote it, and it appeared on 20 May. On 21 May Wakefield replied to his own letter, this time signing it himself. Letters poured into the office, as they had done to the *Daily Mail* fifteen years earlier on the subject of dancing clergymen. All Northcliffe's ingenuity was in vain. Circulation rose from forty-one thousand to forty-seven thousand; in Harmsworth terms this was a barely visible gain. Success didn't come until March 1914. Then, after another spell of long-distance planning conducted from Paris, between visits to his dentist, Northcliffe reduced the price of a remodelled paper to a penny, and circulation quadrupled. The change was cross-advertised in the usual way by articles in the *Evening News* and *Daily Mail*. For five days running the main story in the *Mail* was the sensational news, so-called, from Printing House Square. On the day of the first penny *Times*, the *Mail* and Northcliffe as a headline-writer excelled themselves with: TIMES MYSTERY—WHY?—1896 AGAIN— RUSH OF THE SMALL ADVERTISER.

One of the *Mail* reports said the price was coming down because of the serious political situation in Ireland. This wasn't true, any more than the carefully calculated impression that the *Mail* was printing straightforward reports on the subject was true ('A *Daily Mail* representative obtained admission through the closely guarded portals of the world's chief and largest newspaper office', and so on). Some hand, doubtless Northcliffe's, contributed an anonymous leader-page article to the *Mail* with sly digs at the *Times* ('many of the TIMES: people have never seen each other') and the statement that Lord Northcliffe 'rarely sees and never reads a letter, being mainly nowadays engaged in golf and travel'. It was another of his jokes. The truth was easily blurred with Northcliffe; convenient lies merged into humorous fibs; like the slanted news or the sound and fury about penny dreadfuls years before, they were all part of his machinery of deceit. He thrived on bluff, on a continual high turnover of words that meant as much or as little as he wanted them to mean. His bark could be worse than his bite; just as easily, his bite could be worse than his bark. Words were infinitely expendable. Like everyone else, he had to bend the truth a little in order to survive. The difference was that he bent it more effectively than most. He made deception – frequently mild, often amusing, always insidious – into a system.

The new *Times* was popularised – redesigned and edited with an eye on a larger readership, including women and the fashionable young, who were referred to by Northcliffe as 'distinguished Nuts and Flappers'. The paper lost some of its dullness without losing its character; it's unlikely that Northcliffe ever wished it to be otherwise. He wanted to have it all ways: a paper of authority yet with wide appeal, distinguished for its independence yet prosperous through its advertisements, edited by journalists of vision and wisdom who were nevertheless subservient to the will of the proprietor. This rare amalgam still eludes the men who run Fleet Street, half a century and more after Northcliffe. One of his legacies to the Press was a feeling of false promise; he did so much (and happened to live at the right time to do it) that he misled the next generation of newspaper proprietors into thinking that the Press was stronger and richer than the facts warranted.

As he became more involved with the *Times*, Northcliffe's attitude hardened towards 'vulgarity' in his empire. He had shown how sensitive he was to magazines in 1910. On another occasion he was enraged to hear an executive refer to the comics and novelettes as 'the Hooligan Department', demanding to know the names of those at the Amalgamated Press who used such a scurrilous term. The *Mirror* was another source of anxiety. Amid the mixture of praise and criticism which was his way of keeping editors alert is irritation at the bad taste and low tone of the paper. He had never devoted much time to the *Mirror*, and now it was becoming a liability. Grumbling to Alex Kenealy that a referendum was badly reported at the end of 1910, he added: 'I do not suppose that the *Daily Mirror* staff know what a referendum means.' In the same letter Northcliffe said:

185

Someone told me the other day that your people were all Socialists. I do not at all mind them being Socialists, but I do not think that Socialists ought to take Tory money. I know that I would not take Socialist money.

The *Mirror*, competing with a new picture-newspaper, the *Daily Sketch*, was using stunts that were too reminiscent of the early days of the Harmsworth magazines. They included treasure hunts, prizes for the holders of lucky tram-ticket numbers, and experiments with flour-dusted bees to see how far they went in search of pollen. Picture-reproduction was becoming sophisticated, photographers were developing their own journalism. The *Mirror*'s circulation overtook the *Mail*'s, which was still below a million, and rose to 1,200,000 by 1914. It was the world's largest sale, but Northcliffe was not interested. Early in 1914 he sold his shares cheaply to Harold. The following year, when Kenealy died, one of his relatives tried to sell Northcliffe her *Mirror* shares. He refused, saying he was 'adamant in my resolve not to have any connection, directly or indirectly, with any newspaper that I do not absolutely control'.

Despite their differences, Alfred and Harold had an understanding. Alfred's willingness to help Harold's career is the most likely explanation of the part he played, or failed to play, in a tortuous political scandal of 1912 and 1913, the Marconi affair. Three Liberal Ministers were found to have dealt in shares of the American Marconi Company, while the Government of which they were members was completing a lucrative contract with British Marconi to build a chain of radio transmitters. The three men were Sir Rufus Isaacs, now Attorney-General; the Master of Elibank (a Scots title), Alexander Murray, later Lord Murray of Elibank, who was Chief Whip; and Lloyd George, Chancellor of the Exchequer. Isaacs was offered ten thousand American Marconi shares on favourable terms by his brother Godfrey, who was managing director of both British and American Marconi. He declined the shares, but later accepted them from another brother, and passed some of them on to Murray and Lloyd George. This was in April 1912, a month after the Marconi tender had been accepted by the British Government, but three months before the contract was signed. Rumours got about, and in October, Isaacs and Lloyd George stood up in Parliament and denied that they had trafficked in the shares of

British Marconi. This was literally true, but it was held against them five months later when, during a libel action against *Le Matin* of Paris, it emerged that the Ministers had dealt in American Marconi. The scandal ripened quickly. Lesser revelations about further deals in the shares emerged between March and May 1913, as a Parliamentary Committee heard evidence, adding to the impression that the truth had to be dragged piece by piece from unwilling Ministers. Murray had resigned, for other reasons, and remained abroad on business; this didn't help matters. The official report acquitted the Ministers of corruption or impropriety, but since the Liberals had a majority on the committee, many saw this as a partisan verdict. Today the three men seem to have been so evasive that it is inconceivable they should have stayed in office.

Northcliffe played down the affair in his papers, although he might have been expected to enjoy using it to beat the Liberals with. Early in 1913, when the rumours were smouldering, Winston Churchill (then a Liberal, and First Lord of the Admiralty) visited Northcliffe and pleaded for the three men, assuring him that there was no hidden corruption. According to Russell Wakefield, Northcliffe also listened to Lord Rosebery; he drove over from Sutton Place to see him at Epsom, and when he returned, said to Wakefield: 'Rosebery considers it merely inept – inept, but not corrupt.' Although there is no reason to suppose that Northcliffe questioned this view, it left him ample scope for criticism, if he chose to be critical. But a new reason for keeping quiet emerged: Harold desired it. Harold had previously remarked on the need to stay on friendly terms with Isaacs, who had acted for Northcliffe in the Lever and Kenealy cases. In a letter to Northcliffe dated 8 November 1910, he asked his brother to let Isaac's sister, Madame Keyzer, contribute notes on art and the theatre to the *Mail*. Isaacs, he pointed out, was tipped as Lord Chancellor; it was politic to cultivate such a man by doing a favour for his sister – he was a Jew, and a favour for one Jew in a family was a favour for all. Now (10 March 1913) Harold wrote to Northcliffe from La Dragonnière:

I know you have always thought it judicious and prudent to help Rufus Isaacs, if the occasion arose. The occasion is now here. Isaacs has never asked us to do anything for him. *In your interests* I consider you should help him now. The *Times* and the *Daily Mail* can kill at its birth any effort that may be made by misrepresentation and calumny to raise an agitation which might compel Isaacs to resign office. I know the thing will seem ridiculous trumpery to you, and it is, except for the fact that Isaacs is destined for high judicial office. All that is wanted is a very soft pedal in the *Times* and *Daily Mail*.

Presently Northcliffe applied the soft pedal at the *Times*, when he killed a critical leading article, that was about to go into the paper, between 11 p.m. and midnight, and produced a milder one of his own later in the night. He did this on 19/20 March, immediately after the *Le Matin* libel case. Dawson had already argued about the affair with Northcliffe, but on 19 March he was on holiday, and the proprietor, operating from his house via the telephone and Nicholson, forced the acting editor to accept the new article. This congratulated the Ministers and found nothing worse than a lack of 'delicacy' in choosing their invest-ments.* Northcliffe does not appear to have relished the kid-gloved attitude he was adopting. An undated letter to Dawson says that attacks on Isaacs and his colleagues would 'involve me in directly critical relations with highly placed personal friends for which I know neither you nor I care a twopenny dam' (sic). The meaning is confused; is Northcliffe half apologising for his restraint? In another letter to Dawson, dated 7 May 1913, Northcliffe said he had no intention of 'being associated with an ascription of grave imprudence as roguery'. A reference to Lloyd George and Isaacs as 'a Welsh solicitor and Jew barrister' may be taken as a sign of the irritation he felt with them below the surface. Writing to Churchill on the same day (7 May) Northcliffe said he wanted to see justice for Churchill's 'im-prudent and very inept friends', but that he must deal with the matter in his papers if it went on much longer. He did so the next day, in a leader that spoke of 'amazing ineptitude', but no more. Eventually, when the Parliamentary Committee reported in June, the *Times* spoke of 'whitewash' and censured the Minis-ters without condemning them, and Northcliffe approved.

His role in the episode is confused and out of character. Russell Wakefield said that at one point he was sent to warn

* Early editions of the *Times* for 20 March have 'The Crisis in France' as the second leading article. By the edition marked '4 a.m.' the Marconi leader, headed 'Ministers and the "Matin" ', had been substituted. The story of the switch – in the *History of the Times*, Vol. 4, part 1, p. 133 – says incorrectly that it was on the night of 18 March.

Lloyd George not to attack the Press in a speech, or Northcliffe would retaliate. Wakefield was told exactly what to say: Northcliffe put nothing in writing. The message was delivered to a brazen Lloyd George and a quaking Reading. Wakefield thought that as a result the speech was toned down. The episode might be read as evidence of a desire to punish without really hurting. In public, Northcliffe treated them gently. Harold's plea was probably effective. He had been made a baronet in 1910 by a Liberal Government. He wanted a peerage and Alfred would have wanted him to have one. To help restrain Northcliffe in a scandal affecting three prominent Liberals was a valuable service to his friends.* No direct evidence exists except Harold's letter to Northcliffe, but the explanation fits Northcliffe's actions better than any other. There is no need to suppose that he plotted the affair from start to finish. The ethics were blurred, which suited Northcliffe. A nice tangle of obligations produced the required result. In the New Year Honours List of January 1914, Sir Harold Harmsworth was raised to the peerage and took the title of Lord Rothermere of Hemsted, in Kent. The same list contained the name of Rufus Isaacs, who became Lord Reading; three months before, he had been raised to the second-highest judicial office in the land as Lord Chief Justice of England. Isaacs had survived with a little help from his friends, among them Harold. Gratitude, in a definition that Northcliffe liked to quote, was a lively sense of favours to come.

Scandals came and went; the campaign against Germany, it seemed, would last for ever. Northcliffe never let go. The *Times* had its own long-standing suspicions, which suited the Northcliffe thesis. The *Mail* had been warning Britain to watch the Germans since 1896. Now and then the Kaiser would receive a friendly word (in October 1913 the *Evening News* called him 'a very gallant gentleman, whose word is better than many another's bond'), but in general, Germany was regarded as

---

* Lord Beaverbrook suggested the reward was for a different service. In a 1926 speech he said that in 1911, Harold persuaded Northcliffe to ridicule, in the *Daily Mail*, the diehard peers who sought to halt the Parliament Act. Beaverbrook hinted that this was why the Liberals ennobled him. Perhaps it was a combination of Parliament Act and Marconi.

sinister. Urbane Englishmen were hardened to the warnings. H. G. Wells later wrote a novel, partly autobiographical, about a man who refused to believe that war would ever come.

Some years ago, [Wells made Mr Britling say] I used to believe in the inevitable European war, but it's been threatened so long that at last I've lost all belief in it. The Powers wrangle and threaten. They're far too cautious and civilised to let the guns go off.

Northcliffe didn't agree. One of his German relatives told him: 'We are a nation of land crabs. If you advance, we retreat. If you retreat, we advance.' He quoted the phrase in letters to Churchill, written following the Agadir crisis of 1911, when Germany sent a gunboat to Morocco. The Germans, Northcliffe believed, were a nation of 'greatly misunderstood, hysterical people'. He planned a Berlin edition of the *Mail*. A dummy was prepared in November 1913, and there were discussions in London. Northcliffe was quoted as saying that it might cost a couple of hundred thousand pounds, but that it would be 'worth many times that much if we can knock the war mania out of German heads'. His views on international relations crystallise into headlines, or stem from headline-type ideas – 'We want Eight', 'A nation of land crabs', 'German war mania'. His talk of peace was contingent on his belief in war. In March 1914, four months after the Berlin newspaper was mooted, he was writing to his nephew Vyvyan, who tried to interest him in an Anglo-German friendship club at Oxford: 'You know that I am not one of those who believe in the likelihood of friendship be-tween the English and the Germans.' His mood had hardened, as the mood of Europe was hardening. Germany was making unmistakable preparations for war. Events caught him up. All he could do was detect a climate of rivalry and suspicion, as he had been doing for nearly twenty years, and by dramatising it, make the *Mail* a part of the climate, feeding back half-truths as facts that circulated among the public, only to be further dramatised by publicity. This endless re-cycling of opinion was to be the central function of popular journalism, reproducing, on a national scale, the shapeless, shadowy conversations of ordinary people in parlours, bars, and offices. Democracy was slowly coming true in newspapers. If the results were muddled, it was because people in general were muddled, too. It was Northcliffe's fortune, for good or ill, to be the man who stumbled on this before 1914.

Ireland was the last major issue to concern him before Germany made the warnings come true. Home rule for Ireland, the bugbear of British politics since the days of Gladstone, was again attempted by the Liberals in 1912. It came to grief on the new militancy of Ulster, the north-east portion of the country, where the Protestant descendants of British colonists lived. Championed at Westminster by Sir Edward Carson, they refused to be part of a separate, Catholic Ireland. British politicians found themselves cursed with two Irelands instead of one, neither of which could be appeased without offending the other. A 'private army' in Ulster, the Ulster Volunteers, was formed in 1912, countered by the National Volunteers in the South the following year. Northcliffe's attitude to Irish affairs was never clear. This is remarkable, considering that he was born in Dublin of an Irish mother; perhaps his background inhibited him. At one point in June and July 1914, Rothermere played some part in trying to negotiate a compromise settlement between Westminster and John Redmond, the Irish nationalist leader. He was living in Claridge's Hotel, and saw much of Lord Murray of Elibank and Bonar Law. Northcliffe was not involved. He let the *Times* (where Dawson was on the side of Ulster) pursue its own policy. The *Mail*, too, was opposed to coercing Ulster, and when a group of British cavalry officers stationed at Dublin said they would resign rather than be sent to the north – the 'Curragh Mutiny' – the paper's main headline and contents bill, ordered by Northcliffe, was 'The Bullying of Ulster'. But in private he equivocated. In a letter to Dawson on 13 August 1912, he wrote that 'I have not cared for the violent Ulster language of Bonar Law, Carson, and others'. R. McNair Wilson, a doctor-journalist on his staff, found him luke-warm towards Ulster. Northcliffe agreed with Russell Wakefield that Ulstermen were an 'unlovely race'.

He was more enthusiastic about making preparations to report the civil war that seemed in prospect for Ireland. He drove up and down northern Ireland at the head of a newspaper retinue, the like of which had never been seen there before. McNair Wilson received a telegram instructing him to meet the party at Larne, on the north-east coast. When he arrived,

Northcliffe was in an expansive mood. 'We must have half a dozen cars – Rolls-Royces for preference,' he said. Andrew Caird, an executive at Carmelite House, a morose Scotsman with an eye on editorial budgets, muttered 'Fords' under his breath. Northcliffe decided they needed a ship that could cross from Larne to Stranraer, thirty-five miles distant on the Scottish coast, in any weather, if the Post Office cables were cut. McNair Wilson was sent to Glasgow to hire a tug, which he succeeded in doing, when he had convinced the ship owners that he was serious, for eighty pounds a week. Other newspapers watched with astonishment and envy as the *Mail* spent thousands of pounds on cars, motor-boats, caches of petrol and a permanent team of at least ten reporters. Northcliffe was carried away. He took his combined *Times* and *Mail* party to Craigavon, the residence of the Craigs, a family of staunch Ulster Unionists, and lectured everyone on how little the English knew about Ulster. A correspondent who was in Ireland for the rival *Daily Express* heard about it from Captain Craig, and wrote to his editor on 14 July. Northcliffe was reported to have sat in the drawing room, holding forth, while his staff listened in awe. 'We don't want to reach the man in the street,' he declared, 'we want to reach the man in the tram-car.' He turned to a young reporter and said, 'Tell Captain Craig about the man in the tram-car.'

'I was coming to Blackfriars from Streatham,' said the reporter, 'and I was reading the *Daily Mail*. I saw the man next to me was reading the *Daily Mail* – in fact, everybody on the tram was reading the *Daily Mail*. I said to the man next to me, "What do you think about the Ulster question?" and he replied, "I don't think anything about it." I asked the next man and he said he didn't care, and then I asked everybody in the tram and nobody cared, and then I came to the office and told Lord Northcliffe.'

'There!' said Northcliffe to Craig. 'Those are the people we are going to get at.'

But Ireland was already falling into place as a domestic matter that would have to wait. The assassination at Sarajevo on 28 June had begun the chain of events that would lead to war. H. G. Wells's Mr Britling would try to convince himself until the last minute that it was not going to happen. A German student, staying at his house, would tell him: 'No. It is the war. It has

come. I have heard it talked about many times.' McNair Wilson
wrote later of a feeling of release, of a world passing away. Lovat
Fraser, a highly paid journalist who wrote the Irish leading
articles in the *Times*, gave the true record of a dream in the
Daily Mail on 18 June. He had seen an airship above Constan-
tinople, the city in flames. One moment, roses and sunshine;
the next, destruction and panic. An Englishman in the dream
said: 'They're Germans. None but Germans could do this.
International law ended when airships came in.' The airship
sprayed the city with liquid that smeared his clothes. 'Good
lord,' he cried, 'the brutes are dropping inflammable stuff!
They're going to burn us as well!' Soon Fraser would be writing
an article called 'The March of the Hun', giving the Germans
a new hate-name.

To Cecil Harmsworth, weeding in the garden at Henley,
bird-nesting with his children, slipping off from Parliament in
the middle of the afternoon to fish, bombs from the air were unthinkable. War was a remote contingency. To Northcliffe it was
a culmination. He had a stake in war; it meant a new role for
him and his newspapers. Perhaps for him, as for others, it also
meant a convenient closing of books, a release from petty detail.
His private life was as confused as ever. Mrs Wrohan gave birth
to a daughter, Geraldine, in May 1912, and to a second son,
Harold, in April 1914; so Northcliffe's children had the same
names as he, his next sister, and his next brother. Harold was
christened at St Martin in the Fields, in Trafalgar Square;
described as the adopted son of Francis Wrohan ('Gentleman')
and Kathleen; her Paris address, in the Avenue du Bois, was
given.* As far as is known, neither of the other children was
christened in church. It hints at further changes in her relationship with Northcliffe, who would hardly have welcomed such a
record in a West End church. He and Mrs Wrohan seem to have
become finally estranged. From now on he was to have a succession of minor mistresses. His restlessness deepened. But as a man
of affairs, August 1914 meant a new arena to move in.

On the afternoon of 1 August, a Saturday, Northcliffe

---

* The entry in the parish register says: 'Stated to be born about mid-March
1914.' This is not true. The birth was on 14 April, only eight days before the
christening; someone was in a hurry

was closeted at the *Times* with Dawson, Wickham Steed, and Marlowe from the *Mail*. Austria and Russia had mobilised. Liberal newspapers (the *Daily News*, the *Manchester Guardian*) were urging that Britain stay neutral. The Cabinet was said to be divided, and unlikely to go to war. Lord Rothschild, representing powerful financial interests, had already begged the *Times* to moderate its language. Steed described this as 'a dirty German-Jewish international financial attempt to bully us into advocating neutrality'. Northcliffe agreed with him, and the *Times* had declared, 'We dare not stand aside'. Rothschild and his brother Leopold tried again on the Saturday afternoon but were sent away without satisfaction. The editorial meeting was not unanimous. Marlowe said they should not criticise the Government. Dawson advised caution. Steed and Northcliffe were the hawks. A special Sunday edition continued to argue that Britain must intervene. The news that Germany had invaded France came as the paper was going to press. Doubts about British involvement disappeared. In a day or two, Northcliffe was striding into Steed's office, saying, 'Well, it's come,' ripping out a page from a reference book with a theatrical gesture, ready for the big fight.

17

Northcliffe at War

Most Englishmen thought the war would be over within months. Northcliffe knew that Germany's military preparations went deep, and said from the start that it would last for years. The war satisfied him as a journalist but frustrated him as an amateur politician. He was heard to complain that running it was a slow business beside running a newspaper. His natural tendency was to sweep aside objections and demand that Britain fight as though her life depended on it – as it did. This truth eventually came home to the nation, long after it had been apparent to Northcliffe. Wickham Steed said he had 'the war mind'. Northcliffe began the war by railing against censorship, and ended it by demanding that the Germans be properly punished. In 1914 he was suggesting the techniques of propaganda that were used four years later (the idea of dropping leaflets on the enemy seemed comic in 1914; General Henry Wilson pointed out sternly that the object of a war was to kill people). Northcliffe harassed and vilified politicians if they seemed effete or inefficient, demanded conscription, thundered at 'slackers' and did much to suggest that the only good German was a dead one. In all this he appeared to be successful: politicians tumbled like lead soldiers, millions of men were enlisted, ladies rushed about the streets giving white feathers to those who should have been in uniform, and Germans were seen as brute creatures set apart from humanity. In the last year of the war, the Rev. Innes Logan, Chaplain to the Forces, wrote in *War Illustrated* that he had declined, 'with a feeling of repulsion', a cigarette offered him by a wounded German prisoner. 'One can be kind to wounded men of any race,' wrote Mr Logan, 'but good fellowship with a German is impossible. It is, indeed, cynical and immoral.'

War Illustrated was a Harmsworth magazine. But it would be misleading to see cause and effect in any of their wartime enterprises. Conscription would have come regardless of Northcliffe. Asquith would have fallen and Lloyd George taken his place. Mr Britling would have learned about total war. But without Northcliffe, the pace would have been more sluggish and the realities might have taken longer to dawn on people. He distilled the strange odours of fear, hatred, and love of country that filled the air; interpreting the mood of people before they were aware of it themselves, employing crude arguments about strength and survival that were scorned, condemned, and finally adopted. Most of his energy was used to attack the existing order. He found so much fault with the way the country was being run that his critics were able at first to present him as a monster of sensationalism, blundering from one scandal to another. The Liberal newspapers, which before 1914 had committed themselves to the idea of peace as enthusiastically as Northcliffe had committed himself to the idea of war, were outraged. So were most orthodox politicians. Northcliffe was armoured by his convictions. At times he seemed to court unpopularity. Whether he would have courted it if it had meant turning against the underlying mood of the nation is beside the point, since his actions were governed by what he sensed of the mood in the first place.

The war lent newspapers in general, and Northcliffe's in particular, a new stature. A wider range of people were now accustomed to their morning paper. The biggest, bloodiest war in history became a daily serial. There was no medium to compete with the Press, and no proprietor to compete with Northcliffe. No publicist had ever stood in this position before. His skill in mounting campaigns, in organising the news to suit his purpose, could now be harnessed in the cause of national survival. His theme was to prosecute the war thoroughly, with short shrift for dodgers, slackers, faint-hearts, cowards, fumblers, failures, tired men, and, of course, the Huns. Having warned about Germany for so many years, he was off to a good start. War gave his voice a new resonance. It is not surprising that the results were far-reaching, both for the habits of the Press and the workings of Northcliffe's mind.

His first action misfired, the day after the war began, when he decided that the British Army should stay to defend Britain and not be sent to France. He wrote a leading article for the *Mail* to say so, and handed it personally to the head printer, with instructions that he alone should see the proofs. Northcliffe's headline read: NOT ONE BRITISH SOLDIER TO LEAVE ENGLAND'S SHORES. Marlowe, the editor, disagreed, and refused to be overridden. The compositors made up two pages, one with Northcliffe's article, the other without. There were comings and goings from Whitehall. In the end, probably because his patriotism was appealed to, Northcliffe gave in; Marlowe's page went to press, three-quarters of an hour late. The British Expeditionary Force sailed to France, and Northcliffe, like everyone else, was soon encountering a Press censorship that picked the meat out of war reporting. The new Secretary for War, Lord Kitchener, was no fonder of journalists now than he had been in the Sudan. This set Northcliffe against him, and sowed the seeds for what would have been inconceivable before the war began, an attack on the great Kitchener himself. It was Northcliffe's first full-scale intervention in affairs of State. Like all his wartime acts, it made up in ferocity what it lacked in subtlety. In the early months of 1915, with blunders and carnage at the Dardanelles and in France, the *Times* and the *Mail* were increasingly critical of the country's leadership under Asquith. The papers reflected growing public disenchantment, which came to a head in May with a political crisis that saw the Liberal Government become a Coalition. Northcliffe's part in the crisis has been much argued. He adhered to events like a lining to a coat. Like everyone else, he had heard stories about a shortage of high-explosive shells on the Western Front, denied by Asquith but fostered by the Commander-in-Chief, Sir John French, and believed by many. On 1 May Northcliffe wrote to French, criticising Government secrecy and urging the general to speak about the need for ammunition: 'A short and very vigorous statement from you to a private correspondent (the usual way of making things public in England) would, I believe, render the Government's position impossible, and enable you to secure the publication of that which would tell the people here the truth and thus bring public pressure upon the Government to stop men and munitions pouring away to the Dardanelles as they are at present.' Whether or not as a result of this hint, French put his case in private to the military correspondent of the *Times*, Colonel Repington, a personal friend who was staying with him at headquarters. In the *Times* of 14 May, a report from Repington contained a significant phrase that passed the censor: 'The want of an unlimited supply of high explosive was a fatal bar to our success.' In private, French's emissaries intrigued in London against Kitchener, who, as War Minister, had undoubtedly muddled the supply of munitions.

Northcliffe's role in this was to edit the political complexities into a version fit for headlines. The message was brief: Britain has a peacetime government incapable of fighting a war, and in particular it is hampering our brave soldiers, thanks to Kitchener's obstinacy in ordering shrapnel shells instead of high explosive. In the circumstances this version contained as much half-truth as was necessary. During the week following Repington's dispatch, the Government was beset by internal squabbles that had no direct connection with shells. To Northcliffe's annoyance, other newspapers were better informed than his own about the crisis. On the afternoon of 20 May, when changes in the Government were expected daily, he angrily told subordinates at the *Mail* that they were getting a 'good hiding' at the expense of their rivals, adding that he would go out that night and obtain 'the news' himself. What he did was to write a long leading article for the next day attacking Kitchener, and present this along with a single-column story on the main news page. The articles contained no fresh news, and for that matter no fresh opinion: the *Mail* of 19 May implicitly blamed Kitchener for the shell shortage, while the *Manchester Guardian* of 20 May said bluntly that Kitchener was at fault and should go. The *Mail*'s leader was headed: THE TRAGEDY OF THE SHELLS. LORD KITCHENER'S GRAVE ERROR. The news headline WAS: THE SHELLS SCANDAL. LORD KITCHENER'S TRAGIC BLUNDER. No doubt Northcliffe believed in the story; no doubt also he was anxious to outsmart other papers.

He was with his mother at Totteridge for dinner, telephoning minor corrections that she suggested. When it appeared, the paper aroused great indignation. The *Daily Express* spoke of 'a most vicious, insane, and scandalous attack'. The *Mirror*, under Rothermere, said uncomfortably that attacks on Kitchener were out of place. Three thousand members of the Stock Exchange assembled (after lunch) to give three cheers for Kitchener and burn a copy of the *Daily Mail*. Police guarded Carmelite House. Circulation fell momentarily by a hundred thousand, and the attack on Kitchener was not continued 'day in, day out', as Northcliffe had told Max Aitken it would be. The shell agitation went on. When the Government was reconstructed as a Coalition the following week, with Kitchener retained but Lloyd George created Minister of Munitions, Northcliffe's critics gave him the blame for it, just as later writers gave him the credit for the same thing. It is now accepted that technically the Government collapsed for other reasons, and that the crisis can be seen operating independently of Northcliffe. But behind the fog of decision-making, Northcliffe can be glimpsed groping and clutching, helping to unseat the 'old gang'.

His reputation grew, in some ways for the worse. He was always so busy. There were few aspects of the war in which he did not involve himself. He nagged the Cabinet in private over the Dardanelles fiasco. He visited the Western Front at intervals, returning from one trip with a ten-inch shell in a taxi, which he pretended was live, and put beneath Andrew Caird's office at Carmelite House with a notice saying 'Danger'. Having campaigned for more munitions, he turned to manpower and made the need for compulsory service a constant theme in his attacks on the Coalition Government. These attacks were intense and continuous by the end of 1915, abetted by Dawson at the *Times*. Conscription for single men was announced early in 1916, but produced endless argument about who was in 'reserved occupations' and who was not. In April it was extended to married men. Northcliffe continued to complain about unmarried slackers who skulked at home while fathers went out to be killed; the *Mail* asked readers to report on draft-dodgers, so that the authorities could be told. Northcliffe's view of the war effort in 1916 remained simple: the inept politicians were letting down the clever generals. Kitchener, his ministerial powers waning, was drowned on the way to Russia in June 1916. Lloyd George replaced him as War Minister. The Army was led by the Chief of the Imperial General Staff, Sir William Robertson, and a new Commander-in-Chief in France, Sir Douglas Haig. In July they launched the British Army on the murderous Battle of the Somme, which lasted until November. Towards the end of the battle, sensing public disquiet but wishing to stifle it, Northcliffe became active in his defence of the military. On 10 October he went to the War Office and saw Lloyd George's personal secretary, J. T. Davies. According to Davies, Northcliffe said that he didn't want to see the Minister, but that 'you can tell him from me I hear that he has been interfering with strategy, and that if it goes on I will break him'. Northcliffe's version, in a letter to Sir Philip Sassoon written on 18 October, was that he had telephoned 'our Welsh friend' but found him absent or evasive. As a result he visited Davies to tell him that he could no longer support Lloyd George, and that 'if further interference took place with Sir William Robertson I was going to the House of Lords to lay matters before the world, and hammer them daily in my newspapers. I have heard nothing since, but [Dawson] tells me that General Robertson says that matters are better.' Northcliffe begins to emerge as more of a bully than a critic.

Fresh stories about his health were circulating. The previous year, Dawson had noted 'lunatic rages' in his diary; Lady Northcliffe wrote to Sutton to say her husband was '*much* too excitable and beginning his old habit of abusing his friends at his own table if they venture to disagree with him'. It was one thing when Northcliffe's eccentricities were confined to running newspapers and his private life; if they were to be displayed in high politics, rough times lay ahead. H. G. Wells, writing to him in April 1916 about the need for a social revolution (he thought it would come in the 1930s), suggested that Northcliffe should lead it. He added: 'The war has brought you into open and active conflict with the system as it is.' This was true, but turned out to be irrelevant: as Northcliffe came to be increasingly at odds with the way things were done, he responded by speaking louder but not clearer.

He still backed the generals and suspected the politicians. The *Times* was told on 14 November that Haig's name should appear as frequently in the paper as Kitchener's used to. Haig, said the proprietor, was of a retiring nature, and 'when the great fight between the politicians and the Army occurs he will be handicapped'. Aitken talked with Northcliffe and concluded that he wanted a form of military dictatorship. In the end, he had to be content with the collapse of Asquith's Government, and its replacement by a new Coalition under Lloyd George, in December 1916.

Northcliffe's part in this echoed his part in the crisis of May 1915. Again he was a violent critic of the Government, which fell as a result of moves to which he was not privy, but whose roots he had helped to water. On 1 December, a Friday, he saw Lloyd George; they had been on bad terms since Northcliffe began to threaten. Northcliffe was given no details of the political manoeuvrings. That evening the news editor of the *Mail*, Tom Clarke, visited Northcliffe's house in St James's Place. The Chief was in theatrical mood. 'I am in a hurry,' Clarke heard him say to a secretary. 'I am going to my mother's. Time is short.' He stared at Clarke over the top of his heavy spectacles. 'I thought you were dead,' he said. 'I thought there were no young men left.' He discussed the next day's leading article, devoted to an attack on Asquith, and ordered that the word 'Government' should appear in quotation marks throughout. The headline was to be 'Asquith – A National Danger' (Marlowe later altered 'Asquith' to 'The Limpets'– the men who clung to power) 'The police will be after you all,' said Northcliffe happily. Then he left for Totteridge; crises drew him to his mother. Over the weekend the Government was crumbling, and on Monday an anti-Asquith leader in the *Times* helped to sever any last hope of agreement between Asquith and Lloyd George. The leader was written by Dawson, apparently without consultation. By Thursday evening, Lloyd George was Prime Minister. On the Friday he found time to invite Northcliffe to the seat of power, using Aitken as intermediary on the telephone. Northcliffe's reply paved the way for a stormy future between the Anglo-Irishman and the Welshman: 'Lord Northcliffe sees no advantage in any interview between him and the Prime Minister at the present juncture.' The *Mail* gave a parting kick to Asquith and his colleagues with a page of pictures headed 'The passing of the failures'. It showed the fallen Ministers emerging from the Reform Club in twos and threes, top-hatted and grim-faced, pasted over with sneering captions. There was no doubt in Northcliffe's mind that when he pushed, things fell down. Even before the Government collapsed, he was telephoning Cecil and saying: 'Who killed cock robin?' 'You did,' answered Cecil dutifully. Northcliffe's system of alternate praise and blame was too crude to be called manipulation, but it had a certain effectiveness. The ins and outs of the political power-game were immaterial to his growing opinion of what he could achieve. 'Heaven forbid that I should ever be in Downing Street,' he wrote to a correspondent in January 1917. 'I believe the independent newspaper to be one of the future forms of government.'

With this arrogant philosophy, Northcliffe was a danger to any Prime Minister's peace of mind. In April there was talk of asking him to be Ambassador in Washington; in May Lloyd George invited him to head a permanent British War Mission in the United States, and he accepted. It was suggested that the Prime Minister wanted to remove Northcliffe from the London scene. The appointment was violently attacked, in and out of Parliament, by those who saw Northcliffe as a menace to public life. His standing was low with orthodox politicians. (When Lloyd George came to power in 1916, the Conservative leaders had made it a condition of joining the new Coalition that Northcliffe should not be in it.) But Northcliffe was on his way to New York before the storm broke.

The American post was onerous. It involved co-ordinating the work of British buying agencies, and liaising with the US Government. Northcliffe had prepared for it with a mixture of practical measures and grandiosity. *Times* and *Mail* were instructed to print no criticism of anything American while he was away. He told Lloyd George that he could leave the country only if assured that Sutton (now chairman of the Amalgamated Press), Dawson of the *Times*, and Marlowe of the *Mail*, were not to be called up for military service in his absence; for good measure, the Prime Minister was given details of the £5,350,000 shareholders' capital for which Northcliffe was responsible. He told Sir Robert Hudson, a friend of the Northcliffes, that he had a premonition he would not see England again, and asked him to look after Lady Northcliffe if he was killed. Sir Robert was his wife's lover; perhaps then, certainly later. Northcliffe feared assassination by Germans in the United States, so he said. The risk that his ship would be torpedoed was more real: German submarines were causing catastrophic losses in the North Atlantic, and the convoy system that prevented them was only just being forced on a reluctant Admiralty by Lloyd George. On board ship, he wrote a circular letter to his family, giving a rose-coloured view of his life:

My private objects are selfish. My sweet mother is nearing her eightieth year and she and I have always delighted in each other's companionship. For the last few years I have lived much with her, slept in the room next to her. Her happiness and my happiness and health have benefited by my sleeping at Totteridge, for in London I sleep ill and my health goes downhill. My domestic life, despite the children that never came, is smooth and happy ... We have been married twenty-seven years, not many childless couples so happily. My work has been absorbing, always. My *Times* and *Daily Mail* and other newspapers, my periodicals, the Newfoundland adventure (for which, together with the business side of the Amalgamated Press, the business foundation and success of the *Evening News* and *Daily Mail*, Harold is mainly responsible), all these have been my children. My journals have been burned and banned at times for doing what they believed to be their duty, but they have huge followings. These undertakings are filled with those who have proved to be my friends. I have other friendships of value. Our family is a united one, with the Mother as the centre ...

His watch was kept to 'Totteridge time'. so that he could picture what his mother was doing. 'Wouldn't I like to start straight back to my darling Mum, submarines or not!' he wrote to her. He thought of England, 'green, cloudy England', with lilac and hawthorne in flower. He thought of Elmwood, at one stage settled on his wife, but now his again – he had bought her a house of her own at Crowborough, in Sussex. He wrote to Sutton: 'If anything happens to me I want you to have it, and after you the Boy, if he be a good boy and cares for it. It's the nicest house I know and I love every inch of it, just as much as I shall hate every hour I am away from all my friends and haunts.' Mrs Wrohan's first son was nearly seven years old. The three children – Alfred, Geraldine, and Harold – stayed often at Elmwood; so did Mrs Wrohan. They couldn't be with him at Totteridge, since his mother either knew nothing of them, or chose to pretend they didn't exist. The family thought it unlikely she was ignorant of Northcliffe's girl friends, especially Mrs Wrohan; but she gave no hint of knowing, and everyone was careful to keep off the subject. Some members of the family went for years without learning that Mrs Wrohan had borne Northcliffe three children. Lady Northcliffe said later that she knew nothing of them for years, but probably wasn't telling the truth.

At Elmwood he had the ghost of a family life, in a house that his wife never visited, yet where they had once been happy. Much of his time there was spent in bed, telephoning and dictating. The bed had its back to the window. Brightness hurt his eyes, and it had become an obsession to avoid it; he even disliked white tablecloths. Work at Elmwood went on all the time, mixed up with golf and snoozes. Newspapers and letters arrived by the bagful, secretaries hovered and scribbled, the telephone was engaged for hours on end. Settling down for the night, he was lulled to sleep by a gramophone that a footman played outside his door.

There were no torpedoes; he arrived unscathed. In America, his dreams were of England, not the country where he was. He lived in a creeper-covered house filled with English books, on the shore of Long Island Sound; a painting of his mother, shipped out after him, hung on a wall. No one in London was allowed to forget how hard he worked for love of country, what sacrifices he was making. He undoubtedly worked hard at organising his mission and impressing a sense of urgency on the Americans. He went to and fro between New York and Washington, talked endlessly in private and in public, met President Wilson, Government officials, and industrialists, and dramatised the British need for help. No doubt a principal reason for appointing him was that he should act as a publicist while others wrestled with the technicalities of loans and purchases. His merit was that he was unlikely to offend his hosts by waving a Union Jack in their faces. He had no illusions about Britain's situation: 'I am sent forth literally to *beg* for assistance of all kinds,' he wrote on the voyage, adding that 'on the scale on which I am being sent forth to plead, it looks as though the British nation will be in pawn to the United States.' He had been hearing about American industrial output since 1900. 'These resolute people will not stop till they have Kanned the Kaiser,' he wrote to Sutton later. 'It is my duty to prevent any break between us and them, and to use every ounce of their vast chemical and engineering resources for winning.' His view of business America was the one that persists among many British people today, that the country is rich and dynamic, yet curiously inefficient. 'Much as I delight in these people – and they are a splendid people,' he wrote in another letter to Sutton, 'they are the greatest nation of time-wasters

on God's earth. Life here, as you know, is a combination
of ridiculous rush and waste of time.' According to Russell
Wakefield, who was with him on an earlier trip to the United
States, Northcliffe disliked and rather despised the Americans.
In some moods he probably did. This was not his mood in 1917.
His only recorded quarrel during his five months' tour of duty
was with the British Ambassador in Washington, Sir Cecil
Spring Rice, who resented Northcliffe's presence.

By the autumn of 1917, Northcliffe had done his work as a
public-relations man and was becoming bored. Lord Reading
(the former Rufus Isaacs) was sent out as chief financial
negotiator, and Northcliffe returned in November to the raw
winds and old wounds of London. He had suggested at one point
that Rothermere take his place in America, after Rothermere
suggested it to him. Lloyd George, anxious as he was to placate
the Harmsworths and utilise them for national or personal ends,
thought that people might begin to regard the War Mission as a
family affair. Nothing came of the idea. But the brothers' push-
fulness points to the way the Harmsworths were getting their
foot in the door.

Lloyd George's remark that the War Mission might appear a
family affair was made to Cecil, late one October afternoon as
they walked in Richmond Park, on the edge of London. Cecil's
career had been unexpectedly advanced. From being a back-
bench Liberal MP he became Under-Secretary at the Home
Office in 1915. In May 1917 he joined Lloyd George's private
staff, the first secretariat of its kind to be attached to a Prime
Minister. It was called the 'garden suburb', from the temporary
building of concrete and match-boarding in the garden of
Number 10 Downing Street, where the staff worked. Cecil was
industrious; he was also Northcliffe's brother, and thus a channel, a sounding-board and, hopefully, a hostage. He took to
Lloyd George, who dropped words in his ear about the Press
and how it did him an injustice. They strolled around Knights-
bridge, taking tea in a restaurant, while the Prime Minister
admired pretty babies, and turned the conversation to newspapers and why they hated him. They took the air in Richmond

Park. Lloyd George's car set them down at one gate and they strolled to another, a detective padding behind. An enemy agent, watching with binoculars, might have supposed some scheme of unimaginable secrecy to be afoot. All they did was talk about Northcliffe, and wonder whether the populace could eat chestnuts if driven to it. They paused under a tree where some had fallen, two amiable gentlemen in the dusk, far from the war.

Cecil rubbed shoulders with power but failed to acquire any for himself. His diary shows where his heart was; he preferred to chronicle his family and its doings, not the goings-on at Downing Street. He goes out to Poynters for a Sunday and helps with the weeding; the gardeners are at the war. Playing patience with his mother after dinner, they think they hear gunfire in France, a hundred miles away. He likes family picnics in woods – pork pies and milky eggs and a bottle of claret. London yesterday was nicer than London today. He had bought and restored Dr Johnson's house off Fleet Street. When he hears the 'Sweet Lavender' men outside his house in Montague Square, singing the last of the London Cries, he sends someone down to copy the words:

> Will you buy my sweet blooming lavender,
> Fresh gathered from the valley.
> Gathered fresh every morning.
> There are sixteen blue branches for a penny.

When a bomb hits Lord's cricket ground he is astonished; overwhelmed at such a thing. A bomb! At Lord's!

In politics, Cecil was a wrestler with details. Earlier in the war he had dealt with such matters as drunkenness among the workers and the damage it was supposed to be doing to the war effort. ('I am glad to see that your people are about to tackle the drink problem,' Northcliffe wrote sarcastically in March 1915, 'more especially as the cellars at Elmwood, St James's, and Sutton Place are extremely well stocked, like those, I have no doubt, of many such friends of the people as [Lloyd] George.') On a private visit to Ireland after the Easter Rising of 1916, Cecil acted as go-between with an influential Irish businessman, William Murphy, in an abortive attempt to enlist his help for negotiations that Lloyd George and Northcliffe had in mind.

Cecil was always the willing servant. He irritated Northcliffe by failing to exploit his opportunities for personal advancement. In May 1917, Lloyd George had offered him the post of Chief Whip, an office that an ambitious politician might have coveted. Cecil declined it for the very reason that would have made it attractive to many: it involved the holder in the business, now becoming an industry, of awarding honours and titles. Lloyd George was shrewdly aware of the powers of patronage; he used knighthoods at ten thousand pounds, baronetcies (thirty thousand pounds), and peerages (fifty thousand pounds upwards), to raise money for party funds. Cecil agonised between his inability to accept duties he found repugnant, and the difficulty of saying no without being offensive. He managed it well enough to be invited to join the Garden Suburb instead. It was the most decisive political gesture he ever made, assuring him of respect but little advancement. Northcliffe frequently urged him to speak up for himself. 'Those who don't ask don't get,' he wrote in November 1918, using his favoured phrase. Two months later, though not as a result of asking, Cecil was made Under-Secretary at the Foreign Office; a note from Lloyd George to his Foreign Secretary, A. J. Balfour, described him as 'an able, quiet fellow and the best I can think of'. Northcliffe saw it as a 'cunning Welsh attempt' to buy his support. He grumbled to his brother that he was too old to be an Under-Secretary (he was forty-nine), and it was 'not flattering to our family name'. But Cecil was incurably self-effacing. Colleagues smiled when they noticed that he would never use Foreign Office stationery for his personal letters, or dictate them to an official secretary. His lapses were those of an honest, lazy man. Once, in 1921, he slipped off from the Foreign Office to fish the river Wye near the Welsh border, and forgot to arrange for someone to answer his questions in the House of Commons. Soon he slipped out of politics altogether and devoted the remainder of a long, restful life to being an English gentleman. He scarcely seems to have belonged to the same family as Northcliffe and Rothermere. In 1917 and 1918, these were making themselves heard more than ever. It would have been difficult to find two men in England who were less self-effacing.

18

Public Prosecutor

A MEMBER OF PARLIAMENT who launched an attack on Northcliffe near the end of the war said that 'ten years ago he saw that power was departing from this House. His great conception was to seize it for the Press'. It is unlikely that Northcliffe saw anything of the kind. Wartime politics provided him with another area in which to assert himself. He was, by now, well versed in the ways of crushing opposition. He showed little discrimination; it was simply that he had to master whatever he touched. His nature was raw, egocentric, immature. Its strong appetites, that were often contrary to his outward behaviour, had to be mastered. He was sexually promiscuous. He had a sadistic streak. There was always a need to keep himself in check, to stay in control. His rages welled up from below and people called them 'brainstorms'. One of his staff, Frederick Wile, wrote in 1915 that 'five minutes later he was invariably as gentle as a woman, forgiving as a lover, as generous as a doting parent'.

His breakdown of 1910 may have given Northcliffe a glimpse of the chaos within himself that he dreaded. Alongside his need to rule himself was the need to prove his capacity by ruling others. To impose his will on them was to reassure himself that it was in good working order, ready to deal with his private demons. The way in which the idea of *whiteness* attached itself to Northcliffe through his life can be seen as a reflection of his desire to stay aloof from the black side of his nature, a shining prince on a shining steed, untainted by the mud beneath the flying hooves. It recurs constantly, from the early days when he wore light suits instead of the lower-middle-class black. At Elmwood in the 1890s, a woman writer had noted that he looked as though he played tennis all his life. Thirty years later an essayist saw him 'dressed in white flannels, and looking as if he had just come from a Turkish bath'. A reporter who stayed at Elmwood recalled him rushing down a corridor in the early morning, wearing white pyjamas and trailing a handful of white galley-proofs, looking 'like a snowstorm'. The Pullman-car staff who knew him from Continental trips called him 'the white chief'. His favourite flower was white jasmine. He liked white hats.

From about 1915, when he was fifty years old, the tensions within Northcliffe began to affect his behaviour more noticeably. Stories of his wayward nature had circulated for years. Once, dissatisfied with picture reproduction at the *Mail*, he ordered everyone concerned – block-makers, photographers, sub-editors – to stand in a line, the tallest at one end and the shortest at the other. He lectured them on the defects of the picture page, then announced that he was putting the tallest man in charge, and if necessary would work his way through them all, by height. The tallest man happened to be a technician who did the job to Northcliffe's satisfaction. This appetite for making authority triumph over reason became sharper. Hannen Swaffer saw a troubling episode one day in Northcliffe's room at the *Times*. Swaffer, editor of the *Weekly Dispatch*, had an independent turn of mind; Northcliffe reserved his iron humour for weaker creatures. Swaffer handed him a proof with a joking bow. Northcliffe asked what he was doing, and Swaffer replied: 'Bowing to a peer of the realm.'

'You don't know how to,' said Northcliffe, and told one of his staff – probably a secretary – to show him. The man took the proof and bowed.

'Lower still,' said Northcliffe.

The man bowed lower.

'Kneel, darn you, kneel!'

The man knelt.

'There you are,' said Northcliffe, 'I can make them do anything I like.'

Not everyone saw him like this – or, if they did, they pretended to shrug it off as one of the Chief's amusing quirks. For every man he insulted or humiliated there was another he spoke to encouragingly or soothed with a bonus, a promotion, a free trip abroad. Some were bought; some liked him for himself.

Either way, his undisputed authority within his newspapers makes his need to keep exercising it the more noticeable. Andrew Caird found him the rudest man he had ever met and added that Northcliffe expected his staff to rise from their chairs when he entered a room. The humiliating of senior executives in front of juniors was a routine procedure. Harold Snoad, one of Northcliffe's secretaries (later managing director of Amalgamated Press), remembers it happening to Caird – 'Having to listen was one of my jobs. I disliked him for that intensely.' Lewis Macleod, literary editor of the *Mail*, was regularly persecuted. A 1918 communiqué said: 'This is the last occasion on which I can tolerate Macleod's gross neglect and carelessness. He will read this message out to the editorial conference on Monday.' Presumably he did. Northcliffe was developing into a tyrant. An elderly sub-editor, lunching at Elmwood with the editorial staff of the *Weekly Dispatch*, contradicted him about the number of times he, the sub-editor, had been shipwrecked. He was sacked at the end of the week. The 'telephone spies' were another sign of Northcliffe's rampant will – or rampant fears. For years it had been said, half seriously, that phone conversations at the newspapers were monitored by telephonists who reported anything of interest, particularly about the Chief. He was said to give them presents, including fur coats (not improbable, on his scale of giving: his private accounts while he was in America with the War Mission include the item: 'Gifts to Mission ladies towards fur coats: four hundred and fifty dollars'). By 1918 there was more talk of Northcliffe's 'spies', telephonic and otherwise. A formal order was given to the head telephonists at all the offices, warning staff that 'in the event of any private conversations taking place on any of the telephone lines, they are to be recorded'.

Northcliffe saw himself at the centre of a structure that was utterly his. He was incapable of seeing it otherwise. Evelyn Wrench founded the Overseas Club (later League) and enlisted Northcliffe's support. Soon Northcliffe was calling himself the inventor and founder, using its files to circularise members, asking them to subscribe to the *Overseas Daily Mail*. Wrench eventually disengaged his league from Northcliffe's grasp. The egocentricity hardened over the years until it became a caricature. Northcliffe's face went bleak when he met an American who had crossed the Atlantic more times than he had. He could write to Garvin (January 1918) that a doctor (a 'very famous doctor') had warned him: 'The vanity of middle-aged men hastens their end.' He was capable of interpreting it only as advice to take more leisure. He couldn't see that simple vanity was not his trouble – in the right place, at the right time, he was able to laugh at himself – but that he was morbidly, consumingly self-centred. It was hopeless to expect him to see it. It enclosed him. The only point for speculation was where his egocentricity would lead him.

Without a 1914, Northcliffe might have remained the ego-maniac of Fleet Street. The war fulfilled his prophecies; it created the need for dynamic figures to help focus the moods of an embattled nation, and propelled him into new regions. Once he returned from the American War Mission, he was convinced of his destiny as a statesman who had no need to bother with being a politician. There was much speculation about what job he would be offered. Gossip in the clubs even suggested that he could be Prime Minister: the professional flatterers were at work. The call came soon, but to a more modest appointment. On 15 November, after a few days back in London, he was invited to lunch at Number 10 Downing Street. Lloyd George sounded him on whether he would accept the newly created post of Air Minister. A separate Air Force was about to be formed, to replace the Army's Royal Flying Corps. Northcliffe would take over an enhanced version of the duties performed by Lord Cowdray as president of the Air Board. Lloyd George was left with the impression that Northcliffe would accept the appointment if it was formally offered. The same day, Northcliffe wrote a letter of contemptuous refusal, which he published in the next morning's *Times* and via the Press Association. He referred to the Prime Minister's 'repeated invitation that I should take charge of the new Air Ministry'. Accusing the Government of dallying with urgent matters, he said he could 'do better work if I maintain my independence and am not gagged by loyalty that I do not feel towards the whole of your Administration'. Northcliffe's official biographers suggest he was 'driven to speak out in defiance of formal usage by an overriding sense of the public interest'. This is improbable. He was demonstrating his strength; perhaps he was insulted at being offered nothing better. Cowdray, who learnt what had happened when he read it in the papers, was mortified, and never forgave Lloyd George.

It would be reasonable to suppose that Lloyd George never forgave Northcliffe. But Lloyd George was prepared to put up with a great deal from a Press lord. The relationship between politicians and newspaper proprietors, controlling a large-circulation Press that might (or might not) be able to sway millions of voters, had yet to crystallise. Northcliffe was a force of unknown potential. Presently Lloyd George offered or at least sanctioned another official appointment. In the meantime, the Prime Minister thumbed through the list of public figures who might accept the shop-soiled Air Ministry, and chose Rothermere. Rothermere accepted. Newspaper government was carried a stage further.

Rothermere's story is a distant echo of his brother's. The family's Number 2 man of affairs, he came a poor second. As a newspaper proprietor, he ran the *Mirror*, the Glasgow *Record*, and a new weekly, the *Sunday Pictorial*, without his brother's touch. Early in 1915 he was manoeuvring to buy the *Observer*, and was writing confidently to friends to say that he was about to become the proprietor. Nothing came of it. A few years later he was offered a share in the *Daily Express* by Max Aitken, newly created Lord Beaverbrook, but declined because it would have meant competing with Northcliffe and the *Mail*. He was much influenced by Beaverbrook. Rothermere's ambition, like his character, was both blunter and lighter than Northcliffe's. He saw politicians as important men for whom he would do favours and who would do favours for him: I tell my newspapers to say nice things about you, you let my friends have jobs or honours. The element of cheerful banditry in Northcliffe's dealings with Westminster was absent; Rothermere's were merely sordid. Lloyd George found him more agreeable to work with than his brother, although allowance had to be made for his shifts of direction and his awkward manner.

Lloyd George put him in charge of the army clothing department, where there had been scandals. Rothermere claimed to have ended them. Cecil called to see him in his suite at the Ritz, and found him complaining that soldiers' uniforms were in danger because Jewish tailors were running away from the danger of bombs in the East End. The middle-class prejudice against Jews, strong in pre-1914 England, often stirs under the surface of the Harmsworths. In November 1917 Rothermere accepted the Air Ministry, an appointment that led to nothing but trouble. His private affairs were unhappy; perhaps he hoped to bury them under the labours of office. In November the previous year, his second son, Vere, a naval lieutenant, was killed in a land battle. Now, a year later, Vyvyan, a captain in the Irish Guards, was severely wounded at the Battle of Cambrai. Rothermere's loneliness was intensified; his wife, Lilian, was by now leading her own life in France as a cultural hostess, encouraging soldier poets and painters.

At the Air Ministry, Rothermere met intrigue and obstinacy that needed tact to overcome. He didn't have any. The Army was reluctant to hand over the Royal Flying Corps, under its spiky commander, General 'Boom' Trenchard. Trenchard was recalled from France to be chief of the new air staff. He went to the Ritz to meet Rothermere, and found Northcliffe with him. The brothers spoke ominously of a Press campaign they were about to launch against the generals. Northcliffe had cooled towards generals, perhaps since his nephew was wounded, and had been heard to refer to Cambrai as 'one of the most ghastly stories in English history'. The brothers wanted Trenchard to cooperate with them, but he was horrified at such backstairs intriguing. Everyone behaved with grotesque clumsiness. The RFC and the naval air service were due to amalgamate and become the Air Force on 1 April 1918. Rothermere and Trenchard worked unharmoniously towards that end. Vyvyan Harmsworth died of wounds on 12 February; this and his other bereavement must colour any view of Rothermere, in 1918 and for the rest of his life. Relations with Trenchard worsened. Rothermere was angry because two staff officers at the Ministry were also MPs, who criticised him in Parliament. Trenchard, in turn, justifiably suspected Rothermere of intriguing with other officers. Evelyn Wrench, who was Rothermere's private secretary at the time, heard indiscreet conversations when his chief had been drinking. He told Northcliffe about it. Northcliffe sounded relieved: for a moment he had thought that Wrench was about to say Harold was going mad. There had been insanity in the family, added Northcliffe. Rothermere was involved in disagreements great and small: how to tell one German bomber from another by the sound of its engines; how many aircraft could be spared for anti-submarine patrols. By the middle of March, Trenchard had had enough. He sent his resignation to Rothermere on 19 March, only to be told that Rothermere himself meant to go soon. The matter was further complicated by the German spring offensive, which began two days later. The War Cabinet accepted Trenchard's resignation on 12 April.

Rothermere – having warned that he was going too – then contrived to go in the worst possible manner. Invited to comment on Trenchard's version of why he had resigned, he did so in a memorandum which he sent with a covering letter to Sir Maurice Hankey, secretary to the Cabinet, on 16 April. The memorandum was strongly worded: 'I frankly told [Trenchard] that under no circumstances would I continue in the same office with him and that if my health allowed me to remain, the question of choosing between myself and himself would be a matter for the War Cabinet.' The covering letter, which Rothermere unwisely said could be circulated to the Cabinet, was stronger still: 'As Chief of the Air Staff [Trenchard] was perfectly impossible. He is entirely without imagination, and although he had been in this office for three months he had prepared no strategic plans of any kind whatsoever. If there ever was a case of a square peg in a round hole, it is to be found in the appointment of General Trenchard ...' Bonar Law, the deputy Prime Minister, saw what Rothermere had written, and was shocked at such unparliamentary language. He telephoned him and said: 'Harold, I think you ought to resign.' Rothermere wrote a letter of resignation in which he continued his offensive against Trenchard; was persuaded by Beaverbrook to throw it away and replace it, two days later, with an innocuous version; and departed on 25 April. Passers-by in the Strand heard cheering from the windows of the Hotel Cecil, where the Ministry was housed, and saw Air Force officers leaning out and waving newspapers. Asked what they were celebrating, one of them shouted: 'A victory at home. Lord Rothermere has gone.'

Rothermere's reign was brief and inglorious. Between his

SIGNOR SOAPO TRUSTI, THE CLUMSY MAGICIAN.

Ladies and gentlemen,—This is the most wonderful trick in the world! I take this pound of soap, weighing sixteen ounces, and remove two ounces without you noticing the difference. I also raise the price and you don't know as I do it so cleverly. Then again—" (Loud cries of "Fake!" "Cheat!" "Robber!" "Give us our money back!" etc., etc.)

[*From the "Daily Mirror."*]

The great soap war. One of the many anti-Lever cartoons from the *Daily Mirror* that helped to cost Northcliffe's papers a fortune in libel damages.

Below left: Auntie Miller with Fred Wood, family friend. His diary disappeared mysteriously.

Below right: The faithful George Sutton. He began as Northcliffe's secretary, and ended as confidant and highly-paid executive.

To darling mother from her first 11.4.1913

Northcliffe at the height of his powers. He loved to remind his mother that he was her 'first-born'.

With his mother, just before he left for America in 1921.

bereavement and his clumsy temperament, he had neither the finesse nor the energy to deal with a difficult fellow like Trenchard. He went back to his newspapers, sustained by the promise of a viscountcy, which would match the one awarded to Northcliffe when he returned from the American mission. King George v, who disliked honours for newspaper proprietors, blocked it temporarily. Rothermere had to wait until the following year before the King could be persuaded; meanwhile he wrote to Northcliffe that he 'believed' there was something in the rumour that he was to be made a viscount, adding grandly: 'On the principle of refusing nothing I shall accept it, although this kind of decoration has very little value in these times.'

Bringing up the rear in the matter of family honours came Leicester, fourth youngest in point of age, but ahead of Cecil in push, pull, contributions to party funds, or whatever it was (apart from the name Harmsworth) that decided an honour was due for a businessman and back-bench Member of Parliament nearing the age of fifty. A baronetcy for Leicester was announced on 3 June 1918. His sister Geraldine (who became Lady King the following year, when Rothermere contrived a knighthood for her husband) wrote to Leicester: 'In view of the paper shortage, I think the family ought to issue printed forms like Field Service postcards, viz.: Many congratulations on your being made Archbishop of Canterbury/Pope/Duke/Viscount/ Knight, etc.'

That was a joke. The honours that poured into the Harmsworths' pockets, the influence they saw themselves exerting, were real enough.

By the beginning of 1918, according to Beaverbrook's account, Northcliffe had put himself beyond the pale of office by his rude refusal of the Air Ministry. Northcliffe, on the contrary, let it be known that he was still regarded by Lloyd George as a candidate for a Government job. He told people he had been offered a Cabinet post, unnamed, early in the year. Wickham Steed believed he was offered the War Ministry some time that year. In February a Ministry of Information, in effect a ministry for directing British propaganda overseas, was set up. The post went to Beaverbrook, not Northcliffe, who then accepted a job from Beaverbrook as a propaganda administrator, but insisted that he be responsible direct to Lloyd George. Northcliffe implied that the propaganda post left him free in a way that a job in the Government would not have done.

Appointed Director of Propaganda in Enemy Countries (as opposed to propaganda in neutral countries), he set up office in a London mansion, Crewe House. He was chronically unwell. As his deputy he appointed a Canadian he had brought back from America, Campbell Stuart. Stuart was a personable young bachelor, aged thirty-two, who endeared himself to Northcliffe, and quickly became more trusted than anyone in his circle except George Sutton. He was no sooner back in London with his new employer than he received a knighthood (honours descended in a steady shower on Northcliffe's entourage. Presently Sir Campbell Stuart was joined by, among others, Sir Andrew Caird and Sir George Sutton, Bt). In his new capacity as official propagandist, Northcliffe oiled the wheels for other men's ideas. Wickham Steed, an authority on the Balkans, came from the *Times* and directed the Austro-Hungarian section. He persuaded Northcliffe to persuade the Government to proclaim that after the war, the 'subject races' of the Habsburgs – Poles, Czechs, southern Slavs, and the rest – would get their independence. This propaganda of promises was designed to reassure the enemy and weaken his will to go on fighting. Idealism was mixed up with expediency. H. G. Wells, in charge of the German section, pressed for a 'soft' approach, which envisaged a reformed Germany eventually admitted to the happy family of good countries, a League of Free Nations. Northcliffe, inasmuch as he listened at all to the babble of ideas at Crewe House, was not interested in the prospect of being nice to Germans. When Wells complained in July about the unwisdom of a hate campaign against Germany, adding that Northcliffe's penny newspapers were helping to make Britain 'nervy, hopeless, irritable, and altogether rotten', Northcliffe snapped:

Let me say at once that I entirely agree with the policy adopted by my newspapers, which I do not propose to discuss with anyone. I have not wandered about Prussia for two years without learning something, and if you will wait you will find that I will unearth much sinister and active Prussianism in England.

Northcliffe saw German influences all around him. So did many people in 1918, after four years of war that showed no signs of ending. What Northcliffe did, once again, was to catch the mood and feed it back to the public. His mood was theirs. He personally passed information to Scotland Yard about a man who worked in an explosives factory, because his hobby was photography and German was spoken in his house. He looked for code messages in the personal column of the *Times*. Yet there is suddenly a breath of aimlessness about Northcliffe. For the first time since the war began he seems to pause in his stride in 1918. It was one of those years that in the old days, he might have spent abroad in white villas or fishing on quiet lakes. He was ill when he received the Crewe House appointment in February and was still recovering in May; officially from influenza and bronchitis, though friends talked of acute depression. 'There is an impression about that you are not at all well,' wrote Rothermere in the early summer. Much of his time as nominal boss of Crewe House was spent at Elmwood or fishing in Gloucestershire. His throat troubled him. For the moment he even had little to say about Lloyd George. He wrote to Beaverbrook on 23 April about 'this alleged War Cabinet', but in letters to Lord Reading in March and May, he spoke well of the Prime Minister. 'He is complete master of the country if he only knew it,' he wrote on 26 May.

In August, according to Beaverbrook, Northcliffe applied for office, demanding a leading post in the Cabinet. No one has ever confirmed the story, but Beaverbrook was not writing from hearsay: he and Reading, he said, were Northcliffe's intermediaries. According to Beaverbrook, Sir Campbell Stuart made some phone calls about the matter during a journey to Scotland. Stuart later denied that he made the journey. But this part of the story is not material. Northcliffe, Beaverbrook insisted, sought to become 'Lord President of the Council in a Lloyd George-Northcliffe administration'. Lloyd George said no.

Northcliffe was approaching a crisis of mid-life, perhaps the depression that can go with the final realisation that certain achievements are beyond one's capacity. Some self-control had slackened. He blurted out his heart's desire. But whether he made the demand or not, his acts from now on are increasingly open to sinister interpretation. Many of the things he will do in the next few years are perfectly normal; some, an increasing proportion, are abnormal. The word 'megalomania', like the word 'brainstorm', is whispered about: meaningless in itself, yet reflecting what people feel when they observe his rages, moods, and sweeping demands. The swift turn of world events flung him back into action: having been at the centre of war, he must now be at the centre of peace. In late September, Germany's allies began to collapse. At the start of October, Northcliffe told the Prime Minister that he would support a new Lloyd George administration only if he were shown in advance a written list of those who would be in it, and approved. Again, Lloyd George said no. Rothermere, who saw nothing strange in the idea of government by consent of the Harmsworths, wrote to his brother: 'Of course, at the present he may be elated at the outlook and have a fit of independence.' Lloyd George could afford to brush arrogance aside. He had already referred to Northcliffe in politics as a grasshopper and a flea. Now Lloyd George was about to rise above every one as the man who had won the war.

Northcliffe's next move was through his propaganda department (renamed, during the summer, the British War Mission). At the beginning of November, with the end of the war in sight, he wrote to Lloyd George to suggest that the department should coordinate propaganda, both before and during the victors' peace conference. The two men met on 2 or 3 November. The precise extent of Northcliffe's peace-conference demands has been much argued. Lloyd George said that Northcliffe wanted a place in the British delegation. When this was rumoured, Northcliffe denied it. Steed agreed with Northcliffe. Dawson agreed with Lloyd George. The argument turns on whether Northcliffe formally asked to join the delegation, a matter now inconveniently buried under the shifting relationship between an opportunist Press lord and an opportunist Prime Minister. What is certain is that Northcliffe wanted to play an important part at the peace talks. Writing to Cecil on 4 November he told his brother he should seek higher office, adding: 'I am asking nothing for myself beyond hard work at the Peace Conference.' But he was not appointed to handle the publicity, or whatever it was that he hoped for. A long article called 'From War to Peace' signed by Northcliffe appeared in *Mail* and *Times* on 4 November. This was a straightforward summary of the terms on which the war should end, based on the officially approved propaganda that Crewe House had been scattering behind the German lines in leaflets from the air. It was written by his staff and he showed little interest in its content, which was milder than anything he personally had in mind for the Hun. When a colleague was reading the draft aloud, Northcliffe told him not to bother: he was thinking about how to handle the publicity. Probably he commissioned 'From War to Peace' so as to involve himself publicly in the policy-making. The article was cabled around the world at his expense, and appeared in hundreds of newspapers. The *Daily Mail* at the same time was attacking Lord Milner for having sounded too lenient towards Germany. Northcliffe wanted it both ways; he wanted to speak as a private Press lord one minute, an official propagandist the next. His critics nearly burst.

The war was over; the air buzzed with advice about what to do next. An austere leading article in the *Mail* on 12 November tolled the bell for the dead: 'The bravest and best are under the soil in France. The redeemed land holds its redeemers. The spring has gone out of our year with the loss of that "swift and joyful generation" which welcomed the call and obeyed.' Alongside it was a sprinkling of the 'little articles' that Northcliffe made a feature of the leader page. Two were about women, who were increasingly to be found in headlines: 'Woman Makes a New World' and 'How the Women Waited'. W. L. George, 'the well-known sociologist', soon to incorporate Northcliffe in his novel *Caliban*, wrote about people's perplexity in wondering what they should do next, the fear that 'after so much pain, delight, love, and hatred we may find life rather flat'. For the moment there was to be no shortage of hatred. Northcliffe divined the national mood and played on it. Germany must be made to pay for her sins. A leading article in the *Mail* on 30 October headed 'Our Softies and the German Lie Factory' had warned of German deviousness. It quoted a remark of a German living in Switzerland, 'They will cheat you yet, those Junkers!' Between the Armistice of 11 November and the first post-war election of 14 December, when Lloyd George and his Coalition offered themselves against an Opposition of Labour Party and others, the *Mail* harried the Prime Minister. He was told to make Germany 'pay up', to see that the Kaiser stood trial, and

to introduce rigid immigration laws to keep 'undesirables' out
of Britain. Dawson was nagged into adding the voice of the
Times, though not as whole-heartedly as Northcliffe wished.
Public feeling about Germany edged Lloyd George into promises of retribution that he would have preferred not to make.
Northcliffe's was the popular voice; it was also the loudest. His
post-war campaign for revenge against Germany was the worst
cause he ever advocated. It was not even a simple case of hating
the old enemy. What lent the campaign venom was Northcliffe's
desire to punish Lloyd George, who had dared to spurn him. It
was malice in action, disguised as high principle.

Northcliffe's voice was growing louder. He told a party of
visiting American editors on 29 November that they came from
'a country where the controllers of independent newspapers are
regarded as men of super-Cabinet rank', and went on to speak
of 'the individual newspaper controller like myself who believes
that, except under circumstances which rarely occur, and do not
at this moment exist, it is his duty to decline office'. Any newspaper proprietor who went to the peace conference in an official
capacity, said Northcliffe, 'would be as effectively gagged as he
would be if he were willing to accept a place in this Cabinet'.

He was often at Elmwood, worried about his cough and his
throat, where he had developed a lump. Later on he said that he
had been ill throughout November and December. Dawson was
bombarded with messages – late in the evening, early in the
morning. They talked at Elmwood; met in London. Northcliffe,
telling everyone he had rejected 'high office' so that the *Times*
might be free, was afraid that reactionary Tory Ministers in the
Coalition would hamper Lloyd George's attempts at social reform, and so encourage revolution among returning soldiers: a
real fear at the time. Dawson – who, as his proprietor divined,
was not a particularly loyal servant – told Milner (who promptly
told Lloyd George) that Northcliffe's attacks on the Government were the outcome of his 'restlessness and vanity'. He showed
signs of strain. A journalist arrived at Elmwood while he was on
the phone to the *Times*. 'What have you done with the moon?'
Northcliffe was shouting. 'I said the moon – the *moon*. Someone
has moved the moon. If it's moved again, whoever does it is
fired.' He slammed down the receiver and explained that 'some
wretch' at Printing House Square had moved the weather report.

The result of the general election in December was an over-
whelming victory for Lloyd George. Northcliffe had been successful in prodding the Prime Minister into punitive attitudes,
but he was not pleased to find the voters ignoring his advice. He
told Dawson it was the fault of the *Times* for not having done as
he said. Dawson heard with relief that his owner was to spend
two or three months abroad for health reasons. It was January,
the month in London that Northcliffe hated. He moved south
through France with a valet and a secretary, pausing at
Fontainebleau to fire off more rockets. Dawson's crime in
Northcliffe's eyes was not that he was too kind to the Germans
but that he was too kind to Lloyd George, who, according to
Northcliffe, was both timid and cunning, like all the Welsh. His
list of Ministers, announced in January, infuriated Northcliffe.
There was talk at Westminster that Northcliffe was out to
destroy the Prime Minister; even that he possessed some
damaging Marconi letters written by Lloyd George.

But behind the angry newspaper proprietor, breathing fire at
the politicians, was a tired man looking for somewhere to rest.
He stayed at Harold's villa, La Dragonnière, the only one open
in the area in January 1919. 'From my bedroom window,' he
wrote, 'I looked across the bay of Monte Carlo and suddenly
there came out of the sky a waterplane which literally dashed
down upon the pale blue Mediterranean as a wild duck descends
upon a Norfolk Broad. I never saw anything prettier of the kind.'
He was producing a series of circular letters for his family,
'Leaves from a Peasant's Diary'. His day began with a call at
five minutes to seven. He shaved between 7.20 and 7.29, listening to the bells in the cathedral of Monte Carlo. A throat-session
followed, inhaling 'fragrant steam' from a china device called a
Zeppelin, a German invention, before breakfast: tiny oranges
from the garden, two eggs, fresh fish. Then he read the *Continental Daily Mail*, the only British newspaper available in
Paris on the day of publication. Steed, temporarily resident in
Paris, wrote the leading articles, and sent Northcliffe a daily
private memorandum. Steed's editorials, read with respect by
delegates, owed nothing to Northcliffe. 'It is a bitter disappointment to me not to be there,' wrote Northcliffe in his diary.
'However, the approach of the first anniversary of my throat
reminds me that my first great duty is to get well ... 9 o'clock

sees me en route in my car for Menton, where at my doctor's
all sorts of things are pumped into my lungs and injected under
my skin for nearly an hour.' Presently he moved inland to a
farmhouse and spent days walking in the hills. He noted pro-
cessions of caterpillars and humming-bird moths; a man showed
him a trapdoor spider. 'Yesterday,' he wrote in mid-February,
'I had to go to Avignon to meet the Chief of my Peace Conference staff in Paris'. He stayed the night. 'There is an air of faded
grandeur about the Hotel de l'Europe, which must at one time
have been the home of some great magnate. As I awoke next
morning in the large salon, with faded red silk hangings on the
walls and a huge chandelier which must have held a hundred
candles, I wished myself back at Elmwood, or my little cottage
in the Valley of Gorbio.'

Northcliffe was romancing. The 'Chief of my Peace Conference staff' was Steed; Northcliffe was meeting him on board the
Rhone ferryboat at Avignon to offer him the editorship of the
Times. Dawson had resigned amid the usual flurry of messages.
Rothermere is said to have intrigued against him, repeating to his
brother indiscreet remarks that Dawson, an inveterate diner-out,
had made about Northcliffe. Steed, aged forty-seven but looking
older, the cosmopolitan with the pointed beard, took on, with
relish, the job of editing the *Times* and supervising policy for all
Northcliffe's papers. Steed was more acceptable than Dawson:
he mistrusted Lloyd George; he had no time for the remedies of
reactionary politicians, the 'Old Gang' of Tories that so infuriated Northcliffe. From Avignon, Northcliffe returned to the
Mediterranean, to be sent immediately by his doctor to the mild
air of Pau, in the Pyrenees; it was ten years since he was there
last, with Mrs Wrohan. Soon after this he made a will: his fourth,
not counting codicils, succeeding those of 1908, 1910, and 1913.
Once again this provided for his estate to be turned into a
source of income, divided into one-hundredth parts and various-
ly distributed. He would retain a kind of power over the recipi-
ents, instead of letting them make off with the capital. Lady
Northcliffe was to receive twenty-five hundredths, as well as
ten thousand pounds cash. All his employees were to have
something. Women were still prominent in the named bequests.
There was no mention of the three children, who were already
provided for in settlements. Like its predecessors, the document

was long and unwieldy. It was witnessed by two doctors, one of them an eminent throat man from London who was in attendance, as reported by Northcliffe in a message cabled to twenty-eight members of the family and friends: 'REPORT OF LONDON SPECIALIST ON LORD NORTHCLIFFE'S THROAT WAS MOST SATISFACTORY AND EVENTUAL CURE ONLY A QUESTION OF TIME AND CARE.' Louise Owen, the faithful secretary of nearly twenty years before, was also there; she was down in the will for two hundredths.

Early April saw him still in the south, giving instructions that the housekeeper at Elmwood was to have all the help she needed 'We shall then have the original establishment as it was thirty years ago.' There must be constant hot water; the garden must have melons and violets. But he was not slipping into retirement yet; it might have been better for him if he had. He moved near Paris, to the familiar Hotel de France et d'Angleterre at Fontainebleau, where the waiters, he said, had manners like bishops' chaplains. Still hoping to bluff people that he was privy to the statesmen's deliberations, he wrote to a friend: 'Of course I am on the inside of the conference.' Wickham Steed's reports from the Peace Conference had confirmed his worst fears: Lloyd George did not mean to exact the 'last farthing' from Germany by way of reparations. On 7 April Northcliffe ordered the *Mail* to print daily above its leading article the full version of its earlier warning: 'They will cheat you yet, those Junkers! Having won half the world by bloody murder, they are going to win the other half with tears in their eyes, crying for mercy.'

The leading article on 7 April declared that 'Germany went to war for world dominion ... Having lost the war by fighting, the Germans hope to win a favourable peace by whining.' Northcliffe had exposed Germany and the war; he still meant to expose Germany and the peace. In a letter to Rothermere on 10 April, he noted that Lloyd George saw too many people and had too little time for reflection: charges that could have been laid at his own door for the previous twenty years. 'I do not believe the tales of German hard-upness,' he added. Next day he sent Rothermere a long memorandum of his views, attacking Lloyd George and warning of 'the pressure of the international Jew' at the Peace Conference. 'Thirty-second anniversary of my wedding day' was typed, inaccurately, across the front page.*

* Northcliffe was married in 1888.

Rothermere, who was friendly with Lloyd George, crossed to France to see his brother, perhaps with a conciliatory message. But, within a few days, Lloyd George lost his temper. On 8 April several hundred Conservative Members of Parliament had sent him a telegram, urging him to 'present the bill in full' to Germany; it was forwarded by Kennedy Jones, Northcliffe's former editor, now an MP. Northcliffe probably inspired the telegram through Jones. On 16 April Lloyd George turned on his critics in a dazzling speech to the House of Commons about the Peace Conference, using Northcliffe as a punchbag. For the signatories of the telegram he had bland words; for Northcliffe, scorn and derision, though his name was not spoken once. In a reference to the 'War and Peace' article that Northcliffe had signed, Lloyd George said it made no mention of reparations in the wide sense now being demanded. 'There was no reparation for damaged houses – not even at Broadstairs.' Laughing MPs settled back to enjoy a Lloyd George spectacular. 'Here today,' cried the Prime Minister, 'jumping there tomorrow – there the next day. I had as soon rely on a grasshopper.' Next day the *Mail* reported it verbatim, down to the laughter. When a man was keenly disappointed, said Lloyd George, he was apt to think the world badly run. When he had deluded himself that he was the only man who could win the war, and received no call to direct the destinies of peace, he found it unnerving.

And then the war is won without him! There must be something wrong! And, of course, it must be the Government! At any rate, he is the only man to make the peace! The only people who get near him tell him so constantly, and so he prepares the peace terms in advance and he waits for the call (*Loud laughter*). It does not come. He retreats to sunny climes – waiting! Not a sound reaches the far-distant shore – (*laughter*) – to call him back to his great task of saving the world. What can you expect? He comes back and says, 'Well, now, I cannot see the disease, but I am sure it is there! (*Laughter*) It is bound to come!' Under these conditions I am prepared to make allowances, but let me say that when that kind of diseased vanity is carried to the point of sowing dissension between great allies whose unity is essential to the peace and happiness of the world ... then, I say, not even that kind of disease is a justification for so black a crime against humanity. (*Loud cheers*).

This was the most scathing attack ever made on Northcliffe.

At the words 'diseased vanity' Lloyd George tapped his forehead as though to suggest mental derangement. The *Mail* replied with restraint: 'Mr Lloyd George Overdoes It.' In the *Times* Wickham Steed ignored the jibes at Northcliffe but argued that if a tolerable peace was in sight, some of the credit must go to the Press. Cecil offered to resign from the Government. Northcliffe told him not to bother: 'He is angry because we have found out what is going on in Paris.' Lloyd George's attack was no doubt crude and expedient; the Peace Conference had no need of Northcliffe when it came to 'sowing dissension between great allies'. It was a farmyard of disagreement. But Lloyd George was merely returning like for like; the invective of politics for the invective of headlines.

Northcliffe had always seen his newspapers as instruments of their owner, to be used as he chose. The war had strengthened his reputation because he had been right about Germany. In 1919 he was anxious to go on developing his papers, in particular the *Mail*, as his voice in politics. No one knew how powerful the new-style Press lords would be. Their growing readerships confused the issue. If a paper that sold a hundred thousand copies was influential in the past, was a paper that sold a million copies now ten times as influential? The question was being raised, and answered with a firm 'No', before the war. But no one could be sure. 'Influence' in the old sense meant arguments expressed at length for a handful of important readers. What about the influence of a newspaper that expressed its views, not by argument so much as by the style and colour of its news presentation, for the benefit of millions? In the Northcliffe sense, which by now was widely copied, 'news' didn't mean raw material presented for the readers' intelligent inspection. It meant packaged information, news that was chosen and treated so as to make it attractive. It meant throwing the weight of a newspaper into a political fight, using news reports and photographs to make the case. It was influence by sledgehammer, not argument. Politicians couldn't ignore the dangers.

Yet in the nature of things, Northcliffe faced insuperable difficulties in seeking to influence electorates and governments. His foreign-affairs policy before 1914 was eventually justified by the coming of war. No such apocalypse was in prospect in 1919, unless it was world revolution – a bogey that frightened Rothermere but not Northcliffe. He tried to make it seem that he was still giving precise warnings about the old enemy; instead, he was giving vague warnings about the post-war world. He was out of his depth. Even if he was right about Tory reactionaries who hamstrung the Government, and Jewish financiers who hamstrung the peace talks, these were not matters that could be dealt with by iron remedies, briskly administered. The problems of reorganising the post-war world were beyond Northcliffe, as they were beyond most people, but he clung publicly to a belief in one-paragraph solutions: expel aliens, punish the Kaiser, present bills. This was asking for trouble. He had basked in the popular esteem; in the space where it now warned that 'those Junkers will cheat you yet', the *Mail* had crowed after 1914: 'The paper that persistently forewarned the public about the war.' Now, having received credit for what was seen as prescience, Northcliffe received kicks for what was seen as malice. No doubt he was sustained by the thought that events would prove him right, and Lloyd George wrong. They were to prove only that Press lords were less important than they supposed. Newspapers could contribute to the national mood, the national debate; the 'daily message conveyed to the household in the form of the newspaper', as Northcliffe said in one of his high-flown pronouncements to the *Times*, was 'an essential part of democratic government'. But newspapers, however adroitly handled, were not instruments that could make and unmake men and policies; even in Northcliffe's hands, let alone in those of his successors. In 1918 and 1919, Northcliffe saw himself both able and entitled to wield political power. He failed to do so; events lumbered forward without his permission; 1914 was a special case that would not come again, for him or for anyone else.

At Fontainebleau, where he remained till the end of April before returning to London, Northcliffe was melancholy. His throat worried him. In a letter to his principal private secretary in London, H. G. Price, on 19 April, he spoke of 'my gradual withdrawal from supreme activity in regard to my newspapers', and said that henceforward Campbell Stuart would visit him weekly to relay necessary decisions. He wrote to Rothermere about economic problems: taxes, war debts, wage demands. Northcliffe thought his brother was 'probably the only one in

England' who understood what was happening. The manner was uncharacteristic. 'I wish you would help me,' said Northcliffe, and again: 'I want you to help me. Without advice, I go back rather helpless.' In his letters to Rothermere, he had always sounded strong. Now he sounded lonely.

19

New World

NORTHCLIFFE had the habits of a journalist. He liked soft pencils and limitless supplies of paper to scribble on. When he made notes or drafted letters in his own hand, he was apt to litter the page absent-mindedly with sub-editor's marks – square brackets at the beginning of paragraphs, double lines under capital letters. Someone preserved a page of scribbled slogans from shortly after the war, when the *Daily Mail* circulation went permanently above a million: 'Daily Mail, Million Sale', 'Daily Mail, Never Stale', 'Hail Hail, the Daily Mail'. He loved the paper fiercely. It was 'the world's best newspaper in the world's greatest city'. But they were difficult times for expansion. Northcliffe's health was in its usual unsatisfactory state. Cancer of the throat had been rumoured at Carmelite House. Doctors diagnosed a benign growth, and in June 1919 he was successfully operated on for an adenoma of the thyroid. After this, he hoped, he would be 'really well'. But the adenoma was not a satisfactory explanation for the coughs, the bronchitis, the depression, the loosening of his personality. A heart murmur had been discovered in 1917 and added to his worries, though the specialist had told him it was nothing to be anxious about. After the operation, his general condition showed no improvement. He was overwrought. He sent a verbose reply, veined with self-congratulation, to a get-well message from the *Times*. It repeated how, a decade before, 'I suddenly found myself with the burden of the paper on my shoulders', at a time 'when, as at present, I was in ill health'. Now the *Times* was prosperous, 'a complete recompense for the thousands of hours that I have spent in the service of the Paper'. A few weeks later he ordered that the blackened-brick façade of the *Times* building in Queen Victoria Street should be covered with gilt letters from four to six feet tall, spelling out *The Times*, topped by the Royal Arms in colour. 'Do not delay,' he told the manager. 'They can very easily dominate the street if brains and imagination are used.' Lady Churchill had told him that her taxi driver took half an hour to find the building. In due course the letters appeared, spanning five windows of the nine-windowed frontage. It seemed an aberration.

Physically he was unwell. Recuperating at his bungalow in Surrey, he was struck by 'excruciating agony' down his left side, accompanied by swelling. Doctors rushed to inject morphine, opium, and hyoscine. Later that year, Tom Clarke, newly appointed as news editor of the *Daily Mail*, visited him at his new London house, 1 Carlton Gardens. The Chief lolled in an armchair before the fire. 'From beneath the folds of a spacious dressing-gown peeped a big, fat thigh in pants. He had no trousers on, no collar or tie, but wore slippers and socks. His face looked coppery and fleshy. I thought of Nero.'

If his private condition was unhelpful, so was the condition of the country. Rothermere, whose pessimism had become a byword, had written to him in January 1919 to say that he expected Britain to be in a state of semi-revolution before long. During the election campaign in December 1918, Northcliffe let the Labour Party have a column a day in the *Mail* to express its opinions. It embarrassed Lloyd George and acknowledged the new force in politics. He introduced a five-day week. Andrew Caird complained that it would cost ninety thousand pounds a year at Carmelite House, adding that the men didn't work as they used to. 'What a gloomy devil you are,' replied Northcliffe on 2 September 1919. 'Why should you expect the "workers" to hurry and worry when the capitalists such as myself and you are lying back in the heather listening to the humming of the bees, or waiting at each tee on an overcrowded links for a game that takes four hours to play?' This was admirably cool-headed. They were troubled times. Strikes raged and there was talk of 'Bolshevist risings', fanned by tales of Red terror from Russia and other parts of Europe. When policemen went on strike in Liverpool on 31 July, mobs looted and fought with soldiers, while tanks rumbled through the streets and a battleship steamed at full speed from Scapa Flow. But Northcliffe's philosophical words to Caird were not to be taken too seriously; they were a gesture. The truth, to Northcliffe, was what happened to strike him at any given moment. A few days before the letter to Caird he was writing to Rothermere about plans to raise the price of the *Mail* to a penny-halfpenny. 'I have been plainly told by trade unionists at Carmelite House,' he said, 'that newspapers at that price are going to mean a fifteen per cent demand for advance in wages in every department. I am not afraid of a fight, but this one will be serious.' After wartime inflation, the index of wholesale prices was at three times the 1913 level. Northcliffe's gross personal income for 1919 was two hundred and eighty-six thousand pounds. This was less than three times as much as he earned before the war, and in addition he had to pay a hundred and thirty-three thousand pounds of it in tax. A letter to Sutton on 30 November 1919 complained that

you do not make any suggestion as to how we are to avert the tremendous danger that I foresee as clearly as, in 1890, I foresaw that our policy was to rain paper after paper upon the public and thus raise our prestige and block competition. (You will remember that that policy was then regarded as madness by those inside and outside the office, especially when I said that most of our new papers should be issued for the coin of the lowest denomination.)

If we go on as we are at present, we are building up a Frankenstein – fat to blackmail by workers, most of whom are really very well paid, and fat to tax by Socialistic and squandering governments ...

As for my own state, I have never thought of it in this matter, but I do not wish to be crushed out of existence by the stupendous, direct invitation we give to Labour blackmailers and tax-grabbing governments by lack of foresight in looking ahead.

Sutton was now a dignified and highly paid figure who ruled a magazine empire of more than seventy publications, with *Answers* and *Comic Cuts* still flourishing. He had no panacea for Alfred; there was none. They had arrived at the post-war world of appetites that would never be satisfied. Northcliffe had helped to alert an industrial democracy by giving it interesting things to read. His publications were built around advertising that promised wonders and comforts for all who could afford them. He offered incentive by the column, editorially as well as in the advertisements, encouraging people to better themselves in an exciting mixed-up world of telephones, Dreadnoughts, motor-cars, machine-guns, ready-made dresses, soap-flakes, holidays, and three-piece suites. About this time, the end of 1919, W. L. George was finishing his novel *Caliban* – it was published the following September. His hero, Northcliffe in disguise, looks around him at the Britain of 1919.

He suddenly developed enough imagination to perceive an incredible future, to understand that rising wages meant rising prices, that profits and the spending thereof on the sterile labour of goldsmiths, on motor-cars, on footmen, would go on all the same. He realised the vicious circle, rising wages and rising prices, and nobody any better off... only goaded by envy, exasperated by injustice.

Perhaps the real Northcliffe had some insight into this 'incredible future'; except that he was more of an optimist than George. Perhaps he knew he would have little to do with the future, whatever happened. He seems to have become more elusive than ever – in some moods unnaturally pompous and heavy, in others still relaxed and companionable. Hearing that his bankers, Coutts, are being taken over by a larger firm, he writes angrily to complain that he was not consulted in advance, and lectures the senior partner about conditions in banking: 'if the wages are not improved my newspapers will take the matter in hand'. A month or two later, travelling in France and Spain, he writes amiably to Sutton to ask for news of his son, Alfred, who had been injured in a shooting accident. He goes on:

Salmon good and plentiful now but *no cigarettes* for travellers in Spain, much to Pine's annoyance. Pine smuggled a pound of pipe tobacco in the motor horn ... Cowdray is motoring in Spain with two Rolls-Royces. He says he has at last learnt to depute and to loaf but that it took him seven years to do it. He says I am too punctual. I like him much. He is easy, humorous, thoughtful of others and very careless about money. He is worth they say twenty million pounds. I say five.

On the same trip he wrote to Price, his secretary, in London:

There is a stack of correspondence waiting for me here. Most of it *wants something*. None of it will get anything ... I must be becoming famous. All Biarritz knows I am here, and I could feed free for months. None of your Soho substitutes, but ten-course déjeuners, asparagus, new peas and taters, strawberries. Dinner at 9 p.m. or even worse. How can these people do it?

He felt his age. The need to encourage young men who would enliven his newspapers became something of an obsession. He would send for them to Elmwood or the south of France, telling them, when they reached the Riviera, that they had come to the most expensive place in the world, yet it would cost them nothing. He would talk about the two kinds of news: happenings, which were to be reported, and topics, which were to be stimulated. Older men were liable to be advised they should read Bacon's essay *Of Youth and Age*. He talked more and acted less. His hold on the papers had slackened. Writing to Cecil in September 1919, he said he had had 'practically nothing' to do with them for months. But a stunt was still close to his heart. In the summer of 1920 he thought up a holiday competition for children; they had to arrange the words *Daily Mail* and 'World's record net sale of 1,121,790' in sand or pebbles. He gave his blessing to a sly scheme for sending a local councillor, who had attacked the shamelessness of men and women bathers, on a tour of Britain's beaches. He was called the Mixed Bathing Inspector. It was the 'Swimming and Sex' debate of August 1896 all over again. More novel was the Melba broadcast. She was persuaded by Northcliffe to make the first advertised entertainment broadcast in Britain, on 15 June 1920. Primed with chicken and champagne, she sang in a Marconi hut at Chelmsford, standing with microphone in one hand and handbag in the other, and was heard tinnily by a few hundred listeners. Sir Campbell Stuart, who had driven her there from London, paid local lads to stand outside the window and cheer when signalled. But wireless as entertainment was still officially frowned on.

The stunt lacked the impact of the *Daily Mail* Hat campaign in the winter of 1920. Northcliffe was always interested in news about hats; he liked the etiquette of correct headgear. More anxious than ever to lighten the paper and find new readers, he suggested a prize of a hundred pounds for a newly designed man's hat. Readers sent in forty thousand drawings, and a panel of three chose one that resembled a shortened top hat with a dome, designed by a clerk at the Ministry of Health. Northcliffe was as determined as he had been with Standard Bread to inflict this strange device on the public. But the bread had been tasty; the hat was ridiculous. It was christened 'The *Daily Mail* Sandringham Hat', and photographers combed the streets in search of notabilities wearing it. A picture of Mr Owen Nares, the actor, appeared two days running. Northcliffe was furious when the paper reported that the hat had been observed at Mile End, on the poor side of London; reporters were told to start seeing it in the West End. Ambitious young men at Carmelite House wore a Sandringham Hat by day but kept a bowler or a trilby to go home in. Nothing was allowed to stand in the way of the hat. A week after the prize had been won, the Lord Mayor of Cork died in Brixton Gaol following a hunger strike of seventy-four days – Southern Ireland's post-war troubles had begun earlier in the year. This had unhappy repercussions on the *Mail*'s picture-page. Half the page was headed: 'Dead Lord Mayor: Yesterday's Scenes'. The other half was headed: 'The *Daily Mail* Hat'. Between the hat headlines and the day's hat picture was a photograph of a man covering his face with a hat, though not a *Daily Mail* one. The caption read: 'The Lord Mayor's chaplain, who was present at the last, hiding his face with his hat on returning to the prison yesterday afternoon.' At first sight, it looked as though the Sandringham Hat had been seen with the Lord Mayor's chaplain. This was the kind of blunder that the *Mail*'s professionals were unlikely to make unless they were under orders to keep the hat in the headlines whatever happened. Northcliffe strove in vain to popularise his hat; the campaign died slowly and painfully.

Over the months, circulation rose; the newspaper market was expanding. Beaverbrook's *Express* was becoming a serious competitor, though as yet the *Mail* was well ahead. A younger, fitter Northcliffe might have given the paper a new direction. As it was, the *Mail* coasted along, practised and confident, but no longer a pioneer. Northcliffe himself was losing a sense of proportion. Perhaps the hat was an omen. Leicester, who owned a house on Campden Hill, in west London, bought an adjacent house for his mother in 1919; he furnished it for her, but she didn't like it. Northcliffe was furious; he called it presumptuous of Leicester; what he meant was that *he* should look after his mother. When Mrs Harmsworth became ill with internal pains in September 1920, Northcliffe, according to Steed, was 'hysterical with anxiety'. Steed had to telephone a succession of Harley Street specialists to ask if they had ever heard of a woman of eighty suddenly showing symptoms of cancer. She was not very ill. The same month, Northcliffe attended the funeral of one of Leicester's sons who had died of a heart complaint, infective endocarditis. He went up to his brother and said, without preliminaries: 'You know, Mother is still desperately ill.' He was of an age when the ranks of friends and relatives begin to thin. Auntie Miller, who thought that the Duke of Wellington's nose could be detected in the family, had died in 1918. Fred Wood, his father's friend, who knew family secrets from the Hannah Carter days if he had chosen to tell them, died earlier in the war. Herbert Ward, his boyhood friend, died in 1919; he was fifty-seven, three years older than Northcliffe.

It was not easy to tell whether Northcliffe's new manner was only a more exacting version of the old. He raged at Wareham Smith, his advertising director, 'like a tiger', in front of a sculptor who was modelling his head. Early in 1921 he was reading, in proof, an article about Harry Lauder by the *Mail*'s dramatic critic, William Pollock. He crossed out 'William' and substituted 'Pollock', remarking that William was a good name for a butler (it was the name of his butler at Elmwood). The proof was sent to the printer marked 'Not to be altered', and the article duly appeared, signed 'Pollock Pollock'. Asked about it afterwards, Northcliffe said there were too many Pollocks in the office: it confused the secretaries. At about the same time, his papers were instructed to make no references to Lord Lee of Fareham. Lee and his wife had been personal friends of the Northcliffes since before the war. Northcliffe was offended by an article that criticised him in a magazine, *Outlook*, with which Lee had been connected. The Lees were to visit the Northcliffe villa at Roquebrune in January 1921. Lady Northcliffe and Sir Robert Hudson were already there. A letter from Northcliffe's secretary informed Lee that he and his family were no longer welcome. Astonished, Lee wrote back to say that he had had no connection with the magazine for more than a year. It was no good. Northcliffe had made inquiries; he believed that Lee was one of Lloyd George's 'parasites'. Three months later Lee tried to make up the quarrel through a third party, but Northcliffe would have none of it.

From Roquebrune, during Northcliffe's visit in January from which the Lees were excluded, his wife wrote to their household steward in London: 'His Lordship arrived safely, but I am sorry to say has not been well owing to inoculation. He has now got it into his head that the position of the villa does not suit him – and I shall not be the least surprised if he leaves suddenly. It is very disappointing – but I am afraid he will never settle down anywhere now – and he is never happy except moving restlessly from one place to another, and can't bear to be in a house which is not arranged *entirely* for himself.' Sure enough, after a fortnight he was back in London, supposedly because his mother was grieving over the death of a grand-daughter. In his absence, a rumour that he had died in a car accident at Monte Carlo had gone around Fleet Street. He swept into the *Mail* office growling: 'I'm not dead yet.'

Economic troubles had beset him constantly in 1920. In 1919 the *Times* was prosperous; a year later, it was not. Costs were rising, circulation falling. Wickham Steed and his assistants were advocating a policy for Ireland – separate State Legislatures for north and south – which offended both the southern Catholics and the northern Protestants. Northcliffe was sent a photograph of himself with a bullet-hole in the forehead; detectives guarded him, and police were stationed outside the *Times* It was assumed that the Irish policy was causing the drop in circulation. Northcliffe spoke of the paper's 'partially necessary unpopularity', at the same time calling for economies, as of old. Trouble with the unions simmered. When union militants talked of refusing to print material about Ireland and Russia to which they objected, Northcliffe told them they would be locked-out: 'I am prepared to shut down all my newspapers for a year if necessary. I can soon build them up again.' In November union leaders at the *Mail*, planning a strike in support of a dissident member, were told the same: if they came out, Northcliffe would sack everyone and stop the papers. 'This is not a threat,' he said, reading from a written statement so there could be no mistake. 'I never threaten. It's a fact.' There was no strike. The statement said that profits of Associated Newspapers were forty thousand pounds down on the previous year, and added significantly: 'We have been obliged to sacrifice the news columns to advertisements.' What Northcliffe had resisted and yet foreshadowed since the first issue of the *Mail* – which looked down its nose at advertisements in the leading article on page four, but was glad to have Bovril and Dr Tibbles' Vi-Cocoa occupying most of page eight – was coming true: the advertising tail was beginning to wag the editorial dog. A message to the *Times* five days after the threatened strike at the *Mail* said: 'It is not pleasant to think that, owing to the gigantic wages paid in newspaper offices and the high price of paper, newspapers are now for the first time in their history *entirely* subordinate to advertisers. I see no way out of this *impasse*, other than by maintaining a great daily net sale and thus keeping the whip hand of the advertiser. The situation is such as should make everyone in a newspaper office think.' It was, indeed; but having created it, there was nothing he could do.

The week before Christmas, in a letter to Robert Hudson, he was complaining that other newspaper proprietors were not being strong enough in opposing wage demands; he wanted to 'screw up the wobblers to resist the brigands'. 'We have four demands this week,' he said, 'one from the engineers who demand fifty per cent increase. Next Saturday, Sunday, and Monday we are publishing no newspapers, in order to give the workmen a little liberty – we say; really to teach them a lesson. They tried to blackmail us with a gigantic wage increase at Christmas.' In the spring and early summer of 1921, Northcliffe supported Rothermere in fighting a long strike of paper workers at the Newfoundland mills, who were resisting wage cuts. Yet Northcliffe liked to pretend he wasn't one of 'the bosses': they were someone else. Over the years he had shown genuine concern for employees, both journalists and printers; from the beginning, the *Mail* paid well.

In April he toured the coalfields, where miners were on strike. He wrote to Rothermere:

People said that if I went in a Rolls-Royce (a rather showy one at that) I should be attacked. Far from being attacked, the car was universally admired by the miners, especially when told that it was a hundred per cent British. I immensely admire the fortitude of these strikers. Their only desire seems to be that their children shall get enough to eat. The cut in wages was too sudden. That was the opinion of everyone I met, including some mine owners. The whole question is damnably complex. Except in Glasgow, there is nothing Communistic or Bolshevik about the miners.

He added that 'I don't think we shall ever get back to much cheaper newspapers, railway travel, or advertising'. Northcliffe seemed to be resigning himself to W. L. George's 'incredible future'. He cabled to London: 'HOPE MODERATE TONE WILL CONTINUE IN ALL PAPERS. PRINT BOTH SIDES FULLY.' But the strike was broken; the men went back on the owners' terms. Northcliffe didn't campaign on their behalf – how could he, in his position? He sympathised with 'workers' with one part of his brain and resisted the demands of 'brigands' with another. It was not that he merely paid lip-service to labour relations, taking a kindly view of the workers, as long as they didn't work for him. Rather, he had flashes of insight and sympathy but no conscience. He was astonished, appalled, overwhelmed; five minutes later he had forgotten. It was like his burst of interest in *Red Rubber* and the Congo atrocities: Tuesday's talking-point, Wednesday's fish-and-chip paper. His beliefs consisted of passing fancies and occasional obsessions. Everything counted; nothing mattered.

His behaviour over Ireland – the other burning domestic topic of 1920 and 1921 – points to Northcliffe's indifference; on a subject that might have been expected to arouse him, his words and gestures were wooden. He endorsed Wickham Steed's *Times* policy (which denounced southern Irish gunmen but denounced British reprisals as well), without apparent enthusiasm. The *Mail* followed cautiously, and Northcliffe was blamed or credited in both instances for something he wasn't doing. Cecil pressed him more than once to play an active part over Ireland. In March 1921 he asked him to contact southern Irish leaders. 'Alas,' replied Northcliffe, 'I am leaving for the South of France tomorrow.' In May Northcliffe was writing to Lord Derby, urging concessions to the southern Irish, including an amnesty for the Irish Republican Army leader, Michael Collins. 'I have Irish blood in me and I understand the Irish people . . . ,' he wrote on 7 May. 'We have to live with these southern and western Irish. They have very long memories – these Irish.' Whether as a result of fresh outrages by Sinn Fein revolutionaries later that month in England and Ireland, Northcliffe seems to have reversed his views, and decided it was now time to impose them on Steed and the *Times*. The *History of The Times* says that in the early summer, Northcliffe 'demanded outright that the policy be changed', and gave Steed a month to do it in. But it becomes impossible to follow Northcliffe's changes

of direction. Information about Northcliffe and Ireland is sparse
and contradictory; it is much easier to establish what he
thought about the *Daily Mail* Hat. His mother is known to have
been pro-Ulster. Rothermere was violently opposed to any 'be-
trayal' of Ulster, and declared in private that it was the only
issue in politics on which he had ever held strong views.
Northcliffe's views on Ireland were a muddle. Like the coal
strike, it was 'damnably complex'; probably he would have
preferred to avoid it altogether.

What he thought about Ireland was further complicated by
deteriorating relations with Wickham Steed: after two years as
editor, Steed was being given the Dawson treatment. Northcliffe
spent much of March and April in Paris and at his villa in the
South. Ominous cables arrived at Printing House Square. 'DO
NOT THINK YESTERDAY'S FIRST LEADER VERY WELL WRITTEN,'
said one in mid-March. 'OUR LEADERS ARE NOW STRONGLY
CRITICISED NOT ONLY IN THE GREAT WORLD BUT ALSO FOR
THEIR ALLEGED LACK OF SCHOLARSHIP DISPLAYED. CHIEF.'
Soon he was complaining about the paper's policy over the
ownership of coal mines, and by 23 April he was threatening to
sell his control of the *Times* 'TO A VERY REPUTABLE PURCHASER
WITH WHOM I HAVE ALREADY ARRANGED THUS CONFORMING
TO THE URGENT WISHES OF MY MEDICAL ADVISERS TO GET RID
OF EVERY TRYING RESPONSIBILITY THAT RENDERS IT DIFFICULT
FOR ME TO BE ABROAD.' Now that it had ceased to be profitable,
the *Times* reawakened Northcliffe's feelings of persecution by
the monks of Blackfriars. Irritations were piling up on all fronts.
In a letter dated 20 March from Roquebrune to H. G. Price, in
whom he continued to confide, he had apologised for being so
irritable when in London. He blamed people who kept asking
for money, and 'infernal taxes'. St John and his Perrier Water, in
bad financial shape after the war, were a plague of a special
kind. 'As to a certain mineral water,' he told Price. 'The first
thing that met my gaze on arriving at Carlton Gardens very
tired after a rough crossing [probably from Paris] was a
demand for five thousand pounds. The last thing that happened
to me was that rush to the station in regard to the same matter,
and would you believe it, within a few minutes of arriving at
this villa I had a telegram on the same subject, and this afternoon is to be devoted to conversation about it.'

What Northcliffe wanted, it seemed, was to devote himself to the affairs of the *Mail*. He wanted to go back in time; perhaps to the horizons his mother thought he had lost when he bought the *Times*. In March he was entertaining clever young men at the villa. He said they were there to learn how newspaper readers would like to live. They sat with him on the terrace, looking over the bay streaked with the lights of Monte Carlo, and talked about the question of questions for all journalists: who are the readers, what do they want? Northcliffe said that even if the readers of the *Mail* were not thousand-a-year men, they liked to imagine they were. Was that snobbery? There were worse vices than snobbery. Were the readers to be flattered, then? 'What else have we ever done?' said Northcliffe. 'What's wrong with it? Read Disraeli on the flattery of royalty. Our papers have flattered the ordinary man all along by putting reading matter in his reach, when pompous academic folk who taught him to read had forgotten to provide it. They created a demand and offered nothing to satisfy it. We did.' Northcliffe was moving towards the paper he understood, the *Mail*, away from the paper whose spirit had always eluded him, the *Times*. His messages to Steed, announcing that he had had enough, reached a climax in the third week of April. By now they were coming from an hotel at Versailles. Northcliffe spoke of 'three aspirants' for the ownership of the *Times*. He was impenetrably mysterious. Steed assumed that Rothermere was one of the three. The previous year, Rothermere had persuaded his brother to stockpile newsprint against rising costs; Steed believed that this was part of a plot by Rothermere to gain control of the *Times* for himself. Newsprint purchases cost Northcliffe a hundred thousand pounds, which helped compel him to raise more capital. In the event, newsprint prices fell. Northcliffe, Steed said afterwards, had fallen into a trap.

Steed and John Walter – nominally chairman of the *Times*, with a minority shareholding – shivered and waited. Nothing happened. One minute there were hysterical telegrams from Northcliffe and many rumours that the *Times* was being sold. The next, it was all over. Steed had expected an announcement on Sunday 1 May, when Northcliffe was to preside at a banquet to celebrate the twenty-fifth anniversary of the *Daily Mail*. Instead, he heard via Lady Northcliffe that her husband was not selling. It is doubtful if he ever meant to. He was bluffing, spreading alarm at the *Times* by threatening to fling them all to unknown wolves. He thought shivering was good for people. Anyway, Northcliffe was sick. His thoughts were all of a piece with the fatigue and disenchantment that were overtaking him.

On 1 May came the *Mail* celebration, in the exhibition hall at Olympia. Special editions of Northcliffe newspapers were on sale outside, with contents bills announcing 'The Chief at Olympia'. Seven thousand guests saw a tired-looking Northcliffe escort his wife and mother to the table. He was annoyed to notice some empty seats. Lunch was preceded by grace, spoken by a vicar from Hampstead, the Reverend Basil Bourchier. Students of the *Daily Mail*'s picture page would have seen that Mr Bourchier had been 'one of the first clergymen to wear the Sandringham Hat'. At Olympia, Mr Bourchier called down the Lord's blessing on 'Thy servant Alfred' – 'grant him health and strength, wisdom and power from on high'. In Fleet Street, 'Thy servant Alfred' became a standing joke. At the end of the meal, Northcliffe spoke briefly, via a recording made earlier. He and the seven thousand listened to the clipped, colourless voice thank the Almighty for his blessings; hope that the fiftieth anniversary in 1946 would be as joyful; and propose a toast of 'long life and happy times' to the workers of the Northcliffe Press. Then he hurried back to Carmelite House to supervise the report of the occasion for the next day's paper, demanding a shorthand writer, who was so flustered that he was unable to make notes.

Later that month came his coalfields tour, and his change of mind about Ireland and the *Times*. Steed was left alone, apparently in disgrace. It was understood that on 15 June, his fifty-sixth birthday, the Chief would resign from the boards of Associated Newspapers and the *Times*. He spoke of a long sea voyage recommended by his doctors. He would visit the Far East and learn about Japan: the new Power that was rising, like Germany thirty years before. In June the *Occult Review* printed his horoscope, and he ordered sixty copies; it compared him to Napoleon. Death, it said, might come suddenly. A later horoscope, sent to Northcliffe by an astrologer, was to warn him: beware of travelling. Invited to a lunch by Gordon Selfridge, the department-store owner, Northcliffe discovered he was the last and thirteenth guest to arrive. Selfridge's attempt to make a

joke of it froze in the air; Northcliffe would have left, if a polite
guest hadn't done so first.

As the date of his world tour approached, Northcliffe spoke to
people at the *Mail* of going 'to solve the riddle of the Pacific and
White Australia'. He told his brother St John that he wanted to
see Japan's preparations for war: 'I am going to Australia, but, of
course, that is mere camouflage as to my real object.' He was to
sail in the *Aquitania* on 16 July, the day after his birthday. On
15 July he held a farewell conference at Carmelite House and
asked a sub-editor to name the best story in that morning's *Mail*.
The sub-editor replied: 'Viscount Northcliffe is leaving tomorrow on a world tour and will be away from England for
several months.' After a few seconds of appalled silence,
Northcliffe turned to his secretary and said: 'See that that man
gets a hundred-pound bonus.' He didn't smile. In the afternoon
he was at Fleetway House with Price, tearing up papers from a
safe. The 'Schemo Magnifico' was probably destroyed then. As
he dropped handfuls of paper down the lavatory and pulled the
chain, Price recognised photographs of Northcliffe's children.
In the evening, Lady Northcliffe gave a birthday party for her
husband. Steed was present. His relations with his proprietor
had been chilly for months. Out of the blue, Northcliffe asked
him to sail in the *Aquitania* next day and come as far as America;
the trip would be a preliminary to an American visit that the
editor was to make in any case, to attend a disarmament conference. Steed, the Irish policy and the *Times* were suddenly
back in favour. The editor accepted as gracefully as he could,
packed his bags, and was on the platform at Waterloo Station
the following afternoon as a crowd gathered to wave goodbye to
Northcliffe. Lovat Fraser, now one of Rothermere's writers, but
still friendly with Steed, whispered to him: 'Be on your guard.
Northcliffe doesn't mean well with you.'

Beside his editor, trim and debonair, Northcliffe looked
shabby and out of sorts. He had spent the previous night at his
mother's house. The day he sailed was the thirty-second anniversary of her husband's death; a date she remembered each
year. Among the books Northcliffe took with him was one she
had given him, a little red-bound devotional work called *Daily
Light on the Daily Path*. They had promised one another to read it
at the same time each day.

20

Travelling Man

NORTHCLIFFE WAS ILL. But then, Northcliffe had been ill for years. He was a hot-tempered, self-centred man with frayed nerves. He had had at least one breakdown. He had suffered with his stomach, his lungs and his throat, and he had undergone major surgery in 1919. He had a heart murmur. In addition, he was a hypochondriac. Too many drugs, vaccines, and electric shocks were administered over the years for them all to have been strictly necessary. When he sailed in the *Aquitania* his medicine chest included opium, aspirin, phenacetin, veronal, dover powders, vegetable laxative, soda-mint, bromide, potassium permanganate, chlorodyne, calomel, zinc sulphate, snakebite lancets, mustard leaves, idoform, caustic pencil, thermometer, suture silk and needles, bandages, plaster, lint, ammonia, and a water steriliser. The significant feature of his health by 1921 was the way his judgment faltered. Brain damage caused by syphilis could have had this effect. So could brain damage caused by other factors. Premature arteriosclerosis – hardening of the arteries – might be reducing the brain's oxygen supply. A sub-acute heart infection could be producing similar results. There is no evidence that his doctors suspected any of these conditions in 1921, though they may have done so. In a way, the root cause is irrelevant. The effect of the illness was to coarsen his personality by letting its wilder elements escape. When the controls of a lifetime began to slacken, he had more violence than most people to come bursting to the surface. He became a caricature of what he was. This may be why it took so long for his illness to be recognised: he had always been odd and strong-natured, and it was difficult for his friends to tell the difference between being odd and being very odd indeed. Later, in a family that shrank from the word 'mad', it would be possible to talk hopefully of 'eccentricity' in an attempt to brush away the evidence of psychosis.

As he began his world trip, Northcliffe was just holding the balance. A minor sensation marked his stay in New York. The *New York Times* wanted to interview him on a Saturday, soon after he arrived. It was a hot summer weekend and Northcliffe had gone to stay on Long Island and play golf. Steed was authorised to make some harmless statement in his name. This he did, to a reporter from the paper who called on him during dinner. Steed talked, off the record as he supposed, about the Irish question. He mentioned a conversation that was believed to have taken place between King George v and the Prime Minister, Lloyd George. The King asked if all the people in Ireland were to be shot. 'No, your Majesty,' said Lloyd George. 'Well then,' said the King, 'you must come to some agreement with them. This thing cannot go on. I cannot have my people killed in this manner.' The *New York Times* tucked away the innocuous statement attributed to Northcliffe, but reported Steed's remarks about Ireland and the King on page one. Steed, of course, denied that he had said it. It was his first visit to America. The muddle was made worse on the Sunday when a young journalist in the New York office of the London *Times* telephoned to Northcliffe to ask what he should do about the published interviews. Presumably without having seen what was in print, Northcliffe told him to cable the material back to London, adding, typically, that it should be in his name, not Steed's. The telephone line was bad; Northcliffe was anxious to get on with his golf. The material was passed to London. At the *Times*, where the remarks about the King, now attributed to Northcliffe, were recognised as something Steed had been heard to say in private, they smelt trouble and wouldn't use the story. But at the *Mail* it found its way into the Irish edition, the first to go to press, before Campbell Stuart suppressed it. In the uproar that followed, Buckingham Palace called the King's alleged remarks 'a complete fabrication', and Lloyd George made use of the incident to imply 'criminal malignity' on Northcliffe's part. Rothermere made one of his helpful suggestions: sack Steed. Northcliffe was unruffled. He remained loyal to Steed while denying that he had mentioned the King, and went on with his holiday.

He and Steed moved to Canada, crossing westward to Vancouver. There were too many deputations and reporters for Northcliffe's liking. 'Never, never will I come to the United States or Canada again,' he said. Steed left him at Vancouver and returned to the United States. A couple of small incidents concerning Northcliffe and women had struck him. Formerly he thought Northcliffe a prude, except that he once said: 'Does it stir you when women pull up their skirts and show their ankles while they're talking to you?' ('No,' replied Steed, 'I freeze 'em out.') On this trip Northcliffe mentioned to Steed that he had just been to see one of his girl friends but that 'nothing had happened'. And while they were crossing Canada by private sleeping car, Steed observed that Northcliffe was joined by a married lady whose compartment was next door.

One of Northcliffe's early tasks on the trip was to dictate notes for Ivy Clark, a woman on the *Mail* who was to write an approved popular biography. These were the notes that described imaginary aspects of Northcliffe's boyhood, raising it in the social scale, and pretending he had been delicate as a child. The book was never published; Northcliffe's biographers* had a thin time of it while he was alive. He took two male secretaries on the journey, and kept them hard at work with correspondence and a serial circular letter that was sent to London once a week, and thence to a mailing list of friends and family. Price, channelling messages through London, was embarrassed, early in the trip, to receive a note from Mrs Wrohan, returning the first batch of Northcliffe's travelogue, which, she said coldly, did not seem to be intended for her. By now she referred to him as 'Northcliffe', though she still had his signet ring, with its emblem of dagger and mailed arm, to use on the sealing wax of private letters. Price asked her to accept the weekly reports. Eventually she wrote (from a house near Elmwood) to say that she would, if it helped Price.

The letters were headed 'Strictly confidential. For Lord Northcliffe's private circle only'. He saw much on the trip, but little that was confidential. For once the business was left behind; he became Northcliffe the travel-writer, sailing 'the same brilliant waveless sea' for days on end, writing with pleasure and excitement about the countries he visited and the

* See Appendix 1.

244

interesting things in them. 'On, on, on we go every day,' he wrote to Price as they steamed across the Pacific. 'Curiously enough the days disappear like lightning, as if by magic.' From New Zealand he wrote: 'The whole place is inconceivably interesting. I call it topsy-turvydom – parlour-maids in summertime earn seven pounds a week; tops of mountains are blown away sixty miles; your money in your pocket turns black with the sulphur in the air; there are wingless birds, forty-pound trout, and caterpillars with trees growing out of their heads; and there are ferns as tall as Printing House Square.' He was the simple soul abroad, looking at wonders but remembering Greenwich Mean Time: 'It is five minutes past four in London. The *Daily Mail* conference is beginning.' Receptions and journalists dogged him. With the secretaries, a valet, and a chauffeur, he wandered from country to country – Australia, the Philippines, Japan. Distant relatives and forgotten friends appeared unexpectedly.

Old interests revived. In Borneo he saw a gallows – 'the usual beam and falling trap'. In Japan he read about ritual suicide, and sent back a description of this 'sickeningly painful operation'. The Japanese confirmed his worst suspicions: 'The biggest spy and police force per square mile in the world,' he wrote to Price. In Borneo, the photographer they posed for at Government House was a Japanese, 'a crafty-looking devil. I said to the Governor, "Probably half spy and half photographer".' Seeing signs of Japanese imperialism in China, he cabled to Steed that the *Times* should press for an end to the Anglo-Japanese treaty; which it did. But most of the time, Northcliffe saw the Far East as a display, a pageant; as though he were turning the pages of a richly illustrated book, or perhaps, for once, as though another hand were turning pages of which he was a part. He met a woman somewhere in the Far East (he told Price later) who said innocently that she had not realised Lord Northcliffe was a real person. 'I have often heard people talk about Lord Northcliffe,' she said. 'I have often heard people talk about Thomas Cook and Son and about Jardine Mathieson, but are there such people as Thomas Cook? I thought Lord Northcliffe was someone who had been dead some time, and that he founded some Press to which his name had been given.'

Gliding from land to land, he wrote that he had never been so well in his life. Harold Snoad, the younger of the secretaries, was not so sure. In Bangkok, where he stayed as guest of the king, Northcliffe asked Snoad for a newspaper. Snoad couldn't find it. Northcliffe charged at him, flinging him through the doors and down the palace stairs. The guards picked him up. Snoad was long-suffering. At sea, after dinner, he would sit in Northcliffe's cabin, reading Dickens to him. Northcliffe lay half naked on his bunk, Snoad sweltered in evening dress. Sometimes he was permitted to take off the jacket; the stiff shirt remained. Northcliffe took to long spells of dictation about the day's happenings. One night he began to dictate soon after nine o'clock. His voice ground on, hour after hour, while Snoad wrote shorthand till his arm was numb. It was 3 a.m. before Northcliffe finished: six hours' dictation, with one fifteen-minute break. He never asked to see the sheaf of typescript that his secretary produced. To those on the receiving end of his messages in England, nothing seemed to be wrong. To his mother he cabled daily and wrote twice a week, addressing her as 'Most sweet and precious' or 'Very sweet Mum', signing himself 'Your devoted Firstborn' or 'Your most loving Firstborn'. 'I dream of Poynters or Elmwood or the bungalow every night,' he told her. As in America during the war, his dreams were of England. Each morning at seven he kissed the devotional book. On board ship he 'made a little nest for it in a cigarette box, which rests in front of your picture in my shrine of home photographs. You are always in my thoughts, darling Mother. I think of you wherever you may be – of your rooms and of your movements.' His mother cabled him in a different tone of voice. When he was in Java he received: 'ALFRED I WILL NOT HAVE ULSTER COERCED.' She was objecting to Steed's policy over Ireland. Two members of the *Times* staff were summoned to Totteridge and given a lecture. Another day Northcliffe received: 'ALFRED I CANNOT MAKE UP MY MIND WHICH OF YOUR TWO PRINCIPAL PAPERS IS THE MORE VULGAR THIS MORNING.' If she was 'darling Mum' to him, he was 'Alfred' to her; the old disparity of affection.

Early in January 1922 he was in Ceylon and India, wondering 'What do we want India for? Prestige? Perhaps. Cash? We certainly don't get any from it. The thousands of able men from home could do far better almost anywhere else.' He sent Steed a letter complaining that stories about Japan in the *Times* were twisted. 'I have no doubt in my mind that the *Times* has been got

Owners and editors. *Right,* with Dawson of the *Times* at Sutton Place, before the first world war. *Below,* in America with Steed, Dawson's successor, on the first leg of the ill-fated world trip.

Northcliffe with his sister Geraldine, who became Lady King.

Three generations. Mrs Harmsworth with her grandson, Esmond (later the second Lord Rothermere), and one of his daughters.

at for years,' he wrote. 'By whom and how I don't know.' Conspiracies were afoot; they stirred in Northcliffe's mind as he turned towards Europe. In Delhi he stayed with Lord Reading, now the Viceroy of India. He visited the Taj Mahal; saw snakes being milked of their poison to make serum; described the dust, the monkeys, the prayers. 'But all this life is passing,' he wrote. 'Now we have the swaggering, boastful, whisky-and-soda drinking, horn-spectacled, and fountain-pen-wearing Babu, who likes to think that, because he has the imitative and blotting-paper mind that enables him to pass examinations, he is the equal of the Anglo-Saxon, and, *knowing* his own inferiority, is bitter and dangerous. These are not my words, but the words of an Indian lady who knows her people.' He disliked India. Soon he was aboard a P and O liner bound for Suez – 'filled with Australians, nice hearty people'. He wrote to an Australian friend, Keith Murdoch of the *Melbourne Herald*, with another summary of the trip: 'The *Australian coast*: superb. *Philippines*: America's toy ... *Japan:* much more medieval than we expected. Busy, active, imitative, second-rate people, thoroughly German.' He seemed to need to anchor the experience in words. Since leaving England he had poured out hundreds of thousands. He was afloat on a tide of verbosity. He might have been writing endless descriptive passages for some monumental *Answers*. 'I shall come back with more knowledge than any of my competitors,' he had written to Harold from Peking. Facts, *things*, still held their magical power. Nearing the Mediterranean, the weekly letter is suddenly irritable: 'How stupid are people who write out from home, as to what they say. Many of them rewrite public news from the daily Press; few of them give any private news. I have not, for example, heard one item of news of my Kentish home since I left it! Yet there are between fifteen and twenty people, in whom I take interest, employed there.' A sinister postcard to his sister Geraldine said: 'I have perfect rooms, bedroom like Mum's front sitting room and four kinds of bath. They have awakened.' What had awakened? His spirits drooped. One morning he began to write a cable to Auntie Miller; then remembered she had been dead for years.

He was glad to see the last of Oriental servants: he thought half of them were spies. In the Middle East he paused for sightseeing in Palestine and Egypt. 'How strange to be back in beds

with blankets and hot water bottles!' he wrote. 'How nice to be
back again among the roses and violets and oranges.' He wrote to
his mother: 'I am so close to my Most Perfect now that I could
be with you in six days, which seem like nothing.' His moods
vacillated; at the *Times* and the *Mail*, they were wondering
what to expect. 'I'm mighty keen to help with my newspapers,'
he wrote in the last weekly letter, 'but equally keen on setting
out again and learning more of the world.' He told Price it was
all planned: first to the West Indies and South America; then
across Africa. 'I will be quite willing to start off a week after
arrival,' he wrote. Was Northcliffe to roam the world for the rest
of his life, bathing in new scenes, writing an endless travelogue?
He believed he must travel before he was too old. At fifty-six,
Northcliffe sounded like a man at least ten years senior. He
would have reflected that both his father and his grandfather
were already dead at fifty-two. He listed more than twenty
acquaintances who had died since he left London; among them
his early rival, Sir Arthur Pearson. On 17 February they passed
Corsica, and he saw Napoleon's Elba, snow-covered. Next
morning they were steaming up the harbour at Marseilles, pick-
ing their way through fog. France looked neat, small, orderly.
The Mayor and Prefect greeted him. An unctuous letter, await-
ing him from Wickham Steed, declared that 'you are now in the
position of a statesman, wielding far greater power than you
have ever possessed'. Northcliffe ended Circular Letter Number
32: 'I have resolved that I was not built for any kind of public
life, that I hate crowds, demonstration, ceremonial, and curiously enough, although I am one myself, reporters.' For the next
few days he proposed to rest on the Riviera. His wife joined him
at Cap d'Ail. He had written to Hudson earlier: 'I will do exactly
what she wishes. I should like to go to Avignon for old times'
sake, and to Paris to my dentist. If she likes to stop there a day
or two I shall be delighted. Thence to Totteridge.' His feelings
for her seemed to have mellowed. He may have been hinting to
Hudson, 'my little lady's latest flame' as he had called him to
Steed, that he meant to reclaim her affections. A few days
passed. In London, they were ordering fresh supplies of cigars
from Northcliffe's private reserve at Harrods. Then, like a sudden hammering on the door, telegrams began to arrive from
Cap d'Ail. It was all going to happen again. 'IN VIEW APPALLING

GROSS FIGURES JUST RECEIVED AM RETURNING IMMEDIATELY.
FIGURES ARE WORSE THAN I PREDICTED TWO YEARS AGO.
ALL THOSE EXPLANATIONS AND STATISTICS WITH WHICH IT
WAS ATTEMPTED TO DOPE ME MAKE VERY PATHETIC READING
TODAY. I PREDICT POSITION WILL GET STEADILY WORSE IF
LAST TWO YEARS' FATUOUS OPTIMISM PREVAILS.'

That was his message to the *Times*. The *Mail* was told to
'leave out all top-heavy advertisements which ruin the paper,
such as the bottle in Johnson's Prepared Wax and the large
heading of Quaker Oats'. The news editor received a telegram
demanding to know who used the word 'ectoplasm' in a leading
article; no one at the Grand Hotel Eden knew what it meant.
The offender was Marlowe, the editor. The news editor asked
what he should say to Northcliffe. 'Say what the hell you like,'
said Marlowe, and told Sutton he was ready to resign, if he was
paid enough compensation. Like a strong wind from the south,
Northcliffe blew towards London. Picture postcards arrived,
with jokes. Macleod, the *Mail*'s much persecuted literary editor,
received one that read: 'Suggested head for page four articles:
When the Cat is Away.' Stopping in Paris to see his dentist,
Northcliffe found that the printers at the *Continental Daily Mail*
wanted more money. He sent for the men's leader and told him:
'You're a damned ungrateful swine!' The man protested.
Northcliffe leapt at him and rushed him out of the office by the
collar, giving him a kick for good measure. It was becoming
difficult to spot the 'real' Northcliffe. Back in England, driving
first to Mary's house in Sussex, he was the traveller come back,
drinking in the green spring countryside. He noted gulls driven
inland by high winds; partridges and plovers, violets and wild
arum. Soon he was dictating his impressions, so that the experience could be pinned down in words. To relatives who met him
in London before he went on to spend the night at Poynters
Hall, he said revealingly: 'I am home in time to put things
down, keep things under.' His former valet, Josef, met him by
chance just after he had returned. Northcliffe said he was
becoming religious, adding that his papers were the cross he had
to carry. Sir Charles Russell, one of his solicitors, found him so
abnormal as to be incapable of business. Others noticed nothing.
Northcliffe's condition was as mysterious as ever. He told a publisher, Newman Flower of Cassell's: 'I've been to my thirty-second

specialist today. I'm going to die.' He might have meant anything. He was scattering clues to his condition in letters and telegrams, in communiqués and conversations; as though to satisfy his liking for secrecy and publicity at the same time.

For the first few days in London, he left the papers alone. He attended Princess Mary's wedding in Westminster Abbey. He had meetings with Campbell Stuart. Then, as everyone expected, he bombarded them with messages. The *Times*, where advertising revenue had been falling for a year, was fiercely attacked. On 2 March the editorial staff was summoned to a conference in the board room, where, presided over by Steed, they listened while H. G. Price read out an insulting message about editorial blunders. They were also told that the price of the paper (which had risen from a penny to threepence because of wartime inflation) was being reduced to a penny-halfpenny for readers who registered with their newsagents. Apparently Northcliffe was off on another series of hectic measures to save the *Times*, as he had done before the war. Steed persuaded senior colleagues not to resign, and took legal advice about his own position. Once again there was whispered speculation as to who might take the *Times* if Northcliffe abandoned it. While the talk buzzed on, Northcliffe announced his intention of leaving England again, in search of milder weather at Pau. It was like a film speeding up, the movements becoming faster, the images beginning to blur on the screen. He had been back in London less than two weeks. A parting message to the *Evening News*, which he ordered to be pinned up in the office, was torn down by angry journalists. The editor-in-chief, W. J. Evans, who was near retirement, wrote to say that good men wouldn't stand abuse. 'I don't like some aspects of recent happenings because they put you in a bad light,' he said. Northcliffe told him not to be so touchy.

Delayed at Dover by a storm, he sprayed his editors with instructions. One minute they were told to watch American neswpapers; the next, to liven up the children's 'Teddy Tail' with monkeys and elephants. Proceeding via Paris and Fontainebleau, he set up court at the Hotel Gassion in Pau, and began to send for senior editors and managers, who came and went without much idea why. One director of the *Mail*, summoned at a moment's notice, thought he was needed on urgent business.

Northcliffe told him to enjoy himself; the man went back puzzled a few days later. Apart from the weather, which was wet and stormy, it was like old times on the Riviera. Parties went for car rides or played golf. Over dinner the Chief would talk about spiritualism or Jews or the new men in Fleet Street. 'Watch Beaverbrook,' he said. He was still apparently in control of everything. Messages from Pau about presents he had brought back from the world trip show him half annoyed, half amused at Lady Northcliffe's attempts to take the best for herself. Crate-loads of antiques and fabrics had been arriving at the *Times*, and Mary was complaining that other people had chosen their gifts first. Northcliffe cabled her plaintively to say that it was only a matter of having a few things for relatives, servants, and telephone operators. To Price he wrote that he didn't see what Lady Northcliffe was grumbling about, since in three visits she had taken presents worth several times as much as the rest put together. Other messages concerned a former housekeeper who was dying of cancer, a disease he dreaded. He telegraphed her a hundred pounds, and wrote promising to pay for her daughter's education and to send ninety pounds a month; he spoke of 'the abundance with which the Almighty has blessed me', and told Price that he had read in his mother's devotional book: 'Unto whomsoever much is given, of him shall much be required.' Price was advised to read Bacon's *Of Youth and Age*.

One Saturday near the end of the month, a telegram arrived at Pau while they were having lunch to say that the *Daily Telegraph* was to lower its price to a penny-halfpenny in April. Northcliffe was in his element. Messages were rushed to London by direct cable, radio, and via Paris by telephone (to make sure that at least one got through), instructing the afternoon's *Evening News* to announce in the Late News space that from Monday the *Times* would be a penny-halfpenny to all. The *Times* was instructed how to word the announcement, where it must go in the paper (leader page, top of column five), and what Monday's contents bill must say ('The Times a Penny-Halfpenny to All Today'). The manager of the *Times*, Lints Smith, had just arrived from London. He was turned round and shot back by train and aeroplane. When Wickham Steed arrived on Monday, Northcliffe arranged for him to sit at lunch facing a poster that he had had sent out from London, announcing the *Daily*

Telegraph move. 'Look at that, Steed,' he kept saying. 'That's
the thing you have to think about. Look at it. Look at it.' Next
to Steed, Northcliffe had seated a Jew, Bernard Falk, who was
editor of the *Weekly Dispatch*. He tried unsuccessfully to get them
talking about Jews; he liked to tease Falk – some said, bait –
about his race.

Steed agreed, against his will, to attend a forthcoming world
economic conference at Genoa. He found much of Northcliffe's
talk incoherent. One morning they were by a window, looking
at the rain. Northcliffe was annoyed because he wanted to play
golf. A gust of wind swung a cord that hung from a window
blind. The wooden acorn on the end rapped the glass. Northcliffe
gave a start. 'Somebody shot me!' he said. 'Did you shoot me?'
Steed went back to London and began to make private inquiries
among doctors. Northcliffe remained in Pau a few days more.
One night he asked a companion to join him on the balcony. A
full moon was shining. Northcliffe pointed at the sky. 'How
many moons do you see?' he asked. 'One,' said the man. 'I
thought so,' said Northcliffe, 'but I see two.' The return to
London was via Fontainebleau. Napoleon's chateau, the relics
and memories, were more meaningful than ever. Colleagues
were told to be sure to see Napoleon's hat. 'I once had it on,'
Northcliffe told them. 'It fits me.' When one of them went shopping and bought toy pistols for his children, Northcliffe sent him
back to buy twenty more that he could give as presents. He
mentioned that he had advised a secretary to learn how to use a
real pistol, as his life had been in danger more than once. He
was sending up to twenty telegrams a day. Discussing his plans
for the *Times* with Campbell Stuart, he said, not for the first
time, that it was 'now or never'. He referred to Steed as a
'pinhead'.

Steed reappeared briefly to lunch with him at Fontainebleau,
on his way to Genoa; Hildebrand and St John were there as
well. Steed saw, or thought he saw, certain physical signs in
Northcliffe that matched what he had heard in London.
Northcliffe, he was now convinced, was suffering from tertiary
syphilis. Steed's own doctor had told him so. He was an Italian
called Tallarico with a practice in Wimpole Street, who said
that he had been approached by Northcliffe's doctors about
their patient's illness, which 'as far as he could gather' was of

syphilitic origin. While Steed was in Paris, en route for Genoa, a telegram arrived from the doctor to say that information from two quarters confirmed his suspicion. To any doctor, knowing the symptoms of tertiary syphilis in its neurological form, Northcliffe's disease offered some of the classic signs. As the central nervous system is affected, from ten to twenty years after infection, the personality changes. There may be irritability, loss of memory, failure of judgment, mania, melancholy, paranoia, and delusions of grandeur. But Steed's evidence was hearsay. His own observations at the Fontainebleau lunch, by which he later set store, were irrelevant. He claimed to have seen in one of Northcliffe's eyes 'a kind of light streak, not exactly a cast and not a squint, extending upwards diagonally from the pupil through the iris'. It was similar to one that a friend of his who suffered from syphilis had shown him in his own eye, five years earlier. For good measure, Steed saw this streak or cast not only in Northcliffe but in his brother St John. It appears to have no basis in venereology; there may be abnormalities of the pupil, but they would not show themselves as Steed supposed. But, just as Steed's evidence neither proved nor disproved the evidence, the clinical diagnosis made little difference to the situation for those who were on the receiving end of Northcliffe's behaviour. The paranoid idea that someone was trying to shoot him might be a symptom of neurosyphilis. It might be an aggravation of deep-seated fear about his powers, evidenced for many years by his fondness for 'spies' and his inability to stand criticism. It might be both. A predisposing cause of neurosyphilis – that is, syphilis when it attacks the brain – has been described as 'a life absorbed in ambitious projects with all its strongest mental efforts, long sustained anxieties, deferred hopes, and straining expectation'. On that basis, Northcliffe's life predisposed him to have his brain invaded by syphilis. But whatever the balance between mind and matter, it was now badly upset.

Northcliffe returned to London in the second week of April, in time for Easter. On Easter Sunday he attended the village church at Totteridge with his mother, and became agitated because the sermon lasted longer than he expected. A secretary was sent out three times to telephone the friends who expected him for lunch. Next day, Easter Monday, he was at Carmelite House, his first visit for months, to plan Tuesday's paper. Room

One hummed again. He sat in his old chair, blue pencil in hand, eyes sharp behind heavy spectacles, telling people that soon he wanted to see the *Mail* selling two million copies. In front of him was a make-up dummy of the next day's issue, a big one of sixteen pages. Everyone was exhorted to make it look different. A news story was written to remind readers that the *Times* now cost a penny-halfpenny. The picture page was to be headed 'How the Easter Holiday was Spent'. The leader-page articles were about Bolshevik women, motor roads, and plovers' eggs. Northcliffe wrote the main news-page story: WATCH JAPAN! – SOME SIMPLE WORDS OF WARNING.

It began: 'For what purpose are the great Japanese overseas army and the great Japanese fleet being maintained?' The same story went in the *Times*. After scrutinising heel-clicking Germans for a quarter of a century, it was time to find a new stereotype and begin a crusade against cunning Japs. What else were newspapers for? A glorious future of crusades and campaigns stretched ahead. 'The battle of the Skirts: Long v. Short' had sprung from the Chief's brain only a few days before. 'What a great talking point!' he told the *Mail* news editor. Perhaps his hopes reasserted themselves briefly in Room One that morning. Circulation would soar beyond two million; the world would come into line again. Northcliffe wrote streamers for leader page and the news page opposite: DAILY NET SALES EXCEED 1,668,214 – ONE MILLION SIX HUNDRED AND SIXTY-EIGHT THOUSAND DAILY NET SALE.

Soon he was hurrying off down the narrow marble staircase. He said he was overworked and must leave them to get on with Tuesday's paper. 'This is an emergency – a big day for us,' he added. He had a theory that newspapers were read more on the day after Easter Monday than at any other time of year. He may have been right; in any case, he had ruled by flair and intuition for so long, and been so much better than anyone else at the fickle trade of newspapers, that whatever he said carried weight. He could have told them to print blank pages or put the headlines upside down, and they would have obeyed, winking behind the Chief's back but confident that he had something up his sleeve. When, at the end of the month, he appointed Glover, the hall porter at Carmelite House, to be 'censor of advertisements', there were those who thought it reasonable or at worst whimsical.

Heavy black type and big drawings in advertisements continued to torment Northcliffe. Whatever he said seemed to make no difference. 'After all my criticism,' he told the *Times* once, 'I was very surprised to see the picture of a huge boot.' The more his papers came to depend on the money from advertisements, the less he could bear to look at them. This time he objected to a three-column ad in the *Mail*. Advertising men had to assemble in the music room at Carlton Gardens. Glover, who had previously lunched with Northcliffe, came in puffing a cigar, and made a few embarrassed remarks. He was a burly ex-guardsman; Northcliffe had said he was making the only appeal left, to force. It was a joke and yet not a joke. 'Someone has been saying I'm off my head,' Northcliffe said to Tom Clarke on the phone. 'Not you, is it, Tom?'

In May there were more rumours about his health; more communiqués to the papers. Steed, in Genoa, produced an interpretative report on the conference that was effectively challenged by Lloyd George on grounds of accuracy. Steed's authority was weakened. Campbell Stuart cabled him, to pass on Northcliffe's thoughts: you have been duped again. But apart from the office communiqués, softly worded, Northcliffe was quiescent. He attended and gave lunches. At one of them, a guest mentioned the desiccated corpse of an Egyptian in the British Museum. Northcliffe was fascinated. Cars were ordered and the luncheon party drove to Bloomsbury, marched upstairs, and stood gazing at the shrivelled figure. It would have been a ready-made item for Volume One of *Answers*. At another lunch, he hinted that he would visit Germany soon. In the middle of the month he caused muttering in Fleet Street with a threepenny pamphlet called 'Newspapers and Their Millionaires'. This was the first public evidence, for anyone who chose to read it carefully, that Northcliffe's mind was straying. It rambled on about Press proprietors who had made their money elsewhere, and said rude things about their newspapers. Its message was that planned wage reductions in Fleet Street must not take place; dismay at the prospect of newspapers in the hands of industrialists, instead of journalists, seemed to be the underlying thought. But the message was clouded and confused. He had dictated the pamphlet over the preceding weekend at Elmwood. Oscar Pulvermacher, night editor of the *Mail*, was there. It was

Pulvermacher, years before, who leapt to attention when Northcliffe burst into the newsroom at dawn, goggled and leather-coated, demanding to know what would happen if the King died. Northcliffe showed him the garden bungalow and the lifeboat in the lawn, and sent him back to London with the text, to be rushed out in an edition of twenty thousand. Before Pulvermacher left Elmwood on Monday morning, Northcliffe summoned him to his bedroom. He lay with his back to the window, holding a telephone. 'Here is the *Evening News* early sub-editor,' he said. 'Talk to him. Pretend you are me.' Pulvermacher did as he was told. Northcliffe was unsmiling.

The head gardener at Elmwood and his wife, the house-keeper, resigned that day; he said they could no longer bear Northcliffe's rages. Northcliffe had sent for him one morning and said that he must have fire alarms installed, adding that 'some people may be coming down from London to set fire to the house'. About this time, the middle of May, Northcliffe had a blood test; the results are unknown. Tom Clarke was finding him difficult to talk to by telephone. He shifted from subject to subject, and made long statements, as though he had forgotten he was speaking to anyone. Sometimes he would leave the phone and walk away. Each morning a secretary transmitted the precious communiqués. On 18 May a Pepysian message in his old bantering style told the *Times*: 'Up by very betimes and abroad by road to Gravesend, there to see ye mightie new paper machine being installed for ye benefitt of Printing House Square.' On 19 May he complained that 'getting anything done at Printing House Square is almost impossible'. On 20 May he said he was going away for a long time and that in his absence no charity appeals were to appear unless they came from the royal family. 21 May was a Sunday. On Monday he repeated an earlier complaint about the number of tea ladies in the office. On Tuesday he said he had heard that relatives and friends of employees were being given jobs. On Wednesday he developed the theme: 'As I never myself employ friends or connections in justice to the other proprietors, it is grossly unfair to me that there should be underhand business going on.' The *Mail* was receiving similar messages. H. G. Price drew up a list of 'Relations in the businesses'. (At Associated Newspapers there were thirty-nine names; at the top was 'Sir Andrew Caird – Brother in Overseas Editorial'). On Thursday, 25 May the *Times* communiqué began: 'Before this reaches you all I shall be out of England on a very interesting mission of which you will hear later, and of which you know nothing whatever now, though you may think you do.' As he read his *Times* in bed that morning, lightning flashed and thunder rumbled. His communiqué praised the leader page; criticised the letters. He complained about the photograph of an agricultural show at Guildford because a peer was not identified. 'On the other hand, a Jewish gentleman with an enormous Hebrew nose is marked by a star. Who cares a damn about him? Jews are not liked in country society – as I know. I have a house near Guildford.' Later that day he sailed for Boulogne under the name of Lawrence, later Leonard, Brown, and booked in at the hotel where he had stayed during the *Times* negotiations of 1908. In his luggage was a .32 Colt pistol and two hundred cartridges. He was going back to Germany, the root of all evil.

21

Poisoned Ice Cream

THE *Daily Mail* was experimenting with sky-writing, the
latest thing in publicity, in the early summer of 1922. An
aeroplane looped and dived over London, scribbling *Daily Mail,
Daily Mail* in smoke. Garvin saw the words fade and felt uneasy.
Or so he said later. It was a strange time for those who had
worked near Northcliffe, now that he was drifting out of power.
The papers proceeded day by day. Northcliffe's parting messages were displayed on notice boards. Legally he was still in
absolute control of his properties, except that as long as he
remained out of Britain, George Sutton held his power of attorney. Campbell Stuart, the other trusty, was in Canada, unwell.
    Everyone's deference was undiminished. On the Continent,
Northcliffe and his small party made its usual semi-royal progress, saluted and bowed to by officials and hotel managers. The
Commander-in-Chief of the British Army on the Rhine, General
Sir Alexander Godley, heard of the forthcoming visit to Germany, and invited him to stay at Cologne. Northcliffe accepted
but asked to be met at the frontier, since his life was in danger;
he talked of sending a secret messenger. 'I am not afraid of
attempts on my life as I can defend myself,' he said. He added:
'I shoot from the hip.' Driving from Boulogne to Brussels, he
stopped to look at the battlefields of Flanders and practised
shooting at trees with his pistol. General Godley's staff car met
him on the frontier at Visé, and after an officer had persuaded
him to give up the weapon, they drove direct to Cologne. During the journey, the noise of wartime forts being blown up could
be heard. 'As I expected,' said Northcliffe, 'the fighting has
begun.' His companions from London were his golf professional,
a temporary valet, and Pine, his chauffeur; he was more alone
than usual. In Cologne he was noticeably unwell, blaming it on

ice cream he ate in Brussels. He spent most of his time indoors or in the garden, talking only to staff officers and newspapermen. Godley said he spoke 'incessantly but not foolishly'. One subject that obsessed him in Cologne was the engagement between a niece of Lady Northcliffe and a British officer with the Army on the Rhine. The girl was eighteen. Northcliffe cabled the officer's mother: 'RUMOURS ARE REACHING ENGLAND FROM COLOGNE OF AN ALLEGED AND IMPOSSIBLE ENGAGEMENT BETWEEN MY CHILD NIECE AND YOUR MIDDLE-AGED SON. IF THESE RUMOURS CONTINUE I SHALL MOST REGRETFULLY BE COM-PELLED TO INSERT PROMINENT AND EMPHATIC CONTRADICTION IN THE TIMES DAILY MAIL MORNING POST AND OTHER NEWS-PAPERS.'

After a few days Northcliffe returned to Boulogne, ready to write a series of articles about Germany. On the night train he said he was recognised by two Germans, who spoke offensively about him. He had to request them to stop, or be put off the train by the guard. His mood and temper continued to be erratic in Boulogne. He sacked his golf professional for drunkenness. He insisted he could smell gas in his bedroom, and made Pine sleep nearby. His twelve-year-old son, Alfred, should have been there to meet him, but Mrs Wrohan thought it prudent not to send the boy. This upset Northcliffe. But it would have been better if others in his circle had acted as firmly. Because he often darted from place to place, swiftly and privately, no one thought to check his progress. He maintained his charade of secrecy. He was Mr Leonard Brown, occupying a small rear bedroom for reasons of his own. Douglas Reed, a telephonist at the *Times*, was sent over as temporary secretary. Reed found Northcliffe sick and disillusioned, but it didn't occur to him that the Chief was mad. He was a young man, finding what he had been told to expect, an imperious employer whose orders must be obeyed unquestioningly. A lifetime of imperiousness had put a wall around Northcliffe. Inside it, his fantasies grew unchecked. He showed Reed a black silk purse that was under his pillow. 'Look at this,' he said, 'it was left here for me, for Mr Leonard Brown, by a man who wouldn't give the porter his name. How do they know that I am here? You see the colour? It is the colour of death.' When Reed mentioned that he started work at thirteen, Northcliffe was astonished. The contempt for

effete public-school men which he often expressed was peeled
away; he complained that he should not have been sent a board-
school boy. Reed's luggage was not in order: he lacked a silver-
fitted crocodile-leather suitcase. Northcliffe sent him to London
with a hundred and fifty pounds to buy one. The puzzled young
secretary was not too puzzled to spend the money on suits and
a wardrobe trunk instead, and pay off some bills, before returning to Boulogne. Northcliffe himself was doubting his sanity. He
wrote to Sir Robert Hudson, who was staying at Evian-les-
Bains, on Lake Geneva, with Lady Northcliffe and a fashionable
London doctor, Sir Frederick Treves. The letter, written on
Sunday, 4 June, said:

> You have with you the most distinguished medical man in the
> world. Will you kindly ask his opinion as to my sanity? I have begun
> to have doubts whether it is too little work and too much money, or
> whether it is simply decay of my faculties; I do not know, but I think
> I am going mad. Please wire me at once to relieve my suspicions.
>
> I dreamt the other night that I had run off with Princess Mary and
> started a boarding house at Blackpool, and she said to me: 'Thank
> you, we are doing very well.' That was a dream.

At the *Times*, John Walter would have liked to see that letter.
The events of May had finally convinced him that he could
stand no more of Northcliffe. For years he had remained chairman of the company, bereft of power, a minority stockholder,
putting up with the chief proprietor in the hope of better times.
Northcliffe's will, and an agreement of 1913, gave him an option
to purchase Northcliffe's equity on his death. Now Walter sold
his own two hundred and fifteen thousand shares to Northcliffe
and relinquished the option. He made the first approach to
Sutton on 29 May, while Northcliffe was heading for Germany.
The shares were paid for on 7 June. On 10 June Northcliffe
cabled that he wished Walter to remain as chairman. On 11
June, Walter, having had second thoughts, replied that he
would agree to be chairman if he could maintain his option on
the shares. Perhaps he had got wind of what was happening to
Northcliffe. But by this time, Northcliffe was in no state to
negotiate about anything. All that week he had been firing off
angry and incoherent telegrams, including seven about office
nepotism on 5 June. He had also sent the first of his articles to

London, to appear on 10 June, a Saturday. That morning the *Daily Mail* carried it as the main news story, under a double-column heading: INCOGNITO IN GERMANY. WHY BRUSSELS SHOULD BE AVOIDED BY TOURISTS CROSSING THE FRONTIER.

The article (which also appeared in the *Times*) ran to some two thousand five hundred words. It was very discursive. It described the Flanders scenery, the traffic problem in Brussels, nightingales, and chestnut blossom in the Rhineland. It described a conversation with a builder on the way to Cologne (which could never have taken place, according to the British Army) and remarked that 'the principal feature of the landscape was ladies in an interesting condition. I have never seen them in such profusion and so proud of their state'. In an accompanying leading article, under the 'Junkers will cheat you yet!' epigram, the *Mail* commented hopefully that activity in the building trade and a high birth rate were two of the surest signs of national prosperity. The same morning, Northcliffe was dictating a letter for publication in the *Times*:

Sir, This morning at breakfast, high up in beautiful Switzerland, I was reading the *Journal de Genève*, for Lady Northcliffe only allows me to read local papers when I am away. It is duller than even the worst of my publications and that is saying a great deal, and has even less news. In very prominent type I came across Mr Asquith's remarkable letter about the dangers of the air services. I said to my very small Lady, 'I have never been on Mr Asquith's side before. I should like to write something about it in the *Times* or the *Daily Mail*.' She remarked snappishly, 'You are too much in the papers, Alfred. You are becoming a regular Garve (Garvin, our very dear friend). Please leave off. What with your German articles and very dull pamphlets about the millionaires, I am sure the public is quite tired of you. I have got to the stage when I hate to see our names in print ....'

The letter was never published. Northcliffe was nowhere near Switzerland. He was still at Boulogne. Lady Northcliffe was at Evian, enjoying the June sunshine with the English abroad, waiting for her husband to make his way there from whatever it was that he was up to. The letter rambled on about Mrs Asquith's legs and the length of her skirts; about his dislike of the Jews; about 'Incognito in Germany'. 'I have made a promise that I will not break loose again till I get home,' he dictated,

'except, of course, my German articles, which have been announced and cannot be stopped. As a matter of fact they are all
written, so I am free to pick flowers, watch nightingales, and
play golf in this beautiful valley.' The letter covered eight
quarto pages. The great communicator had forgotten how to
stop communicating. That Friday and Saturday, words poured
out of him as though something had burst in his brain. He told
his mother he was well, he told the women at Carmelite House
to be good. He told Lady Northcliffe about the affair of her
niece and asked Rothermere to publicise 'Newspapers and Their
Millionaires'. A letter was dictated to the assistant editor of the
Times, Geoffrey Brumwell, to say that 'for the first time I shall
have freedom', adding that Steed was to become a travelling
correspondent, and that 'it is not at all sure that we shall appoint
an editor at all'. This mood meant trouble for John Walter, if it
meant anything at all. But the letter was not sent. It became
part of the growing log-jam of messages at Northcliffe's hotel.
An undated letter to H. G. Price, written about the same time,
said the past week had been one of the worst of his life. 'What I
am chiefly anxious about,' wrote Northcliffe, 'is the control of
Carmelite House. I have said again and again that it seems out
of control.' The world was slipping from his grasp; the loss of
authority that he had always feared, over himself and over
others, was becoming a reality. He had failed to 'put things
down, keep things under'. 'After all,' he added plaintively to
Price, 'I am the editor of the *Times*, as you well know.' On 9 and
10 June, Price was deluged with telegrams accusing him of dis-
loyalty and other misbehaviour. One was fifteen hundred
words long. A shorter message read: 'LADYSHIP DOESNT
WISH YOU AND YOUR BEASTLY GREY SUIT OCCUPY HER ROOMS.
SHE MUCH HURT AT YOUR ATTITUDE. PLEASE GIVE THAT SUIT
AWAY TO SOME POOR MAN TIS VERY DIRTY ... WILL YOU
WITHOUT FAIL GET A QUICK TYPIST AND FOR GODS SAKE GIVE
THAT DIRTY SUIT AWAY.' The manager of the *Times*, Lints
Smith, received a telegram at home; it suggested he become
chief reporter. The day-editor of the *Times* was told to stop
walking down Fleet Street in a tall hat. The editor of the *Con-
tinental Daily Mail*, which was not advertising the 'Millionaires'
pamphlet to Northcliffe's satisfaction, was told he would get
punched on Monday. Sir Andrew Caird and another *Mail*

director, Walter Fish, were accused of 'OUTRAGEOUS ATTEMPT
TO CUT DOWN WAGES' and of lying to Northcliffe.

On Sunday, 11 June, Northcliffe prepared to move to Paris,
where he had asked Steed to meet him, before going south to
Evian. Reed was under notice because he was having lunch one
day when he was needed. As Northcliffe left for the railway
station, he told him: 'You will never see me again in this world.'
There was a scene on the platform; Northcliffe insulted railway
officials, and said that God was a homosexual. He also spoke of
an attempt to murder him with a Perrier bottle. More insults
followed on the train to Paris, where he went immediately to the
Hotel Plaza-Athénée. Steed found him there at eight o'clock in
the evening, in bed in a darkened room, chewing a cigar and
drinking a mixture of champagne and brandy. Far into the
night, Northcliffe shouted, groaned, pleaded, and cursed. He
spoke obscenely of his wife and Robert Hudson, referred to
assassination attempts, and said that God spoke to him. At one
point, Steed went down to the lobby to consult with anxious
Times and *Mail* men, and returned to find Northcliffe waving a
loaded pistol in one hand and *Daily Light on the Daily Path* in the
other. He had seen the shadow of his dressing-gown behind the
door, and mistaken it for an intruder. Apart from Steed, said
Northcliffe, the gun was his only friend. Later, when Northcliffe
was in the bathroom, Steed removed the cartridges. Much of the
raving was directed at the *Times*. He said he intended to be the
editor himself, while Steed could travel around the world and
see the Far East, which would make him less of a pinhead. Steed
had been duped at Genoa. He was a fool, said Northcliffe, but
he loved him. Sir Basil Zaharoff, the arms salesman, was the
real ruler of England; he was the man behind Lloyd George.
Northcliffe would expose them all. He would be a Cromwell at
Printing House Square and smash his enemies. Already orders
had been given to dismiss a hundred and fifty Lloyd Georgians.
His solicitors had organised a private detective service at the
Times, disguising their men as bricklayers and clerks; astonishing
scandals had been revealed.

Steed's account of what happened, then and in the days that
followed, was written immediately afterwards and deposited in
the archives of the *Times*. It gives a running account of an episode that normally would be concealed within a family. Cut off

from those who might have protected him, uncontrollably sending letters and telegrams, Northcliffe made sure that his collapse into madness was well documented. Steed believed that once again he saw evidence of advanced syphilis: 'His eyes went wild, and I noticed, when for a moment the light was turned on, that his left eye had a strange squint in an upward diagonal direction.' It was 1.15 a.m. when he left, with orders to be back by 5 a.m., when Northcliffe's barber was to attend; then they would leave for Evian together. When Steed returned, having had no sleep, the barber was at work and Northcliffe produced the manuscript of his second article about Germany. This was worse than the first. Northcliffe had written about the pistol, and said he could shoot seven Germans at sight through his pocket. He was angry when Steed said this passage must be suppressed, but agreed when it was pointed out that otherwise people might think he was afraid. Steed and his colleagues in Paris had asked a doctor to try to persuade Northcliffe not to travel, but Northcliffe refused to see him, and the party caught the 8.30 train from the Gare de Lyon with two minutes to spare. With Northcliffe were Steed; P. A. Goudie, a Paris director of the *Mail*; Sisley Huddleston, recently appointed Paris correspondent of the *Times*; Miss Rudge, a telephonist from London (Northcliffe said she was 'my special telephone spy'); a shorthand writer, and a valet. Pine had gone ahead with the Rolls-Royce. Huddleston soon left, when Northcliffe objected to his red silk handkerchief, his teeth, and his breath; he got off the train at Dijon. Another nightmarish day passed, Northcliffe talking without a pause, insanely one moment and lucidly the next; telling the girl telephonist dirty stories, then asking Steed if he had gone too far, and if this meant he was mad; refusing to eat food prepared by the chef in the railway president's private dining car, which had been attached for Northcliffe's convenience. Goudie was ordered to return to London and dismiss a hundred and twenty of the *Times* staff. A new obsession had appeared, the case of an English murderer called Ronald True who had just been reprieved and sent to hospital as a criminal lunatic. The *Mail*, as directed by telegrams from Northcliffe the previous week, was busy working this up into a scandal, denouncing the psychiatrist who was being held responsible, Sir Maurice Craig, and printing columns of letters expressing disgust that True wasn't to hang. Northcliffe dictated more telegrams to be sent from railway stations.

Robert Hudson met the train at Bellegarde, the nearest station to Evian. Pine had the car ready. 'Oh my dear Pine, I have had a hell of a time since you left me,' said Northcliffe. He leaned on Steed's arm, cursing porters and gendarmes. He was ill and beside himself on the fifty-mile drive to Evian, and when he arrived at the Hotel Royal, he was rude to the manager, the porter, Lady Northcliffe, and Sir Frederick Treves, whom he called an old fool. He agreed to see a local French doctor when told that he was an expert on German poisons, and an injection of morphia quietened him. But he continued to talk until 1 a.m.; as Steed noted, he had then been talking for twenty hours non-stop.

By the Tuesday, Sutton was on his way to Evian; behind him came Sir Leicester Harmsworth and Northcliffe's personal doctor, Seymour Price. Sutton must have realised that something serious was wrong before the weekend, as the hysterical telegrams began to arrive from Boulogne. He had cabled suggesting that Northcliffe was overworked and saying that H. G. Price was broken-hearted at receiving such messages. But there was little sense of urgency. They were like men in a dream, unable to react at normal speed. While Steed waited for Sutton to arrive, on Tuesday evening, he finally moved to neutralise any messages that Northcliffe might send to London before they could be intercepted. He cabled the *Times*: 'DISREGARD ENTIRELY AND UNPUBLISH, TELL CARMELITE DISREGARD AND UNPUBLISH ANY MESSAGES OR INSTRUCTIONS, DIRECT OR INDIRECT, FROM HERE UNLESS SIGNED SUTTON OR ME. SUTTON ARRIVES LATE TONIGHT.' Apart from telegrams to relatives, Northcliffe's messages were now being intercepted at source. Steed held on to telegrams complaining to the *Times* about soap advertisements on the literary page, and accusing the *Mail* of suppressing the name of Ronald True's mother. He stopped a message to Northcliffe's solicitors telling them to be kind or cruel to various journalists and managers. 'WAS POISONED BY THE GERMANS BY ICE CREAM' said one telegram that was not sent. 'I SHALL GIVE YOU ALL HELL WHEN I GET BACK' said another. In an unfinished telegram, Northcliffe referred to one of his office love affairs. But it was not easy to deceive him. He told Steed that someone in London was playing tricks on him, and, as though he knew that Steed had sent the 'disregard and unpublish' message, instructed him to cable Lints Smith in the name of Wickham Steed, to say 'YOU ARE A RASCAL AND A THIEF. I WILL HAVE THE LAW ON YOU. IF YOU DON'T LEAVE THE OFFICE IMMEDIATELY I WILL COME WITH THE POLICE TO TURN YOU OUT.' Steed sent a harmless telegram containing the same number of words; Northcliffe checked the total with the receipt from the Post Office. Part Two of 'Incognito in Germany' had appeared on Tuesday morning. Even as edited by Steed, it was a garbled piece of writing. Part One was still being taken seriously by the European Press. German newspapers, calling Northcliffe the 'great war agitator', were accusing him of being superficial and prejudiced. Sisley Huddleston, insulted on the train on Monday, was telephoning a polite story to the *Times* on Tuesday about French Press reaction. In *Le Temps*, a M. Galtier had commented that there was nothing like first-hand reporting. In the *Times* office that evening, a memorandum to the manager (Lints Smith) from the acting editor (Brumwell) said that 'the request of Sir Charles Russell for a paragraph on the Hospital of St John and St Elizabeth, I am afraid, cannot be granted, as it runs entirely counter to the Chief's wishes'. The shadow still moved behind the scenes. But Northcliffe's powers were now being clipped, though legally nothing had changed. John Walter, hearing the rumours, instructed his bankers not to hand over the share certificates that he had sold a week earlier. He was unable to stop the deal going through.

At Evian on Tuesday afternoon, Steed left to meet Sutton at Bellegarde. When they returned to the hotel, Steed learned that in his absence, a 'nerve specialist' had been brought from Lausanne, in Switzerland, on the other side of Lake Geneva. The Evian doctor told Steed that the specialist had written a certificate to say that Northcliffe was out of his mind. The certificate has never been found. The Harmsworths say it was never written. Steed didn't see it, but insisted that the local doctor told him Northcliffe was 'raving' when the specialist saw him, and that a certificate was definitely written, whose 'tenor' (Steed's word) was that Northcliffe was out of his mind. Someone did come from Lausanne; notes of cash payments made by the family at Evian include twenty pounds for a 'Lausanne doctor'. A male nurse came as well, and remained in attendance. Another consultant who arrived on the scene that week was Dr James Birley, a well-known neurologist at St Thomas's Hospital in London. Dr Birley was at Evian for a few days and was paid five hundred guineas, in cash, on the spot; a large but not abnormal fee. In later years, Lord Horder, the noted physician, responded to family requests by recording that Northcliffe was never certified insane.* Horder was not at Evian. Seymour Price, who was, denied that a certificate of insanity ever existed. There are grounds for treating these statements with caution; they have an air of too much innocence. It may be that the mysterious document was not technically a 'certificate of insanity'. Seymour Price, who owed his prosperity largely to Northcliffe, might have been disposed to interpret the evidence tactfully. Unpublished notes made by Horder for the family in 1954 point out that the question of having Northcliffe certified when he returned to London didn't arise because Horder organised a twenty-four-hour watch by a rota of male nurses. (Horder agreed to amend this revealing remark, but it suggests what he really thought.) Steed, of course, had a vested interest in putting the worst interpretation on Northcliffe's reactions. He was violently insulted for days, about matters which had some foundation in fact. When Northcliffe called him a fool and said he had been duped at Genoa, the remark was too near the truth for comfort. That encounter between Northcliffe and Steed crystallised the ailing proprietor's frustration with the *Times*. He bought it, saved it, instructed it; but the newspaper's spirit remained

---

* Conflicting statements about Northcliffe's mental state at the end of his life have led to much confusion. Fleet Street gossip, and most of the casual commentaries on Northcliffe and the Press, have taken for granted that he 'died mad'. Biographies have been more guarded, sprinkled with hints – for instance, Hammerton's *With Northcliffe in Fleet Street*, which says that 'eccentricity had merged into something much more grave and alarming', and speaks of 'a mysterious and terrible malady'. Pound and Harmsworth's official biography in 1959 set out to demolish the idea that Northcliffe was insane. As well as citing Horder, it quoted a statement by Seymour Price in 1926 that 'there is a world of difference between insanity and the delirium caused by such an illness as his' (i.e. endocarditis). In fact, Northcliffe's behaviour in 1922 leaves little doubt that he was suffering from an organic psychosis: his mental state was affected by physical causes. 'Delirium' is not an accurate term to describe his condition, though it may have seemed so in 1926. In plain English, anyone who suffers brain damage as a result of tertiary syphilis, arteriosclerosis or endocarditis may become psychotic. In Northcliffe's case, I suggest that his final outburst grew out of and was shaped by an unstable personality.

outside his grasp. He never dominated it as he did the *Mail*. Leicester thought that Steed was a disturbing influence on Northcliffe in his illness, and this is probably true. Steed's face, voice, and manner touched raw spots. Northcliffe treated Steed as he treated the *Times*, both wanting him and not wanting him, knowing himself to be a superior journalist and business man, yet lacking some ingredient that made the other more acceptable to the stuffy traditionalists who continued to rule the world – who, indeed, Northcliffe never seriously thought of overthrowing.

At the time, the family, naturally enough, kept Northcliffe's illness as quiet as they could, and abhorred any suggestion that his mind was unbalanced. Looking back, it matters little whether or not he was technically certified; the probability is that he was not. He was effectively out of his mind at least from the end of May. For nearly two weeks he staggered from place to place, a man in a nightmare, behaving so grotesquely that it seems hardly credible that no one of his family heard of it and tried to save him. From Wednesday, 14 June, he begins to glide from sight. The family has him. He will give no more orders, write no more headlines. That morning the *Mail* led the paper (for the third day running) with what it called the 'Ronald True Scandal'. Northcliffe had protested earlier about indications that True might be reprieved. On the previous Saturday he had sent specific instructions from Boulogne, amid the nonsense, to investigate the matter and interview Sir Maurice Craig, the doctor. It was Northcliffe's last campaign. By an odd coincidence, Craig's name is in Mrs Wrohan's address book.

Steed saw him for the last time early on Wednesday evening. Coherent at one moment, he said to Lady Northcliffe, 'My dear, when I'm well again, I shall present my humble duty to the King and ask him to take back our titles. Steed was right not to take a knighthood. We have been wrong. Hudson has been wrong, too. We shall be plain Mr and Mrs Harmsworth again.' A few minutes later came a fresh outburst. The Evian doctor was so aggrieved that he refused to have anything more to do with the case. Steed was venomously abused, while Lady Northcliffe hid her face in her hands and shouted at him to stop. Then it was her turn. Northcliffe had launched into an obscene monologue when Steed left for London with Sutton.

By this time, Leicester was presumably at the hotel. But there are inconsistencies in the dates, no doubt because the less he and Seymour Price remembered about Evian, the better. A telegram from Northcliffe to his mother on the Wednesday read: 'ALWAYS THINKING OF YOU DARLING. THIS IS LOVELIEST PLACE I HAVE BEEN IN. FOR FIRST TIME IN MY LIFE I AM DOING NO WORK. IF THERE ARE RUMOURS ABOUT MY ILLNESS IN LONDON GEORGE SUTTON WILL TELL YOU THAT THEY ARE UNTRUE. I HAVE BEEN UNWELL BUT AM NOW WELL AGAIN.'

There are few messages after that. If Leicester handled other intended telegrams at Evian, he destroyed them. He, not Lady Northcliffe, was in charge. She moved to the sidelines with Hudson, who wrote to Sutton on Friday, 16 June: 'This business is the devil. He is driving everyone round him into a condition which will *soon resemble his own*! Everyone is to be dismissed as soon as he gets back to London, *so pack your kit*!' The melancholy journey to London began on Saturday, after Northcliffe had tried to send a cable to Sutton that said: 'I CANNOT MAKE HEAD OR TAIL OF YOU ALL.' Leicester, Hudson, and Seymour Price travelled with him. The French President, M. Poincaré, provided his private rail coach for the journey from Bellegarde. According to Steed's account, it was he who intervened with the President, through an intermediary, to ensure there was no risk of Northcliffe being seized by the authorities as dangerously insane. Northcliffe was seen alone in the corridor, fingers white against the glass. He wanted to go via Fontainebleau, where, he said, he would make a new will and leave the *Times* to Leicester. Later there were stories, never substantiated, of a strait-jacket.

Reporters were watching for evidence that he was on the move; Fleet Street had had a week of rumour. Caird and Fish had issued writs for libel after Northcliffe's telegrams about wages. The *Mail* had announced on Friday that Lord Northcliffe was indisposed and ordered to rest, and that publication of his articles about Germany was suspended. At Carmelite House, the directors were understood to have taken over the management; presumably Sutton was using his power of attorney. Some of the office relatives, sacked during Northcliffe's drive against nepotism, drifted back. One was heard to complain that he had been pensioned off and would have preferred to leave things as they were. There were many rumours about Northcliffe's return.

On Sunday afternoon the Exchange Telegraph news service reported from Paris that he had passed through on his way to England. On the quay at Boulogne, Northcliffe tried to push a porter into the sea. A man from Thomas Cook's saw him at Dover being held by both arms, propelled along the platform like a paralytic. On the train to London, he drank thirteen bottles of Perrier. Sutton met him at Victoria Station, only to be shouted at. A car took him to Carlton Gardens. He had been away for twenty-four days. Now he vanished, as far as the outside world was concerned, behind a screen of brothers and doctors.

From his bedroom there were four telephone lines. At first he used these to sack people at the *Mail* and *Times*. He spoke to Steed and said he would forgive him. Presently the phones were cut off; then one seems to have been restored to provide a safety valve. Because of his threats to arrive at the *Times* and turn them all out, Lints Smith had the front door guarded by police with instructions to stop Northcliffe if he arrived. The *History of the Times*, which gives this detail, does not explain on what grounds Northcliffe was to be stopped. Legally he was sane and entitled to exercise his powers as chief proprietor. But the conspiracy against him that had been one of his neuroses over the years had come true. He was being kept locked up until such time as he recovered or died. Horder (at that time, Sir Thomas Horder) was called in on the Monday morning, 19 June. A male nurse was with Northcliffe. When Seymour Price said who the new doctor was, Northcliffe shouted, 'One of [Lloyd] George's bloody knights', and snatched a pistol from under his pillow. The nurse restrained him; the gun was not loaded. After this unpromising introduction, Horder was eventually able to examine the patient, finding him very ill, physically and mentally. Northcliffe refused to see him again, but he remained theoretically in overall charge of the case, with Seymour Price in daily attendance. Price and Leicester were on close terms. The brothers – Leicester and Cecil in particular – dictated what should happen. Lady Northcliffe was persuaded not to live at Carlton Gardens; she said later that she had been turned out of the house. After a week of enforced absence, Hudson – who was staying with her, at her house in Sussex – wrote to Leicester to say how upset she was at being kept in ignorance of what was going on. Hudson said she was nearing a breakdown; Leicester, who trusted neither of them, thought she had never looked better. She was certainly being kept in ignorance. On 30 June Seymour Price telephoned her to say that Northcliffe had slept well for six and a half hours and eaten a good breakfast, and that his mental condition was unchanged. Price omitted to tell her that during the night he had attacked and injured a male nurse with a poker. A week earlier there had been optimistic talk about appendicitis being at the root of the trouble. But Horder also noted symptoms that could have been those of endocarditis, an infection of a weakened heart that may persist for months before becoming severe. The heart murmur discovered years previously could have been evidence of valvular damage. Endocarditis can have neurological complications, and Northcliffe's later outbursts could have been associated with the disease. Northcliffe may have suffered brain damage already, either as a result of arteriosclerosis, or of syphilis, which is not infrequently found in association with endocarditis. The presence of a streptococcus in the bloodstream, affecting the heart, was soon established. A Wassermann Reaction test for syphilis was said to be negative. The test has a margin of error of not less than five to ten per cent. No documentary evidence of the test survives.

More male nurses had been engaged at the beginning of July, and sworn to secrecy. One would sit by the bed, another in an adjoining room. Northcliffe promised one of them a thousand pounds a year and a chicken farm. Newspapers and books were not permitted, and Northcliffe frequently asked for paper and pencils. On 7 July he pencilled a will which began: 'I, Alfred Charles William Viscount Northcliffe, being in good mental state, though suffering from one dangerous disease, Indian Jungle fever and another unknown to any doctors in Great Britain, poisoning by ice cream supplied on the Belgian frontier, where I was unfortunately known. First, I bequeath everything I possess to my wife to use exactly as she chooses under Sir Robert Hudson's guidance.' He particularly desired that 'the darling wife should remarry if she wishes'. Of his sister Christabel he said: 'Although the poorest member of our family, she from the outset resisted with energy, vigour, and counteraction the efforts of the foolish members of the Harmsworth family to wreak their vengeance on one who has built up things by originality. The fortunes these men have made with the exception of Viscount Rothermere are purely imitated. I invented the *Daily Mirror*. It was a failure at first, and Rothermere ran for his life. When it became a success, I sold it to him for nothing ...'

The will was witnessed by two male nurses. On 22 July an edited version appeared, in typescript. This was in roughly the same terms as before, with most of the verbiage removed (but not the Indian Jungle Fever and poisoned ice cream), and left everything to his wife. Instead of using his normal signature, 'Northcliffe', he signed it 'Alfred Charles William Harmsworth'. A doctor (not Seymour Price) and a nurse were the witnesses. It was assumed that Lady Northcliffe's hand could be seen in all this. She had insisted on her portrait being hung where her husband could see it, and be reminded of her. The second will was reported to have been slipped in to the sick room while Seymour Price was having a bracing ride in Leicester's car. Horder said afterwards that he was asked twice by a solicitor to act as witness, and refused. The first time, Northcliffe talked about selling Newfoundland; the second, he accused the solicitor of being drunk. On neither occasion could he have understood the nature of a legal document. Later, someone called at Horder's consulting rooms when he was away and tried to bribe his receptionist to produce the notes of Northcliffe's illness – in the hope, said Horder, of finding evidence of spells of normality. An estate of several million pounds was at stake. They were all playing an elaborate game with one another and with Northcliffe, declaring him to be normal or abnormal, depending on whether it suited the purpose of the moment.

At the *Times*, more intrigue was on foot. John Walter, kicking himself for having lost his shares and his option, sought means of retrieving them. Rothermere came into view as a possible purchaser if Northcliffe died. Lloyd George, of all people, became interested in joining a syndicate to buy the paper, perhaps in becoming its editor. He and Rothermere talked about it. Because there was no one to stop him, Rothermere appointed the assistant editor, Brumwell, to a new post of 'associate editor'. Who was running the *Times*? The power of attorney given to Sutton had not been revoked, and in the circumstances of Northcliffe's illness, Sutton was a Rothermere man. Campbell

Stuart also held power of attorney, but he was still in Canada. Rothermere moved into the vacuum. Ever friendly with Lloyd George, he instructed Brumwell to provide a leading article opposing a projected inquiry into the honours system. The market in knighthoods and peerages that flourished under Lloyd George was coming under attack; the previous month, the Prime Minister had been asked in Parliament if he would say 'How much do you give for a baronetcy, and what is the price of a knighthood?' The article was written. The atmosphere didn't improve when Steed returned to the office after dinner, read the article in proof, and rewrote it.

Northcliffe's fifty-seventh birthday was on 15 July. Christabel took him a bunch of jasmine from his mother, and he gave his sister a note to take back, headed 'Our Day'. Northcliffe had told her that he had changed his mind about her husband, Percy, and wanted to make amends in his will. Christabel thus came under suspicion from the Leicester-Cecil camp. Northcliffe had asked her if she would take him to Totteridge, but this was ruled out as impossible. The day before his birthday, the verdict of a heart infection had been confirmed to Leicester. Christabel told her mother for the first time how ill Northcliffe was, but said nothing about his mental state. A week later, on 22 July, Mrs Harmsworth saw him, for the first and only time since he returned from France. He made a scene. A few days later he cried out, 'Tell Mother she is the only one!' He was still able to use a telephone. He called the *Times* one morning near the end of July, and again in the afternoon, with orders and abuse. Steed's telephone was to be cut off; he was a nasty bounder. Northcliffe's mad words were taken down and passed on to the manager, neatly typed, as though they were a normal message. 'Have you seen Gordon Robbins in Fleet Street wearing a tall hat, strutting up and down? He has been trying to become editor of the *Daily Mail* at a salary of five thousand pounds a year. But he won't. He has been rude – that young man has – to my relatives. Find out why he wears a tall hat. Tall hats are only to be worn on special occasions. I know more than you think. My men tell me.'

Like a character from *Alice in Wonderland*, he suddenly asked, 'Are you a shrimp or a brewer?' It was an intricate chain of thought. The journalist who took the call was born at Gravesend;

the brewery there made Shrimp Brown Beer; the pubs at Broadstairs sold it. At the *Mail*, the last phone call seems to have been taken by Pulvermacher, the night editor. Northcliffe came on the line one evening, whispering instructions as to how he must be rescued from Carlton Gardens. It was found that he had used a key to Lady Northcliffe's boudoir, then taken the telephone and crouched under a table with it, so as not to be heard. He was increasingly under sedation. Sometimes he prayed or fasted; often he wept. At the *Mail* the principal obituary was already written and in type, lying on the printers' stone, partly made up into a page. The headlines had been set: DEATH OF VISCOUNT NORTHCLIFFE. THE FOUNDER OF THE *Daily Mail*. Northcliffe had asked that his death be given a full page. Campbell Stuart returned from Canada on 7 August, and new discussions began about the *Times*. Northcliffe alive had ceased to be a factor. On 9 August Horder decided he must have more fresh air, and ordered him to be moved to the roof of the house. The roof of Number 1 was not suitable, but the Duke of Devonshire next door gave permission for his to be used. A wooden hut was built, an echo of the bungalow on the hill where he used to escape from Sutton Place. Perhaps the hut was his idea, not Horder's. Seymour Price produced a version of his last wishes. By now he was comatose, and they were probably a hybrid of scattered remarks: 'I wish to be laid as near Mother as possible at North Finchley and I do not wish anything erect from the ground or any words except my name, the year I was born and this year upon the stone. In the *Times* I should like a page reviewing my life work by someone who really knows and a leading article by the best man available on the night.'

Over the weekend of 12 and 13 August, a policeman was posted outside the house to keep the road as quiet as possible. Fleet Street was just a mile away. News ebbed and flowed: fighting in Ireland; the prospect that Lloyd George would earn a pound a word for his forthcoming memoirs; the start of that once-momentous social and sporting event, the grouse-shooting season. On the Saturday, page four of the *Mail* carried an article, 'Grouse Today', by 'The Diner Out'. Grouse was neither the diet nor the sport of the average *Daily Mail* reader. But the 'Glorious Twelfth', when gentlemen left London for the moors to shoot, had been a favourite peg to hang articles on since the early days. 'Deserted London', said a headline of August 1899, when Alfred used to point the paper at England like a camera. 'The Hammersmith omnibuses still meander in a thin red line down Piccadilly, but then, though the season may come and the season may go, the omnibuses go on for ever. Palace Yard is a desolate waste, and policemen seem to represent the entire population. The park is still very green and pretty; under the lazily waving trees, hundreds of chairs spread their laps invitingly. But nobody comes to sit on them. In Mayfair you may pass hundreds of houses, and the blinds are down in every one of them. There is nobody stirring but a few footmen left behind, who sit upon the doorsteps in the cool of the evening and smoke.' Northcliffe didn't care about the grouse-cult. But he understood the aspirations.

In his hut he lay unconscious, his profile suggesting Napoleon. He was given oxygen on Monday morning as his breathing failed. He died at twelve minutes past ten. It was 14 August 1922. Cecil and Vyvyan were present. The rival *Star* beat the *Evening News* by half an hour with the first report, which announced the cause of death as ulcerative endocarditis; no postmortem was held. Next day his name filled the papers. Steed, the best man available on the night, wrote a two-column leader in the *Times*: 'Lord Northcliffe's greatness, and, indeed, his genius, are beyond question. To his personality none who came in touch with him could be indifferent. Many it attracted, some it repelled, but all felt its power.' Cecil asked to see the article in proof; he found nothing to alter. The funeral service was two days later at Westminster Abbey. Afterwards a procession of ninety cars drove to Finchley, in Harmsworth country, for the burial. Northcliffe's death released many pent-up frustrations. The will had to be contested. The *Times* had to be fought for. The future of the *Mail* had to be decided. One of the first acts of the directors was to recall or buy back every copy of 'Newspapers and Their Millionaires' they could lay hands on. Aides and secretaries had weeks of correspondence to deal with; many explanations to make as discreetly as possible. Somewhere in the mound of letters was one from a Mr Henry Pope, written three days before Northcliffe died, advising him to stop striving like a battalion of men, and go back to golf and fishing. 'But no,' wrote Mr Pope, 'you go your own mad foolish way, write a lot of silly pamphlets, and play into the hands of your enemies. You want a dog collar round your neck with a ship's cable and a padlock to hold you in. Bear in mind I want nothing – I cringe to no one, but I speak my mind. I pray God that you may get better and completely recover.' He had been Alfred Harmsworth's first office boy, in Paternoster Square. But that was a long time ago.

22

Voice from the Grave

NORTHCLIFFE'S GHOST would have enjoyed the intrigues and litigation that followed his death: the fine tangle of affairs he left behind ensured that he would continue to influence many lives and properties. His spirit, indeed, was soon to be in touch with Earth, dressed, it was said, in a grey flannel suit, talking at séances of the need for spiritual reform. But it didn't speak to Lord Rothermere, Sir Campbell Stuart, Sir George Sutton, or any of the others who wrestled with wills, options, and legatees. Everyone was busy in August 1922. The *Times* was the first muddle that had to be resolved. As a commercial investment it was not very desirable; Northcliffe's latest reforms had failed. As a key property in the British communications business, it attracted the usual cluster of interested parties. The manoeuvrings between 14 August, when Northcliffe died, and 23 October, when the *Times* passed into new hands, have never been satisfactorily explained, and are unlikely to be now. John Walter retrieved his option to purchase the paper, on Northcliffe's death, at the 'best price obtainable'. He had relinquished this option when he sold his remaining shares to Northcliffe early in June, just before it became apparent that the proprietor was desperately ill. The original agreement of 1913 was specifically cancelled on 15 June. However, Northcliffe's will of 1919 contained the same option-clause. By an agreement reached between executors and beneficiaries in September 1922, this 1919 will was agreed to be the appropriate one – not the suspect will drawn up a few weeks before Northcliffe died. Since the 1919 will contained the option-clause, it was agreed that this resurrected the option. Walter found a backer in the form of the Hon. John Jacob Astor, the rich younger son of the first Lord Astor, the American business man who had settled in Britain in

1890.* Rothermere also wanted the *Times*. He bid £1,350,000 for it, but Walter and Astor were able to match this 'best price obtainable', and the paper passed to them.

That was the outline; the details were more picturesque. There was the strange affair of Northcliffe's widow and the deathbed wills. She was probably material in having the 22 July will drawn up. Having got it, she used it to the full. It is unthinkable that any court would have endorsed this sad testament. It stemmed from a previous will which was clearly unbalanced; some of the absurdities remained, and it was signed 'Harmsworth' instead of 'Northcliffe'. But for Lady Northcliffe's purposes, its oddness was her strongest card. By propounding the will of 22 July, of which she was sole executrix, she threatened the family with a public scandal when the rival wills came before the court. The executors of the 1919 will – Henry Arnholz, the solicitor, and Sutton–consulted Rothermere. A plan was devised to buy off Lady Northcliffe. The 1919 will gave her ten thousand pounds cash and one quarter of the estate's income, for life. Under the compromise she had a fractionally smaller income, and the ten thousand pounds, with a new legacy of two hundred and twenty-five thousand pounds. From the family's point of view, this was blackmail. From her point of view, it may have been a fair return for years of deception and humiliation. Apart from Rothermere (always a realist) and Christabel (who had her modest share doubled under the compromise, because the July wills spoke of her kindly), her late husband's family cut her dead from then on. The following April she married Sir Robert Hudson; none of the Harmsworths attended; Cecil was asked to give her away at the wedding, and refused. She was rich, but – no doubt aware of the trust funds that would make the illegitimate children still richer – she complained of poverty for the rest of her long life. She used to say that the Harmsworths grudged her happiness and resented her marriage to Hudson (who died in 1927, leaving her widowed a second time). They may also have resented the two hundred and twenty-five thousand pounds and the way she got it.

* William Waldorf Astor, created a viscount in 1917. He and his son bought the *Observer* when Northcliffe and Garvin parted in 1911. His grandson, the Hon. David Astor, was later co-founder of the *Observer* Trust and editor of the *Observer*.

Sir Leicester Harmsworth.
Hildebrand said he was like
a public building coming
into a room.

Vyvyan, the youngest of the
Northcliffe generation. He
took the money that came
his way and settled for a
quiet life.

Viscount Rothermere. He looked like every man's idea
of a capitalist. In many ways he was.

The tale of the *Times* purchase is more tangled. John Walter wished to buy it. Campbell Stuart took his part from the moment Northcliffe died. They travelled to the funeral service at Westminster Abbey in the same car. Stuart acted as go-between with J. J. Astor, whose name had first been mentioned as a possible purchaser in June. But while they were persuading Astor (and concealing his name, as carefully as Northcliffe concealed his in 1908), other would-be purchasers were in the field. Lloyd George was the centre of more than one scheme. Sir John Ellerman, the shipowner, was ready with cash. Most of them called on Stuart – Rothermere, Lloyd George's friends, Lloyd George himself. Stuart says that Lloyd George offered him a peerage. Sir Basil Zaharoff arrived with a genial proposal to put a large slice of shares in Stuart's way if he helped him get the *Times*. Stuart says he told the ageing arms king that he was not a suitable person to be proprietor. He held firm to the idea of allying Walter with a buyer who was not tainted, politically or otherwise. Sir George Sutton, meanwhile – appointed to administer Northcliffe's estate temporarily – was ready and willing to sell the *Times*. The day he was appointed administrator, 22 September, he sold control of the *Daily Mail* to Rothermere for one million six hundred thousand pounds. Because of the Walter option, the *Times* could not go the same way. After Rothermere had formally given notice of his intention to bid for the paper, the matter came before a judge, who had to decide whether, in the circumstances, the Walter offer was going to be the 'best obtainable'. Neither party knew what the other's figure would be. Rothermere's counsel named one million three hundred and fifty thousand pounds. The shares were offered to Walter at this price, and four days later he (in reality, Astor) accepted. One version of the story is that Rothermere only pretended to want the *Times*, and was ingeniously pushing up the price so as to benefit estate and family. The evidence* is contradictory. Rothermere's son Esmond, later the second Lord Rothermere, believed that he was to become chairman of the *Times* when his father took over. But if it *was* all a ruse, the episode would be in character. Rothermere, a low-spirited man in most ways, was quite the reverse when it came to making money.

* See Appendix 2.

With Northcliffe gone, the head of the family was a much plainer, shallower man. Rothermere was dedicated to making money. His purchase of Associated Newspapers – *Mail, Evening News,* and *Weekly Dispatch* – was made through four hundred thousand deferred shares at four pounds each. To exploit these properties, and purchase more, he raised fresh capital with a company called the Daily Mail Trust. Acting surreptitiously with Beaverbrook, his principal rival in Fleet Street, he bought a chain of papers from Sir Edward Hulton. For many years, the Daily Mail Trust and Beaverbrook Newspapers were interlocked by shareholdings. Rothermere in 1923 had surpassed Northcliffe as a Press lord, as far as Stock Exchange values went. In London he controlled three daily, one evening, and four Sunday papers; in the provinces, another nine dailies and weeklies. Presently he sold off the former Hulton properties (at a large profit) to another rising newspaper family, the Berry brothers from South Wales, who were later ennobled as the Camroses and Kemsleys. Newspapers had grown into big business in Rothermere's lifetime, and he understood how to exploit them. At the *Mail,* which in theory was now in competition with his *Mirror,* he applied the methods he would have done years before, if Alfred had given him the chance. He took a knife to the paper's expenses, and sacrificed editorial columns to make way for more advertising. Profits increased, and the holding for which he paid four pounds a share soon shot up in value. Rothermere had let it be known at the time of purchase that he was doing it only to please his mother. Leicester, a sharp businessman himself, believed that by purchasing at the price he did, Rothermere was taking his revenge for the years long before, when Northcliffe had excluded him from control of the *Mail*'s finances. If Rothermere had had his way from 1896, the paper might have been consistently more profitable, so that by 1922 it would have been a far more expensive property. As it was, he bought it cheaply. This was not the version that Rothermere wanted to see publicised. But a suspicion that financial acumen, rather than filial respect for Mrs Harmsworth, had led him to buy the papers, aroused the wrath of one of the numerous ladies who benefitted under Northcliffe's will, Louise Owen.

Louise, employed at Carmelite House since 1902, regarded herself as Northcliffe's special confidante. She was the only mistress to set herself up against Mrs Wrohan; according to a book called *Northcliffe: the Facts*, written and published privately by Louise in 1931, Mrs Wrohan was not his mistress at all. Four years before Northcliffe died, he guaranteed Louise a yearly income for the rest of her life of four thousand one hundred and sixty pounds, tax free. This was a handsome sum, but she would have been aware that Mrs Wrohan's emoluments were handsomer still. Her rival died less than a year after Northcliffe, on 4 July 1923, at a nursing home in Broadstairs. Needless to say, Mrs Wrohan's death was mysterious. Northcliffe, in his last weeks, was supposed to have told his wife: 'Don't worry about her, she'll die of drink.' Louise Owen spoke of 'tragic circumstances, surrounded by a veil of mystery'. Cecil King wrote that she was fatally injured by a car outside Elmwood. The certified cause of death was heart failure; Seymour Price, appearing again at a crucial moment, signed the certificate. Her age was given as fifty-one. Leicester attended the funeral at St Peter's Church,* near Elmwood, hoping to find some clue to her identity among the flowers and mourners. It was a hot, still morning, the sunlight bouncing off the sea. Sutton was there; so was Montague Ellis, her solicitor. Rothermere sent a wreath. Leicester found no clues. Mrs Wrohan's will† showed a respectable fortune of a hundred and thirty thousand pounds. Montague Ellis was to receive three thousand pounds a year for life; Sutton, four hundred. Her death reduced but didn't remove the fear among some of the family that Northcliffe's former women friends might cause trouble. His widow was even afraid that if anyone wrote a biography that suggested a happy home life (presently, some did), former mistresses might be tempted to try blackmail. As it turned out, the only real trouble came from Louise Owen. Labouring under a sense of grievance, she threw sand in the wheels of the Northcliffe estate. The 'compromise' over the 1919 will, under which Lady Northcliffe received two hundred and

---

* Her place of burial became a further mystery. At least one of her children, Geraldine, believed that her mother had died in Paris and was buried at Brockenhurst, in Hampshire, one hundred and fifty miles away. She once pointed out the place to her husband.

† The will, drawn up in 1917, had some Northcliffeian complexities. Nine codicils were added later, revoking various legacies, among them a thousand pounds for Arnholz. Northcliffe was not mentioned, though in an earlier will, dated 1908, Mrs Wrohan had left him everything.

twenty-five thousand pounds, had to be agreed to by the bene-ficiaries. Louise refused to sign at first, and held out for several months. She became convinced that Rothermere had been allowed to buy the Associated Newspaper shares too cheaply, robbing Northcliffe's estate of millions, and eventually brought an action against Rothermere, Sutton, Arnholz, and the Attorney-General. Predictably, she lost, and was described by the judge as 'an extremely dangerous woman'. Her case was probably better than she was able to make it appear. It was not helped by her interest in spiritualism, which led her to suppose she was being guided by Northcliffe's ghost. She claimed to have seen the Chief in Paris and Switzerland. Northcliffe was an attractive source of spirit communications, real or fancied. Mrs Osborne Leonard, a famous spiritualist of the day, was in touch with him more than once. One message said that his teeth no longer bothered him. Sir Arthur Conan Doyle, visiting San Francisco, was informed that only a wave of spiritual reform could save the world from catastrophe. The message added: 'The American people are too busy. That was the mistake I made during my lifetime.' St John, hearing of the ghostly traffic, was haunted by the thought that there might be 'something in it'.

Rothermere, so far as one can tell, was not unduly hampered by memories of his brother. He plunged into action in the early 1920s, not only as a large-scale newspaper financier but as a political manipulator, of sorts. The idea that the Press could dictate successfully to Westminster was a long time dying. A prolonged campaign to reduce public spending, run during Northcliffe's lifetime in his *Mail* and Rothermere's *Mirror*, had considerable success because it matched the national mood. 'Squandermania' by the Government was blamed for everything. Rothermere wrote, or signed, articles condemning high taxa-tion. An Anti-Waste candidate, raucously supported by the *Mirror*, was elected for Dover in 1921. Rothermere's son Esmond, MP for the Isle of Thanet (the constituency that included Elmwood) since 1919, made anti-waste speeches in Parliament. But Rothermere soon moved on from concluding that govern-ments did some things wrong to concluding that they did no things right. His manner with politicians was truculent. In October 1922, when Lloyd George's Coalition had broken up and was replaced by a Conservative administration under Bonar

Law, Rothermere is reliably said to have demanded an earldom for himself and a Cabinet post for his son as the price of support for the new Government. He was shown the door.*Rothermere had fared better under the previous Prime Minister. He once wrote a two-sentence letter to Lloyd George, telling him to arrange for the Minister of Transport to have a vacant post at the Admiralty. His policy, inherited from Northcliffe, of being free to support or condemn politicians without fear, favour, or party-political bias, degenerated into a caricature of independence. One minute he was running a campaign against Bonar Law in the *Mail*, the next (when Beaverbrook intervened on behalf of his friend) he called it off. Had he applied a coherent set of beliefs, his independence might have been worth something. As it was, his criticisms were merely petulant. Northcliffe's actions had been no better rooted in organised belief, but his skill and passion as a journalist enhanced whatever he did, besides leading him to do certain things of importance. His life-long campaign against Germany saw him marching with events. When Rothermere tried·to march, he looked like a stage army. The new situations of the 1920s led many people to feel that the old political solutions were inadequate. Rothermere strove to find fresh answers. Whenever he thought he had one, he flung it in the face of the public. He was usually wrong, and wrong without panache. He became the clumsiest man in Fleet Street.

If his newspaper activities were a caricature of power, his private life was a caricature of affluence. His usual method of travel between Grand Hotels on the Continent was in a small convoy of Rolls-Royces – two for the passengers, one for the luggage. When he grew bored with the conversation of the aides beside him, the cars would halt and the passengers change round. He liked people to tell him stories; if they were far-fetched, so much the better. Girls were supplied as necessary. His wife led her own life. Business was conducted from wherever he happened to be; an editor was often with him on his travels, as political mentor, and secretaries were in attendance to keep

---

* The story was told by Lord Davidson, and incorporated by Robert Rhodes James in his book about Davidson, *Memoirs of a Conservative*. As J. C. C. Davidson, he was Parliamentary Private Secretary to Bonar Law, and said he heard what had passed between Bonar Law and Rothermere 'within seconds' of the latter's departure. Esmond, the second Lord Rothermere, has said he doesn't believe it.

in touch with the financial markets. People who met him for the first time were apt to be intimidated by the way he would sit, a big, gloomy man, listening hard, interjecting 'What, what?' if there was something he failed to understand. Sewell Stokes, a writer, who met him over lunch at a villa in the south of France in 1925, described this cold, stony pessimist, accompanied by an editor who said 'That's right, sir!' whenever his opinion was asked. Another guest mentioned that he owned some houses in the East End of London. 'You do?' said Lord Rothermere. 'Then you'd better sell 'em quickly, or they won't be there to sell. Isn't that right?' 'That's right, sir!' said the editor. The host at the villa that afternoon was Arthur Hendry, son of Auntie Miller – the cousin who had called Alfred a liar and a swindler in the Paternoster Square days. Rothermere now paid him a generous allowance, and he lived comfortably in the hills behind Antibes.

Those who knew Rothermere better found a more agreeable man beneath the bleak silences and moments of bluster. To Collin Brooks, a writer who knew him well in his later years, he once said: 'Ah, you thought I was a brazen-faced old man sitting in a corner counting his gold.' Brooks found him more complex than his outward behaviour suggested. It was Rothermere's misfortune to have the heavy features, hard eyes, crude manner, and enormous wealth of some archetypal capitalist. The increasingly pedestrian tastes in food (a weakness for cakes, scones, and sandwiches), and an aversion to strong liquor in his later years, were evidence of a simpler streak. He would gamble happily, winning money from his secretaries and returning it to them with a bonus next day. He liked his aides to stake money for him on the tables at Monte Carlo or Deauville, saying gleefully: 'I am the pirate.' Simplicity merged into ignorance: art dealers swindled him unmercifully.

Friends detected the sadness of a man who had wanted a large family, like the one he had known as a child, only to be left with one son alive out of three, and loneliness that set around him like concrete. Leicester observed him at a family party, dancing 'grimly and stiffly'. Money provided the light relief. It surrounded him with a golden haze. St John, writing to his sister Geraldine about 1925, advised her to stake her claim. 'Harold is in an expansive mood,' he wrote. 'There is a proverb which says, "Those nearest the fire get most heat". Get near the fire. In days to come my Perrier tree should be full of fruit – in those days you shall have your share. But reach out and get what you can now. There is lots about.' She got near the fire; Rothermere gave her a hundred thousand pounds in 1926. Northcliffe had been generous with allowances. Rothermere looked after people, but gave enormous presents as well. He told an acquaintance in 1924 that he was giving away thirty thousand pounds a year to nephews and nieces, and that he had made a present of one million two hundred and fifty thousand pounds to his son Esmond when he reached the age of twenty-one, a few years before. Women, he added, cost him between ten and twenty thousand pounds a year. He once called on Lady Hudson, after she had been widowed a second time, and remarked that she would doubtless like to have a little garden; the following day he sent her a cheque for five thousand pounds. One Christmas he gave each of his sisters-in-law a Rolls-Royce. He took a fancy to a hat that Leicester's wife, Annie, was wearing, and sent her a hundred pounds to buy some more. His nephew Geoffrey, one of Leicester's sons, who had become a journalist, wrote a *Times* article that pleased him; he received a cheque for five hundred pounds. Beggars were given five-pound notes by secretaries, who carried a supply for the purpose. Cecil was with him one day in 1927, travelling in the north of England. They stopped to visit York Minster, but were prevented from leaving by a thunderstorm. As they waited for the rain to stop, Cecil saw his brother stuffing five- and ten-pound notes into the cathedral contributions box. Good causes were drenched in Rothermere money. The headmaster of his old school, Marylebone Grammar, appealed for a thousand pounds; he was given ten thousand. University chairs at Oxford and Cambridge were endowed in the names of his dead sons, at twenty thousand pounds apiece.

In 1926 he paid a hundred and fifty-five thousand pounds for the site of the Bethlem Hospital in south London, the old Bedlam, and turned it into a park and children's playground in memory of his mother. She had died the previous year, and was buried near Northcliffe in the family grave; the lawn at Poynters was covered with wreaths. After the death of Alfred she had repeated constantly, 'It is the Lord's will, it is the Lord's will'. With Northcliffe and his mother gone, the family had lost both its genius and its conscience. Poynters was deserted; damp crept up the walls and the bells rusted; no one wanted to live in it. Apart from Rothermere, the brothers did little; except perhaps Leicester, who built up his remarkable collection of books and manuscripts. Since 1920 he had owned newspapers in the West of England, which he bought for his sons. Leicester was cynical and astringent, the brother who would have written the best account of the family, if he could have brought himself to tell the truth.

Cecil had retired from politics. He and Aunt Em had moved to a house overlooking Hyde Park, where she organised her own social events without reference to Cecil. They went on cruises, drove about the English countryside eating raspberries and cream, attended royal garden-parties, and never missed Henley for the annual Thames regatta. Cecil talked to everybody in the family except Mary Northcliffe, now Mary Hudson. He moved smoothly from one branch to another, genial and kindly. Everybody trusted Uncle Cecil. Given the shattered pleasures of some of the others, his lack of greed and ambition seems not only a virtue but a practical advantage. Some said he would have gone a long way but for Aunt Em. More likely, Aunt Em was what he wanted. As long as no one tried to reveal unwholesome secrets about the family, he could enjoy his role of literary monitor, writing memoirs and typescript reminiscences in which every Harmsworth was good and true.

St John still pursued a cure, with fading hopes. The family protected him, not without grumbling at the perpetual nuisance of Perrier, which was always about to make him a millionaire but never quite did; but they ensured that he lived in the state to which his tragedy entitled him. Rothermere took over the role of chief provider. Nephews and nieces who stayed with St John at his house on the Isle of Wight used to enjoy themselves acting as protectors of their uncle, who complained that a cripple could never escape from bores. Vyvyan once armed his children with a coal scuttle and posted them on the verandah to pelt unwelcome visitors with small lumps. One summer an old man of the Mudie family which had founded a circulating library in the nineteenth century battened on St John. He wanted Rothermere, or anyone with money, to finance a book that would prove it was Bacon who wrote Shakespeare. St John paid Christabel's children by the hour to sit and listen to the old man and keep him away.

Hildebrand still thrived on preposterous wagers, spending much of his time at an hotel in Brighton, where he used to annoy the management by putting down cheese for the mice. During his long retirement he invested shrewdly and built up a fortune. At one time he farmed in Sussex, and owned a herd of pedigree shorthorns that was written up in the agricultural journals. He shambled about in gym shoes, with hay on the path and weeds everywhere, making children scream with laughter, taking nothing seriously. Now, in Brighton, he lived alone in the little sitting-room of a private hotel, up a side street away from the sea. There had been no fame, no high office; yet he was as rich as he can have dreamt himself in the shameful days when he walked up and down mean streets in smoky cities, selling *Answers* from door to door. He didn't know what to do with his million or two. He liked rice pudding and standing with the crowd at football matches. But bets were real. He bet people they wouldn't do ridiculous things, for the pleasure of seeing them do it for a fiver. He bet strangers they wouldn't walk down the beach and out to sea till their hats floated off. To crown his non-career, Lloyd George had made him a baronet in 1922, at the request of Rothermere, who is supposed to have done it, not for Hildebrand but because he liked his elder son, and wanted him to inherit the title. Sir Hildebrand received sarcastic telegrams from relatives, but probably didn't bother to read them; he ignored correspondence unless it looked like dividend cheques. Having played the fool all his life, he left nearly one and a half million pounds when he died in 1929. He was one of the short-lived Harmsworths, dying (of cirrhosis) at the same age as Alfred, fifty-seven. Relatives noted that he expired at 9.45 a.m., almost the same time of day as Alfred, and within a few days of his age. Living or dead, Alfred was the family's point of reference.

23

Rothermere: The Survivor

WHEN NORTHCLIFFE'S POWERS were waning, he wrote to ask Rothermere what was wrong with the economy. 'I want you to help me,' he said. He didn't understand the post-war world of slumps, trade deficits, high taxation, and bloody-minded workmen. Neither did Rothermere. Rothermere understood stock markets and balance sheets, not the new need to manage national economies. He thought (like thousands of businessmen) that the war had been a temporary setback in the industrial idyll. If governments would only spend less and reduce taxation, leave industrialists alone and stop being soft to the workers, prosperity would return. His own prosperity made him all the more pessimistic about what would happen unless strong measures were taken. He saw advancing columns of Socialists, and behind them dust-clouds of Bolsheviks. In September 1924 he was writing to Lloyd George, by then an ex-Prime Minister, to say that Britain's mounting financial troubles provided a parallel with France, a few years before the Revolution. Soon, he thought, 'we shall be hurried towards our 1789'. A year later he wrote to say it would not be long before Lloyd George was brought back to deal with a national emergency (Rothermere, who was in Deauville, added that he had just seen a letter criticising Lloyd George in the *Daily Mail*; orders had gone to London that such letters were not to be published). When Rothermere thought about the apocalypse, he concluded that strong, business-minded men were necessary. They would impose rigid economies and reduce taxes: knifing extravagance, no doubt, as he had once knifed it on *Comic Cuts* and *Illustrated Chips*. After the General Strike of May 1926 had confirmed his gloomy forecasts, he looked still more favourably on Lloyd George, the politician who won the war, as a possible Man of

Destiny. Rothermere wrote to him in June 1927:

> May I suggest that in your public utterances you should make a move from your present standpoint and travel the road – the road almost invariably pursued by all great democrats – towards a very modified political dictatorship. Even a small advance along this road will secure you the support of the inner core of the Conservative party. Artistically done your movement will be very difficult to detect and almost before you know where you are you will be back to the days of December 1918 when you were regarded as the saviour of the country. It is too early to start a Lloyd George boom but I believe that in six months' time it will be possible for myself to inaugurate such a boom personally over my own signature.

At the same time, Rothermere was casting round for other men of action on whom the new politicians could be modelled. Like many others, he approved of what he heard about Italy's Mussolini, who had supposedly saved Italy from Bolshevism. Rothermere was in a position to publicise his opinions, but this failed to make him cautious. 'Do we need a Mussolini?' in the *Sunday Pictorial* and *Daily Mail* of March 1926 concluded that, despite Mussolini's genius, there were practical objections to a British dictatorship. But it called for an emergency committee of three strong men to run the nation's finances, free from interference by Parliament. There would be 'relentless economy'. Democratic instincts might recoil, said Rothermere; the alternative was worse.

In 1927, Rothermere was sidetracked from his authoritarian crusade by a farcical episode that could have come straight from a comic opera. Without warning, he took up the cause of Hungary. The country, which fought with Germany in the war, had been harshly served by the post-war Treaty of Trianon. This handed over tracts of territory and several million inhabitants to Rumania and the new States of Yugoslavia and Czechoslovakia. The idea of the campaign was suggested to Rothermere by a princess. Princess Hohenlohe-Waldenburg was a woman from (it was said) Vienna, who had married and later divorced a member of a family of fading aristocrats. Princess Hohenlohe and Rothermere met socially. Why she should have wanted him to campaign for Hungary never emerged, nor why he should have been so willing; perhaps, since Northcliffe had been a hammer of the Central Powers, helping to bring about Hungary's ignominy, Rothermere was groping for some magnanimous act that would reflect well on himself. By chance, he stumbled on a cause that was guaranteed to produce a popular response. That Whitsun he was in Vienna. His motorcade drove along the Danube to Budapest. He was there only a few days, before moving on to Venice. Two weeks later, on 21 June, the *Mail* filled its leader page with an article called 'Hungary's Place in the Sun', signed by Rothermere, which condemned the post-war frontiers, urged they be revised, and hinted that Wall Street could bring this about by refusing to lend money to the countries that had robbed Hungary. The Hungarians were delighted. An English milord had dropped out of the sky to champion them. The British Foreign Office was baffled. Rothermere had obviously been got at, but by whom? 'The remedy proposed by Lord Rothermere would be worse than the supposed disease,' said a disdainful minute of 22 June. Czechoslovakia and the other neighbours were incensed, and the topic raged in Balkan newspapers for months on end. Rothermere became a national figure. Officially the Hungarian Government dissociated itself from the Rothermere movement, while privately welcoming it as good cheap propaganda. By the autumn the Foreign Office, still as puzzled as ever, was consoling itself with reports that Rothermere was bored with his campaign, and the *Daily Mail* staff in despair. The *Express* was creeping up on the *Mail*, which could ill afford a campaign like the one for Hungary.

Rothermere was caught up in a private fantasy. For the Hungarians, it was different. They thought they were being taken seriously. While Rothermere's editors in London groaned at the columns of comment and counter-comment they had to carry, Budapest papers thrived on the story. Rothermere seemed like a magician; the *Daily Mail* like a spell. Hungarians named squares and fountains after him. His name was carved in hillsides. Rocks and trees were dedicated to the good Rothermere. In November a delegation came to London and presented him with an address of gratitude, signed by one and a quarter million Hungarians, a sixth of the population. When he was given an honorary doctorate at a university, he sent Esmond in his place, equipped with two open Rolls-Royces and a chartered aircraft. Esmond, greeted by cheering crowds, was entertained privately by the Regent of Hungary, Admiral Horthy, and the Prime Minister, Count Bethlen. Rothermere had been making substantial gifts since the campaign, and during the visit his son handed out a further ten thousand pounds to good causes. Later in the year, the episode reached its climax with a proposal by some Hungarian monarchists to offer the Crown of St Stephen to Rothermere. The country was a monarchy without a king; the idea of Rothermere as a successor to the Habsburgs was seriously canvassed. He pretended to be shocked at this turn of events, possibly because he wanted an excuse to disengage himself from the campaign. Other Harmsworths knew that all along he had been pleased to think he was a candidate for the throne.

By the end of 1928 the Hungary campaign was virtually over, though it smouldered on through the 1930s. It had given him great pleasure. Hardly a popular figure in his own country, he delighted in the praise from abroad. The episode showed Northcliffe's technique, of using the Press for personal ends, being mercilessly abused. If a proprietor felt liverish or magnanimous, his editors would have to reflect his liverishness or magnanimity. The cheapest expediency could govern his policies. In 1928, Stanley Baldwin was Prime Minister. The chairman of the Conservative Party wrote to him on 13 September to report that Rothermere had decided to support the Labour Party at the next general election; but would support the Conservatives instead if Baldwin were to slip a sentence of sympathy for Hungary into a forthcoming speech. It seems extraordinary now that politicians still took so seriously this game of seeking newspaper support. But given a situation where the proprietor's word could change the policy overnight – and where the proprietor was notoriously fickle – it was not so surprising. The noise that Northcliffe made still echoed. People were still influenced by his valuation of newspapers. And circulations continued to rise. The *Mail* was close to two million by 1928. The *Express* under Beaverbrook, another believer in Press power, was expanding rapidly. Rothermere's shifts and turns of policy must have looked more serious to those who thought they could suffer or benefit by them at the time.

After Hungary, Rothermere returned to the domestic battle. His talk of backing Labour was a passing phase; he had guessed, correctly, that Labour was going to win the coming elections.

British politics were going through an empty period; ideas were scarce. Rothermere settled for a straightforward policy: the Socialists must be stopped, and Baldwin and orthodox Conservatives were incapable of stopping them. His pessimism seemed to be justified on all counts. The Labour Party scraped home in May 1929. National economies were faltering. In 1928, staying in Venice, Rothermere had been heard to say: 'Look at those Americans. You won't see them here next year. There's a crash coming.' As it loomed up in October 1929, Rothermere took a third of a page in the *Times* to insert an advertisement, in the form of an interview with the city editor of the *Daily Mail*, telling investors not to panic foolishly and sell their shares in his newspapers (which now included a chain of provincial evening papers, engaged in a ruinous battle with the Berrys, city by city). Rothermere begged the timorous not to be stampeded by baseless rumours about the stock markets. A few weeks later came the Wall Street crash. Rothermere himself, heavily invested in the American market, is said to have lost a fortune; family gossip spoke of millions. A newspaperman met him in the small hours one morning, walking dejectedly in St John's Wood, by the wall of Lord's. He complained he couldn't sleep. The newspaperman took him back to his flat for coffee. Rothermere said he had lost heavily on the stock market that day. Soon, he cheered up; he had wanted someone to talk to.

For a year or two, he tangled regularly with the Conservative Party, expecially with its phlegmatic leader, Baldwin. Both Beaverbrook and Rothermere agitated for his removal. In January 1930, Press power lurched forward: a new political party was launched by Beaverbrook, with Rothermere close behind, designed to put a zip into Conservatism. Christened the United Empire Party, it was mainly a vehicle for Beaverbrook's dream of Empire free trade, his version of the old cry of Protection for British and Commonwealth interests. Tacked on to its programme were vaguer clauses about economy and the defence of national interests. It was these that interested Rothermere. The *Mail* heralded the new party with its biggest headlines. For twelve consecutive days, the United Empire Party was the main news story in the paper. Reports spoke of tens of thousands of recruits, and suggested a national reawakening. Every morning there was a leading article. Then, suddenly, the story stopped as abruptly as it had begun. On a Wednesday it dominated the paper. On Thursday someone had turned off the tap. There might never have been a United Empire Party. Such clumsy handling was likely to devalue any campaign. Two days later, on Saturday, the story began again, with a different emphasis. Baldwin had promised to hold a referendum on the subject of food taxes. This satisfied Beaverbrook for the moment, and he withdrew from the campaign, leaving Rothermere to exploit the UEP along the lines that had interested him from the start. The awkward silence had covered this change of direction. Rothermere came out for 'ruthless economy', together with 'no more surrenders in India' (where Gandhi and civil-disobedience campaigns were causing trouble) and 'no diplomatic relations with Moscow'. Rothermere wanted rampant Conservatism. His campaign stumbled along, losing steam and adherents, changing direction yet again before the end of the year. Having found one admirable strong man in Mussolini, Rothermere now found a second and better candidate in Hitler. The National Socialists were on their way to power in Germany, and Rothermere greeted them in September 1930 with a long article (presented, as usual, as the main news story) headed GERMANY AND INEVITABILITY. A NATION REBORN. YOUTH ASSERTING ITS POWER. This saw the National Socialists under Hitler as a bulwark against Communism. It contained the interesting news that Rothermere (Beaverbrook wasn't mentioned) had set up the United Empire Party with a purpose similar to Hitler's: to organise youth against the 'corruption of Communism'.

For the next few years, Rothermere saw Hitler as a blessing. The United Empire episode was soon forgotten, though Empire-minded Conservatives popped up at by-elections to oppose the official candidates. A by-election on March 1931 provided the last organised battle between Press lords and politicians. Beaverbrook and Rothermere supported an independent Conservative at the by-election in the wealthy constituency of St George's, Westminster. *Mail* and *Mirror* took as their theme, 'Gandhi is watching St George's'. The Conservatives were so anxious about the newspaper threat to the party leadership that they considered starting a new evening paper of their own, and might have done so if anyone would have put up the eight hundred thousand pounds it was estimated to cost. At St

George's, Baldwin decided to treat the by-election as an attempt by the Press to dictate to the Conservatives. Two days before polling he made an aggressive speech in which he accused Beaverbrook and Rothermere of producing, not newspapers in the ordinary sense of the word, but 'engines of propaganda for the constantly changing policies, desires, personal wishes, personal likes and dislikes of two men'. (In fact, Beaverbrook was a model of consistency beside Rothermere.) Baldwin went on to use a phrase that had been suggested by his cousin, Rudyard Kipling: 'What the proprietorship of these papers is aiming at is power, and power without responsibility – the prerogative of the harlot throughout the ages.' On election day a group of editors took up the cry with a statement about 'irresponsible amateur politicians', meaning newspaper proprietors; among the signatories were two former editors of the *Times* who had suffered under Northcliffe and were now getting their own back, G. E. Buckle and Wickham Steed. More to the point, the official Conservative candidate won the by-election. The victory and Kipling's fine phrase rang conclusively in people's ears; apparently the Press lords were not only immoral in their quest for power, they were ineffective as well.

With Hitler and the rise of the Nazis, Rothermere returned to vaguer forms of persuasion. He saw the new Germany as a splendid defence against the creeping Communism he feared, and directed the *Mail* to say so. He was quite right when he drew attention to Russian slave-labour camps, but unwise to see no menace in Hitler's totalitarianism. Northcliffe, whose name he invoked more than once when he wrote about Europe, would hardly have missed the point. In July 1933, six months after Hitler became Chancellor, Rothermere wrote in a *Mail* article headed 'Youth Triumphant' that anyone who visited Germany would soon discover that so-called atrocities 'consist merely of a few isolated acts of violence such as are inevitable among a nation half as big again as ours'. He had little patience with Germany's Jews: 'In the last days of the pre-Hitler regime there were twenty times as many Jewish Government officials in Germany as had existed before the war. Israelites of international attachments were insinuating themselves into key positions in the German administrative machine ... It is from such abuses that Hitler has freed Germany.' Shortly after, Leicester had lunch with the editor of the *Daily Mail* and unburdened himself of fears that 'Hitler worship' in the paper was going to alienate not only Jews and Jewish advertising, but readers who had been brought up to suspect Germany. Leicester wrote in his diary:

Northcliffe had conducted this campaign for years before the war, and the war itself, provoked by Germany as it was, had been the great justification of Northcliffe's campaign. Upon this campaign and the wise direction Northcliffe gave the papers throughout these years and during the war I felt, and always had felt, that the strength of the *Daily Mail* and its reputation was based. To reverse this policy, and adopt one of unnecessary friendliness with Germany and Hitler, and Hitlerism worship, would be contrary to the instincts of British nationality, and would inevitably react unfavourably, and perhaps disastrously, upon the circulation of the *Daily Mail*.

Sales stagnated in the 1930s, and by 1934 the *Mail* had been overtaken by the *Express*. Rothermere harmed the paper and his own reputation. Chance had provided him with a platform for views that would have been best confined to dinner parties and the balconies of Riviera hotels. He sent Princess Hohenlohe around Europe as an unofficial ambassadress, paying her five thousand pounds a year plus other sums to consult right-wing figures on his behalf. She visited the Regent of Hungary and talked to him about restoring the Habsburgs. Another of Rothermere's ideas, when Hitler was on the way to power, was to restore the German monarchy at the same time. The princess went from castle to castle. She saw Hitler more than once. So did Rothermere, who told the princess she would 'live in history'. But it was pure imagination and self-deception. Rothermere, like others at the time, was not manipulating anyone; he was being manipulated.

His enthusiasm for the fascists reached its peak with a clumsy campaign on behalf of the British movement, under Sir Oswald Mosley. This was a grandson of the Mosley whose wholemeal loaves started Northcliffe on his Standard Bread campaign in 1911. The Mosley of the 1930s was a dashing young politician who had begun his career as a Conservative. He later joined the Labour Party, and became a member of the Government in 1929. Two years later, having resigned because his radical solutions to mass unemployment (later seen as soundly based) were rejected, he formed a political party of his own, the New Party.

When this failed, he moved towards authoritarian politics, and founded the British Union of Fascists. Here, at last, was a British version of the strong man, the leader, who would put things right without weak-minded nonsense about democracy. Mosley has written that 'the final act in all real things is will', a phrase that would have appealed to Northcliffe. Rothermere had detected Mosley's shift towards fascism in 1931, while the New Party was still in existence, and in December he offered the support of his papers. Mosley declined for the moment; he wanted to lie low. Three years later, when the British fascists, black-shirted and well organised, were on the way to becoming Mosley's 'instrument of steel', the offer was accepted. A telegram of support arrived from Rothermere in Monte Carlo, followed by a long signed article in the *Mail* on 15 January 1934, headed 'Hurrah for the Blackshirts!' 'We must keep up with the spirit of the age,' wrote Rothermere. 'That spirit is one of national discipline and organisation.'

For five months, Rothermere used his papers to campaign for Mosley, who says that what appealed to Rothermere was not the detailed policy of the British Union of Fascists, but its air of purposeful patriotism. 'He was an ultra-patriot,' says Mosley. 'He was in a state of terror that the Empire would be lost, so he would back anyone who looked like a strong boy.' A blackshirt rally was a 'stirring rally' in the *Daily Mail*. There was much talk of youth and idealism. Rothermere gave money to the Fascists, and also conceived a plan to make a fortune, for the movement and for himself, by using the party's several hundred branches as outlets to sell cigarettes that he would manufacture. He bought machinery and lured a manager away from Imperial Tobacco, telling Mosley that 'one of two things is going to happen: either we're going to do a lot of business, or the tobacco companies are going to pay us a large amount of money not to do business'. But advertisers, already restless at the *Mail*'s fascist campaign, became still more restless when they heard of the cigarette scheme with fascist partners.

Mosley says it was the specifically Jewish advertisers who stopped Rothermere 'at the point of the economic gun'. He recalls Rothermere in a London hotel bedroom, lying on a narrow brass bedstead, looking like a cross between a teddy-bear and a balloon, agonising over his support for the Blackshirts. Mosley told him that his brother would have filled the streets with contents bills saying 'Jews Threaten British Press'. But that would have been Northcliffe, the vim and vigour man; and even he, by 1934, might have been disinclined to do battle with the advertisers. 'Rothermere dithered,' says Mosley. 'The whole bed trembled with the dithering. He said, "I'll let you know, I'll let you know".' The result was a foregone conclusion. Rothermere stopped the campaign; he sold the cigarette machinery. Before he withdrew, the *Mail* had time to print a tendentious report of the Blackshirt rally at Olympia, London, on 7 June 1934, one of the ugliest clashes between Fascists and Communists. In July, the *Mail* published an exchange of friendly letters that Rothermere and Mosley had concocted between themselves to smooth over the parting of the ways. Having urged young men to join the British Union of Fascists (and printed its address) Rothermere now spelt out his aversion to fascism, dictatorship, and anti-Semitism. It was another muddled performance.

Later, Rothermere and the *Mail* hoped that the episode would be seen as part of a campaign to strengthen Britain. It was true that Mosley's policy included strong armed forces, and that Rothermere had been campaigning for a bigger air force since the end of 1933. But Rothermere's support for Mosley, like his lenient view of Hitler, stemmed from his fear of Socialism. It was only from the end of 1933 that his admiration for Hitler as the 'bulwark against Communism' began to merge into the more defensible (if misguided) matter of trying to understand what Hitler wanted, in order to appease him. The rearmament campaign was carried on vigorously enough, with constant demands for more aircraft, which brought accusations of warmongering against Rothermere from left-wing politicians. Taken by themselves, the articles are impressive evidence of foresight and boldness. 'The day of the warship is over,' wrote Rothermere in the *Mail* in December 1933. 'The day of the warplane has come. Our desperate deficiency in these modern weapons puts the very existence of Britain in deadly peril. Fate has never pardoned a people that refused to move with the times.' He even had an aeroplane designed and built by the Bristol Aeroplane Company at his expense in 1935. He called it the 'Britain First', which was one of Mosley's slogans; later, as the 'Blenheim' light bomber, it went into production for the RAF. As the *Mail* kept reminding its readers, the campaign for a bigger air force was reminiscent of the pre-1914 campaign for a bigger navy. But Northcliffe had been single-minded; he understood the mood of the times, and clamoured for arms to fight an enemy whose wickedness he never doubted. Perhaps European politics were more complex in the 1930s; this was all the more reason for an amateur politician to tread carefully. Rothermere's rearmament crusade was an uneasy complement to his soft, extravagant words for Hitler. His policy sprang from fear, not courage. It made him look foolish politically and it made the *Mail* look foolish journalistically. Northcliffe had seen the Germans as 'a nation of land crabs': make concessions and they took advantage; be resolute and they stepped back. This would have been a useful philosophy for the thirties. It meant nothing to Rothermere, who wanted to be nice to Hitler. The charge was laid against many people. I was wrong, said Rothermere in 1939, but so was half Britain. Unfortunately he was wrong at great length, in print, in a tone not far short of adulation for the Nazis. Whoever wrote the articles about Hitler (it is said to have been G. Ward Price) served him badly.

At Christmas 1934 Rothermere was in Germany, visiting Nazi leaders. Earlier in December, Rothermere signed a main news story from the Saar, declaring that the region must be returned to Germany (as it was, before long). A Christmas article described conversations with Hitler in his office, or beside a red log-fire as the winter dusk came down. It spoke of miracles and faith and Germany's new soul, all due to this simple fellow who neither drank nor smoked. It waved aside tales of hunted Jews. Hadn't Rothermere seen happy parties of them in restaurants? The Germans were our friends. 'We have no ground of quarrel with these people ... We and the Germans are blood kindred.' The British Ambassador in Berlin, Sir Eric Phipps, writing to the Foreign Office during the visit, remarked that 'Rothermere's is a strange, rather muddled mentality. He seems to oscillate between panic of Hitler combined with a curious admiration for him.' Ward Price, taken on one side, talked about Rothermere's belief that Germany was heading for war with Britain, which led him to advocate both a strong air force and concessions. Ward Price agreed that the more Germany had, the more she wanted; but it was impossible to convince

Rothermere. The Foreign Office watched Rothermere's excursions with a mixture of amusement and alarm. The visits to Germany continued until 1937. Wordy letters passed between Hitler and Rothermere; pictures and presents were exchanged.* One of Rothermere's themes was that some of Germany's African colonies, taken from her as the price of defeat, should be restored. He pressed this view to such an extent that Hitler wrote to him in December 1935, urging restraint:

> You ask me ... whether I do not think that the moment has now come to put forward the German colonial wishes. May I ask you, dear Lord Rothermere, not to raise this point now because looking forward to closer collaboration with Great Britain I do not want to give the impression as if I wanted to avail myself of the present situation of your Government and its many difficulties, and of the British Empire, to exercise a certain pressure.

Rothermere's Hungarian campaign gave a dying twitch in 1938 when Hungary received back some of her territories as part of Hitler's dismemberment of Czechoslovakia. The Munich settlement in September that year, which averted a European war, substantially diminished Czechoslovakia. The *Mail* of 8 November managed to report, at length, on Rothermere's return to Budapest as guest of honour during the celebrations, without once mentioning Hitler. Four months later Hungary occupied more of her lost territories, as the Nazis marched into Prague, and Czechoslovakia collapsed. This time the *Mail* had nothing to say about celebrations. Hungary was aligned with Germany, and Germany was bent on war. It was 1939. Rothermere was seventy years old, and tired of Fleet Street. He was afraid of war; saw ruin around every corner. The exaggerated pessimism of a letter he wrote to his son from New York in October 1937 would be funny if it were not sad: stock markets are falling, crime is rampant, life is cheap, German bombers are terrifying, food has no flavour, taxes are crippling, the Jews are everywhere. 'What I wish to impress [on] you,' he wrote, 'is to look out for anything and everything. Anything may happen

---

* Rothermere's Nazi phase proved useful during the war for one of his nieces, Christabel Bielenberg, a daughter of Christabel Burton. In 1934 she married a German lawyer, Peter Bielenberg, and went to live in Germany. After the 1944 bomb plot against Hitler, Bielenberg was arrested as a suspected sympathiser. Mrs Bielenberg used her Rothermere connection to help hoodwink the Gestapo.

any day, and everything is sure to happen before the end of next year.'

The coming of war in 1939 fitted the last segment of the nightmare into place. It is said that he destroyed his private papers. In May 1940, Beaverbrook, who had been made Minister of Aircraft Production, asked him to visit the United States on behalf of his department; Rothermere's life was full of faint parallels with Northcliffe's. In New York he seemed well; in Canada during the autumn, there were snow flurries and he missed the sun. One day his legs gave way under him. Doctors sent him to Bermuda to rest. Dropsy was diagnosed. As he grew weaker his manner became gentle. He was anxious about relatives and friends in London, where bombs were falling. News of the air raids distressed him. Just before he became unconscious, he said he no longer wanted to live: 'There is nothing I can do to help my country now.' He died on 26 November 1940; the post-mortem showed cirrhosis. His estate amounted to a paltry two hundred and eighty-one thousand pounds: the man who was good with figures had taken care to avoid death duties by disposing of his money in trusts and settlements.* Cecil wrote the words for his gravestone in Bermuda: 'He was a man of boundless generosity both public and private. He loved his country and died in her service.' But it was his misfortune to have his character measured by that of Northcliffe.

* The Harmsworth brothers and sisters paid duty on eight and a half million pounds between them. Northcliffe's will was proved at £5,248,000; another fortune went into trusts for his children. Hildebrand left £1·4 million, Leicester and Cecil half a million each, Violet £177,000, Vyvyan £107,000, Geraldine £92,000, St John £55,000 and the placid Christabel £26,000.

24

Family Ghosts

THE HARMSWORTHS liked return journeys to places they once knew. They were a harsh family; awkward-minded; secretive; sentimental. Alfred Senior used to walk around the Berkshire villages where Hannah Carter was born. Alfred, Lord Northcliffe, was seen, a year or two before his death, leaning on the gate of Rose Cottage in Hampstead, engrossed in thought. In 1933, a few days after St John died, Leicester got his chauffeur to drive him to Kilburn and West Hampstead; he stopped to potter around a Woolworths, before returning home via Salusbury Road, where his father's last house still looked out over the cemetery. The following year he went to Totteridge with Cecil on a winter's afternoon. Poynters stood empty, as it had done for nearly nine years. The lake at the foot of the grounds was filled in. New houses were encroaching – Northcliffe Drive and Harmsworth Way. 'A strange experience,' he said.

Yet as a family they were anxious to outlive their past. Leicester used all his powers of persuasion on Geoffrey, his journalist son, to deflect him from writing a history of the firm, in case it revealed too much. Geoffrey had access in the early 1930s to Northcliffe's papers. Leicester asked him not to look at his correspondence with Northcliffe, and advised him not to look at his brothers', either; they might resent it. When Evelyn Wrench's autobiography, *Uphill*, was published in 1934, Leicester instructed his West Country newspapers not to review it, because it contained 'ungrateful references' to Northcliffe. Cecil was still more discreet. He was prepared to have parts of Northcliffe's original diaries for the 1890s destroyed if they threw any light on the break with Captain Beaumont and the supposed homosexual scandal. Cecil's daughter, Daphne, once found him tearing up a letter written by his grandfather, William Maffett. 'I've done a good deed,' he said happily. She retrieved the pieces and stuck them together; it was about a family tiff, three-quarters of a century before. Even Printing House Square was influenced. The *History of the Times* (Volume 4, part II) sought to hint that Northcliffe may have been suffering from more than ulcerative endocarditis when he died. The second Lord Rothermere, shown a draft of the relevant chapter, objected to Stanley Morison's qualifying phrase, 'according to the doctors'. The offending words were deleted before publication.

The Harmsworths kept most of their secrets successfully. Alfred Benjamin Smith, Northcliffe's first illegitimate child, went to Australia and died there – in a lunatic asylum, it was said – around 1929. (His half-sister was employed at one time to read and criticise serial stories for Harmsworth magazines.) Mrs Wrohan's three children grew up undisturbed. Occasionally someone would drop a hint about Northcliffe's private life. In a 1930 biography, Hamilton Fyfe wrote that Lady Northcliffe had seen her husband, 'disappointed in his hope of a family, turn from her and solace himself in another home'. That was as far as it went. Louise Owen privately published her *Northcliffe : the Facts* in 1931, which mentioned Northcliffe's son by a maid-servant, but pretended that the other children were neither his nor Mrs Wrohan's. The doctors and solicitors kept their professional secrets. Those in a position to reveal anything about the Harmsworths kept quiet. Thomas Marlowe of the *Mail* left no papers. Fred Wood left a diary covering the period when he and Alfred Senior were young men together; some (perhaps all) of it was shown to the Harmsworth family years ago; later it disappeared. George Sutton, who must have known enough to fill several volumes, remained tight-lipped. After the first world war, he was earning thirty thousand pounds a year as chairman of the Amalgamated Press. As Northcliffe's executor, he had to sell the company to meet death duties. The Berry brothers, who bought it, would have kept him on, but he stayed in the fold as managing director of Associated Newspapers at a reduced salary. He produced no awkward recollections. Sutton had secrets of his own. When he was dying in a nursing home in 1947, his last words were: 'I have seen Northcliffe. He understands everything.' Sutton left four hundred thousand pounds.

The first-generation Harmsworth men had thinned out before

the second world war. St John's death in France in May 1933 came soon after he had made 'a last attempt to break out of my chains', going to the Black Forest in Germany for treatment. He was a few days short of fifty-seven, the age at which Northcliffe and Hildebrand died. The Perrier business went to his brother Vyvyan and his three sisters, Violet, Geraldine, and Christabel. Quarrels about the will broke out immediately. His nurse was thought to have got too much. Lady Rothermere attended the service at Golders Green Crematorium, looking old and haggard; Violet, beady-eyed, said she didn't recognise her at first. Afterwards Lilian Rothermere wanted to visit Violet in her flat, in order, it was suspected, to gauge her style of living so as to guess whether Rothermere was paying for it. The women met, quarrelled, and parted angrily. Later St John's ashes were thrown overboard from a hired cross-Channel steamer, the *Maid of Kent*, midway between England and France, with the family on board. Leicester was unwell and unable to be there; he borrowed a telescope from one of the Kenealys, but it was foggy and he saw nothing.

With worsening heart trouble, Leicester was forced to turn over the management of his papers and the *Field* magazine to his second son, Harold – the elder son, Alfred, was a recluse who had been severely wounded in the first world war. Leicester kept a diary for the few years of his retirement; it is heavy with melancholy. He remembers the anniversaries of deaths. He looks glumly at Rothermere's Hitler campaign. He avoids Northcliffe's widow at a wedding reception, and is irritated to hear from Christabel that Mary Northcliffe, who must be worth not less than forty-five thousand pounds a year, free of tax, plus capital of two to three hundred thousand pounds, is still professing poverty. As always, the family is absorbed in its own affairs, but set against itself. Leicester died four years after St John, in 1937. Alfred inherited the title, to become Sir Alfred Harmsworth, Bt. Leicester's second son, Harold, had been knighted two years earlier, after heroic efforts behind the scenes by his father. There was still a confusing multiplicity of Harmsworth titles.*

---

* At one time there were five Lady Harmsworths: the widow of Sir Leicester; the divorced wife of Sir Leicester's son, Sir Alfred; the widow of Hildebrand; the wife of the second Sir Hildebrand; and Aunt Em, wife of Cecil, who got a barony in 1939. London stores used to send them one another's bills.

Cecil and Rothermere were the surviving 'heavies'. Cecil thrived in retirement; all through the troubled thirties he fished, wrote a little, and sent letters to the *Times* about the neglected mulberry and the still more neglected medlar. Rothermere, whose political wire-pulling was not what it had been in the palmy days of Lloyd George, had tried more than once to get him a title, succeeding finally in 1939, the year before Rothermere's death, when the New Year Honours produced a barony for Cecil Bisshopp Harmsworth, 'for political and public services'. He took the title of Baron Harmsworth of Egham, the town outside London where he lived; cheeky young Harmsworths referred to him as Lord Ham of Egg. He enjoyed his title for nine years; dying in 1948 at the age of seventy-eight.

The most remarkable survivor was Northcliffe's widow. She lived until 1963, when she was about ninety-five. At her house in Surrey she tended the garden and regarded her visitors with flinty blue eyes. To the end of her life she felt she had been hard done by (although she left half a million), and was heard to complain at not being given the *Times*, as Alfred had intended in his last will, because of some 'funny business' that no one would ever get to the bottom of. No one, she said, knew what she had suffered; Alfred could be everything at once, tender and harsh, gentle and ruthless; but he should never, never have married. She would talk coyly about her lovers.

Had Alfred lived as long as Mary, he would have seen the start of the television age. Even if he had lived to Cecil's seventy-eight, he would have seen the coming of the second world war. He would have seen one of his former properties, the *Daily Mirror*, transformed into the next new wave in British journalism, with one of his nephews involved, to the disquiet of certain uncles. Had he lived, of course, he might have been involved in it himself. But he would hardly have been equipped, in late middle age, to make the emotional leap that was needed to produce such a break with tradition.

In the early 1930s, the *Mirror* was a very bad newspaper. Rothermere formally relinquished control early in 1931, and sold off his personal shareholding gradually, though as late as 1934 his influence was strong enough to have his articles in praise of Blackshirts reprinted there. It was genteel, unimaginative, doomed. It was also, by that time, controlled by no one in particular; the shareholdings were dispersed among a variety of owners. Editorial direction passed to a middle-aged executive, Guy Bartholomew. Bartholomew had been with the *Mirror* since it was a few months old. He was originally a photographic technician; a brash, audacious man without much of an education, who in 1934 put his brashness and audacity to work, and aimed the *Mirror* at a lower and bigger layer of the mass market than papers like the *Mail* and *Express* catered for. It was a paper for people who didn't read papers, but who could be tempted with big headlines, human interest, sex, and irreverence. The *Mail* had left out boring speeches; the *Mirror* left out boring topics, or it mentioned them only to say how boring they were. It kicked against the established order in a way that Northcliffe never did. Politically it moved steadily to the Left. Its success was enormous.

The Northcliffe nephew who backed Bartholomew was Cecil King. Cecil, one of Geraldine's children, was a strapping man in his early thirties, with a face that resembled Northcliffe's, and some inner drives – unhappy childhood, bouts of self-hatred – that made him one of the more complicated Harmsworths. He had worked on the papers while Northcliffe was alive, and in 1926 joined the advertisement department of the *Mirror*, where he kept asking Rothermere to make him a director. In 1929 Rothermere said: 'All right, you're a director.' At first he had little power. After 1934, King was able to use a shrewd business sense and his left-wing sympathies to anchor the revolution ('I was the ballast') while the cantankerous Bartholomew and a clever young Welshman called Hugh Cudlipp developed its style.* Far from making himself popular with the family as the brightest Fleet Street hope of the Harmsworths in the second generation, Cecil King was regarded as a vulgar young man who was associating himself with a newspaper in bad taste. His own shyness and awkwardness of manner had tended to separate him from his cousins, in any case. He had a deep vein of uncertainty; another of arrogance. He had the family pessimism, thought often of killing himself, and was to write later that 'life has always

---

* In theory the *Mirror*'s flight to irreverence and the Left could have been stopped. It was sanctioned, but not approved, by the chairman of the company, John Cowley, who joined the Harmsworths when he was inherited as cashier of the *Evening News* in 1894. Cecil King suggests that if the Conservative Party had been astute enough to offer Cowley a knighthood to keep the paper on the path of righteousness, he would probably have accepted.

been difficult because this is not my world'. His association
with a roaringly successful newspaper that found the Honours
Lists boring, and printed photographs of bare breasts, went
against the grain of Harmsworth dignity. He felt himself subtly
ostracised; perhaps more than was really the case. But the
Mirror was certainly deplored by many of the family as a
traitorous sequel to the age of Northcliffe. After the war, Uncle
Cecil – who was once proud to be seen with his godchild, and
have him mistaken for a son – refused to propose him for the
Reform Club.

Already in the thirties, the Harmsworths had been overtaken
in Fleet Street. At Carmelite House, the *Mail*, hampered by the
first Rothermere's misjudgments, failing to be sufficiently 'serious' and incapable of being sufficiently 'popular', was beginning
a long decline, strewn with the bodies of fallen editors. Cecil
King and the *Mirror* prospered, through the war and beyond.
He became chairman of what grew into (yet again) the world's
largest publishing group, the International Publishing Corporation, controlling most of Britain's magazines; among them were
the former properties of the Amalgamated Press, which came
full circle, back to a Harmsworth. He lacked power in the old
sense: he was a member of a board which was a servant of the
shareholders, who were paper mills and insurance companies.
But he was a capable Harmsworth tycoon, with touches of his
Uncle Alfred's drive and wilfulness. It made no difference to
well-brought-up Harmsworths; he was the man who rose to
success with that vulgar newspaper. Cecil King was faintly embarrassing. The old snobberies never die.

Cecil King revived other memories. As chairman of the
Mirror he enjoyed the feeling that he wielded political power; it
was why he wanted to be there. This led to his downfall. It was
one thing for a paper to use its influence politically; the *Mirror*
may have swung the voting to Labour at the elections of 1950
and 1964. But if it were to operate as an expression of one man's
dogma, it ceased to fit the newer, smoother, altogether more
delicate role that was now generally envisaged for the Press.
Cecil King was a part-time governor of the Bank of England,
and privy to the pessimism there in 1968 about Britain's financial situation. The Bank, as it turned out, was unnecessarily
gloomy; so was Cecil King. He wrote a page one article for the

Mirror, 'Enough is Enough', castigating Harold Wilson's Labour Government. This was too much for the newspaper's board. They voted to sack him one evening, and he received the news while he was shaving next morning. In retirement (he would have retired three years later, at seventy, in any case) he wrote a book of reminiscences, *Strictly Personal*, which set a new record of outspokenness about one's own family. Cupboards flew open; skeletons covered the floor. One of Hildebrand's grandsons, reviewing it for a newspaper, wrote: 'He will no longer be in the family address books.' He was not joking. It contained much evidence of private torment. As far as the family was concerned, Cecil King had written the book they could bear least, an attack on their dignity. But he might not have felt such an overpowering urge to write it, except as a violent reaction against two generations of cloaks, veils, and blue-pencils.

Who were the Harmsworths of Northcliffe's generation? They were an ordinary family, propelled to wealth and position by one man's genius, unable to stand the strain. Money flooded in and let them be lazy and dissolute if they felt like it. A number of them became serious drinkers, or married them. There is a feeling spread through the family – difficult to pin down, but unmistakably, sadly there – of uncertainty about who they really were. They were important to one another, but what did the world think of them? They were always groping for a background, a Vice-Chancellor Wickens to provide a professional pedigree, an address in Boundary Road (which was acceptable) instead of one a mile to the west in Salusbury Road (which told one's friends the worst). Perhaps none but the English would care so much and try so hard, instead of making a virtue of what they were. But their snobbery was fed by their uncertainty. In the 1890s, Alfred and his brothers were aflame with the thought of founding a dynasty. Thirty years later, the society that Northcliffe helped to bring about was leaving them all stranded, and the dynasty was already in decline. Eight of Alfred's brothers and sisters married; all had children, nearly forty between them. Talent was spread thin. Cecil King's mother, Geraldine, and Leicester, had been the most astute of the first generation, after Northcliffe. Leicester's son Sir Harold (and after his death in 1952, Sir Geoffrey) ran the West Country papers and some magazines. Esmond, the second Lord Rothermere, ran the *Mail* group, controlling policy through minority shareholdings. The *Mail* of later years lost its excitement, and invited cruel comparisons with its great days. The second Rothermere was little known in Fleet Street, and little talked about outside his own papers. He was cold or shy, depending on one's viewpoint, and rich. He divorced his first wife in 1938, his second in 1952 (when Ian Fleming, the James Bond author was cited). In 1966 he married again, at the age of sixty-seven, and started a new family. His part of the Harmsworths remained close-knit, with a son, Vere, to succeed him in the business, and a son-in-law, Sir Neill Cooper-Key, married to his daughter Lorna, on the board (a second daughter, Esmé, married the Earl of Cromer). The Rothermere millions were still there; a single trust fund, settled on Vere by his father, was worth nearly three million pounds in 1968. The name Harmsworth cropped up often enough in Fleet Street, but it no longer meant the same.

Of the first-generation marriages, only Northcliffe's was childless: as though, even in this, he was ensuring that things began and ended with him. His three children by Mrs Wrohan remained shadows; withdrawn and wealthy. Geraldine, the daughter, who was married three times, died in 1968, aged fifty-six; she became an alcoholic. Dogs roamed her house, gnawing at books and papers; once a great hound was seen coming downstairs with a diamond tiara in its teeth. She told a car dealer to deliver a Rolls-Royce within the hour, and refused to accept it when it failed to arrive in time. She had a violent streak, and stormed out of the room whenever she heard an unkind word about Northcliffe. Watching television, she judged a reporter by whether she thought Northcliffe would have approved. Some nights she dreamt of her father, and insisted on going downstairs to talk to him. Sitting in her nightdress, she conversed with Northcliffe and Mrs Wrohan, turning her head towards the empty chairs. 'Mother,' she said once, 'you ought to tell Father about Lady Londonderry.' Northcliffe's ghost was kept busy. Cecil King and his wife interested themselves in the occult. A medium told her that Mr King had a spirit guide. His name, not surprisingly, was Alfred.

As for the flesh and blood Northcliffe, the short answer is that he was an ordinary person of extraordinary will. His need to rule others made him an abnormal force in the lives of less agitated men. Arriving on the scene when he did, he had the right character to want to impose himself on millions. He embodied many of the traits of the mass-market Press: vigour, cunning, ruthlessness. To say that he brought 'yellow journalism' to Britain makes it sound as though he imported a virus that struck at the innocent. He imported what had to come. If there had been no Alfred Harmsworth, other people and forces would have introduced the new journalism. As it was, the style of his particular revolution passed into common usage. Fleet Street's old-fashioned mixture of expertise and triviality stems from Northcliffe. So does the blurring of 'news' with 'comment'.

He revelled in the crude, harsh business of creating daily entertainments that kept pace with the public. It was necessary to bend the truth to get at the readability. Many of the things he said or caused to be said were true and important; but he was always at work, pushing the news in the direction he wanted it to go. He was expedient, full of bluff and gusto, and without conscience. Journalists who were older, more punctilious or less bold might sneer. Unfortunately Northcliffe was cleverer than they were at recognising that newspapers could afford to be no better or wiser than the public they must serve to survive, whose foibles they had to share. What looked like vices – expediency, glibness, prejudice – were virtues in the new Fleet Street. Since newspapers for millions had to be entertainment, how was a newspaper (or how is a television programme) to be responsible, well-balanced, accurate – and popular? Men in the communications business still argue the puzzle, far into the night. In his day, Northcliffe was supreme at the art or craft of producing news disguised as entertainment, and entertainment disguised as news. In order to do it he had to humour his readers seven days a week, to scratch the ape that never stopped itching. Their aspirations must be played upon; their vanities satisfied.

Everything was grist to his mill, politics and jokes, murder and God, kings and babies. The truth was that the truth was beyond newspapers, anyway. Life was an encyclopaedia: turn the pages, see the paragraphs. Kennedy Jones, observing him sprinkle his beloved items over the *Evening News*, said: 'God, man, you're not going to turn the paper into an evening *Answers*, are you?' Perhaps that was where his heart always lay. Alfred hankered after interesting things. They were truth of a kind.

The Harmsworths are reputed to be descended from kings
Mr Gladstone wears number nine in boots
Viscount Northcliffe died mad
Elmwood has been turned into flats
Everything counts, nothing matters.

Public benefactor. Rothermere with Herbert Morrison at the opening of the Geraldine Mary Harmsworth Park in London in 1934, named after his mother.

Cecil with Emily, his wife. They had to wait until 1939 to become Lord and Lady Harmsworth.

Christmas with the Nazis. Rothermere with Goering, December 1934.

Appendix 1

Northcliffe's Biographers

Eight biographies of Northcliffe have been published in English, together with at least another six books that have 'Northcliffe' in the title, and deal with him to a greater or lesser extent. The only one to appear in his lifetime was an American book, *Northcliffe: Britain's Man of Power*, by William E. Carson (Dodge, New York, 1918). It is polite and innocuous, but Northcliffe threatened Hodder and Stoughton with an injunction if they tried to publish it in Britain.

In 1918, Northcliffe had been toying with the idea of an approved biography for at least eight years. In 1910, while he was having a breakdown, he wrote from the South of France to an editor at the Amalgamated Press, J. A. Hammerton, inviting him to prepare a biography as an antidote to two other books that were supposed to be in preparation – a 'horrible fact that has been revealed to me in the last two years'. Nothing more was heard of the two books, and it was twenty-two years before Hammerton's appeared. At least four other biographies were either commissioned or given a vague blessing before Northcliffe died. H. W. Wilson, a senior writer on the *Mail*, produced an adulatory typescript that exasperated Northcliffe by, among other things, suggesting that he had had 'partners' in his enterprises instead of being a lone figure. This was never published. Hamilton Fyfe, war correspondent and one-time editor of the *Daily Mirror*, was at work on a biography towards the end of Northcliffe's life. A woman on his staff, Ivy Sanders (the wife of Alfred Clark, first head of the HMV gramophone company), collected material in 1921 and produced an unexceptional typescript, never published, after Northcliffe's death.

The fourth biography was *Northcliffe: a Memoir*, by Max Pemberton, who submitted the manuscript for approval about

1916. Because he was a boyhood friend, this was taken seriously, and read by, among others, Cecil; he thought it 'sad rubbish', a harsh judgment, and one that was too easy to deliver on books that were written on slender information, and had to pass the family censors. Northcliffe found it frivolous. It was put aside in his lifetime, but was brought out smartly by Hodder and Stoughton within months of his death. Pemberton's book pretends to inside information it doesn't possess.

Lord Northcliffe: a Study was published in 1927 (Benn). The author, R. McNair Wilson, was a doctor on the *Times* editorial staff. He gave a sharper impression of Northcliffe in his autobiography, *Doctor's Progress* (Eyre & Spottiswoode, 1938). Hamilton Fyfe's book was published as *Northcliffe: an Intimate Biography* in 1930 (Allen & Unwin). This drew on much personal observation. In 1932 J. A. Hammerton's *With Northcliffe in Fleet Street: a Personal Record* was published (Hutchinson). Again, this was based on what the author saw and heard of Northcliffe in action. Leicester Harmsworth thought it the best biography. Nothing more appeared until the 1950s, when A. P. Ryan wrote *Lord Northcliffe* (Collins, 1953, Number 10 in *Brief Lives*), and Harry J. Greenwall wrote *Northcliffe: Napoleon of Fleet Street* (Allan Wingate, 1957). Both were based on published material; Greenwall's book was the first to be openly critical of its subject.

The voluminous private papers were finally utilised in the official biography, *Northcliffe*, by Reginald Pound and Geoffrey Harmsworth, published in 1959 (Cassell). This enormously long book emphasised the 'public figure' at the expense of the journalist. The sexual side of Northcliffe's life is barely hinted at; his widow was still alive when the book was published.

Of the other books that deal directly with Northcliffe, Louise Owen was first off the mark, with *The Real Lord Northcliffe: some Personal Recollections of a Private Secretary* (Cassell, 1922). She said it was written to honour the dead. *Northcliffe's Return* by Hannen Swaffer (Hutchinson, 1925) has a little reporting and a great deal of spiritualism. In the following year *The Coming Again of Northcliffe* by the Reverend J. W. Potter was published (Society of Communion). Louise Owen's *Northcliffe: the Facts* (privately published, 1931) is an unhappy account of her litigation against Northcliffe's executors, mixed up with personal reminiscence. A former news editor of the *Daily Mail*, Tom Clarke, published what reads as a first-hand account of Northcliffe as journalist, from 1912 onwards, in *My Northcliffe Diary* (Gollancz, 1931). Slight discrepancies in the text suggest that Clarke may have been writing from memory and the newspaper files as well as from an actual diary. He later published *Northcliffe in History: An Intimate Study of Press Power* (Hutchinson, 1950).

The Sale of The Times

Sir Campbell Stuart, the last survivor among Northcliffe's executives, denies that Rothermere was bluffing. His account of what happened between August and October 1922 is as follows. Stuart was a small beneficiary under the 1919 will, and so was entitled to contest it. When he and Walter realised that the 1919 will would restore Walter's option to buy Northcliffe's shares, Stuart sought to stop the 1922 will being propounded. He first saw Sir Thomas Horder, who confirmed that he had refused to witness the 1922 wills because of the state of Northcliffe's mind. Then he saw Rothermere. Rothermere was acting in concert with Lady Northcliffe to have the 1922 will propounded, so that when she obtained the *Times* under that will, he would buy it from her. Stuart told Rothermere: 'If you try to propound the 1922 will, I will go into the law courts with Horder and make a scandal.' The compromise over the wills was then reached. Before the purchase came to court on 19 October, Stuart was the subject of a clandestine attempt by Lord Rothermere and his friends to discover how much money the Walter interest would offer. Stuart was invited to dine alone with Sir Robert Hudson. Hudson plied him with drink and pumped him about the price. Stuart said that Walter could afford a million pounds, and if pressed would consider going to one million, two hundred and fifty thousand. After midnight, while they were still talking, the phone rang. Hudson went into the next room to answer it, but Stuart heard him say: 'Is that you, Charles?' This identified the speaker as Sir Charles Russell, a solicitor involved with the estate, and a known associate of Hudson and Lady Northcliffe. Stuart heard Hudson say: 'He started with a million pounds but is obviously prepared to bid one million two hundred and fifty thousand.' This warned Stuart what to expect when the case came to court, so that Astor and his financial advisers were more prepared than they would have been otherwise to meet Rothermere's bid – which was designed to top the Walter figure of one million two hundred and fifty thousand pounds.

According to A. J. P. Taylor, in *English History, 1914–1945* (p. 193, *n*), Rothermere was not outwitted. Taylor says that 'according to a more reliable account, he had no desire to acquire the *Times*, and the telephone conversation was a plant to squeeze more money out of Astor'. Taylor does not enlarge on his source. It is unlikely that Rothermere had been lying from the start when he said he wanted the *Times*. He told Lovat Fraser about 1921 that he wished him to be managing editor of a 'very select' *Times*, price sixpence (Steed in *Times* Archives – 'A Long Memorandum of his Experience of and Relations with Northcliffe'). Rothermere's son, Esmond, described his father's plan, as it existed after Northcliffe's death, to give him complete control of the *Times*, in a letter to Stanley Morison dated 4 July 1950 (*Times* Archives, 'History of the *Times*' file). But it is possible that Rothermere changed his mind.

Bibliography

See also Appendix 1, Northcliffe's Biographers

Angell, Sir Norman, *After all* (Hamish Hamilton 1951)

Beaverbrook, Lord, *Men and power 1917–1918* (Collins 1956)

Beaverbrook, Lord, *Politicians and the press* (Hutchinson 1925)

Bielenberg, Christabel, *The past is myself* (Chatto & Windus 1968)

Blake, Robert, *The unknown prime minister. The life and times of Andrew Bonar Law 1858–1923* (Eyre & Spottiswoode 1955)

Boyle, Andrew, *Trenchard* (Collins 1962)

Brooks, Collin, *Devil's decade. Portraits of the nineteen-thirties* (Macdonald 1948)

Carrington, Charles, *Rudyard Kipling* (Penguin 1970)

Connor Leighton, Marie, *A Napoleon of the Press* (Hodder & Stoughton 1900)

Cooper, Duff, *Old men forget* (Hart-Davis 1953)

Critchley, T. A., *The conquest of violence. Order and liberty in Britain* (Constable 1970)

Cross, Colin, *The Fascists in Britain* (Barrie & Rockcliff 1961)

Cudlipp, Hugh, *Publish and be damned! The astonishing story of the Daily Mirror* (Andrew Dakers 1953)

Cudlipp, Hugh, *At your peril* (Weidenfeld & Nicolson 1962)

Donaldson, Frances, *The Marconi scandal* (Hart-Davis 1960)

Edelman, Maurice, *The Mirror. A political history* (Hamish Hamilton 1966)

Ensor, R. C. K., *England 1870–1914* (Oxford 1936)

Falk, Bernard, *Five years dead* (Book Club reprint 1938)

Falk, Bernard, *He laughed in Fleet Street* (Hutchinson 1933)

Flower, Sir Newman, *Just as it happened* (Cassell 1950)

'Gentleman with a Duster' (Harold Begbie), *The mirrors of Downing Street. Some political reflections* (Mills & Boon 1920)

George, W. L., *Caliban* (Methuen 1920)

Gollin, Alfred M., *The Observer and J. L. Garvin 1908–14. A study in a great editorship* (Oxford 1960)

Howard, Keble, *Lord London. A romance of today* (Chapman & Hall 1913)

Isle of Thanet as a health and pleasure resort (Visitors' guide 1892)

Jenkins, Roy, *Asquith* (Fontana 1967)

Jones, Kennedy, *Fleet Street and Downing Street* (Hutchinson 1919)

King, Cecil, *Strictly personal* (Weidenfeld & Nicolson 1969)

Lloyd George, David, *War memoirs of David Lloyd George*, 2 vols (Odhams n.d.)

Magnus, Philip, *Kitchener. Portrait of an imperialist* (Penguin 1968)

Marquardt, Martha, *Paul Ehrlich* (William Heinemann Medical Books 1949)

Maurois, André, *Cecil Rhodes* (Collins 1968)

Mosley, Sir Oswald, *My life* (Nelson 1970)

Nicolson, Nigel (ed), *Harold Nicolson–diaries and letters 1930–1939* (Fontana 1969)

Nowell-Smith, Simon (ed), *Edwardian England 1901–1914* (Oxford 1964)

Owen, Frank, *Tempestuous journey. Lloyd George, his life and times* (Hutchinson 1954)

Price, G. Ward, *Extra-special correspondent* (Harrap 1957)

Price, G. Ward, *Year of Reckoning* (Cassell 1939)

Rhodes James, Robert, *Memoirs of a Conservative. J. C. C. Davidson's memoirs and papers 1910–1937* (Weidenfeld & Nicolson 1969)

Royston Pike, E., *Human documents of the age of the Forsytes* (Allen & Unwin 1969)

Reed, Douglas, *Insanity Fair* (Cape 1938)

Rothermere, Lord, *My campaign for Hungary* (Eyre & Spottiswoode 1939)

Rothermere, Lord, *My fight to rearm Britain* (Eyre & Spottiswoode 1939)

Sackville-West, V., *The Edwardians* (Hogarth Press 1930)

Stuart, Sir Campbell, *Secrets of Crewe House. The story of a famous campaign* (Hodder & Stoughton 1920)

Stuart, Sir Campbell, *Opportunity knocks once* (Collins 1952)

Taylor, A. J. P., *English History 1914–1945* (Oxford 1965)

The Times, History of, Vol. 3, *The twentieth century test 1884–1912* (*The Times* 1947)

The Times, History of, Vol. 4, parts 1 and 2, *The 150th anniversary and beyond, 1912–20 and 1921–48* (*The Times* 1952)

Turner, E. S., *Boys will be boys* (Michael Joseph 1948)

317

Wallace, Edgar, *Edgar Wallace, by himself* (Hodder & Stoughton 1932)

Wells, H. G., *Mr Britling sees it through* (Cassell 1916)

Wells, H. G., *Experiment in autobiography* (Gollancz 1934)

Williams, Francis, *The right to know. The rise of the world press* (Longmans 1969)

Wrench, John Evelyn, *Uphill. The first stage of a strenuous life* (Ivor Nicholson & Watson 1934)

Wrench, John Evelyn, *Geoffrey Dawson and our times* (Hutchinson 1955)

Wilson, Charles, *The history of Unilever. A study in economic growth and social change* (Cassell 1954)

Wickham Steed, Henry, *Through thirty years 1892–1922. A personal narrative*, 2 vols (Heinemann 1924)

Notes on Sources

The Northcliffe Papers are the source of so much information in the book that individual references are impractical. The same is true of information which has come from interviews with present-day Harmsworths. Unless otherwise stated, it can generally be assumed that letters, extracts from diaries, quoted remarks by or about Harmsworths and all other important details about Northcliffe and his family stem from the Northcliffe Papers or from interviews.

The Northcliffe Papers I have seen consist of the following:

About two hundred files on individuals and subjects.

Typescript copies of Northcliffe correspondence, some of this loose in further files; some of it in spring-backed holders.

About fifty reels of microfilmed material, mainly Northcliffe correspondence.

A large amount of other material, chiefly letters and notes, in envelopes and folders; some of this is not sorted, and none of it is indexed. One deed box contains letters of, and material about, Mrs Wrohan; together with early Northcliffe wills.

Typescript copies of early office memos from Rothermere to Northcliffe.

Northcliffe's diaries for 1886 and from 1891 to 1906.

Alfred Harmsworth (Senior)'s diaries for 1867, 1868, 1870, and 1874.

Sir Leicester Harmsworth's diaries for 1932, 1933, and 1934.

Copies of Northcliffe's communiqués to the *Times* and *Daily Mail*.

A collection of books about or with reference to Northcliffe, some of them annotated by members of the family. Many pamphlets and leaflets.

Transcript of Northcliffe v. Kenealy case, 1910.

Typescripts of two unpublished biographies of Northcliffe, by Ivy Clark and H. W. Wilson.

Cuttings files.

The same letters to and from Northcliffe often appear in more than one of the main sources – files, folders, and microfilm. But lists of Northcliffe correspondence under an earlier filing system, before the papers passed to Sir Geoffrey Harmsworth, include a number of correspondents who do not appear to be represented anywhere in the present papers. Some of these letters may be in the papers given to the British Museum, which are not available at the time of writing (1971).

As an indication of the variety of material in the papers, a single unindexed envelope contained the following: Copy of letter from Sir Thomas Horder to Sir George Sutton, 18.10.22, about an unexplained agreement over a form of words that they have reached. Copy of letter from Sir Leicester Harmsworth to Mary Northcliffe, 26.6.22, about Northcliffe's health. Several letters from Sir Robert Hudson to Leicester, June and August 1922, annotated by Leicester. Hotel bills from the Hotel Royal, Evian, June 1922, and a manuscript note of money spent there by Hudson. Receipt from Holland & Holland, gun manufacturers, for two 32-bore Colt pistols and 200 cartridges. Receipt for bacteriological examination, 15.5.22, and other medical receipts. Sundry cables from Evian to London. Letter from Hudson to Sutton, 22.8.22, asking to meet him and end their 'enforced silence'.

In the chapter notes that follow, these abbreviations are used:

Northcliffe Papers	NP
Northcliffe	N
Sir (Robert) Leicester Harmsworth	RLH
Cecil Harmsworth (first Lord Harmsworth)	CH
St Loe Strachey Papers, in the Beaverbrook Library	SP
Lloyd George Papers, in the Beaverbrook Library	LGP
The *Times* archives	TTA

Notes on Sources

Chapter 2

Early Harmsworth history. NP include the results of extensive genealogical research by the family.

Chapter 3

The childhood of N and his generation is poorly documented in NP. Most of the information there is from letters and interviews of many years after. CH wrote about the family childhood (and some later episodes) in an 88-page typescript, 'Northcliffe and Other Harmsworth Memorials', in NP.

p. 23 Notes for approved biography. This typescript in NP is headed 'Notes dictated by Lord Northcliffe to Snoad on his trip round the world and given to him by Mrs Clark. These notes were to assist her in the popular life of Northcliffe she was writing.' P. 1 is annotated: 'Note in pencil by Lord Northcliffe: Corrected on a steamy day in the Gulf Stream.' The typescript has marginal notes added later by Sir Harold Harmsworth (son of RLH) and CH.

p. 24 Louisa Jane the parlourmaid. Most of the information about her and N's first son, Alfred Benjamin, is in NP, in an envelope marked 'Bluett Duff (re Alfred Smith)'. Bluett Duff was Alfred Smith's first tutor. A 41-page typescript of 'My material relating to Lord Northcliffe', written by Duff in 1933, is among the contents.

Chapter 4

p. 34 The magazine launched in the 1930s was *Lilliput*. Writing in *Picture Post 1938–1950* (Penguin, 1970) Tom Hopkinson said that Stefan Lorant started it on £1,200.

p. 41 London gardens: H. G. Wells in *Experiment in Autobiography* writes of 'narrow strips of blackened garden ... in which at the utmost grew a dying lilac or a wilted privet.'

Chapter 5

p. 50 The woman writer was Ethel F. Heddle. Her 'notes on my connection with the great firm in the early days' are in NP.

Chapter 6

p. 57 N's childhood stories, told to Cecil King: from the latter's *Strictly Personal*.

p. 59 Penny dreadfuls are lovingly dealt with by E. S. Turner in *Boys will be Boys*.

p. 65 Mrs Harmsworth to CH, December 1894; the letter belongs to the second Lord Harmsworth.

Chapter 9

p. 88 The American newspaper interview was in the New York *World*, 17.12.1899.

p. 91 'Pleasure fell like a ripened peach': V. Sackville-West, *The Edwardians*.

Chapter 10

p. 98 Northcliffe and road-mindedness: quoted by R. McNair Wilson, *Doctor's Progress*.

p. 109 N's letters to Strachey: SP.

p. 113 Evelyn Wrench on the Riviera: from his book, *Uphill*.

pp. 114–15 Morel and the Congo: the behind-the-scenes part of the story is from Hamilton Fyfe's *Northcliffe: an Intimate Biography*.

Chapter 11

pp. 122–4 The letters about N's baronetcy and peerage are in the Balfour Papers, British Museum.

p. 123 N to Strachey, SP.

p. 126 N's letter about Mrs Furse's improper postcard, written on *Daily Mail* paper, is in TTA.

Chapter 12

p. 132 The comic dummy phone: Tom Clarke, *Northcliffe in History*, p. 19.

p. 135 N to Strachey, SP.

p. 136–7 St John's engagement: information from Lady Vansittart, formerly Sarita Ward.

Chapter 13

The Lever libel. The case was described by Dr H. Montgomery Hyde in an article in the Unilever magazine *Progress* in 1964; and, with more detail about the company, in Charles Wilson's *History of Unilever* (Vol. 1). Other information is from bound volumes containing verbatim notes of the trial and miscellaneous material in the Unilever library.

p. 144 The postcard to Mrs Furse is in TTA.

p. 144 N to Strachey, SP.

p. 145, etc. N's purchase of the *Times* (and his subsequent proprietorship) is described at great length in the *History of the Times*.

p. 149 Lady N, Nicholson and Wrench: Wrench wrote cautiously about 'the first time that I saw the ugly side of [N]'s nature' in *Uphill*. The other information is from a family interview.

Chapter 14

pp. 152–3 N tells Wrench about Germany: *Uphill*, p. 198.

p. 153 *Times* Berlin correspondent on Germany: *History of the Times*, Vol. 3, p. 366.

p. 154 N to Strachey, SP.

p. 156 'The king's crown is an advertisement', etc.: McNair Wilson, *Doctor's Progress*, p. 120.

p. 157 'Not the slave of the telephone': J. A. Hammerton, *With Northcliffe in Fleet Street*, p. 53.

p. 158 N and the Barber's Secret: G. Ward Price, *Extra-special Correspondent*, p. 193.

Chapter 15

p. 167 N to Nicholson, 'For myself I recover', etc., TTA.

p. 171 N to Strachey, SP.

p. 172 N to Nicholson, 'One can't change a leopard's spots': *History of the Times*, Vol. 3, facsimile opp. p. 738.

pp. 173–4 N to Nicholson, 'Preach the daily text', etc. TTA.

p. 174 N and Bonar Law at Aitken's flat: Beaverbrook, *Politicians and the Press* (Hutchinson, 1925).

p. 177 'The Black Strike': Tom Clarke, *My Northcliffe Diary*, p. 51.

Chapter 16

The diaries of CH, from 1912 until near the time of his death in 1948, belong to the second Lord Harmsworth. Initially I was allowed to see them. I had read from 1912 to 1927 when permission was withdrawn.

p. 185 'The Hooligan Department': J. A. Hammerton, *With Northcliffe in Fleet Street*, p. 159.

p. 188 Letters to Dawson: *History of the Times*, Vol. 4, part 2, pp. 1057, 1058.

Chapter 17

p. 195 N's 'war mind': Steed, *Through Thirty Years*, Vol. 2, p. 33.

pp. 196–7 N and the BEF: Clarke, *My Northcliffe Diary*, pp. 66–7; NP, interview with Tom George.

pp. 197–9 N and the shells: Clarke, *My Northcliffe Diary*; Beaverbrook, *Politicians and the War*: Magnus, *Kitchener*.

p. 205 CH and the 'garden suburb': this description has been used of other buildings; the version here is from CH's diary, 2.5.17.

pp. 205–6 The outing in Richmond Park: CH diary, 4.10.17.

p. 206 CH as go-between in Ireland: there are a number of letters from CH to N in LGP, D/14/1.

p. 207 CH declines Chief Whip: LGP, F/87 (letter from CH to LG); CH diary, 26 April, 1 May, and 2 May, 1917.

p. 207 CH an 'able, quiet fellow': LGP, F/3/4/1.

Chapter 18

p. 209 The essayist who saw N in white flannels was 'A Gentleman with a Duster' (Harold Begbie) in *The Mirrors of Downing Street*.

p. 209 The picture staff in line: J. A. Hammerton, *With Northcliffe in Fleet Street*, pp. 63–4.

p. 209 The bowing episode: Hannen Swaffer, *Northcliffe's Return*, p. 32.

p. 212 Rothermere and the *Observer*: Bonar Law Papers (Beaverbrook Library), 36/2/43; 36/3/4; 36/5/3; 37/5/13. The Astor Papers have some references to this obscure episode, in particular a letter from the Astor Estate Office to Waldorf Astor, 25.1.15.

p. 213, etc. Rothermere at the Air Ministry: Andrew Boyle, *Trenchard*; Beaverbrook, *Men and Power* (Chapter 7); Robert Rhodes James, *Memoirs of a Conservative*, pp. 68–70.

p. 214 Rothermere's memo and letter about Trenchard: Public Record Office, CAB 24/49, GT 4321.

p. 215 Rothermere's viscountcy blocked: Beaverbrook, *Men and Power*, pp. 239–42.

Chapter 19

p. 238 N's telegrams to the *Times*: *History of the Times*, Vol. 4, part 2, pp. 590–2.

p. 239 N on snobbery: Tom Clarke, *Northcliffe in History*, pp. 152–3.

pp. 238–40 N's threats to sell the *Times*; Steed's view is in his 'Long Memorandum of His Experience of and Relations with Northcliffe', TTA. This is a 90-page typescript, undated, with pp. 78–82 missing.

p. 240 N's 'clipped, colourless voice': there is an HMV disc of the recording, made for private distribution, labelled 'Short Address by Viscount Northcliffe recorded April 28 1921, for the luncheon at Olympia on May 1, 1921, commemorating the 25th anniversary of the founding of the *Daily Mail*.'

Chapter 20

p. 243 Steed and the King: Steed, *Through Thirty Years*, Vol. 2, pp. 365–9; *History of the Times*, Chapter 14.

p. 244 N and women's ankles: Steed, *Long Memorandum*, TTA.

p. 247 N's sinister postcard belongs to Cecil King.

p. 249 Marlowe and ectoplasm: Tom Clarke, *My Northcliffe Diary*, pp. 224–5.

p. 252 'Somebody shot me': Steed, *Long Memorandum*, TTA.

p. 253 Steed and N's health: letter from Steed to Stanley Morison 21.7.52; Steed, *Long Memorandum*; both TTA.

p. 253 Prelude to syphilis 'a life absorbed in ambitious projects' etc.; R. R. Willcox, quoting Mickle in *Textbook of Venereal Diseases and Treponematoses*, Wm Heinemann Medical Books, 1964.

pp. 253–4 N at Carmelite House: Tom Clarke, *My Northcliffe Diary*, pp. 263–5.

Chapter 21

p. 258 Garvin and sky-writing: from his obituary of N in the *Observer*, 20.8.22.

p. 258 N in Germany: 'I can defend myself' and 'The fighting has begun', LGP, F/54/2/30.

pp. 259–60 Reed and N: Douglas Reed, *Insanity Fair*, pp. 58–61.

p. 261 N's letter to the *Times*: TTA.

p. 263, etc. Steed and N, 11–14 June: these documents in TTA have been used: Steed, 'Notes of My Intercourse with Lord Northcliffe, June 11 to 14, 1922', dictated 17 June 1922 (44-page typescript); Steed, *Long Memorandum*; Steed, an account of the 'General Situation and of my Relations with Lord Northcliffe', 60-page typescript, dated 6.9.39; letters from Steed to Stanley Morison, 12.7.52 and 21.7.52.

p. 265 'Disregard and unpublish': *History of the Times*, Vol. 4, part 2, p. 680.

pp. 266–66 N's telegrams that weren't sent: Steed, 'Notes on my Intercourse', TTA.

p. 266 'Rascal and a thief': *History of the Times*, Vol. 4, part 2, p. 680.

p. 266 Memo about Sir Charles Russell: TTA.

pp. 273–4 N's phone call to the *Times*: TTA.

Chapter 22

p. 284 Sewell Stokes and Rothermere: the *Listener*, 22.5.58.

pp. 284–5 St John's letter to Geraldine belongs to Cecil King.

Chapter 23

pp. 288–9 Rothermere to Lloyd George: LGP, G/17/1/8, G/17/1/9, G/17/1/17.

p. 290 Foreign Office minute, Public Record Office, FO 371/12185, 22.6.27. There are extensive references to Rothermere and Hungary in the Foreign Office files.

pp. 290–1, Esmond's visit: described in Rothermere's *My Campaign for Hungary*.

p. 291 Rothermere and the sympathetic sentence: Robert Rhodes James, *Memoirs of a Conservative*, p. 296.

p. 292 The newspaperman who met Rothermere was James Drawbell, later managing editor of George Newnes.

p. 296 Rothermere offers Mosley support in 1931: Harold Nicolson, *Diaries and Letters*, p. 95.

pp. 296–7 Rothermere and Mosley: Sir Oswald Mosley, *My Life*, Chapter 18, and information from Mosley.

p. 298 Sir Eric Phipps to Foreign Office: Public Record Office, FO 371/17763, 19.12.34.

p. 299 Hitler to Rothermere: Public Record Office, FO 371/18821. 20.12.35.

pp. 299–300 Rothermere to his son: a copy of this letter belongs to the second Lord Harmsworth.

Chapter 24

p. 302 Second Lord Rothermere and the *Times*: TTA, letter from second Lord Rothermere to Stanley Morison, 4.7.50: *History of the Times*, Vol. 4, part 2, p. 699.

pp. 305–7 Cecil King and the *Mirror*: King, *Strictly Personal*, and interviews with him.

Index

Index

Index

Harmsworth, Vyvyan (son of 1st Viscount Rothermere), 181, 190, 213
Harmsworths' family ancestry, 10–14
Hearst, William Randolph, 82, 100, 108–9
Hendry, Arthur, 30, 31
Hendry, Arthur (son of Sarah Miller), 284
Henley, W. E., 95, 138
History of the Times, 161, 163, 237, 270, 302, 315
Hitler, Adolf, 293, 294, 295, 297, 298, 299
Hobhouse, Emily, 107
Hohenlohe-Waldenburg, Princess, 289, 295
Holland, Hon. Sydney, 166
Home Chat, 116
Home, Sweet Home, 52, 71, 116
Horder, Lord, 267, 270, 271, 272, 274
Howard, Keble, 23, 55
Huddleston, Sisley, 264, 266
Hudson, Lady Mary, *see* Harmsworth, Mary
Hudson, Sir Robert, 202, 236, 263, 265 and Lady Northcliffe, 234, 248, 260, 268, 269, 270, 271, 278; and sale of the *Times* (1922), 314
Hungary, 289–91, 299

Illustrated Chips, see Chips
Imperialism, growth and effects of 64–5, 74–5
Imperial Paper Mills, 157
International Publishing Corporation, 306
Ireland, 191–2, 235, 237–8, 240, 243
Irving, Henry, 182
Isaacs, Rufus, *see* Reading, Lord

Jackson, F. G., 68
Jameson, Leander Starr (Jameson Raid), 74, 75, 76, 77
Japan, 240, 241, 245, 247, 254
Jealous, Mr. and Mrs. George, 21

Jerome, Jerome K., 91
Johannesburg, 75
Jones, Kennedy, 72, 104, 115, 160, 169, 224, 309
and the *Evening News*, 68, 69, 70; and the *Daily Mail*, 79, 81, 83, 104; and the *Daily Mirror*, 122; role in purchase of *Times*, 147, 148
Jones, Dr Vernon, 171

Kenealy, Alex, 185, 186
Kenealy, Annesley, 166
Keppel, Mrs. George, 124
King, Cecil, 57, 134, 134n, 161, 281, 308
at the *Daily Mirror*, 305, 306–7; reminiscences, 307
King, Geraldine (*née* Harmsworth), 32, 41, 215, 247, 284, 300n, 303, 307
childhood, 21; marriage, 62–3, 88; children, 134, 134n;
King, William Lucas, 62–3, 88, 215
Kipling, Rudyard, 95, 294
Kitchener, Horatio Herbert, 104, 105, 106, 107, 110, 197, 198, 199, 200
Kruger, Paul, 74, 75, 77, 104

Law, Andrew Bonar, 174, 182, 191, 214, 282–3
Lee of Fareham, 1st Viscount, 234
Leighton, Marie Connor, 110
Leonard, Mrs. Osborne, 282
Le Queux, William, 64
Lever, William (*later* Lord Leverhulme), 139, 140, 141–4
Lilford, Lord, 24
Lipton, Sir Thomas, 89, 92, 129, 134
Lloyd George, David, 106, 124, 222, 226, 229, 234, 243, 255, 273, 282, 287
and the Marconi affair, 186, 189; and first meeting with Northcliffe (1909), 175; wartime relationship, 200, 201, 202,

335